W9-DEO-071

Assessment
for Instruction

Assessment
for Instruction

■ *Susan S. Evans*
Educational Consultant
Pensacola, Florida

■ *William H. Evans*
University of West Florida

■ *Cecil D. Mercer*
University of Florida

Allyn and Bacon, Inc.
Boston   London   Sydney   Toronto

Series Editor: Jeffery Johnston
Production Coordinator: Sue Freese
Editorial/Production Services: Cynthia Hartnett
Interior Design: Judith Ashkenaz
Cover Coordinator: Linda K. Dickinson
Cover Designer: Lisa Tedeschi

Library of Congress Cataloging-in-Publication Data

Evans, Susan S., 1948–
  Assessment for instruction.

  Bibliography: p. 353
  Includes index.
  1. Educational tests and measurements. 2. Educational
tests and measurements—Design and construction.
3. Educational tests and measurements—Case studies.
I. Evans, William H. 1948–   . II. Mercer,
Cecil D. III. Title.
LB3051.E93 1986   371.2′6   85–28659
ISBN 0-205-08787-6 (pbk.)

Printed in the United States of America

10 9 8 7 6 5 4 3 2 1   90 89 88 87 86

Contents

Preface

Assessment is necessary to make the decisions that influence a student's progress in school. Students are assessed to identify those at high risk for developing learning problems. Students are also assessed for classification purposes, such as determining if a student is eligible for a special program. And when a student is placed in a special program, further assessment is necessary to develop long-range goals suited to that individual's special needs. Assessment also assists in the evaluation of educational programs and teaching methods. Finally, students are assessed on a continuous basis to monitor their progress and make daily instructional decisions.

To determine a student's instructional needs, assessment must provide information in two areas. First, assessment data must be collected to help the teacher determine the goals of instruction—*what to teach*. Assessment must also provide information to help the teacher determine the means of instruction—*how to teach*. To carry out assessment in these two areas, a systematic plan must be developed for collecting and using assessment data.

PLAN FOR THE TEXT

This book provides an integrated approach to assessment for instruction: how to tailor instruction according to individual student needs and learning levels. In mastering this approach, the reader will:

- develop a knowledge of the academic skills, learning variables, and social behaviors that must be assessed to implement an effective instructional program
- learn which assessment procedures are appropriate for periodic and continuous assessment
- learn how to develop and use informal procedures to assess specific areas of curriculum in order to establish instructional objectives
- learn how to establish a recordkeeping system that facilitates the ongoing assessment of academic and social behavior

Using a comprehensive and practical format, this text provides principles and examples to aid in the selection, design, use, and interpretation of informal assessment procedures. Descriptions of formal devices used to assess language arts, reading, mathematics, learning variables, and behavior are provided in the Appendix.

Chapter 1 introduces the purposes and issues that influence assessment. The difference between formal and informal assessment is discussed, and the statistical procedures used to analyze assessment data are reviewed. Chapter 2 presents the three-step model that serves as a framework to collect and use the assessment data systematically. The model is then applied to the assessment of basic academic areas, learning variables, and behavior in Chapters 3 through 7. In each of these chapters, a detailed skill/behavior network is provided. Chapter 3 discusses assessment of the variables that influence learning; Chapter 4 applies the model to language arts; Chapter 5, to reading; Chapter 6, to mathematics; and Chapter 7, to behavior. Chapter 8, the final section, demonstrates how to organize the assessment process for a group of students.

The text is designed as a handbook for present and future teachers, school psychologists, administrators, counselors, and other professionals responsible for implementing instructional programs. Although the emphasis of the text is on students with learning and behavior problems, both special and regular classroom teachers should find the information relevant and useful.

ACKNOWLEDGMENTS

We would like to express our appreciation to a number of individuals who have provided us with encouragement and invaluable assistance in this manuscript preparation: Ann Agnew, Bill Barnes, Sheldon Braaten, Jim DeRuiter, Don Deshler, Allan Frank, Lorna Idol-Maestas, Jeff Johnston, Ann Loper, Tom Lovitt, James McCleskey, Lawren Meacham, Ann Mercer, Stan Scarpati, Pat Schloss, Rex Schmid, Edward Stewart, Elaine Stewart, Kay Stevens, Tom Stritch, Ouina Sutter, Ruth Waugh, Mike Wiebe, and Larry Wynn.

Special thanks go to Susan Peterson for her help in writing Chapter 3.

Assessment
for Instruction

1

Introduction to Assessment

■ Learning Objectives

After completing this chapter, the reader should be able to:

- ■ list several purposes of assessment
- ■ discuss the issues that have had a significant impact on assessment
- ■ differentiate between formal and informal assessment
- ■ describe four scales of measurement
- ■ describe the diagnostic questions that can be answered by analyzing assessment data
- ■ describe the statistical procedures used to answer each diagnostic question

Imagine a family taking a trip in a car in which they had no speedometer, odometer, or road map. They would have little idea as to the direction of their destination, the speed and distance of travel, or even an estimated time of arrival. After aimlessly wandering the roads for a short time, the initial excitement and anticipation associated with taking a trip would be replaced with feelings of anxiety and frustration. This aggravating situation could easily have been avoided if before beginning the trip, a road map had been obtained, and the functioning and accuracy of the car's instruments had been checked. This would have allowed the travelers to continuously monitor their mileage and speed. Moreover, they would have had a clear idea of their destination, travel route, and approximate location. And, barring any unforeseen catastrophies, they would have arrived at their location at the designated time, tired, but happy.

Likewise, accurate data are required to evaluate the strengths, weaknesses, and progress of students in educational settings. This information is often collected through tests, work samples, interviews, observation, and anecdotal reports from numerous individuals. Data gathered in these ways may then be used to assist in making educational decisions that may affect the student.

Assessment, however, involves more than just administering tests and tabulating results. Assessment should not be simply imposed on people, but rather approached as an interactive process involving parents, students, and school personnel. It is a method of inquiry, an ongoing process that results in all parties giving and obtaining information about the strengths, weaknesses, and expectations of a student and his or her environment.

PURPOSE OF ASSESSMENT

■ ■ The scope and form of assessment are necessarily dependent upon the many purposes of educational assessment. Assessment may be done to screen a group of children and identify those who are considered at high risk for developing learning problems. Assessment may be done for classification purposes, to determine if a student is eligible for a special program. If a student is placed in a special program, further assessment is necessary to develop long-range goals for an Individualized Education Program (I.E.P.). Assessment is also used to evaluate educational programs and teaching methods. And assessment may be used on a continuous basis to monitor students in order to make daily instructional decisions.

ISSUES

■ ■ A great number of events have combined to produce changes in education, particularly in the area of assessment. The launching of Sputnik by the Soviet Union in 1957 produced an outcry of concern in the United States about the quality of American education. Many thought that American schools were not rigorous and their graduates not equal to those from other countries and that this accounted for America not being the first to launch a satellite into space.

This perception resulted in a massive federal response that sought to improve the perceived inadequacies in American public education. This interest in education was pervasive and filtered through all aspects of the educational system. By the mid-1960s, this concern for education had been transformed by legislation, litigation, and various social forces into a movement that sought to secure appropriate educational opportunities for special education and academically disadvantaged students. Increased public awareness and litigation led to the enactment of numerous state and federal laws in the 1970s, such as Public Law (PL) 94–142 (Education for All Handicapped Children Act), PL 93–112, Section 504 (Rehabilitation Act), and PL 93–380 (Family Educational Rights and Privacy Act), all of which guaranteed handicapped students equal access to education.

Clearly, the passage of PL 94–142 in 1975 caused many changes in special education. Specifically, this law guarantees a free and appropriate education for all handicapped individuals ages three through twenty-one. The due process provision of this law ensures the rights of students and their parents or guardians in the assessment and educational programming process. Parents, for example, must be given notice of referral, must give permission for assessment, be informed of their rights to inspect all records, receive an independent evaluation, and request a due process hearing if desired. Moreover, any assessment is required to be accurate, valid, nondiscriminatory, and administered by trained personnel.

If the student is placed in a special education program, the law demands that an Individualized Education Program (I.E.P.) be developed within thirty days after eligibility is determined, and before special class services are begun. The I.E.P. is developed by a team that includes parents or guardians, teachers, a representative of the local education agency, and, if appropriate, the student. The I.E.P must include:

1. A statement of the student's present levels of educational performance.
2. A statement of annual and short-term goals.
3. A statement of special services and materials needed by and provided to the student.
4. A statement of the extent to which the student will participate in the regular school program.
5. The date of initiation of services and the anticipated duration.
6. Objective criteria, evaluation procedures, and schedules for determining at least annually if the objectives are being met.

With the enactment of PL 94–142, assessment assumed an integral role in educational programming. Many issues such as minimum competency standards, multicultural assessment, computer-assisted assessment, and adolescent assessment reflect the interest and importance of educational assessment.

■ Minimum Competency Standards

Many states and school districts require that all students complete a battery of tests on basic academic skills. These formal standardized tests are generally administered on a group basis and often take several days to complete. The scores obtained by the students are then judged in relation to national or regional norms that are assumed to reflect minimal competence. Students whose scores are less than satisfactory are deemed to lack competence in that academic area and may not be allowed to advance to the next grade or to graduate.

This type of assessment may be satisfactory for students whose scores meet the minimum competency standards. It is inadequate, however, for students experiencing difficulty in school who do not achieve the minimum criteria needed for advancement. Some authors such as Dickinson (1980) have therefore suggested that this singular testing of academic skills be supplemented with informal assessment procedures that can be frequently administered. By assessing in this manner, it is increasingly likely that any instructional problems will be identified in time to make the appropriate educational interventions.

■ Multicultural Assessment

Culture has a pervasive effect on how we think and act. It dictates standards for behavior and social interaction. Laws, customs, and even the role and function of public institutions are molded by culture. It is not surprising, then, to realize that all organizations take on the values deemed significant by society. These values, however, are generally weighted heavily in favor of the majority group.

This sometimes causes a variety of problems. In a pluralistic society, which is composed of divergent cultural groups, each social group dictates a somewhat different set of values. Nowhere can this be seen more clearly than in the public schools.

Public schools are a unique institution. All children are required to attend school and are expected to obtain a level of knowledge of basic academic skills. This does not happen in a vacuum, however. The rules, procedures, standards of behavior, curriculum, and even assessment procedures reflect the social and cultural values of society. A problem occurs when a student's behavior deviates from the accepted standards. This deviation may indicate a learning or behavior problem, or it may simply reflect a difference between the values of the student's cultural group and those of the school.

Assessment of these differences may be very difficult. Authors such as Mercer (1973) and Sattler (1982) argue that many formal tests are biased against students from minority cultures. This bias may take many forms. Two common examples are test questions that hold little relevance to the minority group (Alley & Foster, 1978) and the failure to include adequate minority group members in the norming population (Salvia & Ysseldyke, 1985). If a test is culturally biased, a disproportionately large number of students from minority groups may do quite poorly on the instrument. This is disastrous if the results of these tests are used to place students in special education or remedial programs.

Alley and Foster (1978) suggest that many of the problems of culturally biased testing can be reduced by using informal or teacher-made tests. Informal assessment techniques are generally not used for the purpose of program placement, but rather are used to assess specific skills in a curriculum while accounting for those unique aspects of the student's background that may affect performance.

■ Computer-Assisted Assessment

Hundreds of years from now when historians write about the last fifty years of the twentieth century, they will note that the computer revolution was perhaps one of the most significant and pervasive of phenomena. It has completely changed the way we live, do business, and interact. It has automated life in such a way that we are now able to record and examine huge amounts of data that before would have been impossible to analyze.

The proliferation of computer technology has also affected education. As witness to this, many states require that high school and college graduates become computer literate. In many thousands of classrooms, some aspect of the instructional program is delivered with the aid of computers.

Assessment procedures have also been influenced by this movement. Computerized tests are being used in public schools with increasing frequency. Generally the student interacts with the computer by typing answers to questions that are visually displayed on a monitor attached to the computer. The student may do this independently, thus freeing the teacher for other instructional duties.

Student responses to computerized test questions may be quickly and efficiently analyzed. Error patterns may emerge that reflect the student's deficiency in some aspect of the curriculum. Moreover, the computer analysis may determine that a specific type of test question or required response results in an increased probability of student error or slower response rate (Bennett, 1982). Taber (1981) notes that these data, combined with the instantaneous feedback given to students by the computer, allow the classroom teacher to swiftly and continuously make appropriate adjustments in the student's instructional program.

Hannaford and Taber (1982) state that the most relevant data for instructional planning are obtained when the computerized activities are compatible with the needs of the learner and the requirements of the curriculum. If, for example, the educational program requires the student to write a response rapidly, the computer program should reflect this requirement and provide an evaluation of the student's skill in meeting these demands.

Computers, however, should be used with caution in educational assessment. Computers will not produce educationally useful information if the test questions and the skills sampled are not relevant to the instructional program. Further, Evans and Stritch (1983) assert that computers should not be indiscriminately used, that is, in a way that would supplant the information that can be obtained by direct human contact and observation.

■ Assessment in Adolescence

Most of the tests and assessment practices currently in use are designed to evaluate elementary-aged students in their school settings. These tests are designed to assess the skills and abilities deemed necessary for success in the elementary curriculum. Many professionals, such as Alley and Deshler (1979) and Cullinan and Epstein (1979), have noted, however, that these tests may be inappropriate for the accurate and valid assessment of adolescents.

As Evans and Evans (1983) suggest, the educational nature and needs of adolescents may differ greatly from those of elementary-aged students. Issues such as vocational education, sex education, and substance abuse become increasingly important during adolescence. As a result, procedures for teaching academic subject areas change during the middle and high school years.

The changes that adolescent students experience in environment, expectations, and curriculum necessitate an alteration in assessment procedures. This is demonstrated by the need to assess, for example, an adolescent's ability to use academic, vocational, and life skills in real life settings. To do this, the assessment procedures must be designed to evaluate the extent of knowledge as well as the ability to use the skill in a meaningful manner. This often necessitates, as Alley and Deshler (1979) note, an examination of the manner in which the student obtains and uses information across settings. A major emphasis in assessment, the authors note, should be in the evaluation of listening, writing, and speaking skills. These skills serve as the major underpinnings of cognitive and social skills for adolescents and therefore should be comprehensively assessed.

TYPES OF ASSESSMENT

■ ■   Historical precedents and concern over a variety of issues have influenced the development and use of assessment procedures. This is perhaps most clearly illustrated in the changing nature of formal and informal assessment.

■ **Formal Assessment**

Formal assessment procedures use *standardized,* or *norm-referenced, tests*—that is, tests that compare an individual's performance to the performance of a peer group on which the test was standardized. Norm-referenced tests usually include only a sample of skills, and the skills included may not necessarily be those emphasized in the student's instructional program or be representative of a student's typical performance.

Formal tests and evaluation procedures are best used for classification and placement purposes, as well as for the measurement of long-term objectives. These procedures may be used to measure learning processes and intellectual, sensory, and academic abilities in order to determine if a student meets the eligibility requirements for placement in a special education program. When used for this purpose, testing often is completed in several sessions, and the results are then evaluated by a team of professionals that may include teachers, a psychologist, counselor, and principal. The assessment data are judged in relation to a preestablished program-eligibility criterion. If the data indicate the existence of severe deficits, the student may then be recommended for placement in a program designed to provide an appropriate education.

Formal tests are accompanied by manuals that provide information essential for the appropriate use of the test. Generally included in the manual is a description of the various parts of the test and directions for test administration. These detailed instructions help to ensure that the test will be administered, scored, and evaluated in a consistent, or standardized, manner.

Formal tests may consist of several components, or subtests, that can be used to measure the specific skills of a subject area. In reading, for example, the *Woodcock Reading Mastery Test* (Woodcock, 1973) has subtests that measure letter identification, word identification, word attack, word comprehension, and passage comprehension. The *Wechsler Intelligence Scale for Children—Revised* (Wechsler, 1974) includes subtests such as picture completion, block design, and picture arrangement that measure various perceptual abilities that many consider to be components of intelligence.

Subtests generally consist of a wide range of test questions of graduated difficulty. The examiner seeks to determine the range of questions that the student can correctly answer. This necessitates finding a point below which it can safely be assumed that the student will correctly answer all questions. After finding the lowest point, or *basal,* in the student's range, testing continues until a point is reached at which it is predicted that the student will not correctly answer any further questions. This is called a *ceiling.* Test manuals provide instructions for determining the basal and ceiling of each subtest.

With formal tests, correct student responses are typically totalled and referred to as a *raw score*. This score can then be converted, with the use of normative tables presented in the examiner's manual, into derived scores such as grade and age equivalents or a percentile rank. These normative scores allow the subject's performance to be compared to that of his or her peers of the same age or grade level. These data then allow an analysis of the extent of the student's deficit in relation to the general population.

Formal tests may also be used to assist in developing and measuring the effect of educational programs. A subject area test given at the beginning of the year in reading, for example, may be used to indicate what general skills should be more closely examined. This is called a *pretest*. When used in this manner, formal tests assist in providing a realistic focus for more extensive informal evaluation. The same formal test may be given at the end of the school year as a *posttest*. The difference between the pretest and posttest scores can then be computed to show the extent of gain that the student has made in one year. A great deal of caution, however, must be taken in interpreting these gain scores. Formal tests necessarily sample a broad range of skills. Because of this range of coverage, certain specific skills directly related to the classroom curriculum may be inadequately assessed. Further, the skills evaluated in the formal test may not be the same ones included in the instructional program. Therefore, certain limitations may exist in the conclusions that can be drawn from the pretest to posttest gain made by any student.

■ Informal Assessment

Assessment procedures must be altered if the purpose of the evaluation is to design and closely monitor an instructional program. While formal test data may be used to indicate the student's general strengths and weaknesses, a stronger emphasis should be placed upon the continuous collection of data from instructional settings. This is often accomplished by using informal assessment procedures.

Informal procedures sample skills and behaviors relevant to the curriculum with the use of teacher-made and criterion-referenced devices. A continuous, fine-grained analysis of the student is the goal, and normative comparisons are not made. The results from informal tests may be used to assess long- or short-term specific curriculum objectives.

Informal assessment procedures may consist of tests, rating devices, checklists, and observation systems. Many of the items on informal devices are selected from instructional materials such as worksheets, games, reading and math basal programs, and flashcards. Each skill that is evaluated in a teacher-made test may be sampled with several items or questions. Student responses to these questions are then judged in relation to a criterion of mastery. This criterion is generally established by the teacher and reflects what is thought to be a minimum level of accuracy needed to succeed at the next level in the curriculum. Typically, criteria are expressed as a percentage of correct answers and/or rate of correct responses and incorrect responses.

When giving an informal test, the examiner should carefully observe and take notes regarding the student's response pattern. It may be noted, for example, that the student responds differently when presented with certain types of questions or reinforcers. An analysis of these observations often yields relevant information regarding error patterns and other factors that can prove to be valuable in instructional planning.

Informal tests may be repeatedly given over time to assess student growth. Used in this manner, and in conjunction with formal test data, a precise educational analysis of the student can be accomplished.

By determining the specific purpose of assessment, appropriate procedures can be judiciously selected from the hundreds of tests, rating scales, and observational systems that may be used in answering educationally relevant questions. This increases the likelihood that any instructional program that is developed will be appropriate and will meet the needs of the student.

ANALYSIS OF ASSESSMENT DATA

■ ■ All assessment procedures yield data about student performance. Statistics can be used to condense and analyze data so they may be more clearly understood. In order to select the most appropriate statistical procedure, it must first be determined which scale of measurement is being used and which diagnostic questions must be answered.

■ **Scales of Measurement**

There are four scales of measurement that may be used in educational assessment: nominal, ordinal, interval, and ratio. Each has different characteristics and is used for different purposes.

In a *nominal scale* of measurement, numbers are used to designate people or objects. This can be illustrated by the example of a math class in which there are three instructional groups. The students in the Laker math group might be designated as ones, the Celtics twos, and the Hawks threes. The number assigned to each group has no numerical value, implies no rank, and cannot be used to add, subtract, multiply, or divide. It is permissible, however, to count the number or determine the percentage of students in each group.

Ordinal scales of measurement may be used to rank-order likes, dislikes, or opinions. In school settings, this may take the form of a rating scale in which a teacher is asked to select, for example, a number from 1 (have not noticed the behavior at all) to 5 (have noticed the behavior to a very large degree) that best indicates his or her opinion of a particular student's classroom behavior. When using this scale it is difficult to determine if a 2 is the same distance from 1 as 4 is from 5. Because this cannot be determined, the numbers cannot be added and subtracted. Additionally, one teacher's rating of 2 (have noticed the behavior to a small degree) may represent a much different set of behaviors than another teacher's rating of 2. While ordinal data may be useful, they should not be added, subtracted, multiplied, or divided. They may be counted, however, and used to compute percentages and percentiles.

Most tests used in education have *equal-interval scales* of measurement in which the magnitude of the difference between any two adjacent points is always the same. That is, the difference between 2 and 3 is the same difference as between 100 to 101. This means that a score of 10 is composed of ten separate intervals, each of which is equidistant. With this scale of measurement, numbers can be added and subtracted because they have the same unit of measurement.

Additionally, equal-interval scales have no absolute zero that would indicate the total absence of the trait or ability being measured. As a result, these data cannot be multiplied, divided, or used to make ratio comparisons. For example, while it is appropriate to note that a student answered 20 more problems correctly than did another student, it is not possible to say that a student who has a grade score of 6.0 on a reading test knows twice as much as a student who received a score of 3.0.

A ratio scale also has equal units of measure. *Ratio scales* differ from equal interval scales, however, in that they have an identifiable and absolute zero that indicates the complete absence of the trait being measured. As a result, numbers from this scale of measurement can be added, subtracted, multiplied, divided, or used to make ratio comparisons. With height and weight, for example, there is an identifiable zero in which the quality being measured is not present. It is also permissible to say that a student who is 6 feet tall is twice the height of a student who is 3 feet tall.

Ratio scales are most often used in the physical sciences. Many of their properties are reflected, however, in ratio charts used to record student performance. These charts are illustrated in chapter 2.

■ **Diagnostic Questions**

Numerous statistical procedures may be used to analyze data. The diagnostic question to be answered dictates which procedure is most appropriate.

☐ *What Is the Central Tendency of the Data?*

A great deal of information can be gathered from analyzing daily student performance. As these daily data accumulate, however, it may become increasingly difficult to identify general trends of performance. Therefore, it is sometimes desirable to condense a large amount of data into one or two numbers that represent the average or most common performance of a student or class.

MEAN SCORES   A mean score $(\bar{x})$ is perhaps the most commonly used method of illustrating the central tendency of data from equal-interval and ratio scales of measurement. Simply stated, a *mean* is the arithmetic average of a set of scores. These scores may represent one student's average performance or that of an entire class.

A mean may be computed by adding all of the scores and then dividing by the number of scores. A student, for example, who got 10, 8, and 24 problems correct on math assignments would have a mean score of 14. This is calculated by adding 10, 8, and 24 and then by dividing by the number of entries (i.e., $10 + 8 + 24 = 42$ and $42 \div 3 = 14$).

As illustrated, mean scores do not necessarily reflect any specific reported scores. The student in the previous example did not score 14 on any of the days in which data were kept. The mean score of 14 does, however, provide a summary of the data.

Mean scores may be greatly affected by one or two scores that are unusually high or low. When this happens the mean is "pulled" toward the unusual score and away from the rest of the data. This may result in a mean that is not truly reflective of the central tendency of the data.

MEDIAN SCORES   A median or middle score may be used to illustrate the central tendency of ordinal, equal-interval, and ratio data obtained from an individual or a group. The median is found by arranging the data in order from smallest to largest and then selecting the middle number. As a result, half of the data points are above this number and half are below. Student test scores of 8, 13, 15, 20, and 23, for example, have a median score of 15. Two numbers, 8 and 13, are below this midpoint, and two numbers, 20 and 23, are above it.

The median is not as easily affected by extreme scores as is the mean. Consider the following group of seven test scores: 10, 12, 85, 88, 98, 98, and 98. The mean of these scores, 69.9, is affected by the two low scores, while the median, 88, provides a more useful analysis of central tendency. Because of this, the median may be a more accurate method of summarizing student performance.

MODE SCORES   A mode is the score that occurs most frequently. If two scores occur the same number of times, then this is called a bimodal distribution. If more than two scores occur the same number of times, it is called a multimodal distribution. Modes are very useful in summarizing nominal and ordinal data, but may also be used with equal-interval and ratio data.

Modes clearly illustrate which test score or rating occurs most often, which can be quite helpful when trying to identify the most commonly occurring opinion. In Table 1–1 this is illustrated with a student who was rated by seven teachers on a 1 (inappropriate) to 5 (appropriate) scale for classroom behavior: While the median for these data is 3, the mode is 5. Although the causes for these divergent scores are quite important, it can be concluded that the rating of 5 (appropriate) was given more frequently than any other rating.

Modes may also be a helpful way of reporting the central tendency of data when there are an inadequate number of middle scores. This is illustrated in a class in which students received scores of 10, 10, 10, 10, 10, 38, 41, and 48 on a fifty-point test. The mode of these scores, 10, is a much more useful measure of central tendency than the mean score of 22.

☐ *How Much Do the Data Fluctuate?*

In order to make appropriate educational decisions, the variability or fluctuation of all relevant data must be carefully and thoroughly analyzed. The examination of variability may assist, for example, in determining how different a student's test score is from those of his or her peers. Also, describing the variability of a set of data adds meaning to measures of central tendency. For example, two students may both have mean scores of 50 correct responses on a series of math assignments. One student's scores, however, may range from 10 to 90 correct responses, whereas the other student's correct responses may only range from 40 to 55.

There are numerous ways of reporting and describing the variability of data. Range, frequency distribution, and standard deviation provide some information as to the degree of fluctuation in data. While this descriptive information is useful, it is perhaps of greater importance in instructional decision making to determine the conditions associated with

TABLE 1–1   Mode of Teacher Ratings

Teacher	Rating
A	1
B	2
C	3
D	3—*(median)*
E	5
F	5—*mode*
G	5

changes in performance. Educational programs can be greatly enhanced if it is noted, for example, that improved performance is associated with certain instructional arrangements or types of reinforcement. Therefore, any statistical description of variability must be accompanied by an identification of the conditions associated with the change in performance.

RANGE   Reporting the range of scores is perhaps the easiest way of illustrating variability. It may be used to illustrate the variability of the scores made by one student or those of a group. The correct responses on a math test, for example, may range from a low of 6 to a high of 31. A score of 10, although near the lower limit, may be considered in a different light if it is known that nine of the ten scores were between 6 and 10 and only one score was 31.

FREQUENCY DISTRIBUTION   The distribution of scores is easily reported by preparing a table that illustrates the number of students or times a particular student received a certain score. These scores may also be grouped in intervals. The interval selected may reflect grade limits, percentage of correct responses, or any desired criteria. Illustrated in Table 1-2 is a frequency distribution of scores grouped in 10-point intervals. These data can be used to identify where a particular score lies in relation to others. From this it can be determined if a certain score is significantly higher or lower than others.

STANDARD DEVIATION   The *standard deviation* is a unit of measure that can be used with interval and ratio scales to illustrate how far one or more scores are from the mean. This statistic may be used to evaluate the variability of the scores made by a large number of students in a class or group.

Standard deviation is computed by using the following formula in which *S.D.* is the standard deviation, ΣX^2 is the sum of the squared deviations, and N is the number of scores:

$$S.D. = \sqrt{\frac{\Sigma X^2}{N}}$$

TABLE 1-2   Frequency Distribution

Intervals	Number of Scores
0–10	1
11–20	0
21–30	4
31–40	8
41–50	9

By adding and subtracting the standard deviation to the mean, the limits of ± 1 *S.D.* can be determined. To determine ± 2 *S.D.* the standard deviation is doubled and then added to or subtracted from the mean. With ± 3 *S.D.*, the standard deviation is tripled and then added to or subtracted from the mean.

The standard deviation then can be used to determine the percentage of scores that may be expected to fall within certain ranges if the scores are normally distributed. This is illustrated with the bell-shaped curve in Figure 1–1. The bell-shaped curve is symmetrical so that while approximately 34% of the cases fall between the mean and $+1$ *S.D.*, approximately 34% also fall between the mean and -1 *S.D.* Additionally, approximately 14% of the cases are between $+1$ and $+2$ *S.D.*'s, while approximately 14% of the cases are between -1 and -2 *S.D.*'s, and so on. After establishing the limits of ± 1, 2, and 3 standard deviations, it can easily be determined how far any particular score is from the mean. This assists in identifying the relative position of any particular score. A score at -1 *S.D.*, for example, is greater than only 16% of the total scores while a score at $+2$ *S.D.* is greater than 98% of the total scores.

When using formal tests, the standard deviation is generally provided in the test manual. This allows the examiner to compare an individual student's test score to a normative population.

FIGURE 1–1 Approximate Normal Distribution—Bell-shaped Curve

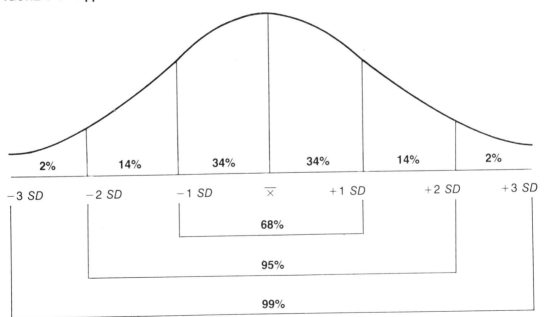

☐ *How Does the Student's Performance Compare to that of Others?*

One of the first indicators of educational problems is the teacher's observation that the student is lagging behind his or her classmates in academic performance. Generally one or two days of poor performance is not regarded as indicative of serious instructional problems. However, if the student's performance is dramatically different from that of others or the problem persists for some time, serious attention may be warranted.

The data obtained from many formal tests allow the test scores of an individual student to be compared to those of students of a similar age or grade. This comparison group is called a norm group. The norm group is generally selected so that its test scores are similar to those that would be made by the entire population of students of the same age or grade. This comparison assists in determining if an individual's test score is unusually high or low when judged in relation to the scores made by his or her peers.

When using a norm-referenced test, there must be a great deal of assurance that the normative group does in fact reflect the population it purports to represent. If the general population has not been adequately sampled, certain groups may be under- and overrepresented, resulting in inaccurate norms.

There also must be evidence that the scores of the normative group are normally distributed in the same proportional manner dictated by the bell-shaped curve. If the scores are not normally distributed, valid conclusions cannot be made about the student's relative standing.

There must also be a great deal of consideration given to selecting a test appropriate for the individual being tested. Many tests are not designed or normed to assess individuals who are exceptional or who differ significantly from the normative population in terms of language or cultural background. Any comparisons that are made for minority populations must be viewed with caution. The following sources may assist in evaluating formal tests: *Assessment in Special and Remedial Education* by J. Salvia and J. Ysseldyke, Houghton Mifflin Company (1985), and *Eighth Mental Measurements Yearbook* by O. K. Buros, Gryphon Press (1978).

The observation of differences may also be made informally over time. Inevitably, these observations lead to the question of exactly how different is the student's performance. Various statistical procedures may be used to answer this question.

STANDARD SCORES   It is very difficult to compare a raw score of 50 on reading test A to a raw score of 60 on reading test B. While 50 is the smaller number, test A may have a mean of 40, while test B may have a mean of 80. Therefore, the score obtained on reading test A is above the mean while the score on reading test B is below the mean.

Even when the mean of two tests is the same, the standard deviation may be different. As a result, it becomes burdensome to compare test results unless the scores can be transformed into similar units of measurement that can be judged in relation to each other. This can be done by using standard scores. Standard scores transform the raw scores of normed tests into scores that have the same mean and standard deviation.

Two of the most common standard scores are *t* scores, which have a mean of 50 and a standard deviation of 10, and *z* scores, which have a mean of 0 and a standard deviation of 1. To calculate a *z* score, the following formula is used:

$$z = \frac{X - \overline{X}}{S.D.}$$

As the formula indicates, the mean score of the test is subtracted from the student's test score. This number is then divided by the standard deviation. The resulting number is the *z* score, which can be thought of as a standard deviation for that particular score.

For example, if a student received a raw score of 110 on a test that had a mean of 100 and a standard deviation of 10, the *z* score would be 1.00. This indicates how far, in terms of standard deviations, the student's score is from the mean. In this case, the score is one standard deviation away from the mean.

This *z* score can also be used in conjunction with a statistical table for *z* scores that indicates the percentage of scores that fall between the mean and the particular *z* score. This information can again be used to establish relative standing.

A *stanine*, or standard nine, distributes a range of standard scores on a scale from one to nine. Each number on this scale represents an interval, or band, of standard scores. Stanine 5 is considered to be at the middle of the distribution, 9 at the upper limits, and 1 at the lower limits. As with *z* scores, stanines can be used to show relative standing.

PERCENTILES   A percentile is a statistic computed from the raw score, and may be used to indicate the percentage of students who received the same or lower score. A percentile of 84, for example, can be interpreted to mean that 84% of those students taking the test received the same or lower raw score. Percentiles do not indicate the percentage of questions answered correctly.

With norm-referenced tests, percentiles are generally provided. Percentiles allow the student's relative standing to be determined in relation to students of a similar age or grade. Percentiles can also be computed by using the following procedure:

1. List the raw scores from high to low.
2. Record the number of students who received each score.
3. Select a score for which you would like to determine a percentile.
4. Calculate the percentage of students whose scores were less than the score you selected. (This is done by dividing the total number of scores into the number of scores that were less than the one selected.)
5. Calculate one-half of the percentage of students who received the score for which you are determining the percentile. Add this number to the percentage of students who scored less than this (step 4).

AGE AND GRADE SCORES With many norm-referenced tests, raw scores can be converted into grade or age scores that reflect the average grade or age at which students in the norm population achieved that raw score. A test manual may indicate, for example, that a raw score of 40 corresponds to an age score of 9–5 (9 years, 5 months), and a grade score of 4.3. This means that the student correctly answered as many items as the average of students in the norm group who were 9 years and 5 months of age or in the third month of the fourth grade.

Grade and age scores are relatively gross measures of performance that can be used to convey to parents and teachers a very general level of achievement. Thus, they may be used to measure global or long-term objectives. They are not sufficient, however, for the purpose of instructional planning. It must be remembered that grade and age scores are derived from the total number of correct responses, and as a result, do not necessarily indicate the specific skills that the student has acquired. Two students with raw scores of 30 could have missed entirely different questions. These two students, therefore, could have dramatically different academic skills and deficits. Age and grade scores may serve, however, as the starting point for the assessment of specific skills in that they assist in identifying students in need of a more extensive analysis.

☐ *To What Extent Has the Student Achieved Certain Skills?*
If educational assessment is to be useful, it must aid in the development and implementation of instructional programs. A crucial first step in this process is determining the degree to which the student has acquired the skills presented in the curriculum. This information can be analyzed in numerous ways so as to assist in identifying student error patterns and variables affecting student performance. From this analysis, effective and efficient instructional programs can be constructed.

As discussed previously, it is sometimes difficult to use a formal norm-referenced test to determine if a student has mastered the specific skills required in the classroom. The primary function of formal tests is to provide information about the student's relative standing. This is not to say that test data are irrelevant for instructional planning. Rather, it is more accurate to say that they assist in identifying the student's general area of skill deficiency. Formal tests may narrow the range of skills that must be examined in the more extensive, informal, criterion-referenced assessment that follows.

An informal, or criterion-referenced, assessment instrument follows the sequence of skills that will be presented in the curriculum. It may be developed by using instructional materials the student will use. The criterion-referenced instrument should contain a sufficient number of questions for each skill. The chances of a diagnostic error occurring are dramatically increased if too few questions or test items are presented. If there is only one question per skill, for example, a careless error may be mistaken for a deficiency in the student's knowledge of the skill.

The informal assessment should probably begin at the point at which the student began experiencing difficulty in the formal test. This point can generally be identified by analyzing the questions that were missed. The formal test data may show, for example, that the student missed all questions involving multiplication but no questions involving addition or subtraction. This would suggest that the informal test should begin with the analysis of basic multiplication. The formal test in this case served to more precisely define the scope of the extensive informal assessment that follows, thus making the process more organized and efficient.

PERCENTAGE Percentage of correct responses is perhaps the most common means of measuring student responses on an informal test. This form of measurement is very useful in determining the accuracy of student responses. Percentage is computed by dividing the number of correct responses by the total number of possible responses. To determine skill competence, this number, or percentage of correct responses, is compared to a preestablished mastery criterion for that skill, such as 90%. Students whose scores are less than the criterion are identified as not having mastered that skill and in possible need of remediation. Students whose scores are greater than this criterion are said to have mastered the skill.

Percentage provides valuable information as to whether or not the student has acquired a skill. It does not indicate, however, how fluently the skill is used. For this, a measure of rate is needed.

RATE Rate is a very sensitive measure of student performance. Whereas percentage measures only number, rate measures number and time. Rate is computed by dividing the number of responses by the length of time it took to complete the task. A student who answered 30 math problems correctly in two minutes would have a rate of 15 correct problems per minute.

Rate can be computed for correct and incorrect responses. This rate may then be judged in relation to a preestablished criterion. The student whose rate surpasses that criterion is said to be proficient. Proficiency rates for various subject areas will be presented in chapters 4, 5, and 6.

Rate allows a distinction to be made between those who have simply acquired a skill and those who can use the skill quickly and fluently. Two students, for example, may both achieve 100% accuracy on a set of addition facts, but be dramatically different in their rate and ability to apply the facts. No differences can be discerned between these students if only percentage of correct responses is examined. This example serves to illustrate that, while percentage is a good measure of accuracy, it cannot be used to determine the speed or fluency of responses. For instructional decision making, it is crucial that this distinction be made.

Proficiency criteria stated in terms of response rate provide a guideline for determining when to advance students to the next, more difficult level of the curriculum. Researchers have stated that progress on subsequent tasks becomes more probable when students are required to achieve high rates on prerequisite skills (Haughton, 1971). By using response rates, curriculum advancement can be systematically and empirically controlled.

In the classroom students experience a great deal of difficulty if their rate of response is slow. The student who reads 35 words per minute must read twice as long as the student who reads 70 words per minute. A slow response rate results in the task of reading becoming tedious and laborious.

All classroom instructional activities have time constraints that reflect the large number of activities that must be completed during the school day. Time limits often mean that the student who has a slow response rate will complete far fewer instructional activities than will others in the class. Unfortunately, this may mean that the student will fall further and further behind his or her peers.

☐ *How Trustworthy Are the Data?*
Imagine the disastrous results and outrage if medical interventions or even automobile repairs were instituted on the basis of inaccurate or unreliable data. Car owners would undoubtably pay for unnecessary and needless repairs. The results for individuals needing medical care could be even more unfortunate. In education, it is just as important that data be precise, accurate, and trustworthy. Without this, the accurate assessment of instructional skills is simply a matter of chance. If educa-

tional programs are based on flawed data, there is no compelling reason why they should succeed.

The trustworthiness of data is the single most important consideration in the assessment of instructional skills. With formal tests, this means that there must be some assurance that the norms are accurate and that the normative population is truly representative. With informal tests, the questions on the assessment instrument must allow for a precise and thorough evaluation of the instructional skills that will be demanded of the student in the classroom. It matters little what statistical procedures are used to report the assessment results if the data themselves cannot be trusted to present a true analysis of student performance. In order to ensure that the data are trustworthy, a great deal of attention must be paid to many issues, including the reliability and validity of the assessment instruments.

RELIABILITY   *Reliability* refers to the consistency of test results. If a student completes a particular test on two separate occasions and receives the same score, the test may be said to be reliable. If a test is reliable, there should be assurance that student errors are due to a lack of knowledge or skills and not the result of a faulty assessment instrument. Educational plans can then be constructed with some degree of confidence that the results do in fact reflect the true nature of the student's skill.

Reliability can be computed by using a variety of statistical procedures and is reported as a reliability coefficient (*r*). This coefficient ranges from +1.0, which indicates perfect reliability, to 0, or total unreliability. A reliability coefficient of +1.0 would indicate that two sets of test scores are perfectly related. In this case, a high score on one test would be related to a high score on another test. Likewise, low scores on the two tests would be related. A score of 0 would indicate that there is no relationship between the two sets of scores. Obviously, it is desirable that there be a great deal of agreement, and thus a greater reliability score between sets of data. Salvia and Ysseldyke (1985) state that a test should have a reliability coefficient of at least .80 if it is to be used in making educational decisions.

Test reliability. There are several methods of determining test reliability. With *test-retest reliability,* the same test is given two weeks apart and the scores are then compared. A difference in scores may indicate that the test is unreliable. However, it may also indicate that instruction and learning have taken place. In this case, the reduction in the reliability coefficient would not indicate as much about the trustworthiness of the test as it might about the extent of instruction.

In *alternate-forms reliability,* two tests measuring the same material, but with different questions, are given at the same time. The results are then compared.

Split-half reliability allows an examination of the degree of agreement or variability between two portions of the same test. The even-numbered items, for example, might be compared to the odd-numbered items. When using this procedure, it is generally advisable that all of the questions pertain to the same or closely related skills. This allows for a more precise examination of the worth of all test items. Howell, Kaplan, and O'Connell (1979) suggest that this procedure can be adapted in the following manner in order to evaluate the reliability of an informal test:

1. Calculate the agreement for all possible pairs of answers.

Possible Question Pairs		Degree of Agreement
1–2 = 7/10	=	.70
1–3 = 3/10	=	.30
1–4 = 5/10	=	.50
2–3 = 6/10	=	.60
2–4 = 9/10	=	.90
3–4 = 9/10	=	.90

These data indicate that seven of the ten students gave the same answer for questions 1 and 2, and three of the ten gave the same answer for questions 1 and 3.

2. Total the degree of agreement of the pairs for each question.

Question 1

Question Pairs	Agreement
1–2	.70
1–3	.30
1–4	.50
	1.50 (Total Agreement)

Question 2

Question Pairs	Agreement
1–2	.30
2–3	.60
2–4	.90
	1.80 (Total Agreement)

Question 3

Question Pairs	Agreement
1–3	.30
2–3	.60
3–4	.90
	1.80 (Total Agreement)

Question 4

Question Pairs	Agreement
1–4	.50
2–4	.90
3–4	.90
	2.30 (Total Agreement)

3. Divide the total agreement for each item by the number of test questions minus 1.

Question 1
$$\frac{1.50}{3} = .5$$

Question 2
$$\frac{1.80}{3} = .6$$

Question 3
$$\frac{1.8}{3} = .6$$

Question 4
$$\frac{2.3}{3} = .76$$

These data can be used to indicate which questions are not yielding consistent information and therefore must be revised. In this case, none of the questions appear to be adequate, although it appears that question 4 is the most reliable. By revising questions 1, 2, and 3, the reliability of all the questions may be raised to an acceptable level.

Reliability of observations. It is often necessary to observe and record the behavior of students. Koorland and Westling (1981) and Bailey and Bostow (1979) have suggested a variety of methods for calculating the *reliability of observational data,* which is often expressed as the percentage of agreement between observers. Observational data may be collected by using permanent product, event, interval, time sample, latency and duration recording procedures. These recording procedures are discussed in detail in chapter 7.

In one method of determining reliability of observational data, suitable for event and permanent product recording, two observers simultaneously record the occurrence of a student's behavior. The degree of agreement (or reliability) is calculated by dividing the smaller number by the larger number and multiplying by 100. If, for example, one observer believed a student talked out 20 times while another observer recorded 21 talk-outs, the percentage of agreement would be 95%:

$$\frac{20}{21} = .95 \times 100 = 95\%$$

Reliability of data from interval and time sample recording—in which observers record the occurrence or nonoccurrence of behavior in a series of time units—can be calculated by using the following formula:

$$\frac{\text{Number of Agreements}}{\text{Number of Agreements} + \text{Number of Disagreements}} \times 100$$

If two observers, for example, agreed that a student was out of seat during 16 thirty-second time intervals, but disagreed on the occurrence of out-of-seat behavior during four other thirty-second intervals, the percentage of agreement would be 80%:

$$\frac{16}{16 + 4} = .8 \times 100 = 80\%$$

The reliability of latency and duration observations, in which the length of time is recorded, is calculated by dividing the shorter number of minutes by the longer number of minutes and multiplying by 100. If one observer, for example, recorded that a student was off task for seven minutes while another observer recorded ten minutes of off-task behavior, the percentage of agreement would be 70%:

$$\frac{7}{10} = .7 \times 100 = 70\%$$

Alberto and Troutman (1982) state that it is highly preferred to have interobserver agreement scores of 90% or higher, while scores of less than 80% may be suspect. These scores provide an approximate measure of the accuracy of observational data. They do not indicate the number of times a behavior actually occurred, but rather illustrate the level at which two observers agree about the occurrence of a behavior.

Standard error of measurement. Reliability provides a great deal of information about the amount of variability in a set of scores. This information about variability can also be useful in calculating a statistic known as the Standard Error of Measurement (*SEM*). This statistic provides a way of measuring the amount of error that inevitably affects any test results. These errors may consist of numerous factors such as mistakes in test administration, technical inadequacies of the assessment device, and even changes in the individual student due to factors such as learning. The *SEM* is generally provided in the test manual, but may be calculated by using the following formula:

$$SEM = S.D. \sqrt{1 - r}$$

The standard error measurement is represented by *SEM*, standard deviation by *S.D.*, and reliability by *r*. This formula indicates that tests with large standard deviations and low reliability coefficients will produce a large standard error of measurement.

Because of the error that always exists, no individual test score can be said to be the true score that precisely identifies the student's level of performance. Due to this, it is helpful to use the *SEM* to calculate a range of scores within which the student's true score may be said to exist.

To determine this range, the *SEM* is added to and subtracted from the student's test score. This establishes the limits of ± 1 *SEM*. This amount is doubled to achieve ± 2 *SEM* and tripled to achieve ± 3 *SEM*. These limits provide a certain degree of confidence that the student's true score is within a certain range of scores. This degree of confidence is usually expressed in terms of percentage. As illustrated in Figure 1–2, there is a 68% chance that a student's true score falls between ± 1 *SEM*, a 95% chance that it falls between ± 2 *SEM*, and a 99% chance that it falls between ± 3 *SEM*.

If a student received a score of 80 on a test with an *SEM* of 2, we would be 68% confident that the student's true score fell between 78 (-1

FIGURE 1-2 Confidence Interval

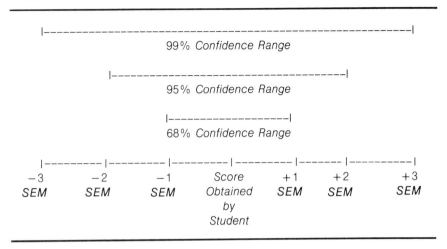

SEM) and 82 (+1 *SEM*). The confidence interval could easily be increased to 95% by adding and subtracting 2 *SEM* from the student's score. In this case, a range of 76 (−2 *SEM*) to 84 (+2 *SEM*) would result.

Suppose that another test on the same skill was given to the student. If the student received an 85, but the test had an *SEM* of 20, the 95% confidence interval would range from 65 to 105. If only test scores were reported, it could be assumed that the student performed somewhat better on the second test. When the range is considered, however, it can be seen that, in the second case, there is a 95% chance that the true score could be as low as 65, while with the first test it could only be as low as 76. This indicates quite clearly the desirability of selecting tests with low *SEM*s and high reliability coefficients.

Generally it is very helpful to report student scores as a range with a specified degree of confidence. This accurately conveys the tentative nature of the test results, and often promotes further investigation and analysis of student performance.

VALIDITY An assessment device could be very reliable and consistently yield stable scores and yet provide an inaccurate and incomplete evaluation of a student's skills. This may occur if the test lacks validity—that is, does not measure what it was designed to measure.

A test with a high degree of validity is reliable and provides a comprehensive, thorough, and accurate analysis of the skill being assessed. The results obtained from such a test can then be used with a great deal of confidence for the purpose of instructional planning.

Content validity refers to the degree to which an assessment procedure measures the ability or skill which it is designed to measure. Content validity is not established by using statistical procedures, but rather by examining the completeness, appropriateness, and method of presentation of the test items (Salvia & Ysseldyke, 1985). A great deal of knowledge about a subject area is required in order to determine if a question is in fact appropriate. The test questions, if they are valid, must comprehensively evaluate the skill being measured as well as the grade and age appropriateness of the items. A question involving the use of calculus, while measuring mathematical skills, is probably not appropriate or useful in assessing the computational skills of a second grader.

In informal assessment it is essential that a great deal of time be spent in evaluating the content validity of the test. There should be a sufficient number of test questions to ensure that the skill being assessed is completely and comprehensively evaluated. An adequate assessment of a student's math skills could not be obtained, for example, if only one question per skill is presented. Likewise, a thorough test of reading would assess more than word-recognition skills.

Also, test questions should be presented in a manner similar to that which will be required of the student in the instructional setting. A valid test, for example, would not be constructed to assess math skills in a multiple-choice format when a written response is required in the classroom.

Criterion validity refers to comparing a test score to the results obtained from another test or form of measurement that has previously been proven valid. Criterion validity may be determined statistically in the same manner as reliability. This allows an examination of the degree of correlation between the two measures. As a result, the criterion validity of a test can range from a correlation coefficient of -1.0 to $+1.0$. A score of 0 indicates that there is no relationship between the two measures, while a score of $+1.0$ indicates that the scores of two tests are perfectly related. A score of -1.0 shows that the test scores are inversely related, which means that a high score on one measure is related to a low score on the other measure. By using this procedure, test scores can be correlated to observations, classroom work, rating scales, and even grades. If the measures are collected at the same time, then concurrent validity, which is a form of criterion validity, can be established. Concurrent validity can be used, for example, to examine the relationship of scores from two reading tests given at the same time. With predictive validity, another type of criterion validity, assessment results are compared to data gathered at a later date. This is illustrated, for example, by using scores from a vocational test to predict later success in a particular occupation.

Construct validity, another type of validity, is used to measure the extent to which a test assesses an unobservable behavior or hypothetical construct such as intelligence or self-concept. Generally, construct validity is determined by examining the degree of correlation between the test in question and other tests previously identified as being valid measures of the construct. It is extremely difficult to make a definitive judgment concerning a test's construct validity because the phenomenon being measured cannot be directly observed, but rather is inferred. Additionally, construct validity is greatly affected if the comparison test is flawed or does not in fact accurately measure the phenomenon in question.

Regardless of why the data are selected, careful consideration must be given to the trustworthiness of the information. There must be a great deal of assurance that the data provide a comprehensive, nondiscriminatory, and accurate analysis of the skill or ability being tested. Once this determination has been made, the data can then be used with confidence to make educational decisions that meet the needs of the student.

CONCLUSION

Educational assessment serves a variety of purposes. The purpose dictates the type of assessment instrument that is appropriate.

Formal devices may be used for the purpose of program placement and to evaluate a broad array of skills. The information from these tests may be helpful in identifying general strengths and weaknesses. Informal assessment procedures may be used to sample skills specific to the curriculum. The results from informal assessment serve to continuously monitor student growth.

The data from assessment may be used to answer a number of diagnostic questions. These questions dictate what statistical procedures should be used in analyzing the data and are summarized in Table 1–3.

TABLE 1-3 Summary of Diagnostic Questions and Statistical Procedures

Diagnostic Question	Procedure Used to Answer Question
What is the central tendency of the data?	mean, median, mode
How much do the data fluctuate?	range, frequency distribution, standard deviation
How does the student's performance compare to that of others?	standard deviation, standard scores, percentiles, age & grade scores
To what extent has the student achieved certain skills?	percentage, rate
How trustworthy are the data?	reliability, validity

ACTIVITIES

1. State four issues in assessment and explain how assessment practices are affected by these issues.
2. How has legislation influenced assessment?
3. State five purposes for educational assessment.
4. Describe how formal and informal tests are best used.
5. Discuss the use of norms.
6. Compare means, medians, and modes as measures of central tendency.
7. Timmy, a second grade student, received the following scores—expressed as percentage of correct responses—on a series of math assignments: 60, 61, 40, 72, 90, 38, 85, 98, 98, 82. For these data, find the a) range, b) mean, c) median, and d) mode. Construct a frequency-distribution table in intervals of 10 percentage points.
8. A reading test has a mean of 100, a standard deviation of 10, and an SEM of 5. Using these data, complete the following:
   a. What are the limits of +1, 2, and 3 *S.D.*?
   b. Frankie received a score of 95 on this test. Within what range could we expect the score to fall 68% of the time? 95% of the time?
9. Mary, a sixth grader, scored at the second grade level on a norm-based math test that was administered in Mr. Smith's class.
   a. Before using this information for educational programming, what factors concerning the adequacy of the test must be considered?

b. Assuming the test is adequate, what does this score indicate about Mary's relative standing?

c. How does this test score indicate which specific math skills Mary has acquired?

d. What additional information must be collected before developing an instructional program?

e. How would this information be acquired?

10. How is rate computed?

2

Assessment for Instruction

■ **Learning Objectives**

After completing this chapter, the reader should be able to:

- describe the three-step model for the assessment process
- describe the steps involved in task analysis
- differentiate between periodic and continuous assessment
- describe criterion-referenced testing (types of tests and development of a test)
- describe methods of data collecting and charting
- describe how data may be used to set objectives

All the major decisions that influence a child's progress in school, including class placement, curriculum selection, and diagnostic teaching, are based on assessment information (Smith, Neisworth, & Greer, 1978). To aid in determining a student's instructional needs, assessment should provide information in two areas. First, assessment data must assist the teacher in determining the goals of instruction—the curriculum decisions, or "what to teach." This may include academic skills and concepts in language arts, reading, and arithmetic, content subjects such as science and social studies, motor skills, personal-social skills, and vocational skills. Assessment should also provide information that helps the teacher determine the means of instruction, or "how to teach" the student. Instructional decisions may involve learning variables such as expectancy factors, stimulus events, response events, and consequent events.

To carry out assessment for what to teach and how to teach, there must be a systematic plan for collecting and using assessment data. The three-step model outlined on the following page provides the framework for this important assessment process.

Step 1: Determine the skills, behaviors, or learning variables to be assessed.
Step 2: Select and administer an assessment procedure.
Step 3: Record performance and set objectives.

This assessment model, detailed in the following pages, describes the sequence of steps that will lead to identifying the educational needs of students and will aid in developing effective instructional programs. In subsequent chapters, this framework will be applied to assessing learning variables, reading, language arts, math, and behavior.

STEP 1: DETERMINE SKILLS, BEHAVIORS, OR LEARNING VARIABLES TO BE ASSESSED

The first step in the assessment process is the precise identification of the specific academic skills, content areas, behaviors, and/or learning variables that will be examined. The behaviors and/or skills that may be selected are dependent upon the student's level of development, the instructional methods used by the teacher, and the teacher's instructional responsibilities.

Skill/Behavior Networks

A skill hierarchy, network, or scope-and-sequence skills list includes a list of skills or behaviors that may be assessed. Detailed networks for the areas of reading, language arts, math, and behavior are provided in their respective chapters in this text. Skill/behavior networks may be found in teaching manuals, in published curriculum guides that accompany basal programs, in published criterion-referenced tests such as the Brigance Inventory of Basic Skills (Brigance, 1977), or in other curriculum guides.

The order of the skills may differ according to the source. Experts frequently disagree on the hierarchical arrangement of academic skills within a curriculum. Furthermore, the acquisition of a task in a hierarchy may not always be dependent upon acquisition of a preceding subtask. Howell, Kaplan, and O'Connell (1979) note that subtasks may at times resemble a task tree. In these cases, many subtasks at the same difficulty level are necessary for the task's successful completion. However, the order of subtask completion may not be important.

The degree of specificity may also vary widely. A teacher-made skill network may reflect that particular teacher's task analysis of a section of the curriculum. For example, in one network, every component prerequisite skill may be listed, whereas another network may list only broad skill categories.

Skill/behavior networks assist in identifying short- and long-term teaching goals for use on an Individual Education Program (I.E.P.). Additionally, the networks may be used as checklists to record the presence or absence of skills or behaviors.

Skill networks provide structure to the assessment process by identifying the skills or behaviors that might be assessed. Then, efforts and resources may be applied in an efficient and organized manner. The end result will be a carefully planned and accurate assessment of the student's instructional needs.

■ Task Analysis

Skill/behavior networks may be helpful in analyzing a particular task. Task analysis is an important step in locating the source of a student's difficulty. When prerequisite skills are determined using a skill network, a student can then be evaluated in those subtasks to pinpoint the skills that are weak. Howell, Kaplan, and O'Connell (1979) define *task analysis* as "the process of isolating, sequencing, and describing all of the essential components of a task" (p. 81).

Task analysis involves three components. First, a behavioral objective or criterion statement must be written. This is a statement describing the task in behavioral or performance terms. A terminal behavioral objective describes what the learner should be able to do at the end of a period of instruction. All behavioral objectives should parallel the instructional goals of the classroom curriculum, so specification of objectives should be done with the aid of the actual curriculum being used. They should be written in precise terms, and be discrete, observable, and measurable tasks that define the behaviors to be demonstrated. To communicate all the information needed for assessment, a behavioral objective should identify the target behavior, the conditions under which the behavior is to be displayed, and the criteria for acceptable performance. Examples of well-written behavioral objectives are:

- ■ Given a graded reader, Brian will read orally 100 words per minute correctly, with two errors or less for three consecutive days.
- ■ Given a set of twenty-six flashcards, each one containing a different letter of the alphabet, Janet will place the cards in alphabetical order in 5 minutes or less with no errors.
- ■ When given directions for a task, Peter will begin the task within 10 seconds, 9 out of 10 times.

A second component of task analysis is determining the subtasks or prerequisite skills necessary to perform a task. Remembering the terminal objective may help to isolate all of the essential subtasks. For example, in a task involving the understanding and use of a clock, prerequisite skills might include the ability to:

- discriminate between the hour and minute hand
- identify all hour-hand placements
- identify all minute-hand placements including intervals of five, exact minute placements, and fractions of an hour
- identify all times correctly (Smith, 1981)

Other prerequisite skills necessary for using a clock might include saying, identifying, and writing numbers from 1 to 60.

The third component of task analysis involves sequencing the steps of the task in order of complexity. For efficient instruction to occur, the order of subtask presentation must be determined. Howell, Kaplan, and O'Connell (1979) state that this sequencing allows assessment to be conducted in a "test down" manner. This means that the student is tested on the most difficult task first. If the task is performed correctly, it is assumed that the student is capable of performing the prerequisite tasks, and valuable time is thereby saved in the diagnostic process. An example of task analysis is provided in Figure 2-1.

FIGURE 2-1 Sample Task Analysis

Terminal Objective: The student will express his/her home mailing address in writing. This should include a house, apartment, or P.O. box number, street, city, state, and zip code.

Subtask 1: able to state orally home mailing address
Behavioral Objective: When asked his/her home mailing address, the student will orally state the correct address within three minutes without any reference aids and with 100% accuracy.

Subtask 2: able to read home mailing address
Behavioral Objective: When shown his/her home mailing address on a sheet of paper, the student will read the words within three minutes without any aid and with 100% accuracy.

Subtask 3: able to spell home mailing address
Behavioral Objective: When given his/her correct home mailing address verbally, the student will spell the correct address within five minutes without any reference aids and with 100% accuracy.

Subtask 4: able to express home mailing address in writing
Terminal Objective: When asked to write his/her home mailing address, the student will write the complete address on a sheet of paper within five minutes without any aid and with 100% accuracy.

Dunlap and House (1976) show how task analysis may be used to identify the prerequisite skills for the task of adding 2¾ and 1⅔. The authors identify nine skills prerequisite to the terminal task:

1. concepts of whole, regions, and sets
2. concept of rational numbers
3. concept of numerator
4. concept of denominator
5. writing fractional numbers
6. principle of addition for whole numbers
7. principle of addition for fractions
8. addition algorithm for whole numbers
9. multiplication algorithm for fractions (p. 17)

Taylor (1984) notes that in task analysis the number of steps depends on the individual student for whom the task was designed. For example, a severely handicapped student might need a more detailed breakdown of subtasks than a mildly handicapped student. The task analysis in both cases, however, is equally valid and useful. Some nonacademic skills, such as making a bed, are much easier to task-analyze than academic skills. Observers are more likely, therefore, to agree on the nature and order of the prerequisite skills associated with nonacademic skills.

Once a skill hierarchy or network has been chosen, the teacher needs to decide at what point in the network to begin the assessment process. To accomplish this, it may be helpful to look at data already available, such as anecdotal information written by past teachers, past report cards, referrals for special education services, work samples, and results of recent standardized tests. This information may be found in the child's cumulative school record. McLoughlin and Lewis (1981) note that parents may also be of help in identifying current levels of academic performance. Also, students themselves may offer an additional source of information by indicating which academic areas are troublesome.

STEP 2: SELECT AND ADMINISTER AN ASSESSMENT PROCEDURE

■ ■ Before selecting an assessment procedure, the purpose of assessment must first be determined. If, for example, the purpose is for placement in a graded textbook, then a standardized test or placement test provided in a basal series may be helpful. Assessing for the purpose of educational diagnosis may require the use of several evaluative instruments. If a severe academic or behavior problem is suspected, a more precise and extensive analysis is warranted. The purpose of assessment and the severity of the problem, therefore, should determine the selection of evaluative instruments.

For the purpose of instruction, assessment procedures may be categorized as either *periodic* or *continuous*. *Periodic assessment procedures* may either be formal or informal and yield global information that may assist in surveying a student's general level of performance and establishing long-range instructional objectives or goals for an I.E.P. This periodic assessment results in summative data. *Continuous assessment procedures* yield formative data and are used to supplement and expand the information obtained using periodic assessment procedures.

As illustrated in Figure 2–2, the extent and frequency of assessment increases corresponding to the severity of the learning and behavior deficits. The student who is progressing adequately need not be continuously assessed throughout the entire year, in which case periodic assessment may serve as the primary method of evaluation. It may only be necessary to use continuous assessment procedures at critical points in the educational program when immediate feedback concerning a particular skill is required. For example, continuous assessment is important when a student is learning a new skill, a time when specific information concerning potential problems would be helpful.

For the student who is not progressing adequately, continuous assessment is important. This frequent and comprehensive monitoring of skills or behaviors allows a comprehensive analysis of the specific elements of the instructional program. This information can then be used to institute changes in the instructional program with some assurance that they are appropriate and will be effective.

■ Periodic Assessment

A periodic test is often administered prior to beginning an instructional program. This initial periodic assessment may occur, for example, at the beginning of the school year and should continue until enough information is obtained to begin an instructional program. This type of assessment can provide an overview of skills and yields information about the starting point for instruction. As a result, it provides a focus for further and more extensive assessment.

This initial assessment can be unnecessarily lengthy if the teacher is not judicious in the selection of appropriate evaluative procedures. At this point it is not necessary to test every conceivable skill with numerous tests. What is called for is a determination of the general area of

FIGURE 2-2 Assessment Continuum Illustrating the Relationship between Periodic and Continuous Assessment to Student Progress

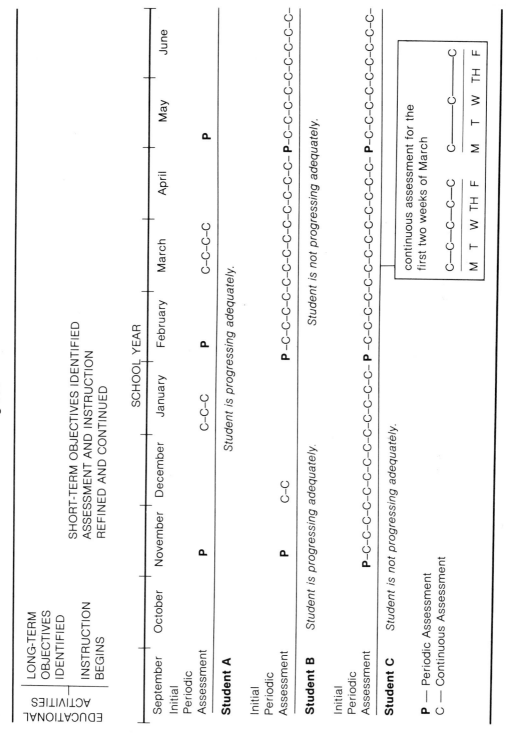

difficulty so that specific curriculum-based tests can be used to analyze the problem and continuously monitor individual growth.

Tests used initially to assess students may also be used periodically throughout the school year. Tests may be given weekly, as is often the case with spelling tests, or they may be given at the end of an instructional unit or at the end of the school year. While the data from such tests may be useful in instructional planning, the primary function of periodic assessment is to evaluate the extent of growth that has occurred over a period of time.

☐ *Formal Tests*

Formal (norm-referenced) tests are often used to assess student achievement prior to beginning an instructional program. The results may be used as one of several criteria for placement in a curriculum. These tests are often readministered after a period of time, such as a semester or school year, to demonstrate how much growth was achieved during the instructional period. Due to the nature of formal tests, the skills sampled may not reflect the objectives of a particular curriculum. As a result, these tests may not provide an adequate explanation of a student's specific academic problems. Formal tests may, however, serve as the beginning point in the evaluative process by identifying areas in need of a more precise and thorough evaluation. A list and description of widely used formal tests is provided in the Appendix.

☐ *Informal Procedures*

Informal procedures are also commonly used as a means of initially and periodically assessing student performance and skills. Informal devices may be used by themselves or as a means of supplementing the information obtained from formal tests. They may be commercially developed instruments such as the Silvaroli Classroom Reading Inventory (Silvaroli, 1982) or teacher-made devices, such as checklists.

Teacher-made devices may be constructed from instructional materials so that the items closely parallel the curriculum being used. Devices of this type may be given at the beginning of the year and/or periodically to assign students to curriculum materials, to form instructional groups, and to plan individual programs. Because the procedures are based directly on the classroom curriculum, the results will be very relevant for use in instructional planning.

Blankenship and Lilly (1981) suggest using a procedure called *curriculum-based assessment* (CBA), defined as "the practice of obtaining direct and frequent measures of a student's performance on a series of sequentially arranged objectives derived from the curriculum used in the classroom" (p. 81). The assessment process is described in the following steps:

1. Select the curriculum materials, such as a basal reading or math series, to be used in the classroom.
2. After carefully analyzing the curriculum materials, develop a CBA. Development includes selecting and sequencing skills to be assessed, writing skill objectives, making assessment materials, planning the administration, designing a scoring and recordkeeping system, and determining rules for making placement decisions.
3. Administer the CBA over a period of a few days. Performance should be measured on more than one occasion.
4. Record performance, noting which skills students have or have not mastered.
5. Analyze the assessment data.
6. Make a decision concerning placement in a grade-level text or further assessment on a lower or higher level.
7. Place the students and form instructional groups.

Many commercial programs include assessment devices with placement and mastery tests, particularly those series used for reading and math. These tests are often very useful for periodic assessment and may be adapted, if necessary, to meet individual needs.

■ **Continuous Assessment**

All students require some form of continuous assessment. For those students progressing adequately through a curriculum, continuous assessment may be used on a limited basis as a means of providing information that would further refine an already appropriate instructional program. There are, however, a number of students who either do not adequately progress or need further diagnosis due to the severity of their problems. These students require a more extensive evaluation that is generally conducted daily over a period of time. This may necessitate the use of an assessment procedure that is administered frequently and assists in precisely identifying factors that affect the student's progress.

Continuous assessment provides a comprehensive examination of a skill or limited number of skills. These procedures are designed to examine a student's response to specific material and to determine the factors associated with success and failure.

Continuous or ongoing assessment procedures are designed to provide frequent measurement of performance over time, allowing a comprehensive evaluation of specific skills and components of the instructional program. By thoroughly analyzing the instructional materials, setting, types of responses, and other factors associated with learning, effective short-term instructional plans may be developed. Discrete changes in student performance that may be due to either planned or unplanned changes in the curriculum and/or environment can then be detected and analyzed. Authors such as Ysseldyke, Thurlow, Graden, Wesson, Algozzine, and Deno (1983) state that the frequent collection of student performance data results in the making of more accurate and appropriate educational decisions. By collecting data in this manner, instructional problems may be precisely identified so that modifications in the school program may then be made.

☐ *Criterion-Referenced Testing*

Taylor (1984) notes that criterion-referenced testing is perhaps the most valuable of all informal assessment procedures. Criterion-referenced testing is a relatively new practice that differs significantly from norm-referenced measurement (Salvia & Ysseldyke, 1985). The purpose of norm-referenced testing is to describe an individual's relative position in a group. In contrast, criterion-referenced measurement allows a comparison of an individual's performance to an absolute standard (Glaser, 1963). Therefore, in criterion-referenced testing, performance is analyzed without making a comparison to others. If the student has achieved the standard, it is assumed that he or she has mastered the skill. The data obtained from criterion-referenced tests therefore may be useful to the classroom teacher in that the measures describe student performance in relation to a fixed criterion of mastery, such as 90 or 95%.

Howell, Kaplan, and O'Connell (1979) note several advantages of the criterion-referenced test. It provides what the authors term "dynamic data" in that the data are collected over time. All test items are on the same instructional skill level so a teacher can determine readily what a child needs to be taught. Often criterion-referenced tests are prepared by a teacher so there is little disparity between test and classroom behaviors.

Skills assessed by criterion-referenced tests are stated in behavioral or performance terms and are usually directly related to instructional objectives. While tests of this type may be used periodically, their primary value is in their ability to provide a relatively continuous assessment of the skills related to a specific curriculum. Highly specific curricular objectives can be tested frequently to measure change.

TYPES OF CRITERION–REFERENCED TESTS   Various types of criterion-referenced tests may be used for continuous assessment. Criterion-referenced tests may be commercially produced or teacher-made. Zigmond, Vallecorsa, and Silverman (1983) suggest two advantages of using a commercial test. First, the information concerning the design and development characteristics of the test will be available. Second, use of a published test will save teachers considerable time and effort that might be used to construct a test. Published criterion-referenced tests are listed in each of the remaining chapters.

Often, however, a teacher will not find a published criterion-referenced test that will meet a student's needs or be closely related to the curriculum being used. In these cases, a teacher-constructed test may be developed to measure exactly what is needed. This type of measure also yields information directly related to curriculum objectives. An example of a teacher-made criterion-referenced test is provided in Figure 2–3. In each of the following chapters, examples of teacher-constructed assessment devices will be provided.

DEVELOPMENT OF A CRITERION-REFERENCED TEST Gronlund (1973) suggests six principles related to the design and construction of criterion-referenced tests:

1. Criterion-referenced testing requires a clearly defined and delimited domain of learning tasks.
2. Criterion-referenced testing requires that instructional objectives be clearly defined in behavioral (performance) terms.
3. Criterion-referenced testing requires that standards of performance be clearly specified.
4. Criterion-referenced testing requires that student performance be adequately sampled within each area of performance.
5. Criterion-referenced testing requires that test items be selected on the basis of how well they reflect the behavior specified in the instructional objectives.
6. Criterion-referenced testing requires a scoring and reporting system that adequately describes student performance on clearly defined learning tasks. (pp. 3–5)

First, the achievement area to be tested should be delimited to a reasonably sized unit of instruction. A manageable unit might be one covering one or two weeks of instruction. Taylor (1984) suggests referring to the I.E.P., if available, to determine appropriate objectives upon which to focus.

The second principle concerns stating instructional objectives in behavior/performance terms. General objectives may be stated first and then be further defined by specifying behaviors a student is expected to demonstrate at the end of a unit. To define specific subtasks, it may be helpful to perform a task analysis of the given skill objectives listed on the student's I.E.P.

Third, standards of performance based on mastery should be clearly specified. There is a wide range of opinion concerning appropriate com-

FIGURE 2-3   Teacher-Made Criterion-Referenced Test

Skill: Sums to 9.

Instructional Objective: Given 75 addition facts with sums to 9, write the correct answers at 60 digits per minute with 0–1 errors for three consecutive days.

5 2 —	1 8 —	4 2 —	6 0 —	3 4 —	2 7 —	4 4 —	0 0 —	5 4 —	0 9 —	6 2 —	2 5 —	7 2 —	5 1 —	1 7 —	(15)
1 2 —	2 2 —	0 9 —	1 7 —	1 1 —	3 6 —	1 4 —	8 0 —	3 4 —	6 3 —	1 2 —	6 3 —	3 1 —	8 1 —	3 4 —	(30)
4 4 —	4 5 —	2 6 —	1 8 —	0 3 —	6 2 —	4 2 —	1 6 —	4 3 —	3 4 —	2 7 —	1 5 —	3 6 —	4 1 —	7 0 —	(45)
2 5 —	1 5 —	2 6 —	1 6 —	7 0 —	5 3 —	4 5 —	0 0 —	0 4 —	1 6 —	4 3 —	6 3 —	3 5 —	2 3 —	3 5 —	(60)
7 2 —	3 4 —	4 2 —	2 2 —	1 1 —	4 3 —	5 4 —	1 8 —	3 4 —	5 3 —	5 2 —	8 1 —	2 4 —	1 7 —	1 0 —	(75)

Score # digits correct/minute _____

digits incorrect/minute _____

Name _____

Date _____

petency/proficiency standards and how these standards should be determined (an issue discussed later in this chapter).

The fourth principle involves the adequate sampling of student performance. A large pool of test items covering as many items as feasible should be developed for each objective so that the student's true ability in an area can be assessed.

Fifth, the items selected should be direct measures of the expected learning outcomes. Tested behaviors should be closely associated with a specific instructional area so that little inference is made when evaluating the test results.

Sixth, a scoring and reporting system that adequately describes student performance on specific tasks should be included. This report conveys what the student can do and the acquired level or proficiency.

OBJECTIVE TEST ITEMS   Various formats for written test questions may be used. Multiple choice, matching, completion or short answer, and true–false questions have been traditionally used as test items in teacher-made tests. These types of test questions may be used to assess various skills on a continuous basis.

Gronlund (1973) suggests ten general rules for writing objective test items. Each test item should:

1. be directly relevant to the specific behavior described in the learning outcome
2. specify the task in a clear, unambiguous manner
3. be concise and free from nonfunctional material
4. be free of irrelevant factors which may prevent the student from responding correctly
5. be free of irrelevant clues (for example, grammatical inconsistencies) which may lead the student to the correct answer
6. be free of clues to the answers of other items in the test (for example, a name or date)
7. be at the proper level of difficulty
8. have a correct answer that experts would agree upon
9. be stated positively

The tenth guideline that Gronlund suggests is to include enough items to adequately sample the learning outcomes to be measured.

Multiple-choice items consist of an incomplete statement or question followed by several alternatives. Many test experts consider the multiple-choice item to be the best type of objective test for measuring a variety of educational objectives (Green, 1975). Because of its versatility, it is widely used. Among several rules suggested by Gronlund (1973) in the construction of multiple-choice items are the following:

1. The incomplete statement should present a single definite problem.
2. The alternatives should be brief, similar in form, and grammatically consistent with the incomplete statement.
3. The alternatives should be placed in alphabetical order.
4. The alternatives should avoid "none of the above" or "all of the above."
5. Distractors that are plausible to the nonachiever should be used—for example, common errors and misconceptions.

Gronlund notes that matching items are best used when a series of multiple-choice questions have a common set of alternatives. It is better, for example, to present matching items than a number of multiple-choice questions with the same possible answers. In constructing the matching item, he suggests several guidelines:

1. The material in the lists should be homogeneous.
2. The lists should be relatively short.
3. The lists of responses should be longer than the list of premises.
4. The brief responses should be placed on the right and in alphabetical order.
5. Directions should be included indicating the basis for matching.

Completion or short-answer tests have a wide range of applicability in measuring factual recall (Green, 1975). This type of test question may be successfully used to assess skills when specific rules for construction are followed. Only significant words should be omitted in completion items, and the item should be stated so that the answer is limited to a word or brief phrase (Green, 1975). Gronlund (1973) suggests that items be stated so that only one response is correct. In addition, the answer blanks should be equal in length to prevent length from being used as a clue.

True–false items should be restricted to those situations that are limited to two alternatives, for example, questions concerning cause and effect or fact and opinion (Gronlund, 1973). There are, however, few situations where only two alternatives are possible. As a result, the multiple-choice item usually is a better type of question to use.

USING CRITERION-REFERENCED TESTS To use a criterion-referenced test efficiently, a teacher should estimate a student's level of competence by referring to previous anecdotal and test records, work samples, and reports of past teachers. Then testing should begin at the highest point in the curriculum at which the student starts experiencing difficulty. The teacher may then continue down to the lower level skills, or backwards in the skill sequence. With this "test down" procedure, if a student masters higher level tasks, it can be assumed that he or she also has mastery of the prerequisite subskills.

PROBES   Probes, another type of criterion-referenced test, may be used frequently to precisely measure curriculum skill objectives. White and Haring (1980) define a *probe* as "a device, instrument, or period of time used by a teacher to sample a child's behavior" (p. 49). The sample provides a reasonable idea of the student's social behavior (e.g., crying) or performance in a skill without having to continuously record behavior throughout the day. Probes may take many forms. Arranging letters in alphabetical order, reading orally, identifying numerals, and writing answers to math problems are examples of probes. Skills assessed on a probe are usually stated in terms of the stimulus that is presented and the response that is required of the student (e.g., see–write answers to math facts).

A probe sheet is perhaps the most commonly used type of probe. The name of the child, the number correct and incorrect, and the date should be included on a probe sheet. The items selected for the probe should be representative of the skill to be assessed. The items in the probe shown in Figure 2–4 assess one specific instructional objective.

PRECISION TEACHING   Probes are often used as part of a measurement system called Precision Teaching. Precision Teaching includes a set of standard procedures for the direct and daily measurement of behavior.

FIGURE 2–4   Probe: See–Say Dolch Words (Preprimer Level)

a	and	my	run	can
three	look	help	in	for
down	we	big	here	it
away	me	to	said	one
where	is	yellow	blue	you
go	two	the	up	see
play	funny	make	red	come
jump	not	find	little	I
a	down	where	play	and
we	is	funny	my	big

Name _____

Date _____

Time _____

Number Correct _____

Number Incorrect _____

White and Haring (1980) describe five basic steps that are part of this procedure:

1. selecting an instruction pinpoint (e.g., oral reading speed or sight words read correctly)
2. developing a probe sheet to evaluate progress on the pinpoint selected
3. collecting rate data and recording these data on a standard behavior chart, also called an equal-ratio or proportional chart
4. making instructional decisions such as a change in instructional methods
5. continuing to alter the antecedents, the behavior, or the consequences until positive change occurs

☐ *Observation*

Observation permeates all other types of assessment. Teachers spend much of their time directly and indirectly observing students. Whether giving a diagnostic math test, using a checklist in language, administering an informal reading inventory, or taking a frequency count on times out of seat during the day, the teacher is continuously making observations about student behavior. McLoughlin and Lewis (1981) note that observation allows a teacher to gather information about specific student behaviors, such as social and academic skills, study habits, and self-help skills, and may produce information that often cannot be obtained from other procedures. Following an observation, a written record should be made that can be used to further clarify the results of assessment and aid in planning instructional objectives. Various observation techniques will be described in each of the following chapters.

STEP 3: RECORD PERFORMANCE AND SET OBJECTIVES

■ Record Performance

All of the diagnostic data concerning the student's strengths and weaknesses in academic skills, behavior, and learning variables must be organized in order to lead to effective instructional planning. The Periodic Assessment Record, a form presented in later chapters, is specific to each content area and assists in organizing the data obtained from periodic assessment procedures. The Periodic Assessment Record is a form on which scores from formal tests and data from periodic informal procedures may be recorded. By recording the data in a comprehensive manner, an analysis can be conducted that will indicate what aspects of the skill, behavior, or learning variable network require more extensive and continuous assessment. This record serves as a guide to further identify individual needs. In addition, the record can be easily used to generate instructional plans or teaching objectives and to develop and update I.E.P.'s.

Kerr and Nelson (1983) suggest that to "be an effective teacher—i.e., to ensure that your students are progressing as rapidly as their capacities and present educational technology allow, you need a system for monitoring their progress on a frequent and regular basis" (p. 29). Specific skills or behaviors that will serve as the focus for further and more frequent assessment and instruction should be listed on the Continuous Assessment Record, illustrated in Figure 2-5. Commercial or teacher-made continuous assessment devices may then be used to evaluate student performance precisely in each of the targeted areas. The following information should be recorded on the Continuous Assessment Record: 1) the date of assessment, 2) the conditions associated with assessment (such as the setting), mode of task presentation and/or reinforcers, 3) the skill or behavior required of the student, 4) current performance results, and 5) the proficiency goal, often expressed as either a percent or rate per minute. If assessment indicates that the student is deficient in a skill or behavior, that skill/behavior may serve as an instructional objective. The Continuous Assessment Record can be easily used as an aid in choosing short-range lesson plans or objectives.

To justify frequent data collection, the data collected and recorded on the Continuous Assessment Record must be meaningful. Data must be of comparable scale so that one day's performance can be judged against another day's performance to accurately determine if progress has been made (Smith, 1981). Data are commonly collected in one of two ways: 1) percent of correct responses, or 2) a rate of correct and/or incorrect responses. Depending on the skill or behavior being measured, one type of measurement system might be more appropriate than the other.

☐ *Percent Scores*
Percent scores (percent correct or percent of occurrence) provide an indication of the quality or accuracy of a performance, and an analysis of the number of correct or incorrect responses. Percent data do not provide information about the quantity or amount of work completed. When accuracy rather then speed is the primary aim, such as when a student is acquiring a skill, a percent score is a useful measure.

Percent is often more appropriate to use, for example, when giving a spelling test to a group of students when the speed of writing the answers is determined by the teacher. Assessing reading comprehension skills might also be better accomplished with only a percent measure because of the task complexity and various subskills used to answer questions (Eaton, 1978).

There are several limitations to the use of percent measures. While

FIGURE 2-5 Continuous Assessment Record

Date	Conditions	Skill/Behavior	Current Performance	Proficiency Criterion/Goal	Date Attained
	may include: mode of task presentation (prepared tape) instructional materials (probe) setting (regular class) learning style or preferred modality (auditory materials) motivators or reinforcers (praise)	target response being assessed	might be expressed in percent or rate		

Student's Name _____
Grade/Teacher _____

percent is an excellent measure of accuracy, it yields little information concerning the speed (fluency) of a response. Additionally, percent does not account for the number of opportunities the student has to respond to a task. For example, if there are ten words to be spelled one day and fifty words to be spelled the following day, a student who misses two words each time receives quite different percentage scores (80% and 96%). For the purpose of assessment, it is more helpful if the opportunities to engage in a particular task remain constant.

☐ *Rate Data*
Rate or frequency data indicate the period of time in which a behavior occurred. This type of measure is more sensitive than a percent measure because both accuracy and fluency (speed) are specified. White and Haring (1980) note that percent serves as an adequate measure of performance until the student stops making mistakes. While the student may continue to improve in the use of the skill, percent measures are incapable of detecting such change. According to Blankenship and Lilly (1981), rate is one of the most overlooked measures of student performance and should be the measure of choice when speed is concerned. Rate allows a discrimination to be made between the students who have acquired skills with 100% accuracy but are slow, and students who have acquired skills with 100% accuracy but are fluent (proficient). The student who performs tasks accurately, but slowly, may not be able to keep up with classroom tasks or use skills in a functional manner. Results from research at the Institute for Research on Learning Disabilities at the University of Minnesota indicate the following: "Clear and consistent differences exist between the performance of learning disabled resource program students and regular class students on one-minute samples using simple measures of reading, spelling, and written expression. Given that these measures reliably differentiate students, they also are useful for referral and assessment decisions." (Ysseldyke, Thurlow, Graden, Wesson, Deno, & Algozzine, 1982, p. 16) Thus, measurement based on rate may be very useful in making an educational diagnosis because problem learners—such as the accurate, but slow students—can easily be identified.

Rate data are easy to collect and are especially useful when administering probes. Teachers may time children in a group for many written skill objectives. Students may also learn to time themselves using a tape-recorded tone. Often students can be taught to (and are eager to) time themselves and their peers.

☐ *Charting*
The data collected concerning the skills and behaviors that are established as daily or weekly objectives generally require some form of on-going or daily display such as a chart or graph. Because a visual display is provided, charts enable teachers to easily document changes in pupil

performance over time. Student progress may also be effectively summarized on a chart and then communicated efficiently to students, parents, and other school personnel.

A student's percent or rate of correct and incorrect responses on a
probe may be recorded daily on a chart. There are a variety of charts
used to continuously record student performance. Equal-interval and
proportional charts are commonly used for this purpose. Graph paper
may be used as an equal interval chart. As illustrated on the equal-
interval chart in Figure 2-6, time or days are represented on the horizontal line—the x-axis—and levels of behavior on the vertical line, or

FIGURE 2-6   Equal Interval Chart

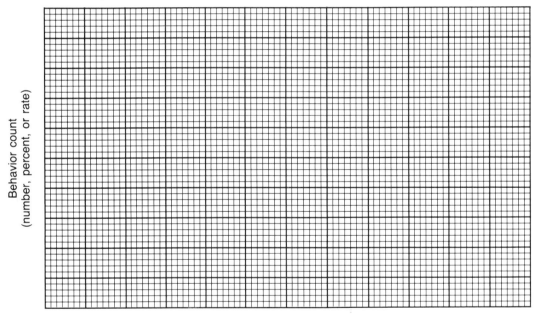

Behavior count
(number, percent, or rate)

Days of the Week

Name _____

Grade/Teacher _____

Target Skill/Behavior _____

Goal _____

y-axis. Each day the teacher records correct and incorrect responses and then connects the dots from day to day.

Responses are recorded in a similar manner on the proportional chart presented in Figure 2–7. This chart differs, however, in that the distance from 1 to 2 is the same as from 5 to 10 or 50 to 100. The equal-ratio property of this chart allows proportional growth to be clearly illustrated. Using the equal-interval chart, student growth from 1 to 2 correct responses per minute would appear to be less significant than a change from 5 to 10 responses, even though 100% growth occurred in both cases. On the equal-ratio chart, however, the ratio of growth is clearly illustrated.

CHARTING CONVENTIONS   When changes in a student's program are made, phase lines are inserted. Changes may consist of an alteration in the classroom environment, a change in the presentation of the task, the reinforcement, or the curriculum. (See Figure 2–7.) Phase lines are vertical lines drawn between day lines or sessions from the top of the y axis to the x axis, and indicate a change in instructional conditions or teaching techniques. Other charting conventions to be aware of are:

- Use a pencil when charting so that corrections can be made easily.
- Connect data points by drawing a straight line from one plotted day to the next.
- Do not connect data points over weekends, holidays, absences, or across phase lines.

LEARNING LINES   A pattern may emerge after several days of collecting and charting data. Changes in performance over time may also be illustrated by what has been termed a learning or celeration line, also displayed in Figure 2–7. Celeration may be used to measure past growth and predict future growth. The celeration or learning line is the line drawn through the daily data on a chart so as to reflect the general trend or central tendency of the data. It results in half of the data points falling above the line and half below the line. In their purest form, learning lines are drawn across data that has been recorded on an equal-ratio chart because this type of chart allows ratio comparisons to be made and, as a result, a numerical value to be assigned to the line. This numerical value can then be compared to other values to determine the magnitude of growth. In order to determine the extent of change, the following procedure may be used:

1. Select any two days that are seven days apart, for example, days 4 and 11.
2. On those days, record the number crossed by the learning line; day 7 = 50; day 14 = 85.

FIGURE 2-7 Proportional or Equal Ratio Chart

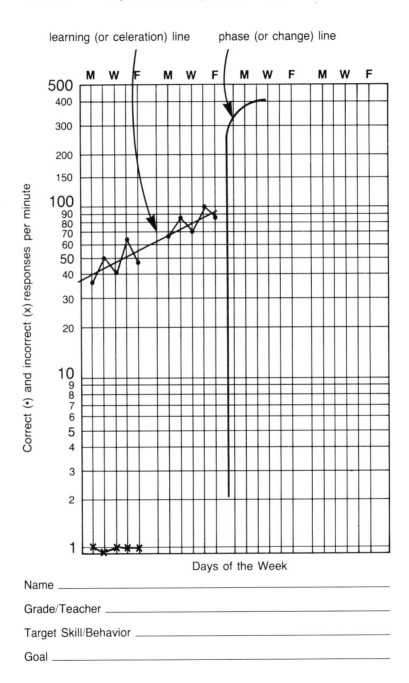

3. Using the number from step two, divide the smaller number into the larger number: 85 ÷ 50 = 1.7
4. If the line is moving up the chart (accelerating), assign a times sign (×) to the number. If the line is moving down the chart (decelerating), assign a divide by (÷) sign to the number.

In the example on page 50, the learning (celeration) line indicates a growth of ×1.7. This line can then be compared to previous performance or learning lines to determine the magnitude of change.

Learning or celeration lines summarize and represent the changes in a student's behavior over time. Often these lines form data trends. Presented in Figure 2–8 are some of the most common data trends that occur. By using these data trends, instructional changes may be quickly and efficiently made.

FIGURE 2-8   Data Trends

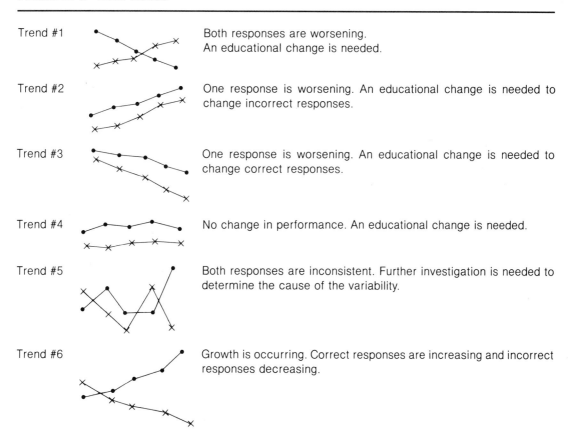

Trend #1   Both responses are worsening. An educational change is needed.

Trend #2   One response is worsening. An educational change is needed to change incorrect responses.

Trend #3   One response is worsening. An educational change is needed to change correct responses.

Trend #4   No change in performance. An educational change is needed.

Trend #5   Both responses are inconsistent. Further investigation is needed to determine the cause of the variability.

Trend #6   Growth is occurring. Correct responses are increasing and incorrect responses decreasing.

CHARTING GUIDELINES   Objections to using a systematic data collection or charting procedure sometimes arise (Kerr & Nelson, 1983). Teachers may complain that there is not enough time to collect all the different types of data that are required. King, Wesson, and Deno (1982) note, however, that trained teachers require only two minutes to prepare for, administer, score, and graph student performance. Kerr and Nelson suggest that teachers make sure the data they keep are data they can, and will, use.

Another solution is to simplify the data-collection procedures. Someone else, such as an aide, another pupil, or a volunteer, can be trained to observe and collect data. Although daily measurement and charting is the ideal procedure, research has indicated that satisfactory educational decisions can be made on the basis of data collected three times a week (Ysseldyke, Thurlow, Graden, Wesson, Algozzine, & Deno, 1983).

Teachers may also argue that collecting data doesn't help them teach. This suggests that the teacher is not collecting useful data. Kerr and Nelson recommend collecting only those data that can be used in educational decision making.

A third objection to charting data concerns the problem of support or reinforcement from others for frequent and systematic data collection. To alleviate this problem, the data must be shared with the student, parents, other teachers, and administrators—those to whom student progress is reported. This sharing is enhanced if the data and the charts are presented in a manner that is easily understood by parents and school personnel (Evans & Evans, 1983). Valuable feedback and cooperation may be gained from sharing the data with others.

☐ *Raw Data Sheets*
Although a visual display on a chart is essential to effectively evaluate student progress, additional information may be needed. If the teacher also wishes to know the specific types of test items that were answered correctly and the types of errors made, it may be necessary to record that additional information on a raw data sheet. This information assists in identifying specific examples of content weakness and will prove to be of great assistance when developing instructional programs. An example is provided in Table 2–1.

■ **Set Objectives**

All of the methods and forms used for data collection and recordkeeping aid the teacher in summarizing information, generating instructional plans, and identifying further assessment needs. Long-range intervention goals may be established from behaviors targeted on the Periodic Assessment Record or from the I.E.P. These goals then may be refined

TABLE 2–1   Raw Data Sheet

Date	Condition	Number of Items Correct/Incorrect	Error Types
10/2	baseline	50/4 per minute	6 × 7, 7 × 6, 8 × 7, 7 × 8
10/3	baseline	51/4	6 × 7, 7 × 6, 8 × 7, 7 × 8
10/4	feedback	50/2	8 × 7, 7 × 8
10/5	feedback	51/2	8 × 7, 7 × 8
10/6	feedback	51/0	
10/9	feedback	50/1	7 × 8
10/10	feedback	55/0	
10/11	feedback	57/0	
10/12	feedback	58/0	
10/13	feedback	58/0	

and analyzed to determine short-term objectives. The short-term objectives should be stated in terms of well-written instructional objectives or criterion statements.

☐ *Mastery, Proficiency, and Instructional Aims*
Student performance should be measured frequently until mastery or proficiency of the skill has occurred. Proficiency is often considered to be a stage of learning (Haring & Eaton, 1978; Lovitt, 1977; Smith, 1981; White & Haring, 1980). Haring (1978) notes that stages of learning may be detected through a precisely displayed continuous record of learning. Authors have described these stages as ranging from initial exposure and gradual acquisition to proficient and fluent performance of a skill. Later stages that build on acquisition and proficiency include generalization, application, and adaptation of acquired skills.

Many authors consider a highly accurate performance to demonstrate mastery, whereas proficiency implies a level of fluency beyond mastery in which performance is automatic, consistent, and comfortable (Evans & Evans, unpublished paper). For example, Smith (1981) notes that mastery may be demonstrated when a student achieves a criterion above 90% or more correct responses for three consecutive days. During this acquisition stage, the aim is for the student to perform the skill with accuracy. The aim at the proficiency stage is both high accuracy and sufficient speed. Lovitt (1978) notes that the reason to establish the extent to which a skill should be developed is to avoid underteaching or overteaching.

There are many ways to determine mastery and proficiency. Teacher judgment is perhaps the most popular evaluative method. However, making decisions solely on personal opinion creates the likelihood that students could be advanced before mastering a skill. Moreover, research indicates that educational progress is enhanced when skill advancement is based on data rather than solely on teacher judgment (Ysseldyke, Thurlow, Graden, Wesson, Algozzine, & Deno, 1983). This necessitates the identification of specific goals that indicate mastery or proficiency. This can be accomplished in various ways.

Eaton (1978) recommends using normative data. By collecting individual data for a large number of children on the same skill, the central tendency of the data may be found. However, the criterion derived using central tendency might not be appropriate for all students, and there is no guarantee that it will represent the optimal performance necessary for adequate progress.

Other methods include the use of performance rates of peers who are progressing acceptably or using a student's previous performance rate to set an aim for a new, but similar task (Eaton, 1978; Haring & Gentry, 1976). Smith (1981) notes that, in general, students should be able to function academically at the same level as their classmates.

Although these guidelines may be helpful, enough data are now available to suggest tentative proficiency levels for many academic tasks. These data are based on an extensive sampling of student performance and have resulted primarily from several Precision Teaching projects. Mercer, Mercer, and Evans (1982) compiled these data on suggested proficiency aims for selected academic tasks. Among the results are the following examples:

> see–say words in a list: 80 + words per minute
> see–write math facts: 55–75 digits per minute

Additional data are presented in table form in chapters 4, 5, and 6.

☐ *Using Data to Make Instructional Decisions*
Kerr and Nelson (1983) define data-based decision making as "using direct and frequent measures of a behavior as a basis for comparing student performance to a desired level, and making adjustments in the student's educational program based on that comparison." (p. 344) To effectively use data to make instructional decisions (i.e., the test–teach, test–teach cycle), the following procedure should be followed:

1. State the short-range instructional objective in terms of specific aims or levels of performance.
2. Collect baseline data (the level of the behavior before an intervention is implemented) for at least three days. If the data are moving in the direction of the desired aim, continue collecting data until the aim is attained, or until stability in the data is noted (i.e., little change in the frequency of the behavior).

3. Institute an intervention. Continue to collect data and record performance.
4. Evaluate progress. Introduce other interventions if the student hasn't made progress in 3 to 5 days.
5. When the aim is attained, maintain that level of performance for 1 to 3 days. Assess on a variable schedule after the aim is achieved.
6. Return to step 1. Proceed with more advanced objectives or aims.

An example of this procedure is provided in Figure 2–9.

☐ *Using the Data to Communicate*

With the data-based decision-making procedure, the data may be used for many purposes. Blankenship and Lilly (1981) suggest four ways to use data collected on a student's performance in a classroom:

1. for referring a student for special education services
2. to advocate appropriate educational services
3. to develop goals and objectives in planning instructional programs
4. to communicate student progress to students, parents, and other school personnel

Data may also be used to monitor the effectiveness of daily instruction.

When referrals are made for special education services, formal testing is usually done, and the results are used to determine if a student meets eligibility requirements for a specific educational program. If continuous measurement and data-based decision-making procedures have been used, the teacher can be more involved in the placement decision made by the staffing team. Data based on day-to-day performance should be the deciding factor. Charted data may be used to corroborate or refute other information provided.

The data collected by the teacher may also serve as the basis for developing accurate goals and objectives for an I.E.P. Other school personnel, parents, and even the student may participate in the data-collection process. If organized appropriately, the data and goodwill generated greatly enhance the effectiveness of any intervention.

Communicating student progress to others is an extremely important aspect of the assessment process. Teachers often are able to comment on a student's progress only in generalities. Without systematic methods of data collection, teachers can only provide limited information concerning student progress (Blankenship & Lilly, 1981).

By collecting data frequently and in a systematic fashion, the task of communicating with others will become easier. Students, parents, and other school personnel, if actively involved in this task, will react favor-

FIGURE 2-9 Using the Data to Make Instructional Decisions

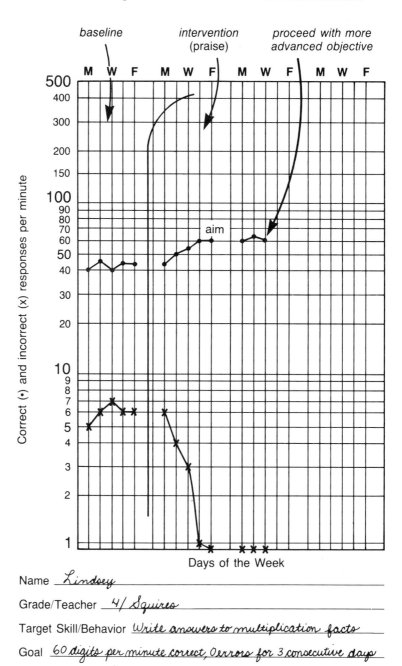

Name *Lindsey*

Grade/Teacher *4/ Squires*

Target Skill/Behavior *Write answers to multiplication facts*

Goal *60 digits per minute correct, 0 errors for 3 consecutive days*

ably to seeing specific behavioral objectives measured continuously and displayed on a chart. When data are shared, others may more readily assist with feedback and cooperation.

CONCLUSION

Assessment, for the purpose of instruction, must be organized in such a manner that the instructional skills required of the student can be comprehensively and accurately evaluated. This necessitates that a skill hierarchy or network be established. If students are experiencing educational problems, data must be collected on a continuous basis. This allows for changes in student performance to be immediately noticed and instructional programs to be altered to ensure student progress.

ACTIVITIES

1. A three-step model provides the framework for the assessment process. List the steps.
2. Define task analysis.
3. Give three examples of behavioral objectives (include the conditions, the target behavior, and the criterion for acceptable performance).
4. Complete a task analysis for an academic and a nonacademic task.
5. Describe periodic assessment and continuous assessment. Discuss how each is best used.
6. Discuss the importance of curriculum-based assessment procedures.
7. State the six principles related to the design and construction of criterion-referenced tests. How are these tests best used?
8. Describe a ''probe.'' How are probes used?
9. Why is it important to chart data? State three guidelines that will assist in collecting and using classroom data.
10. Discuss the importance of percentage and rate as measures of performance.

3

Assessment for Determining How to Teach

■ **Learning Objectives**

After completing this chapter, the reader should be able to:

■ describe the direct instruction model
■ list four learning-related factors included in extended assessment and describe how each factor influences learning
■ describe four types of expectancy factors and how they influence learning outcomes and student behavior
■ describe assessment using learning preferences, metacognition, and learning strategies
■ discuss the influence of teacher-response style on student behavior
■ describe how to record the data collected on periodic and continuous instructional records and how to develop a teaching prescription

The instructional needs of students are typically determined by assessing which skills to teach. However, the assessment process must go beyond this step to facilitate comprehensive educational programming. After the teacher determines *what to teach*, the very important process of determining *how to teach* begins. This second assessment process focuses on environmental and individual factors that influence student achievement.

Since student progress determines the frequency and often the extent of assessment for how to teach, it is very important for the daily instructional program to include good teaching practices. If daily instruction is fundamentally weak (e.g., it includes reinforcement of inappropriate behavior, limited practice of skills, poor class control, poor organization), many students, including students who would make good progress if good teaching principles were used, will not progress well.

The next section presents a direct instruction sequence of empirically based teaching practices that serves as a good instructional foundation from which assessment of how to teach can be efficiently used.

GUIDELINES FOR DETERMINING HOW TO TEACH

■ ■ An analysis of factors that influence learning becomes important when students fail to learn appropriately from daily instruction. If a student is making good academic and behavioral progress, the teacher does not have to spend a lot of time searching for factors that provide insight into how to teach the student. However, when a student consistently fails to make adequate progress, the teacher must examine learning-related factors such as motivation, physical setting, instructional arrangements, and reinforcement, which may provide clues about how to best teach the student. Thus, the frequency of systematic assessments of learning-related factors depends on a student's progress.

■ **Direct Instruction**

Direct instruction has received much support in recent literature. Rosenshine (1978) describes *direct instruction* in the following passage:

> Direct instruction refers to high levels of student engagement within academically focused, teacher-directed classrooms using sequenced, structured materials. . . . [D]irect instruction refers to teaching activities focused on academic matters where goals are clear to students; time allocated for instruction is sufficient and continuous; content coverage is extensive; student performance is monitored; questions are at a low cognitive level and produce many correct responses; and feedback to students is immediate and academically oriented. In direct instruction, the teacher *controls* instructional goals, *chooses* material appropriate for the student's ability level, and *paces* the instructional episode. Interaction is characterized as structured, but not authoritarian; rather, learning takes place in a convivial academic atmosphere. (p. 17)

Research supporting the use of direct instruction has been extensive. Studies investigating the effectiveness of direct instruction for teaching academic skills have reported positive results (Carnine & Silbert, 1979; Chadwick & Day, 1970; Hartman, 1974; Lovaas, 1968; Smith & Lovitt, 1973; Stephens, 1977; Stephens, Hartman, & Cooper, 1973).

FIGURE 3-1   Direct Instruction Sequence

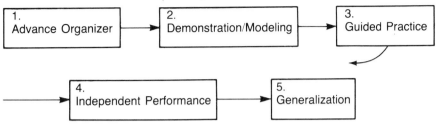

The sequence in Figure 3-1 presents the basic steps of direct instruction. Learning progress is assessed at each stage of the direct instruction sequence to determine if teaching is effective.

☐ *Advance Organizers*

Advance organizers are used to enhance the student's comprehension of content area material (Lenz, 1982) and to prepare the student for the instructional process. For example, giving the student an outline of a lesson serves as an introduction to the material and helps prepare the student to follow the sequence of instruction. Mercer and Mercer (1985) note that an advance organizer should:

- provide background information
- motivate students to learn
- identify topics and/or tasks
- provide a structured framework for the class period
- clarify required activity
- introduce vocabulary
- state concepts to be learned
- clarify concepts to be learned
- state expected outcome

☐ *Demonstration/Modeling*

During this stage of direct instruction, the new skill is demonstrated for the student from start to completion, and each step is specified aloud. The student is encouraged to ask questions to ensure understanding after observing the teacher perform the desired task. Once the skill is demonstrated, the teacher instructs the student to imitate or model the skill as the teacher repeats the task a second time.

☐ *Guided Practice*

During the guided practice stage, the student practices the new skill with teacher assistance or other available resources (e.g., peer tutors, self-correcting materials). Corrective feedback is an important aspect of guided practice. Such feedback corrects initial misunderstandings and prevents the practicing of errors. Verbal praise should be used generously during this stage of instruction.

☐ *Independent Performance*
The independent performance component of direct instruction allows the student to practice the new skill. This practice continues until the skill is mastered using a percent or rate criterion. At this stage of instruction, the student should have very little difficulty performing the academic task. If student problems persist during independent performance, recycling the student through the first three stages may be helpful.

☐ *Generalization*
The generalizaton stage occurs when the student has mastered the skill and is able to apply the newly learned material to other tasks and settings. For example, if a student masters the measurement unit in his or her math class and then uses the newly acquired skills to assist in baking a cake, one can assume that generalization is taking place.

☐ *Summary of Direct Instruction*
The five components in the direct instruction sequence are characteristic of effective instruction. Their success has been documented through commercially produced programs such as *Distar Reading* (Engelmann & Bruner, 1974), *Corrective Reading Program* (Engelmann et al., 1978), and *Corrective Spelling Through Morphographs* (Dixon & Engelmann, 1979). In addition, Deshler and his colleagues at the University of Kansas have validated a similar teaching sequence. The basic tenets of these components focus on providing the student with the knowledge, motivation, and practice required to apply a skill or strategy to various learning situations (Alley & Deshler, 1979; Shumaker, Deshler, Alley, & Warner, 1983; Warner, Schumaker, Alley, & Deshler, 1980).

Since direct instruction includes a continuous assessment across several stages of student learning, it provides a direct measure of student progress over time. When student progress is not satisfactory, the teacher readily realizes it and the need for additional assessment of learning-related factors becomes apparent (see Figure 3–2). Factors included in this extended assessment are discussed next.

DETERMINING AREAS TO BE ASSESSED

■ ■ The direct instruction program provides a good framework for teaching skills to students and assessing their progress on these skills. The assessment of progress identifies students who fail to learn satisfactorily and alerts the teacher to the need to assess factors that indicate how to

FIGURE 3-2 Assessment of Oral Reading Progress

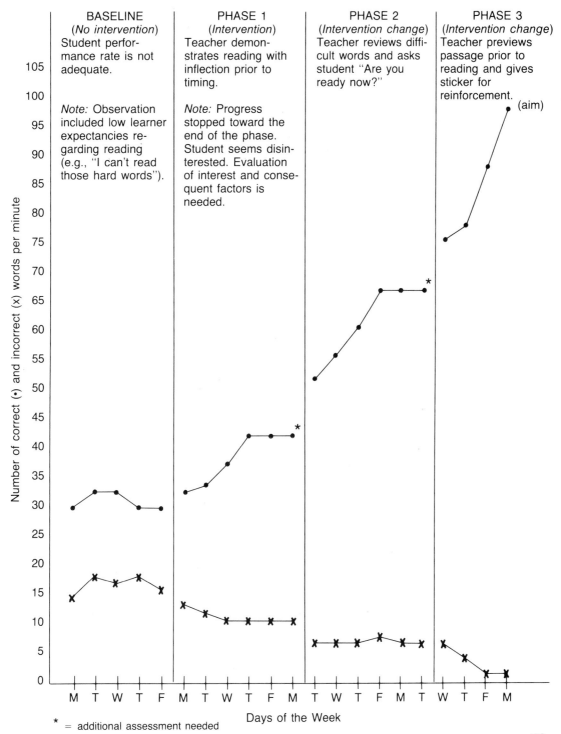

* = additional assessment needed

best teach the students. When the teacher has determined how a student learns best, he or she can arrange variables such as physical set-up of the class, social interaction patterns, and reinforcement strategies to make the instructional program most effective. The assessment for how to teach includes an analysis of ecological (see chapter 7) and student factors. Some of the many variables analyzed in an assessment for how to teach are presented next in a model of learning-related factors. The model (see Figure 3–3) features four categories of variables: (1) entry-level motivation factors, (2) instructional factors, (3) response factors, and (4) consequent factors.

■ **Learning-Related Factors**

☐ *Entry-Level Motivation Factors*
Many students with learning difficulties have serious school-related motivational problems (Adelman & Taylor, 1983; Deshler, Schumaker, & Lenz, 1984), so including techniques to enhance motivation is essential to foster effective instruction. Much literature emphasizes the relationship of motivation to problems in learning and performance. Adelman and Taylor (1983) express it simply:

> If a student is motivated to learn something, (s)he often can do much more than anyone would have predicted was possible. Conversely, if a student is not particularly interested in learning something, resultant learning may not even be close to capability. (p. 384)

Therefore, there are times when motivation, not academic development, has to become the focus of an intervention program. Determining how to teach in such situations is based on what successfully motivates the student. When motivation factors seem to be critical to a particular student's instruction, the teacher may want to consider the relevance of out-of-school factors, interest factors, and expectancy factors. Each of these can affect student performance and influence instructional needs.

OUT-OF-SCHOOL FACTORS Out-of-school influences on student performance remain a variable that educators must consider. Parents, peers, religion, and community all contribute to student behaviors and attitudes that may or may not facilitate the teacher's efforts. Teachers who understand the out-of-school factors influencing a student's life are better prepared to plan meaningful instruction. Moreover, understanding the home situation can foster better communication between teacher and parent.

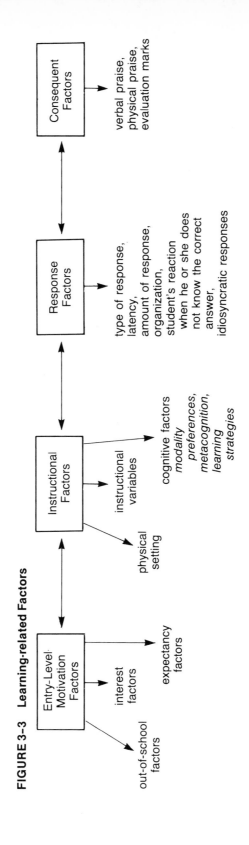

FIGURE 3-3 Learning-related Factors

Numerous methods exist for teachers to obtain out-of-school data. Information may be gathered from other teachers, the guidance counselor, the student's cumulative folder, a parent interview, a conversation with the student, or a home visit. Various forms can also be used to gather data from parents. Rating scales and checklists are easy to design and complete. Such forms provide a structured method for organizing useful assessment information. (See chapter 7 for a more complete discussion of out-of-school factors.)

INTEREST FACTORS   Learning occurs best when the child agrees with and acts upon that which he or she considers to be of most value (Humphrey, 1966). In other words, the student accepts as most valuable those things that are of greatest interest to him or her. Thus, it becomes the teacher's task to assess students' interests so that lessons can be developed that will engage students in the learning process. Information about student interest can be helpful in selecting materials and can be used to make routine drill work more appealing by pairing the task with interest-related reinforcers (Zigmond, Vallecorsa, & Silverman, 1983). When determining how to teach a student, it is important to remember that a student who is not motivated to learn in one setting using certain techniques may become an active learner if certain elements of the program are manipulated to consider her or his individual interests.

Several methods are available for assessing student interest. Prior to designing extensive assessment procedures it is often helpful to ask the student directly what his or her interests are. When direct questioning of the student fails to yield enough information, other methods are helpful. The following questions can be answered by direct observation: "What does the student do in his or her free time?" "What does he or she discuss with friends?" "Which television shows does he or she talk about?" "When does the student seem the happiest?"

Structuring time for informal conversation with the student is another way to learn about his or her interests. Most students enjoy discussing things they like and appreciate adults who listen.

Informal teacher-made inventories are also useful for assessing student interests. Older students can complete these inventories independently, and interest inventories may be administered orally to younger students. A typical inventory would include open-ended questions:

My favorite television show is . . .
My favorite movie is . . .
My favorite food is . . .
My favorite sport is . . .
My favorite school subject is . . .
When I am at home I like to . . .
I collect . . .

A checklist format can also be used. In the following sample the student is instructed to check the things he or she likes:

games   _____
sports   _____
music   _____
television _____
reading   _____
cooking   _____
computers _____

Interest inventories can be adopted for young children using pictures of various items (e.g., animals, games, candy) with instructions to circle the things they like. Facial expressions can also be used to assess the interests of young children. In the following interest inventory, students are told to circle the face that shows how they feel about specific items.

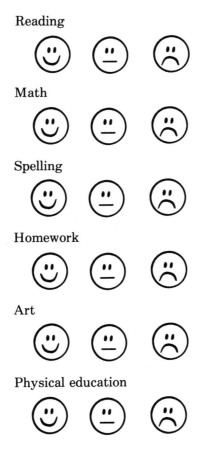

Reading

Math

Spelling

Homework

Art

Physical education

EXPECTANCY FACTORS Expectancy factors, or expectations, refer to the anticipated outcomes of future events. Expectancy factors greatly influence student motivation, learning outcomes, and student behavior. They may serve as an incentive or deterrent for approaching, continuing, or avoiding learning tasks. For example, if a student receives verbal praise for writing his spelling words, he begins to expect that if he writes the words, some desirable event will follow. Conversely, if a student receives a low grade or criticism for writing her spelling words, expectancy can serve as a deterrent, and the student may avoid the learning task. Thus, expectancy of success or failure can influence the student's motivation toward the learning activity. Mercer and Mercer (1985) identify four expectancies that significantly influence learning outcomes and student behavior: learner expectancies, teacher expectancies, peer expectancies, and parental expectancies.

Learner expectancies will undoubtedly affect the instructional process. Negative reactions of the student are often characterized by negative comments regarding his or her abilities, avoidance remarks, and comments that reflect the anticipation of failure or problems. An observant teacher is able to ascertain the situations about which the student has negative expectations for learnings. For example, a student may consistently verbalize dislike of oral reading. This information can be helpful when planning positive instructional experiences for the student. It may indicate the need to allow the student to record his or her reading on a tape recorder or read with a friend or alone with the teacher.

Teacher expectancies can greatly influence student behavior. Teachers develop perceptions of a student which, in turn, create certain expectations. When the teacher expects less from the student than he or she is capable of producing, the teacher expectancies may impede both learning and social development. If a teacher expects inappropriate behavior or poor academic progress, it may likely occur. Fortunately, the reverse of this phenomenon holds much promise. Smith, Neisworth, and Greer (1978) affirm the importance of the teacher's influence:

> The teacher's attitude toward children and education determines to a very real degree how children perceive school, themselves, and each other—and how much progress they actually make. Teachers can make learning pleasant or punishing; they can create motivation or fear; they can produce excited anticipation or dread. A teacher's personal style and approach, more than anything else, create the climate and mood which will characterize the classroom. (p. 84)

The *expectancies of peers* result in students learning to view themselves as leaders, followers, or isolates (Archer & Edgar, 1976). Acceptance by peers helps children gain confidence and self-assurance which, in turn, foster better performance on academic tasks. Peer rejection can produce anxiety and self-doubt. Archer and Edgar (1976) report that teachers must recognize student leaders and understand classroom alliances if they wish to promote a healthy social climate. The teacher also must be aware of peer values, especially those relating to academic achievement and social behavior. Once the social climate is ascertained, the teacher can use peer tutoring, modeling, role playing, seat assignments, and the control of peer attention to promote peer expectancies that foster the growth of students.

Parental expectancies greatly influence a student's academic and social growth. Parental support is often a key factor in maintaining a student's motivation and achievement. Positive parental expectations can be very helpful in the development of the child; however, parental expectations that are negative, too high, or too low can be harmful to the child's academic and social development. Given the trend toward more parental involvement in the identification, placement, and educational programming of mildly handicapped learners, school personnel must prepare themselves to work more closely and effectively with parents.

Teachers can assess all expectancy factors using direct observation techniques; interviews with students, other teachers, peers, and parents; checklists; and rating scales. Information gathered through direct observation and/or interviews should be recorded in a useful manner. Behavior observation forms can be designed to record negative learner expectancies (see Figure 3–4). A tally is made each time the behavior is exhibited during the observational period. Patterns frequently emerge from the data that assist in planning appropriate instruction.

A narrative recording system may be used for summarizing interview data. Teachers can take notes during the interview and later document the information relevant to instructional needs of the student.

As mentioned earlier, checklists can be devised to assess expectancy factors. Questions appropriate for student assessment of the teacher, for example, include the following:

	Often	*Sometimes*	*Never*	*Don't Know*
1. Teacher uses books and assignments that students can understand.				
2. Teacher assigns "busy work."				
3. Teacher makes negative or sarcastic remarks about students' work.				
4. Teacher is fair.				
5. Teacher gets students interested in learning.				

FIGURE 3–4   Behavior Observation Form

Name Nicole B.		Observation Date 10/4	
Observations	*8:00–9:00*	*12:00–12:15*	*1:30–2:30*
Complaints about work			
Complaints about teacher		//	
Complaints about peers	⊬⊬ //	///	
Complaints about school			
Verbal insult toward teacher			
Verbal insult toward peer	/		⊬⊬
Negative verbalization about self			
Noncompliance			

Summary of Observation: Student exhibits difficulties getting along with peers. Opportunities for appropriate peer interactions should be structured.

Rating scales can also yield information useful for assessing learner, teacher, peer, and parental expectancies (see Figure 3–5). Summarizing data accumulated from rating scales and checklists leads to a better understanding of factors influencing a student's performance and to a more comprehensive plan for determining how to teach the student.

☐ *Instructional Factors*
A variety of instructional factors influence student performance. The physical setting and instructional variables (i.e., methods and materials) often need to be assessed for their appropriateness. Cognitive factors to be assessed include learning preferences, metacognition, and learning strategies.

PHYSICAL SETTING   The physical setting of a classroom can influence both the instructional program and the attitudes of the students. Aspects for the teacher to consider include the physical arrangement, classroom noises and sounds, temperature, and lighting.

One of the most important considerations in planning the physical arrangement of a classroom is to designate areas for specific activities (e.g., math area, reading area, and language arts area). Space also must be provided for small-group instruction, individual student storage, in-

FIGURE 3-5 Sample Rating Scale Items for Assessing Expectancies

	Key:	3—always happens		
		2—frequently happens		
		1—sometimes happens		
		0—rarely happens		

I. *Learner Expectancies*

   A. Student comments about not being as smart as peers.   3   2   1   0

   B. Student comments about anticipating failure on tests, seatwork, etc.   3   2   1   0

   C. Student comments about disliking certain activities.   3   2   1   0

II. *Teacher Expectancies*

   A. Teacher assigns work that is too difficult.   3   2   1   0

   B. Teacher assigns work that is too easy.   3   2   1   0

   C. Teacher expects the student to misbehave.   3   2   1   0

III. *Peer Expectancies*

   A. Peers view the students as smart.   3   2   1   0

   B. Peers expect the student to misbehave.   3   2   1   0

   C. Peers tease the student.   3   2   1   0

IV. *Parental Expectancies*

   A. Parents tell the student not to worry about assignments.   3   2   1   0

   B. Parents criticize school (teacher) in front of the student.   3   2   1   0

   C. Parents insist the student be placed in a higher reading or math group.   3   2   1   0

dividual work areas, interest centers, and material display and storage. (See Figure 8-3 for a sample classroom arrangement.)

Sound may also contribute to the performance of students. Some individuals turn on the radio, television, or stereo while they study. For some students, such devices seem to block out extraneous sounds that might otherwise interrupt their thinking (Dunn & Dunn, 1978). Other students find nearby conversations distracting and prefer to work in silence.

The temperature of a classroom also affects student performance. Reactions to temperature differ among students. Studies have shown that some people concentrate better when the environment is cool or cold. Warm temperatures make them feel drowsy and listless (Dunn & Dunn, 1978). Other individuals do not concentrate as well when they are cool.

Since it is frequently difficult to regulate classroom temperature, it becomes important for the teacher to determine which sections of the room provide the most and the least warmth at various times of the year.

Lighting affects the learning environment of some individuals. Some students are light-sensitive and prefer subdued lighting. Others are more comfortable reading and writing in brightly lighted areas.

Analyzing the classroom's physical setting results in information helpful for determining how to teach. Teacher-made checklists and rating scales assess which variables to manipulate to suit the student's preferences. A checklist can include statements directly related to student learning preferences (see Figure 3-6). When options are available for changing the physical setting in a classroom, the student and/or teacher can choose a setting suitable to the learning activity and individual preferences. Either checklists or rating scales can facilitate the assessment of relevant factors.

INSTRUCTIONAL VARIABLES   When a teacher observes the need to manipulate elements within an instructional program, he or she will undoubtedly examine the materials and methods used for teaching. Familiarity with available resources and student needs provides a foundation

FIGURE 3-6   Physical Setting Preferences

Student's Name _____

Teacher's Name _____

Date _____

Check statements that accurately describe the student.

_____   1. Completes more work when room is quiet.
_____   2. Works more accurately when room is quiet.
_____   3. Can block out noise and confusion.
_____   4. Prefers background noise (e.g., music).
_____   5. Becomes lethargic when classroom is warm.
_____   6. Complains about being cold.
_____   7. Complains about being hot.
_____   8. Prefers to sit near classroom windows.
_____   9. Wears corrective lenses.
_____ 10. Selects seat in dimly lighted areas of classroom.
_____ 11. Works best in learning carrel.
_____ 12. Likes to work near other students.
_____ 13. Needs uncluttered work space.
_____ 14. Likes to work in close proximity to teacher.

for selecting appropriate materials. Wise and careful selection of materials increases the likelihood of successful instruction. To maintain the appropriate use of materials, it is important to evaluate their effectiveness with students on a regular basis (Hargrove & Poteet, 1984).

In addition to materials, it is also helpful to evaluate instructional methods. Hargrove and Poteet (1984) define an *instructional method* as an approach to instruction with a set of identifying characteristics. Table 3-1 presents various instructional alternatives.

It is helpful for a teacher to have an extensive repertoire of instructional methods so, if one method is not effective with a student, another can be tried. This prevents feelings of hopelessness and supports the individualization of instruction.

Some instructional methods require specific types of materials. For example, computer-assisted instruction may be a viable method for a particular student. Its implementation, however, requires access to a computer and appropriate software. Thus, there must be a match between student characteristics, instructional methods, and selected materials. In some cases, the teacher may have to devise his or her own materials

TABLE 3-1   Instructional Alternatives

Delivery Methods	Instructional Methods	Independent Practice Methods	Testing Methods
large group	oral	computers	verbal
small group	written	worksheets	written
one-to-one with teacher	oral and written	self-correcting materials	demonstration
independent seat-work	demonstration	instructional kits	time allotted
peer tutoring	modeling	mechanical devices	length of test
teacher directed	cuing	homework	format
student directed	self-recording	tests	
frequent task changes	self-correcting	amount of practice	
frequent location changes	computer-assisted instruction	copying from board	
length of task	built-in reinforcement	instructional games	
	advance organizer		
	previewing questions		
	using manipulatives		
	precision teaching		
	multisensory		
	instructional games		
	active involvement of students		
	audiovisual aids		

and techniques or modify those that already exist to obtain the desired results.

Materials and methods for teaching students should be selected with care. If a skill is being taught for the first time, it may be appropriate to use the student's textbook. If, however, a skill is being retaught because the student did not comprehend what his or her book presented, it may be necessary to use supplemental materials or a different method. If the student needs additional practice on a newly learned skill, it may be more effective to provide the extra drill through a game format rather than dittoed worksheets (Beattie & Algozzine, 1982; Stephens, Hartman, & Lucas, 1978). When instructional tasks are designed and presented properly, student success is the likely outcome.

Assessment procedures used to explore other components (e.g., out-of-school factors, interest factors, expectancy factors, and physical setting) in the model shown in Figure 3–3 can assist in determining appropriate materials and methods. For example, information on student interest can aid in the selection of reading materials, writing assignments, and instructional games. Knowledge of the home environment can assist in selecting appropriate methods for instruction. Students from homes that provide little tutorial support may need homework assignments that feature self-correcting materials in order to avoid frustration on difficult work.

COGNITIVE FACTORS   A teacher who suspects that the instructional factors component in the learning-related factors model (Figure 3–3) is responsible for student problems may consider cognitive factors in addition to the physical setting, materials, and methods. Some cognitive factors that warrant attention include student learning preferences, metacognition, and learning strategies.

Determining learning styles and/or modality preferences has received much attention. Diagnosticians and teachers may administer various tests (e.g., *Mills Methods Learning Test, Illinois Test of Psycholinguistic Abilities, Detroit Tests of Learning Aptitudes*) to determine a student's modality or learning preference and to make instructional decisions. If the student performs better in the visual modality, visually oriented techniques are recommended. Although the strategy of determining modality preferences is commonly practiced, some research (Arter & Jenkins, 1977) asserts that it is ineffective. Salvia and Ysseldyke (1985) provide reliability data on many modality-preference tests and point out that the reliability coefficients are too low for use in applied settings. Foster, Reese, Schmidt, and Ohrtman (1976), Hammill and Larsen (1974), Larrivee (1981), Lyon (1977), and Tarver and Dawson (1978) also question the reliability of standardized tests designed to diagnose modality preferences.

The use of informal measures to determine student learning preferences can be helpful. Stephens (1977) uses a criterion-referenced approach to assess modalities used in classroom tasks (see Table 3–2). Rating scales such as the one shown in Figure 3–7 also assist in assessing student preferences and planning instruction.

Moreover, through direct observation teachers may note that some students prefer certain input and output modes during instruction. For example, a student with fine-motor problems may perform much better

TABLE 3-2 Summary of Modality Assessment

Sense Skill		Stimulus	Criterion Score	Performance Score	Analysis Code
A U D I T O R Y	Discrimination	20 pairs of similar words read aloud	18/20	20	+
	Immediate Recall	Read primer story and answered 4 questions	4	4	0
	Delayed Recall	Referred to—five days later previous story	4	4	0
V I S U A L	Discrimination	10 pairs of words	9/10	9	0
		10 picture words identifications	9/10	9	0
	Immediate Recall	5 tests of removing different letters	4/5	4	0
		Study 4 words and then identify correct spelling	4	3	—
	Delayed Recall	4 words repeated in 45 minutes	4	3	—
H A P T I C	Discrimination	Recognize 10 upper-case letters by touch only	9/10	4	—
		Recognize 8 lower-case letters	7/8	5	—
	Immediate Recall	Identify 8 lower-case letters	7/8	6	—
	Delayed Recall	45 minutes later	7/8	5	—

Note: 0 = at criterion; − = below; + = above.

Source: From *Teaching Skills to Children with Learning and Behavior Disorders* (p. 193) by T. M. Stephens, 1977, Columbus, OH: Charles E. Merrill. Copyright © 1977 by Bell & Howell Company. Reprinted by permission.

FIGURE 3-7   Student Learning Preferences

Student's Name _____

Teacher's Name _____

Date _____

Key: 3—almost always
2—frequently
1—sometimes
0—rarely

I. *Visual Preferences*
   A. Student enjoys reading a book. _____
   B. Student enjoys films. _____
   C. Student enjoys filmstrips. _____
   D. Student needs someone to demonstrate behavior. _____
   E. Student remembers material from blackboard. _____
   F. Student remembers what he or she has written. _____
   G. Student enjoys playing concentration games. _____

II. *Auditory Preferences*
   A. Student enjoys records. _____
   B. Student enjoys taped lessons. _____
   C. Student enjoys hearing a story. _____
   D. Student follows auditory directions. _____
   E. Student remembers what the teacher says. _____
   F. Student likes talking to people. _____
   G. Student likes to study with friends. _____

III. *Tactile/Kinesthetic Preferences*
   A. Student likes to draw. _____
   B. Student likes to manipulate objects. _____
   C. Student likes to trace vocabulary words written on sandpaper. _____
   D. Student likes to trace pictures. _____
   E. Student likes to use clay. _____
   F. Student likes to use tape recorder, typewriter, calculator, Speak & Spell, computer, or other machines. _____
   G. Student likes to play motor games. _____

on see–say tasks (e.g., reading a passage and stating the main idea) than on see–write tasks (e.g., reading a passage and writing the main idea on paper). Systematic probing into various combinations of input and output modes (e.g., see–say, see–write, hear–write, hear–say, see–touch) provides useful information for instructional planning.

The concept of *metacognition* is also receiving extensive attention. *Metacognition* is defined as "individuals' awareness of their own cognitive performance and their use of the awareness in altering their own behavior" (Hallahan et al., 1983, pp. 96–97). In other words, metacognition essentially is one's awareness of one's systematic use of efficient strategies for learning (Wiens, 1983).

Two approaches, mechanical and elaborative, can be used to train a student in metacognition (Loper, 1982). The mechanical approach involves routine recording of behavior in a repetitive manner. For example, at designated times the student might be instructed to ask himself, "Was I on task?" and then write the response on a record sheet. The elaborative approach uses more extensive verbal behavior. This method typically involves a self-interrogatory scheme in which the student asks open-ended questions and responds appropriately. For example, while reading a science chapter the student may stop at the end of each paragraph and ask, "What was the main idea of that paragraph?"

Numerous metacognitive techniques are available to students. Included among these are verbal mediation, organization, and visual imagery. Verbal mediation uses language to assist with recall tasks. For example, the student may practice spelling a word by repeating the letters in his or her mind rather than just looking at them. The student may also use mnemonic devices, such as the sentence "A rat in the house may eat the ice cream" to aid in spelling the word *arithmetic*.

Organization techniques are primarily used when students are required to memorize large amounts of information (e.g., in high school and college courses). Material to be learned is grouped into related clusters or categories.

Visual imagery, in which visual images are used to help the student make associations about the content to be learned, is also an effective strategy for some students. For example, in learning the word *bed*, the student may associate the configuration of the word—

with the image of a bed (McLoughlin & Lewis, 1981).

Advocates of metacognitive training suggest that such interventions can be of practical use in increasing the abilities of learning-disabled students to deal more successfully with school (Brown, 1979; Flavell, 1978). Students who learn to use their cognitive abilities efficiently may improve their problem-solving skills, their attention to task, and their overall academic performance.

Another area of instructional consideration is learning strategies. Alley and Deshler (1979) define *learning strategies* as "techniques, principles, or rules that will facilitate the acquisition, manipulation, integration, storage, and retrieval of information across situations and settings." (p. 13) This approach to instruction focuses on teaching students how to learn and how to demonstrate command of their knowledge in performing academic tasks. For example, a learning strategy might be taught to a student with fifth-grade reading skills that would enable him or her to obtain relevant information from a textbook chapter written at the tenth-grade level.

Deshler and his colleagues at the University of Kansas Institute developed a learning strategies curriculum that emphasizes organization skills and storage of information. The strategies are organized into two strands that correspond to the demands of secondary school settings: 1) strategies for gaining information from written and oral materials, and 2) strategies for expressing information permanently (e.g., in reports, tests, class assignments). Components within a learning-strategy curriculum are designed to help students and teachers discover techniques to facilitate learning. Assessment and instructional components are designed to enhance study skills, time management, test taking, information gathering, organization skills, and note taking. Student deficits may occur in only one of these curriculum areas, although it is more common to find difficulties existing in several components.

Implementation of learning strategies can reveal useful information for determining how to best teach a student. Early learning-strategy field testing and evaluation support good student progress (Schumaker, Deshler, Alley, & Warner, 1983). Cronin and Currie (1984) provide a comprehensive resource guide of materials on learning strategies.

□ *Response Factors*

Instructional tasks usually require students to make either a motor or verbal response, or both. Selecting the type of response for an instructional activity can be crucial in designing classroom activities. McLoughlin and Lewis (1981) suggest six aspects of student response style to consider when assessing for teaching purposes. The first is the *type of response*: verbal, pointing, gestures, and writing. It is sometimes helpful to note which response a student uses when given a choice.

Latency is the second aspect of response style to be assessed. *Latency* is the delay between presentation of a task and the beginning of a response. Teachers should take note of students with very long or very short latencies. Minor alterations in the presentation of tasks may prove helpful.

The third aspect of response style is *amount of response*. Some students will give very brief responses to academic tasks, while others seem to continue at great length. Appropriateness for the given situation must be considered.

Organization is the fourth important aspect of response style. The student may or may not be able to logically organize his or her answers, a skill necessary to achieve success on instructional tasks.

The fifth aspect of response style is *the student's reaction when he or she does not know the correct answer*. Some students simply say "I don't know," while others offer lengthy explanations concerning their lack of knowledge. It is important to note cases when students quickly say "I don't know" without really listening to the question.

The fifth aspect of response style is *idiosyncratic responses*, that is, student responses that seem to have no relationship to the question. In such cases it may be helpful to ask the student to explain his or her answer further to determine whether the response had meaning to the student or whether he or she was playing games.

In addition to assessing these six elements of student responses, it is also helpful to listen to questions the student asks. For example, students who continuously ask "Did I get that right?" may be demonstrating a need for immediate feedback. This could have implications for effective teaching procedures (e.g., selection of peer teaching, self-correcting materials). Students who frequently ask "What's next?" or "What do we do after this?" are also providing valuable information related to their instructional needs. These cues may suggest a need for structure, advance organizers, or daily task sheets. Student questions may also signal boredom. "How soon can we go to music?" or "When is lunch?" or "Do we have to do all of these?" may indicate disinterest in the task at hand.

Diagnostic listening to student questions and student responses can be very helpful when determining how to teach. Diagnostic listening requires that the listener set aside personal concerns while the student is talking. Attention must be focused on the student, and clarification needs to be sought when communication is unclear.

Direct observation can be used to obtain meaningful information regarding student response styles. A sample response observation form is displayed in Figure 3–8.

☐ *Consequent Factors*

The fourth category to consider when using the model of learning-related factors is consequent factors. Consequences greatly influence behavior. Polloway, Payne, Patton, and Payne (1985) report that consequences motivate students and manage their behavior. Social praise, special activities and privileges, evaluation marks, positive physical expression, awards, tokens, and tangible objects are some positive consequences frequently used to reinforce—and therefore influence—student behavior.

Stephens, Hartman, and Lucas (1978) suggest that successful classroom management requires the judicious use of reinforcement. Moreover, the rewards used for developing appropriate behavior must be related to task difficulty. Initially it may be necessary to provide reinforcement

FIGURE 3-8 Observation of Response Style Form

Name _____

Date _____ Observation Time _____

I. Type of Response
   A. Verbal
   B. Pointing
   C. Gestures
   D. Writing
   Comments _____

II. Latency
   A. Too long
   B. Too short
   C. Appropriate
   Comments _____

III. Amount of Response
   A. Too much
   B. Too little
   C. Appropriate
   Comments _____

IV. Organization
   A. Good
   B. Fair
   C. Poor
   Comments _____

V. Reaction When Student Does Not Know Answer
   A. Says "I don't know"
   B. Displays anger
   C. Offers excuses
   D. Gives no response
   E. Appears embarrassed
   Comments _____

VI. Idiosyncratic Response
   A. Made sense to student
   B. Did not make sense to student
   C. Manipulative to end work session
   D. Seeking attention
   Comments _____

Summary of Response Style _____

every time the behavior occurs. As the task becomes easier, however, the behavior can be rewarded less often.

Awareness of consequent factors certainly enhances teacher effectiveness in the classroom. Providing positive reinforcement in a planned, systematic way is a powerful tool to increase desired social and academic behaviors. To use consequent factors most effectively, the teacher must consider timing, amount, and ratio of reinforcement. Student needs differ greatly. Some students need immediate reinforcement to maintain performance; others can tolerate delays. Differences also occur regarding the amount of reinforcement needed to evoke behavior changes. Thus, assessing consequent factors is very important when deciding how to best teach students.

Reinforcement surveys are designed to help teachers determine consequent factors that will effectively motivate students. The survey should be completed in the student's presence. The student answers each question aloud, and the teacher records the response on the survery form. Multiple-choice and/or open-ended questions can be included (see Figure 3–9).

Another method for analyzing consequent factors is to record behavior observations while systematically changing the antecedents (e.g., instructional materials, verbal directions, advance organizer) and/or consequences (e.g., primary reinforcers, verbal priase, free time). Figure 3–10 shows a sample behavior observation form designed to collect data on consequent behavior factors. The teacher records antecedents, behaviors, and consequences and then indicates whether instruction was effective, needs change, or requires further observation. (Chapter 7 includes an antecedent, behavior, and consequent observation form for use with students who exhibit behavior problems.)

RESPONDING TO STUDENT ANSWERS   Reaction to student responses is a consequent factor that deserves special attention. Teacher praise is basic to managing and motivating pupils. Positive results occur when teachers praise students in a systematic manner immediately following a correct or desirable response. Responding appropriately to incorrect answers is more challenging. How the teacher reacts to errors can easily influence the mood, motivation, and participation of the student. An insensitive reaction can discourage the student, promote frustration, and create behavior problems. On the other hand, a sensitive reaction helps maintain motivation and interest. Responses to incorrect student answers should avoid degrading the student and provide encouragement for effort. Mercer (1983) suggests some useful response methods:

1. *Develop sensitive responses.* "Let's look at it together." "That's close." "You have almost mastered that." "One more time and you'll have it." "Nice try." "Let me help you." "Look again." "Almost—let's try again."

FIGURE 3-9   Reinforcement Survey

Name _____

Date _____   Recorder _____

Multiple-Choice Questions
1. *The special job I like to help the teacher with the most in this class is:*
   a. Handing out papers
   b. Putting away supplies
   c. Decorating a bulletin board
   d. Running the filmstrip projector
   e. Writing the assignment on the chalkboard
   f. Straightening up cupboards and book cases

2. *The best privilege I could earn in this class for good work would be to:*
   a. Sit anywhere I want in the class
   b. Help the teacher grade papers
   c. Put an assignment on the chalkboard
   d. Give the class announcements
   e. Pick a partner to work with

3. *When I do well in this class, I like it most when the teacher:*
   a. Smiles at me
   b. Informs the class of my good work
   c. Writes a note on my paper
   d. Tells me privately in words
   e. Draws a big happy face on my paper
   f. Puts my good work on the bulletin board

4. *My favorite free-time activity in this class is:*
   a. Playing checkers or a card game
   b. Listening to the radio or playing records
   c. Working a puzzle or doing a craft activity
   d. Visiting with a friend
   e. Reading a favorite book
   f. Playing a computer game

5. *The nicest thing that could happen to me for doing good work in the class would be:*
   a. Receiving an award in front of the class
   b. Receiving an A+ on a project
   c. Having my parents receive a phone call describing my good work
   d. Having my work displayed in the hall
   e. Earning free time for the whole class

6. *If I had $1.00 to buy anything I wanted, I would buy:*
   a. A yo-yo
   b. A frisbee
   c. A poster
   d. Some silly putty
   e. A comic book

FIGURE 3-9 *(continued)*

7. *The way I best like to learn about something new in this class is:*
   a. Lecture
   b. Books
   c. Pamphlets
   d. Films
   e. Tapes
   f. Language master
   g. Small-group work
   h. Guest speakers

Open-Ended Questions

8. My favorite way to learn new information in this class is . . .
9. My favorite instructional equipment to use in this classroom is . . .
10. The special jobs I like to help the teacher with the most in the class are . . .
11. If I could change one class rule for one hour in this class, the rule I would change would be . . .
12. If I were to choose two students in this classroom to do a fun activity with, I would select . . .
13. If I went to the store and had $1.00 to spend on whatever I wanted, I would buy . . .
14. The person in this school I like most to praise me when I do good work is . . .
15. In this class, I feel proudest of myself when . . .
16. The thing that motivates me the most to do well in this classroom is . . .
17. The nicest thing that has ever happened to me in this class for doing good work is . . .
18. The very best reward in this class that the teacher could give me for good work is . . .
19. My favorite toy or game is . . .
20. My favorite computer program is . . .

2. *Delay feedback.* Some children answer before they have time to think. Simply pause and wait for a second response.
3. *Repeat the instructions with emphasis.* For example: "4 × 4 is what?"
4. *Use synonymous rephrasing.* Repeat the question or task using different words. For example: "Lift the box" can be rephrased as "Pick up the box."
5. *Partially complete the task.* For example: "Where did Bob hide the cookie? He hid the cookie under the ch _____."
6. *Provide ridiculous alternatives and the right answer.* For example: "Did the dog bite the rock? Did the dog bite the bridge? Did the dog bite the stranger?"

FIGURE 3-10 **Behavior Observation Form**

			Instruction Effective	Changes Needed	Further Observation Needed

Name _____

Date _____

Observer _____

Observation Time _____

Target Behaviors _____

Antecedents	Behavior	Consequences	Instruction Effective	Changes Needed	Further Observation Needed

Observation Summary _____
_____

Effective Antecedents _____
_____

Effective Consequences _____
_____

7. *Model the correct answer and instruct the student to imitate.* For example: "4 × 4 is 16. What is 4 × 4?"

☐ *Teaching Prescription*

Motivation factors, instructional arrangements, response factors, and consequent factors may be individually assessed when planning how to teach. This is particularly useful when the teacher informally observes or suspects a problem area in one of these four components.

Time is often saved when assessment addresses only the suspected problem area. In some cases, however, it is necessary to consider all four components to form instructional strategies that best facilitate learning. When the right variables are manipulated from each component, an appropriate teaching prescription will result. A newly devised teaching prescription must be monitored closely to ensure its efficacy and the student's progress. The case study presented at the end of this chapter illustrates implementation of assessment procedures for teaching.

SELECTING AND ADMINISTERING AN ASSESSMENT PROCEDURE

■ ■ As noted earlier, there is little information on the topic of assessment for determining how to teach. The emphasis instead has been on what to teach. Nevertheless, procedures for determining how to teach are evolving. These procedures may be used in either a *periodic* or *continuous* manner. Periodic assessment procedures occur intermittently (i.e., weekly, monthly, or quarterly) and may be formal or informal. Continuous assessment procedures range in use from daily to weekly and usually involve formal procedures designed to monitor a student's progress on a specific skill or behavior.

■ Periodic Assessment

Periodic assessment for determining how to teach efficiently and effectively is advantageous in numerous situations. It is usually used for students experiencing learning and/or behavior problems. For a student with a history of school problems, it is very helpful to conduct a periodic assessment at the beginning of the school year. Assessment at this time saves much trial and error.

Periodic assessment is also useful when placement changes are being considered for a student. Having specific information regarding the student's motivation, preferred instructional arrangements, response factors, and the effectiveness of various consequent factors enhances the decision making of staffing teams. Moreover, this information is invaluable to the student's new teacher when the placement change occurs.

In addition, periodic assessment should be implemented when the teacher notes that a student's performance is inconsistent or puzzling. It is not uncommon to hear teachers discuss the erratic performance of students with learning or behavior problems. Often teachers try an assortment of techniques with little success and become confused about what is needed to reach a student. For example, a student may perform most skills with ease but block on selected skills, or a student may initially learn a skill quickly but fail to retain it. In such cases, periodic assessment provides helpful data for planning instruction.

☐ *Formal Tests*
Formal tests are typically used to determine what to teach a student rather than how to teach. There are, however, some published tests designed to help determine how to best teach particular students (see the Appendix). These tests are most useful as screening devices for potential problem areas; their results are not precise enough to use in making teaching decisions. However, low scores on particular subtests can indicate a need for more direct and precise assessment in specific areas.

As mentioned earlier, the reliability data on some standardized tests are questionable. Thus, most teachers and diagnosticians must rely on their clinical skills and informal inquiries to supplement test results. Occasionally modification of norm-referenced, standardized tests can provide useful teaching information. When the tester suspects that the results of a test do not adequately reflect a student's ability to perform, she or he may decide to alter certain administration procedures. For example, a student may be able to complete test tasks if time constraints are removed or if positive reinforcement is given for responding to test questions. Table 3–3 lists various aspects of test administration that may

TABLE 3–3   Alterations for Administering Tests to Obtain Information for Instruction

Test Elements	Alterations
Instructions	Paraphrase into simpler language. Repeat instructions several times. Have student read the instructions aloud.
Time	Remove time constraints. Lengthen allotted time.
Input Channel	Read items to student. Allow student to read items.
Output Channel	Allow student to say answers rather than write them or visa versa.
Aids	Use manipulatives for math. Provide calculators. Provide scrap paper. Give verbal and/or written cues. Give positive reinforcement.

be altered to provide additional information about the student's abilities and thus how to teach him or her more effectively.

■ Informal Procedures

The informal devices (checklists, observation forms, rating scales, surveys) discussed throughout this chapter can be used for periodic assessment. Teachers should select only those instruments that facilitate gathering information that is needed. Occasionally it may be necessary to assess students with complex problems by using all four components of the model of learning-related factors (Figure 3–3). In such cases, a composite informal assessment form is helpful (see Figure 3–11). On this form, assessment and results of the four learning-related factors are recorded in one place, facilitating instructional planning and providing a comprehensive view of the student's needs.

■ Continuous Assessment

Continuous assessment is the most sensitive measure available for determining how to teach a student with learning and/or behavior problems. The frequent measurement of performance over time provides reliable data on the effectiveness of instruction. Continuous assessment takes the guess work out of teaching. It ensures that students having difficulties will be detected. Once difficulties are identified, the teacher can manipulate instructional variables until student learning proceeds as planned. Continuous assessment should be used when the direct instruction teaching model does not produce desired student progress or when periodic assessment does not specifically target needed instructional changes.

☐ *Criterion-Referenced Testing*
As discussed in chapter 2, criterion-referenced testing can be used to provide continuous assessment. If, for example, a multisensory method is being used to teach sight words, frequent criterion-referenced testing will show how quickly a student is able to learn the new words. For example, if testing reveals that a student is learning only five new words a week, an instructional change should be made. Periodic assessment of consequent factors may have shown that the student performs best for tangible rewards. Thus, the teacher can arrange a token economy system whereby the student earns points for learning new words and later trades the points for tangibles. After the new system is implemented, criterion-referenced testing will indicate the increase in words learned per week, a difference that would go undetected without continuous assessment.

FIGURE 3-11 Composite Informal Assessment Form

Name _____ Date _____

Teacher _____

	Yes	No	Not Sure	Comments
I. **Entry-Level Motivation Factors**				
A. *Out-of-School Factors*				
1. Student has good relationship with family.				
2. Student exhibits good behavior at home.				
3. Home discipline is effective.				
4. Student demonstrates self-care abilities.				
5. Student has good relationship with peers.				
6. Student has satisfactory health.				
7. Student has normal sleeping habits.				
8. Student has good eating habits.				
9. Student completes home chores.				
10. Student participates in extracurricular activities.				
11. Student has a place to complete homework.				
B. *Interest Factors*				
1. Student likes television.				
2. Student likes sports.				
3. Student likes games.				
4. Student likes music.				
5. Student likes reading.				
6. Student likes cooking.				
7. Student likes art.				
8. Student likes animals.				
9. Student likes cars.				
10. Student likes movies.				
11. Student likes computers.				
12. Student likes working for money.				
13. Student likes school.				
14. Student likes to be alone.				
15. Student likes spelling.				
16. Student likes math.				
17. Student likes asking teacher for help.				
18. Student likes taking tests.				
19. Student likes making new friends.				
20. Student likes homework.				
C. *Expectancy Factors*				
1. Student comments on his or her abilities.				

FIGURE 3–11 *(continued)*

	Yes	No	Not Sure	Comments
2. Student comments about liking certain subjects.				
3. Student talks about having friends.				
4. Student anticipates success on work.				
5. Teacher uses verbal praise.				
6. Teacher listens to students.				
7. Teacher is fair when handling discipline.				
8. Peers really like the student.				
9. Peers view the student as smart.				
10. Peers include the student in their activities.				
11. Peers view the student as a leader.				
12. Parents support the teacher's efforts.				
13. Parents encourage the student to achieve.				
14. Parents have realistic goals for the student.				
15. Parents give the student responsibilities.				

D. Summary of Entry-Level Motivation Factors ⎯⎯⎯⎯⎯⎯⎯⎯⎯⎯⎯⎯

⎯⎯⎯⎯⎯⎯⎯⎯⎯⎯⎯⎯⎯⎯⎯⎯⎯⎯⎯⎯⎯⎯

⎯⎯⎯⎯⎯⎯⎯⎯⎯⎯⎯⎯⎯⎯⎯⎯⎯⎯⎯⎯⎯⎯

	Yes	No	Not Sure	Comments
II. Instructional Factors				
A. *Physical Setting*				
1. Classroom lighting is adequate for the student.				
2. Room temperature is comfortable to the student.				
3. Student has adequate storage space.				
4. There is evidence of positive teacher–student interactions.				
5. Student studies best when it is quiet.				
6. Student can block out noise.				
7. Student works well in small groups.				
8. Student works well in large groups.				
9. Student can see the chalkboard easily.				
10. Student can work independently at his or her desk.				

(continued)

FIGURE 3-11 *(continued)*

	Yes	No	Not Sure	Comments
B. *Instructional Variables*				
1. Required tasks are interesting.				
2. There is enough repetition to ensure learning.				
3. Student remains on task.				
4. Student enjoys instructional games.				
5. Student enjoys self-correcting materials.				
6. Student enjoys computers.				
7. Student is satisfied with amount of feedback he or she receives.				
8. Student has the necessary prerequisite skills to be successful.				
9. Student works slowly.				
10. Scope and sequence of the material are clearly specified.				
11. Program provides a method to determine initial placement into the material.				
12. Initial placement tool contains enough items to accurately place the student.				
13. Student enjoys being timed.				
14. Multisensory approaches benefit the student.				
15. Concrete experiences increase learning.				
C. *Cognitive Factors*				
1. Student displays learning preferences.				
2. Visual imagery is effective with the student.				
3. Verbal mediation is effective with the student.				
4. Organization techniques increase the student's learning.				
5. Learning strategies assist the student.				

D. Summary of Instructional Factors _____

_____

_____

	Yes	No	Not Sure	Comments
III. **Response Factors**				
A. *Response Style*				
1. Student has good motor skills.				
2. Student uses subvocalizations effectively.				
3. Student appears relaxed.				
4. Student appears self-confident.				
5. Student attempts to answer all questions.				

FIGURE 3-11 *(continued)*

	Yes	No	Not Sure	Comments
6. Student thinks before responding.				
7. Student handles frustration well.				
8. Student is adaptable to changes.				
9. Student accepts praise well.				
10. Student handles errors adequately.				
11. Student's response latency is appropriate.				
12. Student's amount of response is appropriate.				
13. Student's responses are organized.				
14. Idiosyncratic responses are rare.				
15. Student is alert.				
16. Student functions well with little feedback.				
17. Student remains on task with difficult items.				

B. Summary of Response Factors _____

_____

_____

	Yes	No	Not Sure	Comments
IV. Consequent Factors				
A. *Reinforcement*				
1. Student enjoys time with peers.				
2. Student enjoys time with teacher.				
3. Student enjoys time with counselor.				
4. Student enjoys time with principal.				
5. Student has a best friend.				
6. Student has a favorite school subject.				
7. Student has favorite school activities.				
8. Student has a favorite food.				
9. Student has a favorite game.				
10. Student likes working for privileges.				
11. Student likes to earn tangibles.				
12. Student likes to receive tokens.				
13. Student likes verbal praise.				
14. Student likes evaluation marks (e.g., letter grades, checks).				
15. Student likes awards.				

B. Summary of Consequent Factors _____

_____

_____

☐ *Weekly Checkups*

Many teachers use weekly checkups to facilitate continuous assessment. Perhaps the most common example of this is a weekly spelling test. The student usually receives spelling words to learn on Monday and takes a test on the words the following Friday. The spelling-test scores provide feedback on the effectiveness of spelling instruction. Poor scores may indicate the need for more practice activities before the test, or perhaps reinforcement for good performance would be helpful. Also, strategies for teaching spelling memorization may improve weekly test scores.

Teachers can try various approaches and use the weekly checkups as feedback. This prevents the continuation of student failure and encourages efficient teaching.

RECORDING PERFORMANCE AND SPECIFYING LEARNING-STYLE INSTRUCTIONAL INTERVENTIONS

The diagnostic data that have been gathered about how to efficiently and effectively teach a student must be organized to ensure appropriate instructional planning. The Periodic Instructional Record presented in Figure 3–12 assists in organizing data obtained from periodic assessment. Recording data in this manner assists in the identification of the areas needing more extensive and continuous assessment.

The areas identified as requiring more extensive assessment should be checked on the Continuous Instructional Record shown in Figure 3–13. A systematic evaluation of these areas is then conducted using appropriate continuous assessment procedures (e.g., criterion-referenced testing, charting, weekly checkups). Once successful teaching interventions are identified, they are recorded in the teaching prescription summary at the bottom of Figure 3–13.

Recording periodic and continuous assessment data greatly facilitates instructional planning. Teaching effectiveness is systematically evaluated based on student performance in the classroom. Thus, individual learning needs of students are considered and incorporated into instructional planning.

CASE STUDY

This section features a case assessment for determining how to teach with data recorded on the Case Study Periodic Instructional Record (Figure 3–14) and the Case Study Continuous Instructional Record (Figure 3–15).

FIGURE 3–12 Periodic Instructional Record

	Scores/Result	Date
A. *Formal Tests*		
B. *Informal Measures*		
1. Entry-Level Motivation Factors		
a. Out-of-school factors		
b. Interest factors		
c. Expectancy factors		
2. Instructional Factors		
a. Physical setting		
b. Instructional variables		
c. Cognitive factors		
3. Response Factors		
a. Type of response		
b. Latency		
c. Amount of response		
d. Organization		
e. Reaction when student does not know answer		
f. Idiosyncratic response		
4. Consequent Factors		
a. Social reinforcers		
b. School activity reinforcers		
c. Material reinforcers		
d. Other		

Student _____

Grade _____

Teacher _____

FIGURE 3-13 Continuous Instructional Record

Model Component	Instructional Change	Effectiveness	Assessment Date: Began Completed	Results
Entry-Level Motivation Factors				
Instructional Factors				
Response Factors				
Consequent Factors				

Teaching Prescription Summary _____

_____

_____

_____

Name _____

Teacher _____

Grade _____

By examining the data in these figures, it is apparent that Derrick, a second grader, is having some difficulty in the school setting. Formal test data revealed weaknesses in see–write tasks and visual-motor integration. The informal measures reported similar problems. Noncompliance, off-task, and incomplete work were noted during written assignments. Negative self-expectancies and withdrawal behaviors were also observed. Some factors within Derrick's school experience have been positive. These include computer-assisted instruction, verbal mediation, oral class discussions, *DISTAR*, and consequent factors (teacher praise and stickers).

The data on the Continuous Instructional Record (Figure 3–15) display the effectiveness of several instructional changes within the four

FIGURE 3–14 Case Study: Periodic Instructional Record

	Scores/Results	Date
A. Formal Tests		
1. Classroom Learning Screening (see–write)	21 (learning index = ÷ 1.06)	2/6
2. Developmental Test of Visual-Motor Integration	9 (5 years 4 months age equivalent)	2/10
B. Informal Measures		
1. Entry-Level Motivation Factors		
a. Out-of-school factors	Parents report good behavior at home.	2/6
b. Interest factors	Enjoys situation comedies on television	2/13
	Uses home computer daily	
	Dislikes sports	
	Dislikes most school work	
c. Expectancy factors	Learner expectancies are low (negative verbalizations about self). Teacher, peer, and parental expectancies are appropriate.	2/13
2. Instructional Factors		2/14
a. Physical setting	No obvious preferences	
b. Instructional variables	Noncompliant during writing tasks	
	Off-task behaviors are high during large-group, independent work sessions	
	On-task behavior increases with computers, *Distar*, language master.	
	Rarely completes assignments	
c. Cognitive factors	Metacognitive techniques (verbal mediation) are successfully used for learning spelling words.	
3. Response Factors		2/15
a. Type of response	Frequently contributes to class discussions	
b. Latency	Verbalizations appropriate	
c. Amount of response	Appropriate when verbal; too short when written	
d. Organization	No problems	
e. Reaction when student does not know answer	Easily embarrassed; withdraws	
f. Idiosyncratic response	Not observed	
4. Consequent Factors		2/6–2/16
a. Social reinforcers	Teacher praise is effective	
b. School activity reinforcers	Being teacher's helper	
c. Material reinforcers	Comic books, stickers	
d. Other	Loves computers	

Student   Derrick

Grade   2

Teacher   Ms. Anderson

FIGURE 3-15   Case Study: Continuous Instructional Record

Model Component	Instructional Change	Effectiveness	Assessment Date: Began	Completed	Results
Entry-Level Motivation Factors (learner expectancy)	Introduced self-report method—student counts negative verbalizations he makes (using a wrist counter) and tries to reduce the number each day	Negative statements reduced from approximately 50 to 5 per day	2/17	2/28	Student makes less than 5 negative verbalizations about self per day.
Instructional Factors	Used small group for written assignments Used mechanical teaching devices (e.g., computer, calculator, Speak & Spell, Data Man) for independent work	Written tasks were completed more frequently On-task behavior increased	2/17	2/28	Student now completes 80% of written assignments. Off-task behavior has decreased to 2 times per 30-minute work samples.
Response Factors	Allowed student to give oral answers to weekly exams	Test scores improved	2/20	2/20	Student's grade improved from C to B+. He was very proud and anxious to tell other peers.
Consequent Factors	Allowed student to earn stickers for completing written assignments accurately	Number of completed assignments increased.	2/21	2/22	Student is collecting stickers on his work folder and is very motivated.

Teaching Prescription Summary (1) Student needs reinforcement for written tasks.
(2) Alternatives to written instructional modes should be used when possible.
(3) Self-report is effective for decreasing verbalized negative learner expectancies.
(4) Small-group arrangements increase work completion.

Name   Derrick

Teacher   Ms. Anderson

Grade   2

model components. These targeted areas needed further ongoing assessment to determine how best to teach Derrick. Overall, it appears the changes in Derrick's instructional program are effective. He is making good progress on objectives designed according to his individual needs.

CONCLUSION

The ability to assess learning-related factors is a very critical skill. Teachers who analyze how a student learns are better able to make timely and appropriate instructional decisions that influence a student's motivation and learning successes. It is perhaps the foremost skill that distinguishes the professionally trained teacher from other supportive instructional personnel. The direct-instruction teaching sequence and the assessment of learning-related factors provide teachers with some very effective techniques for helping students with learning and behavior problems to experience success and growth. Although it is impossible for an evaluation team or teacher to evaluate all the factors that influence learning, it is feasible to examine many of the most apparent ones. The four areas listed in the model of learning-related factors in this chapter are some of the most important variables that influence the learning process.

ACTIVITIES

1. List the steps of direct instruction and use a specific academic skill to illustrate the stages.
2. Discuss why good teaching practices provide the foundation for the assessment of learning-related factors.
3. Describe the four primary components of the learning-related factors model.
4. Assess the entry-level motivation factors of an elementary-age student.
5. Briefly describe ten instructional alternatives that may be used in how to teach planning.
6. Describe the three cognitive factors discussed in this chapter that may influence learning.
7. Discuss the influence of teacher response style on student behavior.
8. Discuss the influence of consequent factors on student behavior.
9. Review three commercial tests used to collect information on how to teach.
10. Conduct an assessment of learning-related factors for an elementary or middle school student and write an intervention plan. Use the case study to guide you.

4

Assessment of Language Arts

■ **Learning Objectives**

After completing this chapter, the reader should be able to:

■ identify the communication skills included in language arts and the sequence of development of these skills
■ describe the structure of language, including phonology, morphology, syntax, and semantics
■ identify the three components of written expression and examples of skills that should be assessed in each area
■ describe procedures used to assess listening and written language skills
■ describe how to record the data collected in language arts assessment and set objectives for instruction

The ability to create and use language is one of the most distinctive features of human beings, an essential aspect of human behavior (Wallace & Larsen, 1978). Language arts involves the development of the communication skills of listening, speaking, reading, and writing. The effective use of these skills is crucial to social, economic, and political well-being (Petty & Jensen, 1980). Cohen and Plaskon (1980) note that "the ability to communicate with one's peers, to read for information or pleasure, and to express oneself in writing are daily necessities." (p. 6)

Language art skills are of enormous importance because they influence the student's total educational program. The use of language is an essential prerequisite to all phases of academic achievement (Wallace & Larsen, 1978). Language arts should not be considered self-contained subjects, but rather the tools that are fundamental to learning in all subject areas (Petty & Jensen, 1980). Teachers often integrate the teaching of writing with other subjects such as science, social studies, and

FIGURE 4-1   Development of Language Arts Skills

Sequence of Development

Listening———→Speaking———→Reading———→Written Expression

math. Otto and Smith (1980) stress the use of an integrated approach to language arts instruction because if all the language processes are developed simultaneously, they will be mutually reinforcing.

Language arts tools are being used constantly to acquire new skills. Language arts are the foundation of the school curriculum, and the development of these skills occupies a large portion of the school day. Most academic tasks assigned to students are dependent on a student's language facility (Cohen & Plaskon, 1980), and therefore any language-related difficulty may be reflected in the student's academic and social/behavior growth. For example, Lerner (1985) notes that language deficits of one form or another are the basis for many learning disabilities.

Language arts include two expressive activities (productive or output skills) and two receptive activities (input skills). With expressive activities, communication occurs by speaking or writing. With receptive activities, communication occurs by listening and reading. Acquisition of these skills usually follows a hierarchy of development. As illustrated in Figure 4-1, the oral skills of listening and speaking develop first. The third element to be developed is reading, and written expression is usually the last skill to be mastered. Experience is the basis of language growth, and effective receptive and expressive language development depends upon meaningful observations and interactions within the environment. Moffett and Wagner (1983) note that to gain experiential readiness for language arts, children need to be talked with, read to, and taken places. Lerner (1985) notes that a large quantity of input experiences (listening and reading) is important before the output skills (speaking and writing) can be effectively executed. Additionally, the appropriate use of written communication skills such as reading and writing depends on a firm foundation of oral language skills such as speaking and listening.

DETERMINING SKILLS TO BE ASSESSED

■ ■   To assess language arts skills effectively, it is important to understand the structure of language and the many factors that influence development in listening, speaking, reading, and written expression. Skill networks are helpful in determining specific skills to assess and the approximate grade levels at which these skills are acquired.

■ The Structure of Language

Language may be viewed as having four components: phonology, morphology, syntax, and semantics. These elements are basic to understanding and using language and to assessing language arts skills.

Phonology is the study of the smallest units of speech sounds. For example, the word *hat* contains three phonemes: *h, a,* and *t.* Phonemes are meaningless by themselves. To be meaningful, they must be combined properly into words to conform to the standards of usage in a particular language. Receptive phonology involves listening to, discriminating, and comprehending speech sounds. Expressive phonology involves producing or articulating these sounds.

Morphology refers to the study of the smallest meaningful units in a language. The smallest unit, a morpheme, cannot be divided into smaller units without losing the meaning. For example, the word *girl* is one morpheme, but the word *girls* contains two morphemes, *girl* and *s,* which are both essential to indicate the meaning of two or more girls. Receptive morphology involves comprehending meaningful units, whereas expressive morphology involves producing meaningful units.

Syntax refers to the grammatical system of language—the arrangement of words in sentence formation. In the English language, the ordering of words can make a significant difference in the meaning of a sentence: "the cat ate the mouse" has a different meaning than "the mouse ate the cat." Receptive syntax refers to comprehending the grammatical aspects of language, while expressive syntax refers to producing sentences that are grammatically correct.

Because morphology and syntax both involve elements of grammar, many assessment instruments measure morphology and syntax together. Salvia and Ysseldyke (1985) note that both areas should be included in any valid language assessment.

Semantics refers to the meaning of words. Wallace and Larsen (1978) report that the study of semantics has received much less attention than the study of the other components of language. To date, no theory adequately explains the acquisition of meaning (Cohen & Plaskon, 1980). Moreover, unlike the other components, the development of the semantic system continues through life (Lerner, 1985). Meaning is acquired as concepts are developed. For example, when the concept of time is acquired, the words *Saturday* and *Sunday* take on added meaning for a child. Semantics includes receptive and expressive vocabulary—comprehending the meaning of spoken language (vocabulary and concepts) and producing meaningful speech.

An additional term, *pragmatics,* refers to the study of language in the context in which it occurs. Pragmatics concerns the speaker's intent—knowing what language is appropriate for the setting and purpose. For example, young children learn that they are expected to talk politely when making a request. Semantics and pragmatics are closely related; the development of pragmatics is a refinement of semantic understanding (Cohen & Plaskon, 1980). Research in pragmatics is in its early stages (Petty & Jensen, 1980). However, it is important that students gain knowledge in this area to communicate appropriately in various social contexts.

Proficiency in the four basic components of language is necessary for success in the language arts skills. The relationship between these components and language arts is presented in Table 4–1.

■ **Factors that Influence Language Development**

Language development is a complex process sensitive to the many differences in children. Wallace and Larsen (1978) note that if children are to develop language proficiency, they must be physiologically mature and receive appropriate stimulation and reinforcement. Other factors may influence language development: 1) intelligence—intellectually gifted children may often exhibit accelerated language development; 2) sex—girls usually get a head start in language development; 3) physical condition and central nervous system functioning—speech organs and hearing

TABLE 4-1   The Relationship of the Four Components of Language to Language Arts Skills

Component	Receptive Activities	Expressive Activities
Phonology	listening to, discriminating, and comprehending speech sounds	producing speech sounds
Morphology	comprehending meaningful language units	producing meaningful language units
Syntax	comprehending grammatical aspects of language	producing grammatically correct sentences
Semantics	comprehending meaning of language (vocabulary and concepts)	producing meaningful language (vocabulary and concepts)
	↓	↓
	listening and reading	speaking and writing (handwriting, spelling, and written expression)

must function effectively; and 4) emotional development—children that are emotionally impaired may be language delayed. Morsink (1984) reports that cultural and dialectical differences may also have an impact on language development.

Atypical language development may be reflected in speech and language disorders. A *speech disorder* is an abnormality in speech—in articulation, voice, or fluency. A *language disorder* encompasses "disorders of the entire spectrum of communication and verbal behavior, including such problems as delayed speech, disorders of vocabulary, word meanings or concept formations, the misapplication of grammatical rules, and poor language comprehension." (Lerner, 1985, p. 319) Children with language disorders may not have acquired the typical amount of language expected at certain developmental periods, may be using incorrect speech patterns, or may have vocabulary disorders or poor comprehension. In contrast, a *language difference* refers to a cultural or dialectical difference. Language is subject to many variations—social and regional, and in most cases, Cohen and Plaskon (1980) note, language-different children are not language deficient. A child's use of language must be analyzed to determine if the language problems are due to dialectical differences or delays in acquisition of the standard rules of language.

■ Approaching Assessment and Instruction

Within the school setting, language arts teachers and specialists generally focus on spoken and written language and the four related curriculum areas: listening, speaking, reading, and writing. At the elementary school level, the language arts program is developmental (Burns & Broman, 1983). In the primary grades (K–3), the four language arts curriculum areas are closely interwoven. These individual elements become more clearly delineated during the intermediate grades (4–6). Language deficits that were previously overlooked may surface in the upper grades (Wiig & Semel, 1980). The student at this level may show negative emotional reactions to the widening gap in academic achievement due partially to language difficulties.

☐ *Spoken Language*
The two oral language skills, listening and speaking, begin to develop before written language. Children establish the foundation for oral language during the preschool years and are expected to enter school with linguistic functioning that is becoming refined and more adult-like. These oral language skills are the basis for all communication skills and are crucial to competent written expression. Wallace and Larsen (1978) indicate that by the time a child is five or six years of age, over 2500 words

have been incorporated into his or her vocabulary, and the average length of spoken sentences is approximately 4.5 words.

LISTENING   Listening is the foundation of language growth. Experiences in listening precede speaking. Listening involves the receptive skill of translating spoken words into meaning. Petty and Jensen (1980) discuss the listening process in terms of hearing first, then understanding, evaluating, and responding.

There are four types of listening: literal, interpretive, critical, and creative listening (Burns & Broman, 1983). Listening is an important skill in language arts because a large proportion of a student's day is spent in listening activities. However, research in this area is lacking perhaps because children's listening abilities have been taken for granted in the past.

Proficiency in listening skills is very important in learning to read. Sound discrimination is essential to phonetic analysis, and listening skills are important to the interpretation of reading material. Berger (1978) cites research studies that show a high correlation between the skills of listening and reading, so instruction in listening skills is likely to result in improvement in reading comprehension.

Poor performance on listening tasks may be due to a number of factors: 1) inadequate auditory acuity, 2) below average intelligence, 3) inadequate development in the acquisition of vocabulary, 4) inadequate development in acquiring English syntax, and 5) dialectical differences between the speaker and the listener (Harris & Sipay, 1980). Cohen and Plaskon (1980) describe possible listening-related characteristics of the mildly handicapped child:

- a mild hearing loss
- difficulty with auditory attention
- difficulty with sound identification and discrimination
- failure in isolating, organizing, and recalling information that has been presented orally
- a low tolerance for frustration with tasks that require responses to oral questions or instructions
- problems with misinterpretation or missequencing information
- problems with generalizing and conceptualizing
- failure to appreciate stories, poems, and music for their rhythm and composition.

Alley and Deshler (1979) suggest the following listening skills be included in the secondary school curriculum:

1. understanding of words, concepts, sentences, and large linguistic elements

2. listening comprehension including listening for details, relationships of details to main idea, following directions, sequencing, active listening, and summarizing
3. critical listening including detecting bias, distinguishing fact from opinion, drawing inferences, recognizing absurdities and propaganda, correcting others, finishing stories, distinguishing emotive from report language, evaluating speaker's argument, drawing inferences and making judgments, and recognizing repetition of an idea
4. appreciative listening including listening to visualize, listening for rhythms of speech, recognizing tone and mood, appreciating speaker's style, interpreting character from dialogue, and understanding the effect of the speaker on the listener and the audience.

SPEAKING As previously noted, children usually enter school with mastery of grammatical fundamentals and with linguistic functioning that is becoming refined and adult-like. If a child does not follow the normal pattern of language development, speaking difficulties may be encountered. Speaking is the oral production of language. Its instructional objectives include speaking clearly, expressively, and effectively.

Hargrove and Poteet (1984) cite several factors that may interfere with oral expression including the following: 1) auditory disorders involving auditory acuity and auditory-processing skills; 2) disorders in the speech mechanism and abnormalities of speech including articulation, fluency, and voice problems; 3) lack of appropriate communication models and opportunities to interact with them; 4) inadequate cognitive skills; 5) inadequate development of morphology, phonology, syntax, semantics, or pragmatics; 6) neurological disorders; and 7) emotional disorders. Speech disorders in articulation, voice, and fluency interfere with the flow of communication and often make learning more difficult.

Students with spoken language problems may exhibit difficulties in oral expression or communication. A student who has an expressive problem may pause often and become frustrated trying to recall words, may use a small vocabulary and make inconsistent grammatical errors, may have difficulty forming complex sentences, or may use gestures instead of words (Morsink, 1984). Cohen and Plaskon (1980) note that students with expressive language problems also may lack the ability to respond appropriately to questions.

Assessment and intervention in spoken language may require the expertise of a speech and language clinician who may obtain detailed information about a child's early development and background experiences through a case-history interview. Formal tests may also be administered. (Tests designed to provide a comprehensive survey of language functioning and tests designed to measure individual components of spoken language are presented in the Appendix.) Speech and language clinicians or teachers also collect and analyze spontaneous and structured-language samples in terms of phonology, morphology, syntax, and semantics. Temple and Gillet (1984) suggest using sentence-modeling tasks and measurement of utterance length in language assessment. However, in using these procedures, it is helpful to have a basic background in normal language development and speech and language pathology. For further information about speech and language, see *Language Development and Language Disorders* by L. Bloom and M. Lahey (John Wiley & Sons, 1978); *Language Assessment and Intervention* by E. Wiig and E. Semel (Charles E. Merrill Publishing Company, 1980); or *Children and Communications: Verbal and Non-verbal Language Development* by B. Wood (Prentice-Hall, 1976).

The teacher may assist in determining whether further assessment of speech and language is necessary by being aware of the oral expressive language skills used in the school curriculum. Petty and Jensen (1980) list twelve functional objectives to use in the classroom to appraise oral language performance:

1. to converse with classmates and adults easily and courteously
2. to participate in discussions, sticking to the point and respecting the opinions of others
3. to organize information and report it effectively
4. to plan an interview and carry it through courteously and effectively
5. to use the telephone correctly
6. to conduct a meeting by means of parliamentary procedures
7. to give clear directions, explanations, and announcements orally
8. to tell a story or personal experience effectively and interestingly
9. to greet others properly in various social situations
10. to participate in choral speaking
11. to make use of parliamentary procedures as a member of a group
12. to take part in a dramatic activity (p. 356)

☐ *Written Language*

Written communication includes the skills of reading and writing and is dependent upon a solid foundation of the oral communication skills of listening and speaking. The receptive activity of reading, the third element to develop in the language arts hierarchy of skills, is so important in the school curriculum and in today's society that chapter 5 is devoted entirely to this area of language arts.

The fourth area of language arts is written expression, often considered the most complex stage of language development, more complex than oral language, and the last to be mastered. Written expression may be defined as "a visual representation of thoughts, feelings, and ideas using symbols of the writer's language system for the purpose of communication or recording." (Poteet, 1980, p. 88) It is an extremely important skill for self-expression and communication. Otto and Smith (1980) note that a "successful school experience depends in large measure on the ability to produce a comprehensible written communication." (p. 383) The process of written expression integrates all areas of language arts and includes handwriting, spelling, and composition.

HANDWRITING   Handwriting is the most concrete of the written language skills. It involves the ability, through visual and motor skills, to produce correctly formed letters, or graphemes.

Instruction in handwriting begins in the primary grades at which time the major objective is legibility. Generally, handwriting instruction begins with manuscript writing. Cursive writing is usually introduced at the third-grade level. There is some difference of opinion, however, about whether writing instruction for the learning disabled should begin with manuscript or cursive writing (Lerner, 1985). Cursive writing minimizes spatial judgment problems, allows a rhythmic continuity, and almost eliminates errors in reversals. Also, the need to transfer from manuscript to cursive writing in transitional handwriting is eliminated if the student begins with cursive writing. However, manuscript writing is easier to learn and closer to the form used in printed materials. Also, some educators believe that it is not necessary to teach cursive writing at all because manuscript writing is legal, legible, and just as rapid.

Difficulty with handwriting is called dysgraphia. Mercer and Mercer (1985) note a variety of handwriting problems that children may exhibit: "a) slowness, b) incorrect directionality of letters and numbers, c) too much or too little slant, d) spacing difficulty, e) messiness, f) inability to stay on a horizontal line, g) illegible letters, h) too much or too little pencil pressure, and i) mirror writing." (p. 415)

Left-handed students may also present a few special problems. Because the hand covers up the writing, left-handed students may have difficulty seeing what they have written, may smudge their writing, or start hooking the hand to avoid smudging. A child who shows preference for left-handedness should be allowed to use that hand. Generally, the same techniques used with right-handed students should be used with left-handed students with slight variations. For example, the left-handed student's paper should be rotated in the opposite way in which a right-handed student rotates his/her paper. A suggested handwriting skill network is presented in Table 4–2.

SPELLING   Spelling involves the ability to form words by sequencing letters correctly. Phonemes, the smallest units of oral language, are represented by graphemes, the smallest written units of language. The phoneme–grapheme relationships in English are less consistent than other languages. There is not a one-to-one correspondence between the spoken

TABLE 4–2 Handwriting Skill Network

Kindergarten and First-Grade Skills

establishes preference for left- or right-handedness
draws basic shapes used in writing
writes first and last name using manuscript capital and lowercase letters
writes with correct posture, paper position, and pencil grip
writes upper and lowercase manuscript letters
writes numbers to ten
copies words neatly from chalkboard

Second- and Third-Grade Skills

demonstrates good spacing between letters, words, and sentences
writes clear, legible manuscript letters at an appropriate rate
identifies cursive upper and lower letters of the alphabet
begins transition to cursive writing
uses writing paper, which is standard for cursive writing

Fourth-, Fifth-, and Sixth-Grade Skills

writes all upper and lowercase cursive letters properly
slants, joins letters, and uses proper spacing between letters
begins using pen with ease and fluency
uses clear, legible, and proper-sized cursive writing at an appropriate rate
uses manuscript writing for labeling, map work, and charts
evaluates handwriting objectively to identify own strengths and weaknesses
presents neat work

sounds and the written form in that forty phonemes are represented by twenty-six letters of the alphabet. Although there are many inconsistencies, English orthography (spelling) presents enough consistent phoneme-grapheme rules or predictable patterns to effectively use in diagnosis and instruction (Hanna, Hanna, Hodges, & Rudorf, 1966).

Introduced in the primary grades, spelling instruction is an essential skill in the language arts curriculum because it allows a student to read correctly and because poor spelling detracts from the effectiveness of written communication.

There are four important prerequisite skills that influence a student's spelling ability: 1) adequate visual and auditory acuity, memory, and discrimination skills, 2) adequate fine-motor skills, 3) acceptable knowledge and application of phonics generalizations, and 4) ability to read the words.

Two approches to teaching spelling are commonly used (Lerner, 1985). The linguistic approach stresses phonological, morphological, and syntactic rules and is considered a phonics approach to spelling. The spelling curriculum is organized so that phonological generalizations can be made; for example, in teaching a pattern of *vowel-consonant-silent e*, the spelling lesson might include words like *ride*, *came*, and *tube*.

The second approach often used to teach spelling is based on the frequency of use of words. Sixty percent of our writing consists of 100 words being used over and over again (Lerner, 1985). The frequency-of-use approach assumes that the majority of exceptions to spelling/phonics rules occur in the most frequently used words. It is, therefore, difficult with this approach to convey rules or patterns to beginning spellers.

A suggested spelling skill network is displayed in Table 4–3. Scope-and-sequence skill lists for spelling may also be found in spelling textbooks and other curriculum materials or may be teacher-made to conform to the school curriculum.

WRITTEN COMPOSITION   Written composition refers to the generation and expression of ideas in written form. Composition skill includes the ability to write meaningful sentences and paragraphs with correct grammar and punctuation.

Written composition is the most complex of the language arts skills and is based on the prerequisite skills of listening, speaking, reading, handwriting, and spelling. Three competencies are taught in the written composition curriculum (Hammill & Poplin, 1982): 1) the skills needed to succeed in the school curriculum; 2) the writing skills necessary for survival outside of school—for example, completion of forms and letter writing; and 3) creative expression in written form such as poetry and stories. Tierney, Readence, and Dishner (1985) report an increasing interest in teaching writing, which "has included a swing towards providing students with many more opportunities to write, including writing in response to what they read and even interacting with each other about their writing." (p. 97) Alley and Deshler (1979) state that "facility with written expression is a prerequisite for successful performance in the secondary schools and in postsecondary situations. The curriculum in the secondary schools demands that students take notes from lectures, complete essay examinations, and write themes and research reports." (p. 104)

Learning-disabled students often have difficulty in the prerequisite skills needed for written composition, and consequently many teachers have customarily avoided writing assignments for these students (Reid and Hresko, 1983). Although instruction in composition should not be delayed for mildly handicapped learners, intervention in the prerequisite skills is often necessary before proficient written composition may be accomplished. To create a positive learning environment for written composition, Morsink (1984) suggests that the mechanics of writing not be emphasized too early in the writing program. Excessive correction of

TABLE 4-3   Spelling Skill Network

Second- and Third-Grade Skills

spells regular consonant sounds
spells "sh," "ch," "ng," "wh," and "th" sounds (fi*sh*, *ch*ild, si*ng*, *wh*ile, wi*th*)
uses the following irregular spellings correctly:
  "x" spelling of "ks" sound (bo*x*)
  "c" spelling of "k" sound (*c*ept)
  "ck" spelling of "k" sound (du*ck*)
  "nk" spelling of "ngk" sound (dru*nk*)
  "s" spelling of "s" and "z" sounds (*s*un, a*s*)
  "x" spelling of "ks" sound (ne*x*t)
  "gh" spelling of "f" sound (lau*gh*)
spells silent consonants (*k*now, wou*l*d)
spells consonant blends (*st*op)
spells the following vowel sounds:
  short vowel in initial or medial position (*a*m, d*i*d)
  long vowel spelled by single vowel (b*e*, g*o*, p*a*per)
  two vowel combinations (m*ea*t, r*ai*n, b*oa*t)
  vowel sounds before "r" (*er*, *ir*, *or*, *ur*, *ar*)
  "ow" spelling of long "o" (sn*ow*)
  "ay" spelling of long "a" (d*ay*)
  "oo" spelling of u̇ and ü (g*oo*d, s*oo*n)
  "ow" and "ou" spellings of the "ou" sound in *ow*l and m*ou*se (d*ow*n, fl*ow*er)
  "oy" spelling of the "oi" sound (b*oy*)
  vowel–consonant–silent "e" (h*ome*, r*ide*)
  final "y" spelling of long "e" (bab*y*)
  final "y" spelling of long "i" (m*y*)
  unexpected spellings:
    single vowels (fr*o*m, c*o*ld, *o*ff, c*o*st)
    vowel–consonant–silent "e" (g*ive*, s*ure*, d*one*)
    two vowels together (b*ee*n, fr*ie*nd, s*ai*d)
    other unexpected spellings (they, say, eye)
uses "le" spelling of the "l" sound (peop*le*)
uses morphemes to make structural changes
  "s" or "es" plural (cat*s*, bus*es*)
  changes "y" to "i" before adding "es" (cry, cr*ies*)
  "s" or "es" for third-person singular (live, lives)
  "s" to show possession (our*s*)
  "d" or "ed" ending for past tense (play*ed*)
  "ing" endings with doubled consonant (cla*pping*), with dropped silent "e" (mov*ing*)
  "er" as noun agent ending (sing*er*)
  "er" and "est" endings (old, old*er*, old*est*)
uses syllabication to aid spelling recall (yel-low)
recognizes compounds to aid spelling recall (air • plane)
recognizes rhyming words to aid spelling recall (pet, get)
spells simple homonyms (to, two, too)
spells simple antonyms (last, first)
spells number words (one, two, . . . ten)
sequences words in alphabetical order

TABLE 4-3 (continued)

Fourth-, Fifth-, and Sixth-Grade Skills

spells voiced and unvoiced "th" sounds (six*th*, lea*th*er)
uses the following irregular spellings:
  "ch" spelling of "k" sound (e*ch*o)
  "wh" spelling of "hw" sound (*wh*istle)
  "g" spelling of "g" or "j" sound (brid*g*e, ci*g*ar)
  "c" spelling of "k" or "s" sound (*c*abbage, jui*c*e)
  "qu" spelling of "kw" sound (*qu*een)
  "ph" spelling of "f" sound (ele*ph*ant)
spells the following vowel sounds:
  "ow" spelling of the "o" sound (unkn*ow*n)
  "oi" and "oy" spelling of the "oi" sound (n*oi*se, enj*oy*)
  "o," "al," "au," and "aw" spellings of the "o" sound (n*o*rth, t*a*ll)
  "el" and "l" spellings (cast*le*, barr*el*)
  "y" spelling of long "e" (worr*y*)
uses morphemes to make structural changes:
  irregular plurals (geese, calves, feet)
  plurals of nouns ending in "o" (pian*os*, potat*oes*)
  "ly" ending (especial*ly*)
  number suffixes (thir*teen*, six*ty*)
  suffixes to change parts of speech (play*ful*), harm*less*, attrac*tive*)
  prefixes to change meaning (*re*place), *dis*honest)
uses unexpected spellings (minute, thread)
spells contractions (aren't, they're)
spells higher number words (eleven, twelve,. . . .)
spells days of the week
spells months of the year
uses guide words in the dictionary

Seventh-Grade and Above Skills

spells silent letters (*b*, *h*, *m*, *g*, *p*)
spells hyphenated words (tongue-tied)
uses the following letter combinations (-*ient*, -*ian*, -*ium*, -*iasm*, -*iable*, -*ure*)
uses the following word endings (-*ance*, -*ence*, -*ense*, -*ogy*, -*cede*, -*ceed*)
interprets diacritical marks in the dictionary

grammatical and punctuation errors should be avoided at the beginning. Reid and Hresko (1983) state that children's attempts at writing should not await mastery of form. Rather, emphasis should be placed on the meaningful but simple expression of ideas with ample opportunities for expressive writing integrated into the entire curriculum. A rich amount of experiences is also necessary and most likely to yield a rich output of written productions (Lerner, 1985). Experiences such as class discussions and field trips may be provided to stimulate the production of ideas.

The language experience approach is often used in teaching written composition, particularly at the elementary level. In this approach, the student first dictates a story based on objects or events. The teacher writes the story and then reads it back to the student. The content of the story is then discussed and gradually the mechanical aspects are introduced. The student may copy the dictation into his or her notebook and then read the story independently or to the teacher. As the student progresses, he or she assumes more responsibility for generating and expressing ideas, sentences, and paragraphs. Attention is given to proper sentence and paragraph construction, and proofreading for capitalization, punctuation, spelling, and overall appearance. The language experience approach is best used when it can be integrated with all areas of the language arts curriculum. Mallon and Berglund (1984) report that language experience programs "effectively demonstrate for students the connection between spoken and written language and will emphasize reading as a meaningful process." (p. 870)

Teachers who are successful in their attempts to improve their students' writing usually fail because of inadequate attention to one or more of the following principles:

1. writing is basically a thinking process and must be conceptualized as such by students and teachers—an idea poorly clarified in the mind of the writer will also be unclear on paper
2. writing is always done for a particular purpose and a particular audience, both of which the writer should be aware of at all times
3. desire to commit an idea to writing is basic to writing improvement
4. development in writing can proceed only on a base of oral language development
5. frequent practice and audience feedback are essential to the improvement of written composition (Otto & Smith, 1980, pp. 383–384)

In the assessment of written composition, three areas are considered in the skill network (see Table 4–4): 1) capitalization and punctuation skills, 2) skills in grammar and word usage, and 3) skills in composition format and creative expression.

TABLE 4-4   Written Composition Skill Network

First-Grade Skills

Capitalization and Punctuation

capitalizes first word of a sentence
capitalizes own first and last name
capitalizes name of teacher, school, town, and street
capitalizes the pronoun "I"
uses a period at the end of a declarative sentence

TABLE 4-4 (continued)

First-Grade Skills (continued)

uses a period after numbers in a list
uses a question mark after a written question

Composition Format and Creative Expression

writes simple sentences
presents neat writing on paper with margins on left and right and spacing at top and bottom of page

---

Second-Grade Skills

Capitalization and Punctuation

capitalizes the date
capitalizes first and important words of titles of books read
capitalizes proper names
capitalizes titles of compositions
capitalizes titles of people (Mr., Mrs., Ms., Miss)
uses comma after salutation and closing of friendly letter
uses comma between day of month and year
uses comma between names of city and state

Composition Format and Creative Expression

writes sentences from dictation
copies sentences correctly from chalkboard
recognizes different kinds of sentences (statements and questions)
writes a simple paragraph of three to five sentences
indents first word of a paragraph

Third-Grade Skills

Capitalization and Punctuation

capitalizes names of months, days of week, special days, common holidays, first word in a line of verse, appropriate words in titles of stories and poems, names of special places
uses correct punctuation with abbreviations, initials, contractions, items in a series, quotations, and exclamations

Grammar and Word Usage

recognizes singular, plural, and possessive nouns
recognizes verbs
uses correct verb forms in sentences (is–are, did–done, was–were, see–saw–seen, ate–eaten, went–gone, came–come, gave–given, rode–ridden, took–taken, grow–grew–grown, know–knew–known, bring–brought, drew–drawn, began–begun, ran–run, throw–threw–thrown, drive–drove–driven, wrote–written, tore–torn, chose–chosen, climbed, broke–broken, wore–worn, spoke–spoken, sang–sung, rang–rung, catch–caught
uses correctly *a* and *an, may* and *can, teach* and *learn, let* and *leave, don't* and *doesn't, there is* and *there are, any* and *no*)

(continued)

TABLE 4-4 *(continued)*

Third-Grade Skills (continued)

Composition Format and Creative Expression

recognizes exclamatory sentences
uses a variety of sentences
combines short choppy sentences into longer ones
avoids run-on sentences
correctly sequences ideas to form sentences and paragraphs
begins to learn to proofread
uses variety of descriptive words
writes simple thank-you notes or friendly letters
addresses an envelope
writes a simple, original poem

Fourth-Grade Skills

Capitalization and Punctuation

capitalizes streets, roadways, cities, states, countries, special groups and organizations, proper
  nouns; knows seasons as common, uncapitalized nouns
uses apostrophe to show possession
uses hyphen to separate parts of word at end of line
uses period following a command, after numerals and letters in an outline
uses commas to set off an appositive (Mary, my cousin), after an introductory clause or phrase,
  between introductory words and a quotation, to separate coordinate clauses
uses colon after salutation in business letter

Grammar and Word Usage

recognizes common and proper nouns in complete subjects
recognizes verb in complete predicate
recognizes adjectives
recognizes adverbs modifying verbs, adjectives, and other adverbs
recognizes singular and plural pronouns
uses correct agreement of subject and verb
uses *she, he, I, we,* and *they* correctly as subjects
uses bring and take correctly
uses correct verb forms in sentences (blow-blew-blown, drink-drank-drunk, lie-lay-lain, take-
  took-taken, rise-rose-risen, teach-taught-taught, raise-raised-raised, lay-laid-laid, fly-flew-
flown, set-set-set, swim-swam-swum, freeze-froze-frozen, steal-stole-stolen)

Composition Format and Creative Expression

writes sentences with simple and complete subject and predicate
writes improved paragraphs
develops a simple outline
writes invitations and simple business letters correctly
writes a paragraph that tells a story

TABLE 4-4 *(continued)*

Fifth-Grade Skills

Capitalization and Punctuation

capitalizes in outlining, position titles (President Lincoln), commerical trade names, first word of direct quotation

uses colon in writing time (2:00 P.M.)

uses quotation marks around title of an article, chapter of a book, and title of a poem or story

underlines title of a book

uses periods and commas correctly

Grammar and Word Usage

recognizes prepositions, prepositional phrases, conjunctions, and interjections

recognizes nouns as object of preposition and predicate nouns

recognizes predicate adjectives and proper adjectives (e.g., nationality)

conjugates verbs to note changes in tense, person, number

uses correct verb forms in sentences (am–was–been, say–said–said, fall–fell–fallen, dive–dived–dived, burst–burst–burst, buy–bought–bought, and additional verb forms of words such as climb, like, play, read

Composition Format and Creative Expression

uses variety of sentences

uses correct subject and verb agreement

uses compound subjects and predicates

writes paragraphs from an outline

writes paragraphs with clearly stated main idea and three supporting facts

outlines using main topics (I, II, III) and subtopics (A, B, C)

begins to use more than one paragraph

compiles list of books (authors and titles) to use for reference

proofreads writing for correct spelling, capitalization, punctuation, and word usage

writes a story with a simple plot

Sixth-Grade and Above Skills

Capitalization and Punctuation

capitalizes proper adjectives indicating race, nationality, etc., and abbreviations of proper nouns and titles

uses correctly punctuated dialogue

correctly punctuates dictated paragraphs

uses hyphens in compound numbers, nouns, and adjectives

uses semicolons correctly with coordinate clauses

uses colons to introduce a list

uses apostrophes in plural of letters and numbers

uses parentheses to show related material

(continued)

TABLE 4-4 *(continued)*

Sixth-Grade and Above Skills (continued)

Grammar and Word Usage:

understands noun clauses and nouns used as indirect objects

understands verb conjugation

understands uses of nouns, verbs, adjectives, adverbs, pronouns, conjunctions, prepositions, interjections

uses homonyms correctly (its–it's, their–there–they're, there's–theirs, whose–who's)

uses correct verb forms in sentences (beat–beat–beaten, learn–learned–learned, leave–left–left, lit–lit–lit, forget–forgot–forgotten, swing–swung–swung, spring–sprang–sprung, shrink–shrank–shrunk, slide–slid–slid)

Composition Format and Creative Expression:

uses concise statements avoiding wordiness

uses complex sentences

writes well-constructed paragraph with a topic sentence, supporting details, and a conclusion

uses transition words to connect ideas

checks paragraph for accurate statements

shows improvement in complete composition—introduction, development, and conclusion

develops a paragraph in different ways—with details, facts, reasons, examples, contrasts, and comparisons

outlines using main topics, subtopics, and details

Source: This sample network was developed from many sources including the *Brigance Diagnostic Comprehensive Inventory of Basic Skills* (Brigance, 1983), *Developing Children's Language* by Petty and Jensen (1980), *Teaching Children with Learning and Behavior Problems* by Hammill and Bartel (1982), and *Teaching Students with Learning Problems* by Mercer and Mercer (1985). Networks may also be found in language arts textbooks and in curriculum materials used for language or may be teacher produced.

SELECTING AND ADMINISTERING AN ASSESSMENT PROCEDURE

Because language arts includes four basic communication skills—listening, speaking, reading, and writing—and their subskills, many tests and techniques have been developed to assess communication skills. The first step in the assessment of language arts is to determine whether to use *periodic* or *continuous* assessment procedures.

Periodic Assessment

Periodic assessment in language arts, which may be either formal or informal, yields global information to assist in continuous assessment and establishing long-range instructional objectives. Periodic tests may be given at the beginning of the school year to identify general areas of need, periodically throughout the year as needed, and again at the end of the year to measure student progress in language.

☐ *Formal Tests*

Formal (standardized) norm-referenced tests are used for periodic assessment, and many are available that provide a comprehensive survey of language functioning. Other tests are designed to measure individual components of language such as phonology, morphology, syntax, and semantics. Most of the oral language tests require individual administration. It is useful for those conducting formal assessment to have a basic background in speech and language pathology.

Fewer formal devices are available to assess written language. Survey measures assess several written expression skills including, for example, handwriting, spelling, and the skills involved in written composition. Other tests are available to measure in depth the individual components of written language such as spelling or handwriting.

Some group and individual intelligence and achievement tests include subtests to assess components of language arts. Tests commonly used for the assessment of oral and written language are presented in the Appendix.

Formal language arts tests usually identify general areas of need but do not provide an indepth diagnosis of language problems. To gain useful data closely related to daily instruction, a teacher should focus upon informal procedures.

☐ *Informal Procedures*

Informal, nonstandardized procedures are very useful for periodically assessing student performance in language arts. Informal devices may be used to extend the information obtained from formal tests and are often helpful in determining strengths and weaknesses and error patterns observed in spoken and written language.

Some informal assessment devices are commercially produced while others are teacher-made. *DISTAR* (Engelmann & Osborn, 1976), a commercially produced language program, is a structured approach designed for students in preschool through third grade. *DISTAR* provides placement or entry tests to determine where students should begin the program and work checks for daily evaluation of skills.

Informal assessment devices may also be teacher-produced from instructional materials so that the skills assessed closely parallel the language arts program used in the classroom and are therefore relevant to instructional objectives. As previously indicated, the assessment of spoken language disorders may require the expertise of a speech and language clinician, but that is beyond the focus of this text.

In the following sections, informal procedures for assessing listening and written language skills are presented, including checklists, handwriting error analysis, informal spelling inventories and spelling error analysis, the cloze procedure, written work samples, and structured observation.

CHECKLISTS   Checklists usually consist of skill statements with spaces to record the presence or absence of a behavior. While checklists do not provide information concerning the frequency or quality of performance, they are useful for evaluating and monitoring language arts growth. Checklists are very useful tools to informally assess listening behaviors. A teacher may gain important information by observing various listening behaviors in a student. A checklist to note listening behaviors is presented in Figure 4–2.

Students who display problems in listening skills may need to be prompted or reminded of the appropriate behaviors. Cohen and Plaskon

FIGURE 4-2   Listening Behavior Checklist

Item	+ yes − no
1. Does the student attend to oral directions the first time they are presented?	☐
2. Does the student follow directions in the sequence given?	☐
3. Does the student wait to begin a task until all the directions are given?	☐
4. Does the student understand the assignment?	☐
5. Does the student complete the correct assignment?	☐
6. Does the student appear to understand stories read aloud?	☐
7. Does the student attend well during oral presentations in class?	☐
8. Does the student maintain eye contact with the speaker?	☐
9. Does the student shift attention to different speakers in a group discussion?	☐
10. Does the student appear interested in what the speaker is saying?	☐
11. Does the student frequently participate in class discussions?	☐
12. Does the student wait for his or her turn to speak?	☐
13. Does the student interpret correctly information presented orally in the form of rules, requests, or messages?	☐
14. Does the student always hear you?	☐

(1980) suggest developing a personalized checklist that the student can frequently consult. The checklist presented in Figure 4-3 is a modification of a student checklist for listening behavior developed by Kopp (1967).

Checklists may also be developed to assess all the skills of written expression. Scope and sequence lists included in language arts textbooks may be modified to be used as a checklist. The networks presented in tables 4-2, 4-3, and 4-4 for handwriting, spelling, and written composition are also very appropriate for assessing written expression.

Guerin and Maier (1983) offer several suggestions for writing the items on a checklist. The list should be comprehensive enough to cover the critical elements in the subject area. The items should be concise and clearly descriptive of the element to be examined. The items should be grouped so that all those items related to a particular area fall in consecutive order. A portion of the written composition skill network in Table 4-4 has been converted into a checklist presented in Figure 4-4.

Checklists may also be developed to assess a small group or entire class of students on various skills. The checklist presented in Figure 4-5 is designed to record the date on which each student mastered the use of a punctuation or capitalization skill.

FIGURE 4-3 Student's Listening Checklist

Item	+ yes − no
1. Am I ready to listen? (seated comfortably in a location where I can see and hear)	☐
2. Am I ready to concentrate? (not talking or playing while listening, tuning out distractions and other thoughts, and calling to mind any knowledge about the topic)	☐
3. Am I able to discover the central theme in the speaker's message?	☐
4. Am I able to pick out details that support the main idea?	☐
5. Am I able to use extra listening time to organize or summarize the presentation mentally or on paper?	☐
6. Am I able to listen carefully so I can ask questions to clarify specific information?	☐
7. Am I able to avoid making automatic judgments based on personal biases? (able to wait until all the facts are given before making judgments or stating opinions)	☐
8. Am I able to evaluate what was said and form an opinion?	☐

Source: Adapted from Kopp, O. W. "The Evaluation of Oral Language Activities: Teaching and Learning," *Elementary English* 44 (1967).

FIGURE 4-4 First-Grade Written Language Evaluation Checklist

Skill	Observed + yes − no
preference established for left- or right-handedness	☐
draws basic shapes used in writing	☐
writes first and last name using manuscript upper- and lower-case letters	☐
writes with correct posture, paper position, and pencil grip	☐
writes upper- and lower-case manuscript letters	☐
writes numbers to ten	☐
copies words neatly from chalkboard	☐
capitalizes first word of a sentence	☐
capitalizes own first and last name	☐
capitalizes name of teacher, school, town, and street	☐
capitalizes the pronoun ''I''	☐
uses a period at the end of a declarative sentence	☐
uses a period after numbers in a list	☐
uses a question mark after a written question	☐
writes simple sentences	☐
presents neat writing on paper with margins on left and right and spacing at top and bottom of page	☐

Name _____

Grade/Teacher _____

Date _____

FIGURE 4-5 Punctuation and Capitalization Checklist

(Record the date on which the skill is mastered.)

Student Names	Period	Comma	Question mark	Quotation mark	Apostrophe	Exclamation point	Hyphen	Colon	Beginning a sentence	First/last name	Special days	"I"	Date/weekdays	Proper names	Streets	Cities	Titles	First word in salutation	First word in closing	States	Race and nationality	Commercial products	_____		_____

HANDWRITING ERROR ANALYSIS The use of formal handwriting tests provides a very general evaluation of a student's level of competence. The *Zaner-Bloser Evaluation Scale* (1984) also may be used to assess on a general level the manuscript and cursive handwriting of students in grade one through high school. For the *Zaner-Bloser Evaluation Scale,* students are asked to copy a sample sentence, which is then matched against a series of five specimen sentences appropriate to the student's grade. Each sentence represents a different quality of penmanship.

To accurately determine specific strengths and weaknesses in handwriting, a thorough analysis of errors is necessary. In Figure 4–6 the proper formation of uppercase and lowercase manuscript and cursive letters is presented. Lewis and Lewis (1965) report the following frequent types of errors in the manuscript writing of first graders:

1. Errors in letter forms including both curves and vertical lines of *J, U, f, h, j,* and *m*
2. Incorrect size with the letters *p, q, y, g,* and *j*
3. Reversals with the letters *N, d* (and *b*), *q* (and *g*), and *y* (and *s*)
4. Partial omissions in the letters *m, U,* and *I*
5. Additions with the letters *q, C, k, m,* and *y*
6. Incorrect relationship of letter parts with *k, R, M,* and *m*
7. Incorrect alignment with descending letters
8. Incorrect shapes with the letters *j, G,* and *J*

Newland (1932) studied the cursive handwriting of 2,381 people and noted the most common errors made:

1. Illegibilities involving the letters *a, e, r,* and *t* (accounted for approximately 50% of the illegibilities)
2. Failure to close letters (*a, b,* and *f*)
3. Top loops of letters closed (*l* like *t, e* like *i*)
4. Looping strokes that should be nonlooped (*i* like *e*)
5. Straight-up strokes used instead of rounded strokes (*n* like *u, h* like *b*)
6. Problems with end strokes

Burns and Broman (1983) also note that the Arabic numerals that cause difficulty are 5, 0, 2, 7, 9, and 6. In Figure 4–7, several methods of assessing handwriting errors are presented. In Table 4–5, the most common defects in writing and possible contributing causes are presented.

Students may also be encouraged to analyze their own handwriting samples to identify the errors. A commercial device useful for self-evaluation is the "Peek-Thru" by Zaner-Bloser. A plastic overlay with manuscript or cursive writing is placed over the student's writing and letter formation to allow alignment to be analyzed.

FIGURE 4-6   Formation of Uppercase and Lowercase Manuscript and Cursive Letters and Numbers

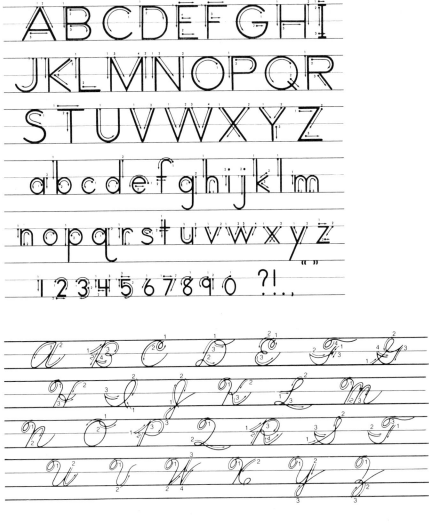

Source: Used with permission from *Handwriting: Basic Skills and Application.* Copyright © 1984, Zaner-Bloser, Inc., Columbus, Ohio.

FIGURE 4-7 Handwriting Error Analysis

Error Type	Method of Evaluation
1. Position of hand, arm, body, and/or paper	Observe to see if the pencil is held correctly, paper is in proper position, head is not too close or far away from paper, posture is correct when seated, and hand preference is always the same.
2. Letter formation (strokes used to form letters)	A card with a hole cut out slightly larger than a single letter may be used to examine letters individually. Illegible or improperly formed letters stand out clearly when this device is used.
3. Letter size and alignment (size of letters may be too large, too small, or varying; letters may not be aligned evenly along the baseline)	A ruler may be used to draw lines that touch the tops and bottoms of letters to analyze size and alignment.
4. Spacing (letters, words, or lines may be too crowded, too far apart, or varying)	Observe to see if there is a space of about one letter (small *o*) between letters in manuscript and cursive writing, as well as consistent spacing between words and sentences.
5. Line quality (may be too heavy, too light, or varying thickness and/or steadiness)	Observe eveness of writing.
6. Slant (should be uniform—manuscript letters are usually formed perpendicular to the baseline; cursive letters may have too much, too little, or varying slant)	Lines of a uniform slant may be drawn through all letters to note inconsistencies.
7. Speed (may be too fast or too slow)	Speed of handwriting may be determined by asking a student to copy a passage as well and as quickly as possible. Suggested proficiency goals for handwriting are presented later in this chapter.

TABLE 4-5 **Common Handwriting Defects and Possible Causes**

Defect	Causes
1. Too much slant	a. Writing arm too near body b. Thumb too stiff c. Point of nib too far from fingers d. Paper in wrong direction e. Stroke in wrong direction
2. Writing too straight	a. Arm too far from body b. Fingers too near nib c. Index finger alone guiding pen d. Incorrect position of paper
3. Writing too heavy	a. Index finger pressing too heavily b. Using wrong type of pen c. Pen too small in diameter
4. Writing too light	a. Pen held too obliquely or too straight b. Pen too large in diameter
5. Writing too angular	a. Thumb too stiff b. Pen too lightly held c. Movement too slow
6. Writing too irregular	a. Lack of freedom of movement b. Movement of hand too slow c. Pen gripping d. Incorrect or uncomfortable position
7. Spacing too wide	a. Pen progresses too fast to right b. Excessive sweeping lateral movement

Source: W. Petty and J. Jensen (1980). *Developing Children's Language.* Newton, MA.: Allyn and Bacon, p. 496. Used with permission.

Another approach involves students checking the relative size of letters they have written by remembering only four different letter heights:

Loop letters and capitals are almost a space tall.
Intermediate letters (*d, p,* and *t*) are 2/3 of a space tall.
Small letters (*a, c, e,* etc.) are 1/3 of a space tall.
Lower loop letters go half a space below the line (*f, p, g,* etc.)
(Petty & Jensen, 1980, p. 481)

INFORMAL SPELLING INVENTORIES AND SPELLING ERROR ANALYSIS An informal spelling inventory (I.S.I.) may be used to assess a variety of spelling skills and to determine an approximate grade level. To construct an I.S.I., graded word lists should first be developed. Words may be selected from a basal spelling series by randomly choosing 15 words from a first-grade book and 20 words from each book for grades two through eight (Mann, Suiter, & McClung, 1979). To select words randomly, divide the total number of words presented in the text by 20. For example, 400 words divided by 20 is 20, so every twentieth word would be selected for a graded list.

Words are next presented in a dictated format using the following procedure: 1) say the word in isolation (e.g., porch), 2) use the word in a sentence (Grandfather is sitting out on the front *porch*), and 3) say the word again (porch). Testing should begin at the first level for children in grade four and below. For students above grade four, testing should begin at the third-grade level and continue until the student incorrectly spells six consecutive words. Wallace and Larsen (1978) recommend determining the achievement level by finding the highest grade-level word list at which a score of 90–100% is obtained. The teaching level is determined by noting the highest level at which a score of 75–89% is obtained.

Dictated tests may also be designed by selecting words from a list of words most frequently used such as the Dolch list (Dolch, 1948) or the *New Instant Word List* by Fry (1980). Word lists such as these are often already grouped according to grade level.

After a dictated test is administered, spelling errors are analyzed to note possible patterns of strengths and weaknesses. An analysis of various spelling errors is presented in Table 4–6. Errors often noted include:

■ omissions of silent letters, sounded letters, double letters, syllables, or endings

TABLE 4-6   Sample Spelling-Error Analysis

Correct Spelling	*Student's Spelling*	*Error*
freight	frate	phonetic substitution
knee	nee	omission of silent letter
laugh	lef	phonetic substitution
roping	ropin	mispronunciation
crush	crusht	addition of unneeded letter
winner	winer	omission of double letter
giraffe	jiraffe	phonetic substitution
alphabet	alfabet	phonetic substitution
quart	kwart	phonetic substitution
guitar	geetar	mispronunciation
broil	brol	incorrect sound/symbol association
purple	purpel	missequencing letter order

- additions of unnecessary letters or syllables
- substitutions, including phonetic substitutions for vowels, consonants, syllables, or words, and nonphonetic substitutions for vowels or consonants
- reversals or missequencing, including letter shapes, letter order, syllables, or whole words
- incorrect sound/symbol association
- dialectical patterns or mispronunciations reflected in spelling of words
- homonym confusion
- other errors, including spellings that bear no relationship to the dictated words

Ganschow (1984) suggests three questions to consider when making a decision about the spelling errors to remediate:

1. What errors seem to be most prominent?
2. Which error patterns will yield the most generalizability if worked on?
3. Which types of errors best lend themselves to ease of correction for this child? (p. 291)

Hammill (1982) suggests that students who have difficulty in spelling keep their own list of frequently misspelled words. Temple and Gillet (1984) suggest that teachers compile a spelling-error log that might include misspelled words from various sources such as tests, worksheets, or creative writing. The teacher may then focus on these words for daily remediation.

Commercially produced tests are also available for informal assessment of spelling. *Spellmaster* (Cohen & Abrams, 1974) is a comprehensive diagnostic spelling test that includes three categories of words: regular words, irregular words, and homonyms. Six levels for grades one through six and one level for grades seven and eight are available. This program also includes a scope and sequence chart, a chart that relates skills tested to seven basal spelling programs, and a method for specific error analysis.

Kottmeyer's (1959) *Diagnostic Spelling Test* (see Figure 4–8) measures a variety of spelling skills and is presented in a dictation format. Two tests are available—one for the second and third grades and one for fourth grade and above. The examiner says a word and an illustrative sentence using the word. Each of the 32 items measures a spelling skill. An analysis of the student's errors is then completed and a grade-level score computed.

CLOZE PROCEDURE FOR ASSESSING SPELLING   The cloze procedure is another informal method used to assess spelling. The student is asked to fill in a missing word of a sentence or supply missing letters of a word. The following examples assess a student's understanding of various "vowel plus r" combinations.

(ar, er, ir, or, ur)

1. Jack is in the th___d grade at school.
2. Did you b___n the toast?
3. Please come aft___ six o'clock.
4. My brother is tall, but I am _____.
5. The _____ shine brightly on a clear night.

The cloze procedure is useful in noting a student's knowledge of spelling rules or sound/symbol generalizations (Cartwright, 1969). Wallace and Larsen (1978), however, note two limitations of this technique: If the words used are not a part of the student's oral language, he or she will not be able to fill in the blanks. And, if the reading level in the test is too high, the student with limited reading skills will be penalized.

FIGURE 4-8   Diagnostic Spelling Test

DIRECTIONS FOR DIAGNOSTIC SPELLING TEST

Give list 1 to any pupil whose placement is second or third grade.
Give list 2 to any pupil whose placement is above Grade 3.

Grading Scoring, List 1:
    Below 15 correct: Below second grade
    15–22 correct: Second grade
    23–29 correct: Third grade

Any pupil who scores above 29 should be given the List 2 Test.

Grade Scoring, List 2:
    Below 9 correct: Below third grade
    9–19 correct: Third grade
    20–25 correct: Fourth grade
    26–29 correct: Fifth grade
    Over 29 correct: Sixth grade or better

Any pupil who scores below 9 should be given the List 1 Test.

FIGURE 4-8 (*continued*)

DIAGNOSTIC SPELLING TEST

List 1

Word   Illustrative Sentence

1. not—He is *not* here.
2. but—Mary is here, *but* Joe is not.
3. get—*Get* the wagon, John.
4. sit—*Sit* down, please.
5. man—Father is a tall *man.*
6. boat—We sailed our *boat* on the lake.
7. train—Tom has a new toy *train.*
8. time—It is *time* to come home.
9. like—We *like* ice cream.
10. found—We *found* our lost ball.
11. down—Do not fall *down.*
12. soon—Our teacher will *soon* be here.
13. good—He is a *good* boy.
14. very—We are *very* glad to be here.
15. happy—Jane is a *happy* girl.
16. kept—We *kept* our shoes dry.
17. come—*Come* to our party.
18. what—*What* is your name?
19. those—*Those* are our toys.
20. show—*Show* us the way.
21. much—I feel *much* better.
22. sing—We will *sing* a new song.
23. will—Who *will* help us?
24. doll—Make a dress for the *doll.*
25. after—We play *after* school.
26. sister—My *sister* is older than I.
27. toy—I have a new *toy* train.
28. say—*Say* your name clearly.
29. little—Tom is a *little* boy.
30. one—I have only *one* book.
31. would—*Would* you come with us?
32. pretty—She is a *pretty* girl.

List 2

Word   Illustrative Sentence

1. flower—A rose is a *flower.*
2. mouth—Open your *mouth.*
3. shoot—Joe wants to *shoot* his new gun.
4. stood—We *stood* under the roof.
5. while—We sang *while* we marched.
6. third—We are in the *third* grade.
7. each—*Each* child has a pencil.
8. class—Our *class* is reading.
9. jump—We like to *jump* rope.
10. jumps—Mary *jumps* rope.
11. jumped—We *jumped* rope yesterday.
12. jumping—The girls are *jumping* rope now.
13. hit—*Hit* the ball hard.
14. hitting—John is *hitting* the ball.
15. bite—Our dog does not *bite.*
16. biting—The dog is *biting* on the bone.
17. study—*Study* your lesson.
18. studies—He *studies* each day.
19. dark—The sky is *dark* and cloudy.
20. darker—This color is *darker* than that one.
21. darkest—This color is the *darkest* of the three.
22. afternoon—We may play this *afternoon.*
23. grandmother—Our *grandmother* will visit us.
24. can't—We *can't* go with you.
25. doesn't—Mary *doesn't* like to play.
26. night—We read to Mother last *night.*
27. brought—Joe *brought* his lunch to school.
28. apple—An *apple* fell from the tree.
29. again—We must come back *again.*
30. laugh—Do not *laugh* at other children.
31. because—We cannot play *because* of the rain.
32. through—We ran *through* the yard.

(continued)

FIGURE 4-8 *(continued)*

List 1

Word	Element Tested	Word	Element Tested
1. not 2. but 3. get 4. sit 5. man	Short vowels	18. what 19. those 20. show 21. much 22. sing	*wh, th, sh, ch,* and *ng* spellings and *ow* spelling of long o
6. boat 7. train	Two vowels together	23. will 24. doll	Doubled final consonants
8. time 9. like	Vowel-consonant-e	25. after 26. sister	*er* spelling
10. found 11. down	*ow-ou* spelling of *ou* sound	27. toy	*oy* spelling of *oi* sound
12. soon 13. good	long and short *oo*	28. say	*ay* spelling of long *a* sound
14. very 15. happy	Final *y* as short *i*	29. little	*le* ending
16. kept 17. come	*c* and *k* spellings of the *k* sound	30. one 31. would 32. pretty	Non-phonetic spellings

List 2

Word	Element Tested	Word	Element Tested
1. flower 2. mouth	*ow-ou* spellings of *ou* sound, *er* ending, *th* spelling	15. bite 16. biting	Dropping final *e* before *ing*
3. shoot 4. stood	Long and short *oo*, *sh* spelling	17. study 18. studies	Changing final *y* to *i* before ending
5. while	*wh* spelling, vowel-consonant-e	19. dark 20. darker 21. darkest	*er, est* endings
6. third	*th* spelling, vowel before *r*	22. afternoon 23. grandmother	Compound words
7. each	*ch* spelling, two vowels together	24. can't 25. doesn't	Contractions
8. class	Double final consonant, *c* spelling of *k* sound	26. night 27. brought	Silent *gh*
9. jump 10. jumps 11. jumped 12. jumping	Addition of *s, ed, ing; j* spelling of soft *g* sound	28. apple	*le* ending
13. hit 14. hitting	Doubling final consonant before *ing*	29. again 30. laugh 31. because 32. through	Non-phonetic spellings

Source: From *Teacher's Guide for Remedial Reading* by William Kottmeyer, pages 88–90. Copyright © 1959 by William Kottmeyer. Webster Division, McGraw-Hill Book Company. Reprinted with permission of the publisher.

WRITTEN WORK SAMPLES AND STRUCTURED OBSERVATION   Work-sample analysis through structured observation may be used to evaluate all aspects of written language, including handwriting, spelling, and written composition. A representative sample of a student's written work should first be obtained. Wallace and Larsen (1978) note that although a subjective interpretation is required when analyzing written work samples, it is helpful for a teacher to try and standardize his or her observations to obtain a reliable and valid assessment. The major components of written expression to be assessed are listed below. Descriptions of each component are only suggestions of specific skills to evaluate in each area.

1. purpose—main ideas unclear or missing, too broad, lacking in significance, or poorly stated
2. content—ideas unsupported, lack specifics, unrelated to the subject, or taken from another source
3. organization—introduction and conclusions poorly stated, ideas randomly presented, transitions inappropriately used
4. paragraphs—paragraphs inadequately developed
5. sentences—sentences are fragmented, consist of dangling modifiers, lack variety, show problems with tense, subject–verb agreement, and pronoun–antecedent agreement
6. word choice and usage—vocabulary inappropriate, cliches, tone ineffective
7. capitalization—incorrectly used in titles, proper nouns, words for deity, etc.
8. punctuation—italics, period, comma, exclamation point, quotes incorrectly used
9. handwriting—does not permit quick and easy reading in either manuscript or cursive style (Wallace & Larsen, pp. 409–410)

Correctness of spelling is another factor to be assessed using written work samples. Figure 4–9 is a fifth-grade student's writing sample. At this level, students should begin to use more than one paragraph in their writing, so this skill might be targeted for instruction. In evaluating a written sample, it would be beneficial to use a profile to show the continuous progress of an individual student. An example is provided in Figure 4–10.

In a study by VanHouten, Morrison, Jarvis, and McDonald (1974), fifth graders were evaluated and reinforced for improvement in three areas of writing: 1) the number of words written, 2) the number of different words, and 3) the number of new words. These three areas could also be targeted in the analysis of written work samples.

Cartwright (1969) suggests analyzing written samples in terms of four components: fluency, vocabulary, structure, and content. Fluency, that is, quantity of verbal output, is measured by analyzing sentence length and complexity. The average sentence length in a writing sample

FIGURE 4-9 Fifth Grader's Writing Sample

Why I Don't Eat Lima Beans.
About The Author

My name is Jill Johansen. I am 11 years old. I am in 5th grade.

One day my mom asked me to go get some groceries from the store. When I got outside it was very hot. So I went and changed my clothes. Then I was on my way! When I got there, there was only a few people there. So I went down the aisle, the first thing on the list was milk so I went and got 1 gallon of milk. The next thing on the list was crackers, So I went and go the cheepest baby crackers there were. The next thing on the list was cheese so I went and got some chedder cheese. Then the very last was lima Beans.

I looked all over the store for lima Beans, I finally found them. But when I piched up the bag a ugly undiscribable hand reached out and grabbed me. What a sight! I screamed And when I noticed there was no body in the store I almost had a stroke! I tried to get free but it had my wrist to hard. Then finally I got free. I ran, and ran, and ran. I finally made out what that ugly thing was... A Lima Bean. Then I ran down Mallory Street then down 12th avenue. I went to the police station And they thought I was a dumb regular Kid who liked to make up imaginary stories. I was really in alot of trouble. This lima bean was the ugliest thing, when I looked around I had ran so fast I forgot which way to go. I was lost, Here I am in the middle of nowhere I was starting to get mad mad and get real mad. My face was turning red and my feet were swelling up. Finally I got so mad that I punched the Lima Bean and squashed him. He was no more alive, And that's why I never ever eat Lima beans

The End

Source: Used with permission from J. Johansen, K. Smith, and P. Smith

FIGURE 4-10 Profile of Continuous Progress in Written Expression

Student _____

+ satisfactory
− unsatisfactory

Date	Writing sample description	Purpose (main idea clear)	Content (adequate ideas with support)	Organization (intro., body and conclusion)	Sentences (complete with proper grammatical form)	Paragraph (development adequate)	Word choice and usage (appropriate and varied vocabulary)	Capitalization (appropriate use of capital letters)	Punctuation (appropriately placed throughout sample)	Handwriting (legible throughout sample)	Spelling (correct throughout sample)

is calculated and compared to age expectations. First count the number of words and sentences in the writing sample. Then divide the total number of words by the total number of sentences. The average sentence length for an eight-year-old is eight words, for a nine-year-old, nine words, and so on through age thirteen. Complexity of sentences is judged in terms of four sentence types: incomplete, simple, compound, and complex—the use of compound and complex sentences increasing with age.

Vocabulary may be evaluated in terms of the variety of words used in the written sample. The type–token ratio (Johnson, 1944) represents the number of different words used (*types*) over the number of total words (*tokens*). In the sentence, "The boy in the car waved to the lady in the car," there are seven word types and twelve tokens, a fairly low type-token ratio (7/12 = .58). The lower the type–token ratio, the more vocabulary words are repeated, a possible indication of inadequate vocabulary development. When used to compare an individual student's writing samples or to compare samples of several students, the first fifty words of the sample should be used.

Vocabulary variety may also be evaluated using the index of diversification (Carroll, 1938). Cartwright (1969) suggests an easy method of calculation: divide the number of words in the sample by the number of "the's," or by the number of times the most frequently used word occurs. The higher the value, the more diverse the vocabulary.

Mercer and Mercer (1985) suggest assessing vocabulary by measuring the number of unusual words. A student's writing sample is compared with a list of frequently used words (e.g., the Dolch word list). The words used by the student that do not appear on the list indicate the extent of his or her vocabulary.

Cartwright's third component used in analyzing written composition, structure, is measured by studying the mechanical aspects of writing, including punctuation, capitalization, and grammatical rules. The total number of grammatical errors are calculated and the types of errors (e.g., subject-verb agreement) recorded to pinpoint specific weaknesses. Teacher-made test items may be used in addition to spontaneous writing samples to adequately assess a variety of grammatical forms, punctuation, and capitalization skills. For example, students may be asked to write a sentence correctly from dictation or correct a sentence when presented in an unpunctuated written form (such as "mr brown was flying to albany new york").

Content is the fourth component to analyze in a written work sample. Cartwright (1969) suggests dividing content into accuracy, ideas, and organization, and rating each factor on a scale from 0 to 10. The particular assignment determines how different factors should be weighed; for example, accuracy would be very important when historical facts were presented. Wallace and Larsen (1978) say that content is an abstract component of written expression and should be evaluated in relation to the student's intelligence, experiences, and motivation to communicate.

Students also may be taught to evaluate their own written work. This technique is particularly useful at the secondary level. Alley and Deshler (1979) state that students should be taught "how to translate their thoughts about everyday observations into writing. Writing should be based on an inquiry method; students should be taught to ask questions, manipulate data, and extrapolate from data." (p. 116) Irmscher (1972) has identified several basic types of questions students should ask themselves to generate writing ideas. Questions relate to a description of the event or action and actor or agent, details about the scene, a description of what occurred, and the purpose. These same questions can be useful for self-evaluation of written composition.

Through a structured observation and analysis of written work samples, much information can be informally obtained concerning student's writing abilities. A student's attitude toward writing is also important to assess. Alley and Deshler (1979) suggest determining whether students have the motivation to write or have emotional blocks to writing assignments.

MICROCOMPUTERS AND WRITTEN LANGUAGE Microcomputers are also excellent tools to use with written language assessment and instruction. Newman (1984) states that word processing holds enormous potential for literacy development because student users can generate and manipulate language. Dudley-Marling (1985) notes that word processing makes editing easy. Students can insert, delete, or move text around and are free of concern about making errors since they are so easily corrected. Language-experience stories can be produced, revised, printed, and distributed using simple word-processing programs. Tutorials may be designed to help students with editing, providing sentence openers, and developing arguments (Woodruff, Bereiter, and Scardamalia, 1981–1982).

After a written-language sample has been developed, microcomputers may allow teachers to more efficiently analyze various aspects of written composition. Lovitt (personal communication, June 1985) notes that computer programs can be developed to determine the total number of words in a story, the number of different words, the number of misspelled words, and the like.

■ Continuous Assessment

Formal and informal periodic assessment should suggest skills to be targeted for a more precise analysis, an analysis obtained using continuous, criterion-referenced assessment. Skills listed in the language-arts networks presented earlier may be assessed and the results compared to a mastery or proficiency criterion. Periodic use of dictated spelling tests may indicate, for example, that a student is weak in spelling words with nonpredictable spellings (words that are not linguistically consistent). However, it is still important to further determine specific error patterns (e.g., words with silent letters may be misspelled more often than other nonpredictable spellings). This specific skill may be continually assessed through use of criterion-referenced procedures until a determined level of mastery is attained.

In the following sections, several procedures for the continuous assessment of language arts skills are presented. These criterion-referenced techniques may also be used for periodic assessment, although they are designed and best used to obtain frequent data and to aid in an ongoing, formative, and comprehensive assessment of language arts skills.

☐ *Commercial Criterion-Referenced Tests*
Commerical criterion-referenced tests may be used to measure a variety of academic skills on a continuous basis. The four Brigance diagnostic measures assess a large variety of language arts skills. The *Brigance Diagnostic Inventory of Early Development* (Brigance, 1978) is designed for use with children from birth to age seven, the *Brigance Diagnostic Inventory of Basic Skills* (Brigance, 1977) is designed for children in grades K–7, the *Brigance Diagnostic Inventory of Essential Skills* (Brigance, 1981) is appropriate for students in grades 7–12, and the *Brigance Diagnostic Comprehensive Inventory of Basic Skills* (Brigance, 1983) is designed for students in grades K–9. The Brigance inventories are easy to administer and can be used to establish instructional objectives and monitor progress of these objectives. The major language arts skills assessed in each inventory are presented in Table 4–7.

☐ *Teacher-Made Tests*
Although commercially produced inventories such as the Brigance measures may be very helpful in ongoing assessment, it may be necessary at times to develop a test to measure skills related specifically to the classroom curriculum or to a student's particular problem. Skills to be assessed should closely parallel those required in the language arts curriculum. Textbooks, workbooks, worksheets, flashcards, and manipulative materials are helpful in designing criterion-referenced tests. Various formats for written test questions may be used (e.g., multiple-choice, matching, and short-answer formats). It is always important to remember to include a sufficient number of test items.

Often criterion-referenced tests designed to assess receptive or expressive oral language skills necessitate individual assessment. But tests used to assess written language skills often do not require individual administration. A group of students may be given a spelling test at the same time or be asked to provide a written work sample for analysis.

TABLE 4–7 Language Arts Skills Assessed in the Brigance Measures

Brigance Diagnostic Inventory of Early Development

prespeech, including receptive language, gestures, and vocalizations

speech and language skills, including syntax, length of sentences, personal data responses, social speech, verbal direction, picture vocabulary, articulation of sounds, repetition of numbers, sentence memory, and singing

general knowledge and comprehension skills

readiness skills

basic reading skills

manuscript writing skills

Brigance Diagnostic Inventory of Basic Skills

reading readiness skills

reading, including word-recognition skills, word-analysis skills, and vocabulary skills

language arts, including handwriting skills, grammar/mechanics skills, spelling skills, and reference skills

Brigance Diagnostic Inventory of Essential Skills

word-recognition skills

oral reading skills

reading comprehension skills

functional word-recognition skills

word-analysis skills

reference skills

skills using schedules and graphs

writing skills

skills using forms

spelling skills

oral communication and telephone skills

TABLE 4-7 *(continued)*

*Brigance Diagnostic Comprehensive
Inventory of Basic Skills*

readiness skills

speech skills

word-recognition skills

oral reading skills

reading comprehension skills

word-analysis skills

functional word-recognition skills

listening skills

spelling skills

writing skills

reference skills

skills using graphs and maps

PROBES   Probes are often used for ongoing assessment of language arts skills. Previously discussed in chapter 2, probes are a type of criterion-referenced procedure used to obtain a sample of a student's behavior. Language arts probes may be designed in a variety of ways and used to assess handwriting, spelling, and written composition skills.

When probes are used to assess handwriting, the student may be timed on a writing task for one minute. He or she may be asked to trace letters, copy letters, write single letters, write letters joined together, or write words. An example of a handwriting probe sheet is provided in Figure 4–11.

Many spelling skills can also be assessed using a probe. Students may be asked to circle the vowels in a group of words, mark the vowels long or short in a group of words, divide words into syllables and mark the accented syllable, write abbreviations for a list of words, change single words to plural forms, or show the contraction or possessive form of a group of words. Examples of spelling probes are presented in Figure 4–12 and Figure 4–13.

FIGURE 4-11   Handwriting Probe

A B C D E F G

H I J K L M N

O P Q R S T

U V W X Y Z

Name _____

Date _____

Time _____

Correct _____

Incorrect _____

FIGURE 4-12   Probe for Spelling Contractions

Directions: See words—write contractions.

am not _____	he is _____
are not _____	she is _____
can not _____	it is _____
is not _____	you will _____
has not _____	he will _____
had not _____	she will _____
have not _____	we will _____
did not _____	I will _____
does not _____	I am _____
will not _____	we are _____
do not _____	they are _____
we would _____	could not _____
he would _____	should not _____
she would _____	I have _____
they would _____	they have _____
I would _____	we have _____

Name _____
Date _____
Time _____
Number correct _____
Number incorrect _____

FIGURE 4-13   Probe: Words Often Misspelled

Directions: 1) see and copy or 2) hear and write (timed or untimed)

ache	buy
afraid	by
again	Christmas
all right	color
already	coming
although	couldn't
among	cousin
answer	didn't
anyway	don't
asks	eighth
beautiful	enough
because	February
believe	for
birthday	fourth
boy's	friend
build	getting

(continued)

FIGURE 4-13 (*continued*)

good-bye	that's
guessed	the
hear	their
heard	there
here	there's
hour	they
I'll	they're
I'm	thought
its	through
it's	to
know	tonight
mother	too
one	tried
our	truly
piece	two
pretty	until
receive	very
right	wait
said	want
school	were
sense	when
separate	would
since	write
some	writing
sometime	you
studying	your
Sunday	you're
sure	yours

Name _____

Date _____

Time _____

Number Correct _____

Number Incorrect _____

Spelling probes may also be designed to assess differences in a child's performance based on sensory modality preferences (Westerman, 1971). Using the auditory-vocal channel, the teacher spells the word aloud first and the student then spells the word aloud. Employing the auditory-motor channel, the teacher spells the word aloud and the child writes the word. Using a visual-vocal channel, the teacher shows the word on a flashcard, then the student spells the word orally. In the visual-motor channel, the teacher shows the word on a flashcard and the student writes the word. In the multisensory combination channel, the teacher shows the word on a flashcard and spells it aloud; then the student spells the word aloud and writes the word. This sensory modality preference assessment calls for teaching eight words in each of the five modality combinations and then assessing the student on all of the words. A preference for learning style may then be indicated that will be helpful in planning daily instruction.

Probes are an excellent means of assessing written composition. They can be designed to sample many skills, including sentence-formation skills, grammar and word usage, capitalization skills, and punctuation skills. Examples are provided in figures 4–14, 4–15, 4–16, and 4–17.

FIGURE 4–14   Probe: Subject/Verb Agreement

Directions: Circle the word in each example to complete the sentence correctly.

1. Jack and I (is, are) going to visit grandad tomorrow.
2. A cat (was, were) in our trash today.
3. You (were, was) the first in line.
4. My sister's children (is, are) traveling by bus.
5. (There's There are) two more sandwiches in the box.
6. (Is, Are) the girls going with us?
7. The children (was, were) ready for school at 8 o'clock.
8. The cause of his trouble (was, were) his rude behavior.
9. Where (was, were) you when I called?
10. We (was, were) waiting for you at the library.
11. They (is, are) so glad that you dropped by to see them.
12. It (was, were) a funny story.
13. You (was, were) a great help to us.
14. She (is, are) a mountain climber.
15. (Was, Were) you asked to help with the painting?
16. He and I (was, were) lost.
17. Rover (is, are) a friendly dog.
18. (Is, Are) you coming?
19. She (was, were) at school when you called.
20. I (were, was) not a big help.

Name _____

Date _____

Time _____

Number Correct _____

Number Incorrect _____

FIGURE 4-15 Probe: Fragments and Complete Sentences

Directions: After each word group, indicate whether it is a fragment (*F*) or a complete sentence (*S*).

1. The flag flying in the breeze _____
2. Although I don't believe you took it _____
3. He was about to answer when the bell rang _____
4. A boy with green eyes _____
5. At last the package came _____
6. Spending many days at the mountains _____
7. They placed the paddle in the canoe _____
8. Don't wait for me_____
9. Because she felt like it _____
10. Tired and dirty after our long hike _____
11. They found the keys and drove home _____
12. Isn't this wonderful _____
13. Rounding the dangerous corner _____
14. I left the party early _____
15. At the end of the day _____
16. Don't make fun of her _____
17. Quickly he responded to the call _____
18. Please, be quiet _____
19. In the vacant lot where we played baseball _____
20. Running as fast as I could _____

Name _____
Date _____
Time _____
Number Correct _____
Number Incorrect _____

RECORDING PERFORMANCE AND SETTING OBJECTIVES

■ ■ The language arts assessment data that have been gathered must be organized in order to lead to efficient instructional planning. Record-keeping systems may be provided through curriculum guides, but often a teacher wants to modify a system to meet individual needs. In the following section, guidelines for recording data in language arts are suggested.

■ **Record of Periodic Assessment Data**

Periodic assessment data collected for language arts can be recorded on the Periodic Assessment Record (see Figure 4–18), a summary that can be

FIGURE 4-16   Probe: Forming Complex Sentences

Directions: Write a complex sentence by adding one of the following words: *when, while, after, since, because, as, although, who, whom, which, that, whoever, before, if.*

1. Some of the children left early. The movie was too long.

_____

2. They are going to the restaurant. She has some money.

_____

3. He went home. We were finished eating dinner.

_____

4. She'll go to the store for you. You ask her nicely.

_____

5. This tie doesn't match my shirt. It is the wrong color.

_____

6. I know you are a good secretary. You never make a mistake.

_____

7. The boys bought two new toys. They have enough already.

_____

8. Janet plays the piano. The rest of the group sings.

_____

9. The lady complained all night. The music played.

_____

10. He is the one. I waited for all evening.

_____

Name _____

Date _____

Time _____

Number Correct_____

Number Incorrect_____

FIGURE 4-17 Punctuation Probe

Directions: Write the correct punctuation mark at the end of each sentence.

1. Why did you go
2. Don't hit her
3. Hand me that book, please
4. Where is it, Jack
5. Didn't they live in New York
6. When it is sunny, we go to the beach
7. Let's win this football game
8. Please move right now
9. Please close the door
10. Have you seen my jacket
11. Help me or I'll fall
12. I saw you at the show last night
13. We won the championship
14. Will you attend that meeting
15. Run for safety
16. Send for the waiter
17. I hope you have a good time
18. Is that your sister
19. This is my new friend
20. What a terrible mistake

Name _____
Date _____
Time _____
Number Correct _____
Number Incorrect _____

---

used in determining the language arts skills requiring more extensive and continuous assessment. Sections are provided to record data related to formal test results, language checklists, handwriting error analysis, informal spelling inventories and spelling error analysis, spelling cloze procedure, and written work samples. A sample use of this form with a case study is provided at the end of the chapter (see Figure 4-20).

■ Record of Continuous Assessment Data

Results from periodic assessment procedures indicate which skills to be targeted for continuous assessment. These skills may be listed on the Continuous Assessment Record (see Figure 4-21). Criterion-referenced procedures and probes should then be used to evaluate student perfor-

FIGURE 4-18 Periodic Language Arts Assessment Record

A. Formal Tests   Scores
_____
_____
_____
_____
_____
_____
_____
_____
_____
_____
_____
_____

B. Checklist Information
_____
_____
_____
_____
_____
_____
_____
_____
_____
_____

C. Handwriting Error Analysis
___ position of hand, arm, body, or paper
___ letter formation
___ letter size, alignment
___ spacing
___ line quality
___ slant
___ speed
Comments _____
_____
_____
_____

D. Informal Spelling Inventory and Spelling Error Analysis
___ omissions
___ additions
___ substitutions
___ reversals
___ incorrect sound/symbol association
___ mispronunciations/dialectical patterns
___ other spelling errors
Other comments _____
_____
_____

E. Spelling Cloze Procedure
_____
_____
_____
_____
_____
_____
_____
_____
_____

F. Written Work Samples
_____
_____
_____
_____
_____
_____
_____
_____
_____
_____
_____
_____
_____

Student Name _____
Grade/Teacher _____

mance in the language arts skills that have been targeted as needing improvements. Conditions related to assessment, the target skill/behavior required, current performance results, and the proficiency goal should be listed. A skill may be targeted as an instructional objective if continuous procedures indicate that a student has not met proficiency in a particular skill within a skill network.

☐ *Charting*
Results of continuous assessment may be entered on an equal-interval or proportional chart. As discussed in chapter 2, charting provides a clear visual display of growth in the targeted skill/behavior. An example of a charted language arts skill is Figure 4–19.

☐ *Proficiency Aims*
The precise recording of periodic and continuous assessment data greatly assists the teacher in summarizing information, generating instructional plans, and identifying further assessment needs. Long- and short-range instructional objectives may be determined from the behaviors targeted on the periodic and continuous records. Short-term objectives are often stated in terms of proficiency aims.

Results from the charted language arts probes should be compared to selected proficiency criteria. Rate criteria have been suggested for handwriting and spelling skills (see chapter 2). These instructional goals are presented in Table 4–8.

For many language art skills, proficiency is more easily expressed by percentage of correct responses. Percentage is particularly useful in measuring oral language skills and many written composition skills (e.g., using correct verb forms in writing or writing a paragraph correctly). Three days of 90–100% accuracy may be used as a guideline for setting these aims (Smith, 1981).

CASE STUDY

An example of a student's periodic language arts assessment record is provided in Figure 4–20. Periodic assessment results indicate that Sarah, an eighth grader, has difficulty in several aspects of written language. Weaknesses in sentence formation, paragraph development and organization, word choice, and word usage were noted in three written work samples. The *Test of Adolescent Language* confirms these problems. Additionally, it was indicated that Sarah does not respond well to writing assignments and is weak in two important behaviors related to listening: attending to oral directions and participating in class. Her achievement in handwriting, spelling, capitalization skills, and punctuation skills is satisfactory.

FIGURE 4–19 Spelling Progress on a Proportional Chart

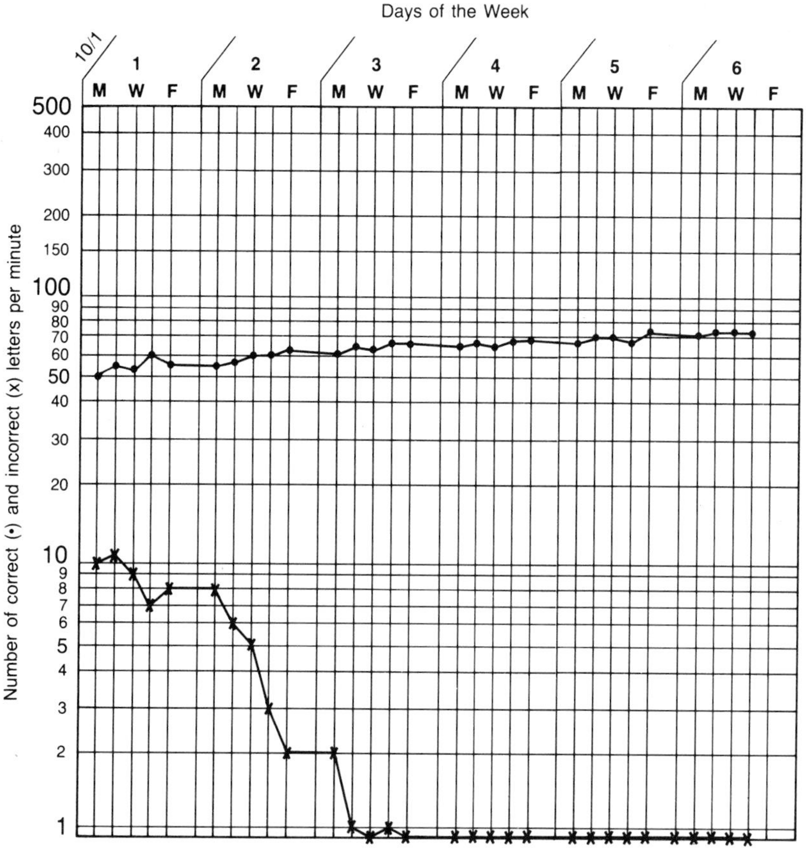

Correct/Incorrect Response

	M	T	W	Th	F
1	50/10	54/11	53/9	60/7	55/8
2	55/8	58/6	60/5	60/3	62/2
3	60/2	65/1	63/0	68/1	67/0
4	66/0	67/0	65/0	68/0	69/0
5	67/0	70/0	70/0	68/0	72/0
6	70/0	72/0	73/0	73/0	

Name *Kyle* Grade *4*

Behavior *hear-write spelling words*

Goal *70 letters per minute correct with 0 errors*

Results from these periodic assessment procedures suggest specific written composition skills that should be monitored on a continuous basis. An example of Sarah's continuous assessment results is provided in Figure 4–21. Using the Continuous Assessment Record, the following skills were targeted for continuous assessment:

1. forming complex sentences by using transition words to combine two sentences

TABLE 4-8 Some Proficiency Goals for Handwriting and Spelling

	Handwriting
Zaner-Bloser scales	grade 1: 25 letters per minute
	grade 2: 30 letters per minute
	grade 3: 38 letters per minute
	grade 4: 45 letters per minute
	grade 5: 60 leters per minute
	grade 6: 67 letters per minute
	grade 7: 74 letters per minute
Precision Teaching Project	think-write alphabet: 80–100 lpm
	see-write letters: 75 lpm
	(count of 3 for each letter
	including slant, form, ending)
	see-write numerals random: 100–120 digits
	per minute
	see-write connected cursive letters: 125 lpm
	(count of 3 for each letter)
Koenig and Kunzelmann (1980)	see-write letters or numerals: 70 letters/ numerals per minute

	Spelling
Starlin and Starlin (1973)	kindergarten–grade 2: 30–50 lpm
	with two errors or less
	grades 3 and above: 50–70 lpm
	with two errors or less
Koenig and Kunzelmann (1980)	grade 2: 60–90 lpm correct
	grade 3 : 90–100 lpm correct
	grade 4: 100–120 lpm correct
	grade 5: 110–130 lpm correct
	grade 6: 120–140 lpm correct

2. thinking and saying or writing ideas about a given topic (a brain-storming activity)
3. outlining using main topics, subtopics, and details
4. writing paragraphs using a clearly stated main idea with three or more supporting details

As seen in Figure 4–22, Sarah has had twelve days of probes on forming complex sentences by using transition words to combine two sentences. These data indicate that she is improving in this skill. No instructional change is required.

Sarah is having difficulty outlining a given list of ideas using main topics, subtopics, and details. As indicated in Figure 4–23, the percent

FIGURE 4-20   Case Study: Periodic Language Arts Assessment Record

A. Formal Tests   Scores
   Test of Adolescent Language
   (TOAL)
   Writing/Vocabulary   93
   Writing/Grammar   93
                    (scaled scores)

B. Checklist Information
   does not attend to or follow oral directions
      well
   does not participate in class
   has poor attitude toward writing
      assignments

C. Handwriting Error Analysis
   __ position of hand, arm, body, or paper
   __ letter formation
   __ letter size, alignment
   __ spacing
   __ line quality
   __ slant
   __ speed
   Comments _____

D. Informal Spelling Inventory and Spelling
   Error Analysis
   __ omissions
   __ additions
   __ substitutions
   __ reversals
   __ incorrect sound/symbol association
   __ mispronunciations/dialectical patterns
   __ other spelling errors
   Other comments Dictated Test administered–
   8th grade ach. level

E. Spelling Cloze Procedure

F. Written Work Samples
   excellent handwriting; capitalization,
      punctuation, and spelling skills satis-
      factory
   observations from three writing samples
      indicate difficulty with sentence for-
      mation, paragraph development and
      organization, word choice and usage.

Student Name   Sarah
Grade/Teacher   8th/Green

FIGURE 4-21 Case Study: Continuous Assessment Record

Date	Conditions	Skill/Behavior	Current Peformance	Proficiency Criterion/Goal	Date Attained
10/2	probe sheet (self-correcting)	writes complex sentences	75% correct	90% correct 3 days/week	10/20 see chart
10/2	topic on card—praise as reinforcement	says ideas	7 ideas/min.	15 ideas/min. 3 days/week	
10/2	list of ten ideas (self-correcting)	develop an outline (using main topics, subtopics, and details)	40–50% correct	100% correct 3 days/week	see chart
10/2	topic on board—praise as reinforcement	write a paragraph (using main idea and 3 supporting details)	50% correct	100% correct 3 days/week	

Student's Name _____ Sarah _____
Grade/Teacher _____ 8th/Green _____

FIGURE 4-22   Chart Showing Progress on See-Write Sentence Probe

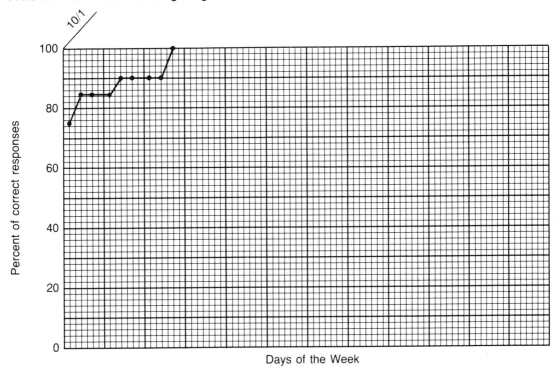

Name _____Sarah_____

Grade/Teacher _____8 / Green_____

Target Skill _____see-write sentences (combine two sentences using transition words)_____

Goal _____90% correct — 3 days in a week_____

of correct responses is not increasing with this task. A step-down to the task of outlining using only main topics and subtopics may be helpful.

Based on all the assessment information collected, the following objectives were developed for Sarah:

1. Given a worksheet with twenty items consisting of two sentences in each item, Sarah will write complex sentences using transition words (when, because, which, etc.) correctly 90% of the time for three days in a week.

FIGURE 4-23 Chart Showing Data on See Ideas-Write Outline Task

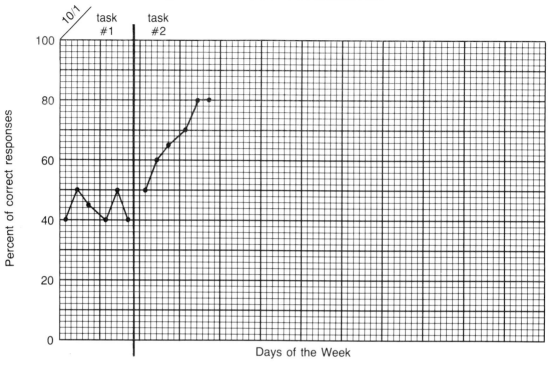

Name _Sarah_

Grade/Teacher _8/Green_

Target Skill _Task #1. See ideas - write outline using main topics,_
subtopics, and details. Task #2. See ideas - write outline
using main topics and subtopics.

Goal _100% correct - three days in a week._

2. Given a topic by her teacher (e.g., spring), Sarah will think of and orally state at least fifteen ideas related to the topic in one minute for three days in a week.
3. Given a list of five ideas, Sarah will develop an outline using main topics and subtopics with 100% correct for three days in a week.
4. Given a topic, Sarah will write a paragraph using a clearly stated main idea and three supporting details with 100% correct for three days in a week.

Two of the objectives described involve see–write tasks and two involve think–write tasks. The data collected may indicate a preference on one type of task that would help in developing further instructional strategies.

Sarah's progress on the four objectives was monitored three times each week. She worked with a peer on the second objective, thinking and saying ideas related to a given topic. Objectives 1 and 3, writing complex sentences and outlining, were self-correcting. Sarah used a teacher-made answer sheet to check her responses. The last objective, writing a paragraph, was checked by her teacher before class ended. Sarah was able to chart her progress on all four objectives three times a week and show the charts to her parents at the end of each week. When she reached her goals, Sarah's teacher assessed her again individually on each objective. The ongoing process of assessment, analysis, instruction, and student and parent involvement will greatly enhance Sarah's performance in school. The end result will be a successful experience in language arts.

CONCLUSION

The effective use of the language arts skills—listening, speaking, reading, and writing—is not only a daily necessity, but is of enormous importance in the total educational program. Appropriate use of written communication skills—reading and writing—depends on a firm foundation of oral language skills—speaking and listening. All of these skills build upon experiences, that is, upon the student's first-hand observation and participation in the environment.

Periodic and continuous assessment techniques are both very helpful in the assessment of language arts. The goal is to gather information, monitor progress, and generate instructional plans and further assessment needs.

ACTIVITIES

1. Describe the sequence of development of communication skills.
2. List examples of receptive and expressive activities for each of the four components of language (phonology, morphology, syntax, and semantics).
3. Describe five factors that may influence language development.
4. Identify the three components of written expression and give examples of skills to be assessed in each area.
5. Discuss the types of formal tests available for the assessment of language arts (e.g., survey measures, tests of individual components, etc.).
6. Describe the following informal pro-

cedures and how each is best used in periodic assessment: checklists, handwriting error analysis, informal spelling inventories and spelling error analysis, cloze procedure, and written-work samples and structured observation.

7. Evaluate the handwriting and spelling of an elementary or middle school student using the guidelines described in this chapter.

8. Obtain a representative sample of an adolescent's written composition. Analyze the sample using the components suggested to assess written expression.

9. With curriculum materials used in a classroom, design probes for a handwriting skill, a spelling skill, and a written expression skill. Administer these probes to an elementary school student.

10. Generate instructional objectives based on the probes administered in the previous question.

5

Assessment of Reading

■ **Learning Objectives**

After completing this chapter, the reader should be able to:

■ identify the stages of reading development
■ list the major components of reading and describe six approaches to reading instruction
■ identify the factors that influence a student's reading ability
■ list skills that might be included in a reading network
■ describe procedures used to assess word-recognition and comprehension skills
■ describe how to record the data collected in reading assessment and how to set objectives for instruction

Reading is perhaps the most important of academic skills, and reading instruction is possibly the most important activity in elementary classrooms (Carnine & Silbert, 1979). Success in daily living and further academic endeavors is dependent, to a very great degree, on the ability to read fluently and to comprehend printed material. Harris and Sipay (1980) state that "poor reading has been recognized as a major barrier to economic advancement, and it interferes in many ways with everyday living." (p. 80) In order to complete everyday tasks such as driving, shopping, working, and bill paying, the ability to read is required. Moreover, nonreaders may not have access to information required to function successfully in a technologically sophisticated society. Those who do not have adequate reading skills are at a gross disadvantage and, as a result, often fail to become productive members of society.

The relationship between reading and achievement is apparent in the public school setting where reading difficulties are a major cause of failure in school (Kaluger & Kolson, 1978). Haring and Bateman (1977) report that 15% of all school children have trouble reading. This failure often adds to a student's frustration, feelings of inadequacy, and dissatisfaction with school. Carnine and Silbert (1979) note that reading failure strongly influences children's self-images and feelings of competency. Feelings of inadequacy often result in poor attitudes toward school and a range of inappropriate school behaviors.

Reading is a very complex process. Experts disagree about the nature of this process—as evidenced by the number of reading models and definitions of reading proposed over the years. Most experts agree, however, that word recognition and passage comprehension are the most essential components of reading (Carnine & Silbert, 1979). Ekwall and Shanker (1983) describe reading "as a process of recognizing words and of understanding words and ideas." (p. 62) They further categorize the scope of reading skills in Figure 5–1. In Figure 5–1, "recognizing words" is broken down into two major categories: sight words and word-attack (i.e., word-analysis) skills. Sight words are words that are instantly rec-

FIGURE 5-1   Scope of Reading Skills

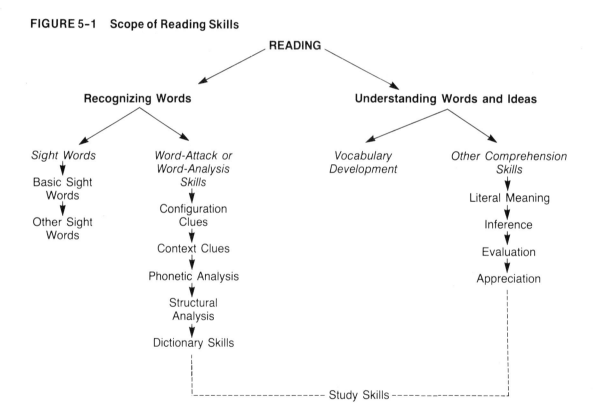

Source: "Scope of the Reading Skills." Reprinted by permission from E. E. Ekwall and J. L. Shanker. (1983). *Diagnosis and Remediation of the Disabled Reader* (2nd ed.)   Newton, Mass.: Allyn and Bacon, p. 69.

Note: Dotted line indicates less direct relationships.

ognized. Basic sight words are high-utility words, that is, words that appear often in print. Other sight words include all other words discerned without the use of word-attack skills.

Word-attack skills are used when a reader does not instantly recognize a word. The subcategories listed in Figure 5-1 include skills that may be applied to analyze a word—configuration clues, context clues, phonics, structural analysis, dictionary skills, and study skills.

Ekwall and Shanker (1983) note that "understanding words and ideas" (comprehension) is much more complicated and less clear cut than the word-attack skills. Unlike word-attack skills, there is little research to support a hierarchy or ordering of many separate comprehension skills (Heilman, Blair, & Rupley, 1981). The most commonly used measures of reading achievement are vocabulary and reading comprehension. Therefore, in Figure 5-1 "understanding words and ideas" is further broken down into "vocabulary development" and "other comprehension skills." The subcategories of "other comprehension skills" are derived from Barrett's Taxonomy of Cognitive and Affective Dimensions of Reading Comprehension. As Heilman, Blair, and Rupley (1981) note, this taxonomy should not be viewed as a means for specifying development stages, but instead as a means for providing a framework for comprehension activities. The subcategories of "other comprehension skills" include:

1. *literal meaning* (the ideas and information explicitly stated in the text)
2. *inference* (the use of stated information and the reader's intuition and personal experience as a basis for interpretation and hypothesizing)
3. *evaluation* (the judgments derived from the comparison of ideas presented in the reading selection (e.g., judgments of reality or fantasy, fact or opinion, adequacy, validity, appropriateness, worth, desirability and acceptability)
4. *appreciation* (the emotional and aesthetic reaction to the selection)

The subcategory "study skills" is connected with a broken line to "word-attack skills" and "other comprehension skills" to indicate that study skills contribute to both of those areas, but the relationship is not as direct as the other subcategories.

Reading is a multifaceted process consisting of a large number of interrelated skills that develop gradually as a child progresses from a less mature to a more mature level. Therefore, it is necessary to define clearly the skills involved before beginning reading assessment or instruction.

DETERMINING SKILLS TO BE ASSESSED

■ ■ Because of the crucial role reading plays in society, difficulties must be precisely diagnosed in terms of the child's level of reading development. Different skills and concepts are emphasized during each stage of reading development. The particular skills taught and method of presentation are also dependent upon the instructional approach being used. Therefore, assessment, if it is to be effective, must be related to the child's developmental reading level and to the teacher's method of instruction.

■ Reading Development

Harris and Sipay (1980) discuss the development of reading in terms of five stages of reading instruction: 1) readiness for reading, 2) beginning to read, 3) rapid development of reading skills, 4) wide reading, and 5) refinement of reading.

☐ *Readiness for Reading*
During this stage, a child develops many abilities that are necessary prerequisites for later effecient reading. When readiness is reached, a child should have the ability to learn to read without excessive difficulty. Kirk, Kliebhan, and Lerner (1978) mention a number of factors that contribute to reading readiness:

1. mental maturity
2. visual abilities
3. speech and language development
4. thinking skills
5. motor development
6. social and emotional maturity
7. interest and motivation

A student's achievement during the readiness stage may not be uniform in each of these areas. Usually there is a diversity of performance, with some skills being strong while others are weak.

The ability and skills required for reading readiness vary with the instructional procedure being used (Durkin, 1983). Different teaching approaches take advantage of the different abilities and interests of individual children. According to Harris and Sipay (1980), "the trend seems to favor a slow, gradual start in beginning reading instruction with readiness skills embedded in the context of reading rather than readiness first and reading afterward." (p. 46) The authors also note the strong support for a relaxed introduction to reading in kindergarten for children who are ready.

☐ *Beginning to Read*
The beginning-to-read stage generally occurs between kindergarten and second grade; success at this level is crucial to later reading development. Four instructional tasks represent the thrust of this stage (Heilman, Blair, & Rupley, 1981). Tasks involve helping the child:

1. to understand that reading is a language process
2. to develop and expand sight vocabulary
3. to learn to associate visual symbols with speech sounds
4. to realize that reading is always a meaning-making process

The main focus of instruction at the beginning-to-read stage is with forming sound–symbol associations and developing decoding skills, which children learn with a variety of materials and methods. These skills serve as the foundation upon which fluent reading and comprehension are based. Students who fail to master skills at this level may be inappropriately advanced through the curriculum, compounding and aggravating their reading problems.

☐ *Rapid Development of Reading Skills*
The rapid development stage occurs at about the second or third grade and serves as a foundation period for later reading success and enjoyment. The skills acquired during the initial stages of reading development are refined. There are several skills that should be accomplished by the end of the rapid development period:

1. recognition of a large number of words by sight
2. successful pronunciation of many unfamiliar words
3. fluent silent reading with good comprehension
4. fluent and expressive oral reading
5. simple factual reading
6. reading for pleasure

If a child has a severe reading problem, however, he or she may not reach proficiency at this stage of development.

☐ *Wide Reading*
The reading program during the intermediate grades is characterized by a greater emphasis on functional reading. Also called study skills, *functional reading* includes:

1. the ability to locate needed material
2. comprehending informational material
3. selecting materials needed

4. organizing and summmarizing the information obtained (Harris & Sipay, 1980)

Recreational reading is also emphasized at this stage. Students are encouraged to select books relevant to their wide range of interests. Less time is spent on developmental activities, and as children become more competent in reading, more emphasis is placed on independent, individualized reading and vocabulary development.

☐ *Refinement of Reading*
During junior high school, senior high school, and college, students continue to practice reading skills previously acquired. Reading increases in amount and difficulty. Vocabulary, comprehension, critical reading, and reading rate gradually improve. Reading is no longer a separate subject in school, but rather various aspects of reading instruction are integrated into all subjects.

■ **Approaches to Reading Instruction**

Many facets are involved in teaching children to read. Approaches differ concerning which reading skills to stress and when to introduce particular skills. Traditionally, reading approaches fall into two groups: a "code emphasis" group and a "meaning emphasis" group (Chall, 1967). The "code emphasis" group believes that initial reading instruction should teach children to break the alphabetic code, the sound–symbol relationships. The "meaning emphasis" group believes that children learn to read best when meaning is emphasized from the beginning—that is, whole words and sentences are learned by sight.

A synthesis has resulted from these divergent views and has been tempered by the knowledge that students may learn by a variety of methods. Heilman, Blair, and Rupley (1981) note that no single approach to teaching beginning reading is successful with *all* children. As a result, many current reading methods reflect features of both the "code emphasis" and "meaning emphasis" approaches and are generally packaged in a flexible program that can be adapted to meet the individual needs of the learner.

Material currently available is indicative of the differing views of reading instruction held by professionals. A large number of commercially prepared beginning reading programs is available. Most approaches, however, differ in two or three of the following ways:

1. how the child is first taught to read words
2. whether the initial emphasis is placed on comprehension or decoding

3. the preplanned structure
4. materials used to develop reading skills
5. the number and type of words used (Harris & Sipay, 1980)

In addition, the skill of the teacher, the pupil's abilities, and the learning environment are important.

In spite of this diversity, most reading instruction can be categorized generally into six methods of instruction: 1) meaning-emphasis approaches, 2) code-emphasis approaches, 3) programmed approaches, 4) a language experience approach, 5) an individualized approach, and 6) skill-management systems. Many current reading programs fit one of these categories while at the same time utilizing aspects of other instructional procedures. Each reading approach stresses somewhat different skills and abilities, and as a result dictates in many ways the procedures used to assess skill strengths and weaknesses. The specific assessment procedures used should be contingent upon the classroom curriculum.

☐ *Meaning Emphasis Approach*

The meaning emphasis approach focuses primarily on teaching children to associate printed words with their spoken counterparts. Proponents of this approach believe that if words and their meanings are known, then instruction in sentences and stories will be easier.

The basal reading series is widely used as the core of a reading program, and initially stresses whole words, which leads quickly to meaningful sentences. However, the assumption of the basal approach is that children learn best through an eclectic method (Heilman, Blair, & Rupley, 1981), so most basal systems try to achieve a balanced reading program.

A basal reading series usually includes a sequential set of texts ranging from preprimer to eighth-grade levels, along with supplementary materials such as workbooks, duplicating stencils, group practice cards, charts, filmstrips, storybooks, and a management system including mastery tests, recordkeeping sheets, and a teacher's manual. A daily lesson, the directed reading activity, might typically involve preparation, reading a story, and follow-up activities. The main orientation of the basal system is the development of comprehension. A controlled vocabulary is frequently repeated in the texts. Skills in word recognition, comprehension, and word attack are all developed in a comprehensive, systematic, and sequential manner. The basal reader series permits teachers a great deal of flexibility in dealing with individual differences, and if used properly covers all aspects of the reading program (Heilman, Blair, & Rupley, 1981).

☐ *Code-Emphasis Approach*

In the code-emphasis or skill-centered approach, the primary focus of instruction is on teaching decoding skills, especially letters and letter combinations that have the same sound in different words. Two major teaching methods fall under this category: the phonics method and the linquistic method.

The phonics approach teaches the recognition of unfamiliar words by associating sounds with letters or letter combinations. In teaching the word *cat* for example, the sounds of the letters would initially be taught in isolation and then be slowly blended until the learner could pronounce the whole word when it was presented. All phonics methods stress word recognition through learning phonemic equivalents of letters and letter groups, and by applying phonic generalizations.

Phonics instruction has received much criticism over the years. Opponents of the phonics approach argue that it interferes with comprehension. Phonics is best used to establish the identity of a word so that a passage can then be read with meaning.

Phonics has been integrated into most basal reader programs. The conventional basal reader format is used, but instruction also stresses sound–symbol associations.

The linguistic approach may also be considered a code-emphasis approach. Bloomfield, a noted linguist critical of phonics and whole-word approaches, recommended an approach that used whole words with a minimum of variation, using "word families" (Bloomfield & Barnhart, 1961). Charles Fries (1963) expanded and modified Bloomfield's philosophy when developing the *Merrill Linguistic Reading Program*, a linguistic basal system.

In the linguistic approach, the letter sounds are not taught directly. Rather, the child learns words by identifying minimal differences in them, such as "Nan can fan Dan," or "A cat sat on a rat." Children are taught to break the written code before concentrating on comprehension. Words that have phonemically irregular spellings are introduced later as sight words.

Kaluger and Kolson (1978) note advantages and disadvantages of the linguistic approach. Words initially learned are phonemically regular and frequent repetition ensures overlearning. However, lack of emphasis on comprehension is a major disadvantage of the method.

☐ *Programmed Approach*

The programmed approach greatly facilitates individualized instruction in the various skills that make up the reading process. Breen (1979) notes the basic premises of this method:

1. objectives are stated as observable behaviors
2. the learner makes a response at each step
3. the learner receives immediate feedback
4. the learner works at his or her own pace
5. the program focuses on specific skills
6. all skills are carefully sequenced

When using the programmed approach, the student works independently at his or her own pace and on his or her own level on a series of systematic and sequential tasks. Each task builds on the preceding one and the student is reinforced immediately after each step. Programmed workbooks such as the *Sullivan Programmed Readers* (Buchannon & Sullivan Associates, 1963) and computer-assisted instruction such as the PERC Project developed at the University of Illinois are examples of the programmed approach. Gillespie-Silver (1979) notes that although programmed instruction may be an effective means of individualizing instruction, it should not be used exclusively to teach reading.

☐ *Language Experience Approach*
The language-experience approach is based on the interrelatedness of language and reading and uses the experience of the learner as the core of teaching (Hall, 1981). Usually, the focus of instruction is on teaching reading in close correlation with language arts activities of listening, speaking, and writing. In the language-experience approach, children dictate stories to the teacher who writes them down so that they may be used for reading instruction. Themes for experience stories are based on class trips, school activities, and happenings at home. A major benefit of this approach was noted by Huff (1979) who stated that children decode printed words more easily when the words are a part of their everyday language and personal experience.

The language-experience approach is widely used as an informal introduction to basal readers and also may be used as supplementary reading material. The language-experience approach can be used from early childhood through adulthood (Stauffer, 1980). However, the language-experience method requires a great deal of initiative, creativity, and planning in the teaching of word-recognition and analysis skills because there is no preplanned sequence of instruction.

☐ *Individualized Approach*
The individualized reading approach emphasizes reading instruction geared to an individual pupil's needs and interests. In this approach, a child selects reading material according to his or her interests and abilities, and then progresses at his or her own rate. The ability to work independently is crucial. Heilman, Blair, and Rupley (1981) also note that the success or failure of the program rests almost exclusively with the teacher as it is the teacher's responsibility to determine how to structure the program. Stoodt (1981) states that an individualized approach to teaching reading includes:

1. the use of trade books for reading selections
2. pupil–teacher conferences in which the student and teacher discuss the reading material and check reading skills
3. small, flexible, and informal groups formed for skill instruction

In addition, a wide variety of reading material on many levels should be available in the classroom.

☐ *Skill-Management Systems*
Skill-management systems stress the diagnosis of the reader and the individualization of skill development based on this diagnosis (Harris & Sipay, 1980). They may be used as primary or supplementary programs. Skill-management systems usually include:

1. a list of sequenced behavioral objectives for the reading skills in the system
2. criterion-referenced tests for each skill objective, pretests, post-tests, placement tests, and mastery tests
3. sources of instructional materials
4. a recordkeeping procedure (Harris & Sipay, 1980)

Among many skill-management systems available are the *Fountain Valley Support System* by Zweig Associates (1971), *High Intensity Learning System* by Random House (1972), and *Prescriptive Reading Inventory* by CTB/McGraw-Hill (1977). These systems are particularly useful for providing highly individualized instruction, but the extensive testing and recordkeeping procedures can be very time-consuming. For further information, see a detailed comparison of all objective-based (skills management or criterion-referenced) reading programs by Stallard, *Journal of Reading*, October 1977.

The most important aspect of diagnosis is that it should uncover information to improve instruction (Durkin, 1983). For reading instruction to be effective, an interaction between assessment and teaching must exist. The particular reading approach dictates what types of assessment questions to ask. If assessment indicates that the child is deficient in the skills or abilities germane to a specific method, then the reading program for that child may be altered.

■ Reading Problems

A classic 1946 study by Helen Robinson suggests that a student's reading ability may be related to four factors: 1) physical factors, 2) psychological factors, 3) socioeconomic factors, and 4) educational factors (Ekwall & Shanker, 1983). Robinson used the services of many specialists in the field of reading disabilities to determine the kind and number of problems that each of her cases possessed. The results of her studies are generally in agreement with more recent studies. Robinson's and later studies indicate that it may be difficult to attribute reading problems to any one of the four factors listed above in that a reading disability is not usually the result of a single factor, but rather the end result of a variety of problems. Teachers should not spend a great deal of time searching for the cause, but rather attempt to correct the reading problem.

After eliminating factors such as psychological and physical disabilities, assessment procedures should seek to identify the specific areas of reading difficulty. Bond, Tinker, and Wasson (1979) suggest that the following difficulties are most prevalent:

- faulty word identification and recognition
- inappropriate directional habits
- deficiencies in basic comprehension abilities
- limited special comprehension abilities (e.g., inability to locate and retain specific facts)
- deficiencies in basic study skills
- deficiencies in the ability to adapt to the reading needs of content fields,
- poor oral reading
- deficiencies in the rate of comprehension

Samuels (1983) uses a cognitive approach to classify the factors that influence learning to read and reading comprehension. He discusses two categories. *Inside-the-head factors* include intelligence; knowledge of the language of instruction—technical terms such as "paragraph" and "sentence"; decoding ability; background knowledge; text structure; anaphoric terms—word(s) used as a substitute for preceding word(s); metacognitive strategies—monitoring one's own reading to ensure the goals of reading are fulfilled; language facility—vocabulary and syntax; graphic literacy—interpretation of figures and graphs; and motivation and attention. *Outside-the-head factors* include: quality of instruction—teaching style, practice, and so on; clarity of writing style in the reading selection; text readability; format design and structural text elements; time allowed student for reading and comprehending.

Opportunity to practice reading is an issue of concern to other researchers also (Allington, 1984). Ysseldyke and Algozzine (1983) note that many students do not learn to read well because they are not actively engaged in reading for a sufficient period of time daily.

☐ *Reading in the Content Areas*
Another important issue facing many students with reading problems is reading in the content areas. Many content textbooks are substantially more difficult in terms of readability than basal readers at the same grade

level. In addition, special skills are required to read subject matter such as science, mathematics, and social studies. Children may progress adequately in beginning reading instruction but have difficulty in the upper grades with content subjects (Gillet & Temple, 1982). Chall (1979) states that the focus in the early years is learning to read (decoding, learning sight vocabulary, and acquiring basic comprehension skills), whereas in the upper grades the focus is on reading to learn (reading that can be used in a functional task or discussion).

Allington (1984) notes that effective academic instruction in reading content areas is directly related to the student's opportunity to learn. Additional time for instruction is sometimes needed, along with better teaching, rather than a different curriculum. Two primary types of content should be stressed: 1) content knowledge, including vocabulary development and 2) learning strategies, including strategies for identifying, organizing, remembering, retrieving, and analyzing information.

■ **Reading Skill Network**

A reading skill hierarchy or scope-and-sequence skill list helps to determine reading skills to be assessed. Many scope-and-sequence skill lists are available, the content, complexity, and ordering of skills differing from material to material. There are, however, some skills commonly acknowledged, such as vocabulary, word analysis, perception, oral and silent reading, and comprehension, which are included in many scope and sequence lists.

Table 5–1 includes a sample reading network that reflects various stages of reading development and a variety of instructional approaches. It was developed from many sources, including the *Barbe Reading Skills Checklist* (Barbe, 1975) and the *Brigance Inventory of Basic Skills* (Brigance, 1977). Many of the basic reading skills that should be assessed before initiating a remediation program are included in this skill network. Because most reading problems occur early in the developmental period, the skills included in the network are those usually taught during the readiness, beginning reading, rapid development, and wide reading stages. Corrective or remedial programs at the secondary level are generally aimed at students who read one or more years below their potential level. Therefore, these programs also focus on basic word-recognition skills, comprehension skills, and application of general study skills (Roe, Stoodt, & Burns, 1978). These skills are also included in the sample network (Table 5–1). Because comprehension cannot be broken down into a hierarchy of subskills, the skills listed in the Table 5–1 network are provided to assist the teacher in specifying activities aimed at the major comprehension goals (literal, inferential, evaluative, and creative thinking).

TABLE 5-1   Reading Skill Network

Word-Recognition and Analysis Skills

Readiness for Reading Stage

recognizes common colors
identifies common body parts
sees likenesses and differences in shapes, directionality, letters, and words
hears differences in words (same or different? hat–hit)
recites alphabet
names upper and lowercase letters
matches letters (uppercase to lowercase letters)
recognizes own name in print
counts from 1 to 10
identifies numerals 1 through 10

Beginning Reading Stage

identifies words with both upper and lowercase letters at the beginning
identifies words usually found in preprimers
identifies single consonant sounds in initial, final, and medial position
identifies sounds of two-letter consonant blends in initial position (*bl, br, fl, fr, gr, st, tr, cl, dr, pr, sl, sp, pl, gl, sk, sm, sn, sw, wr, tw, sc, dw*)
identifies sounds of two-letter consonant digraphs in initial position (*sh, wh, th, ch*)
knows common word families (*all, at, it, et, en, in, an, ill, ell, ay, ake*)
recognizes word endings (*d, ed, t, s, ing*)

Rapid Development Stage

recognizes complete list of 220 *Dolch Basic Sight Words*
uses word-form clues (configuration and visual similarity)
knows contractions
recognizes and uses synonyms, antonyms, and homonyms
can use elementary school dictionary to find word meanings
alphabetizes words to the second letter
knows additional word families (*ou, er, ow, ur, ir, oi, oy, oo, eck, ick, aw, ew, ight, ind, ack, uck, ing,* and *ike*)
knows short-vowel sounds (*a, e, i, o,* and *u*)
knows long-vowel sounds (*a, e, i, o,* and *u*)
understands function of *y* as a consonant at the beginning of a word and as a vowel anywhere in a word
knows soft and hard sounds of *c* and *g*
knows two-letter consonant blends in final and medial position
knows two-letter consonant digraphs in final and medial position
knows three-letter initial blends (*str, sch, thr, spr, spl, chr*)
understands silent consonants in *k*n, *w*r, *g*n
recognizes root words

(continued)

TABLE 5-1 *(continued)*

Word-Recognition and Analysis Skills

recognizes word endings (*en, er, est, ful, y, ly*)
recognizes compound words
recognizes and uses possessives
knows basic phonics rules:
    1) a single vowel in a word or syllable is usually short
    2) a single *e* at the end of a word makes the preceding vowel long
    3) a single vowel at the end of a word is usually long
    4) where there are two vowels together, the first is long and the second silent
    5) in attacking a vowel sound, try first the short sound, then the long sound
knows basic rules for changing words (adding *s, es, d, ed, ing, er, est;* dropping final *e* and adding *ing,* doubling the consonant before adding *ing,* changing *y* to *i* before adding *es*)
knows basic rules for forming plurals (adding *s, es, ies,* by changing *f* to *ve* before adding *es*)
knows basic syllabication rules:
    1) there are usually as many syllables in a word as there are vowels
    2) where there is a single consonant between two vowels, the vowel goes with the first syllable (*pa-per*)
    3) when there is a double consonant, the syllable break is between the two consonants and one is silent

Wide Reading Stage

knows new vocabulary in content areas (math, science, social studies)
knows multiple meanings of words
uses context clues
knows accent clues
    1) first syllable is usually accented, unless it is a prefix
    2) endings that form syllables are usually unaccented (skipp*ing*)
    3) *ck* following a single vowel is accented (ra*ck*-et)
knows and uses prefixes and suffixes
recognizes similarities of known words such as compound words, root words, suffixes, prefixes, plurals, hyphenated words
knows additional rules for syllables
    1) each syllable must contain a vowel; a single vowel can be a syllable
    2) suffixes and prefixes are syllables
    3) root words and blends are not divided
    4) if the first vowel is followed by two consonants, the first syllable usually ends with the first consonant
    5) if the first vowel is followed by a single consonant, the consonant usually begins the second syllable
    6) if a word ends in *le* preceded by a consonant, that consonant begins the last syllable
    7) the letter *x* always goes with the preceding vowel to form a syllable
    8) the letters *ck* go with the preceding vowel and end the syllable
    9) when there is an *r* after a vowel, the *r* goes with the vowel
understands homophones and homographs
understands and recognizes figurative expressions including metaphors and similes

TABLE 5-1 *(continued)*

Comprehension Skills

Readiness for Reading Stage

wants to learn to read
likes to be read to
can work independently for short periods
can follow three-part directions
can sequence events logically
can recall main ideas and names of characters from story read aloud

Beginning Reading Stage

can follow printed directions
can draw conclusions from given facts
can recall major details and sequence of story read aloud
can recall main ideas, names of characters, major details, and sequence of story after silent reading
can distinguish between real and imaginary events
can suggest or select an appropriate title for a story
can relate story content to own experiences

Rapid Development Stage

can draw logical conclusions
can predict outcomes
can see relationships in story
can classify items
can read for a definite purpose (for pleasure, to answer a question, to obtain general idea of content)
can use table of contents, index, glossary, encyclopedia (to locate a topic), telephone directory
knows technique of skimming
knows technique of scanning
can determine what source to use to obtain information (dictionary, encyclopedia, index, glossary, etc.)
uses maps, graphs, charts, diagrams, and tables

Wide Reading Stage

can take notes from lectures and reading
can outline using main idea headings (I, II, III) and subordinate idea headings (A, B, C)
can talk from an outline
can locate information (periodicals, reference materials, other library skills)
reads creatively to a) interpret story ideas, b) see relationships, c) identify the mood in a story,
  d) identify the author's purpose, and e) identify character traits
reads for pleasure from a variety of sources

(continued)

TABLE 5-1 *(continued)*

Oral and Silent Reading Skills

Readiness for Reading Stage

Oral Reading Skills:
  gives name and age
  speaks in complete sentences
  is able to remember a five-word sentence

Beginning Reading Stage:

Oral Reading Skills:
  uses correct pronunciation
  uses correct phrasing
  uses proper voice intonation to give meaning
Silent Reading Skills:
  reads without vocalization, lip movements, or whispering
  reads without head movements
  reads without pointing

Rapid Development Stage

Oral Reading Skills:
  reads clearly and distinctly
  reads with adequate volume
Silent Reading Skills:
  reads more rapidly silently than orally

Wide Reading Stage

Oral Reading Skills:
  reads with understanding and expression
  varies rate depending on reading material
  reads without constantly looking at reading material
Silent Reading Skills:
  reads with good comprehension
  adjusts rate depending on reading material

SELECTING AND ADMINISTERING AN ASSESSMENT PROCEDURE

■ ■ There are hundreds of ways to test various aspects of reading. Numerous catalogs and textbooks provide extensive listings of assessment procedures and devices. This diversity is intended to provide assessment alternatives, but often it leads to confusion when developing a diagnostic plan. Too much or too little time may be spent assessing a problem with inappropriate instruments that yield irrelevant information.

Before specific procedures are selected and implemented, the teacher/diagnostician should be familiar with a number of important operational procedures. Among several noted by Ekwall and Shanker (1983) are: 1) gather enough initial diagnostic information to begin a remediation program and to serve as a data base for measuring improvement, 2) test in a situation analogous to actual reading if possible, and 3) be as efficient as possible in making the diagnosis.

■ **Periodic Assessment**

Periodic reading assessment procedures may be either formal or informal and yield global information that assists in establishing long-range instructional objectives. Periodic tests are often given at the beginning of the school year, periodically throughout the year, and again at the end of the year to measure student performance and growth in reading.

☐ *Formal Tests*
Formal (or standardized, norm-referenced) tests may be used for periodic assessment to measure a student's general knowledge and skills in reading. Some formal tests are designed for group administration, others for individual administration. Ekwall and Shanker (1983) note that group tests can be useful for initial screening of students for remedial reading programs and for measuring overall class achievement, and are less time-consuming to administer than individual tests. However, individual tests can be given in situations more analogous to actual reading, and therefore are more likely to measure what they purport to measure. Formal tests are also sometimes used for grade placement in readers, but do have the tendency to overestimate children's instructional levels. They should not be the sole criterion for placement, but should be used in combination with other sources of information, including teacher judgment (Coleman & Harmer, 1982; Kaluger & Kolson, 1978).

In the Appendix, formal tests commonly used to assess reading are presented. General achievement tests with reading subtests are often administered in a group and provide measures of vocabulary and comprehension. Group reading survey tests assess a general range of reading abilities. Diagnostic reading tests focus on identifying reading strengths and weaknesses, are individually administered, and are usually given if a more severe reading problem is indicated. Specialized word-analysis tests, which may be collectively or individually administered, provide an assessment of specific word-analysis skills.

☐ *Informal Procedures*

Informal procedures are also commonly used as a means of initially and periodically assessing students' strengths and weaknesses in reading skills. They may be constructed from instructional materials so that the items closely parallel the curriculum used. An example of a curriculum-based model is one developed at the University of Illinois for informally assessing reading skills (Idol-Maestas, 1983). The procedure for constructing a reading assessment consists of 1) selecting 100-word passages from the reading series used in the child's classroom, 2) taking timed oral-reading samples, 3) recording errors, and 4) asking comprehension questions. Students are tested over a three-day period, placed at the appropriate curriculum level, and then provided with daily data-based instruction.

Basal reading series also usually include placement and progress tests. However, Turner (1984) reported various teacher concerns about the basal series tests, including unclear directions, insufficient items to measure a skill/concept, poor item formatting, and poor match between assessment device and information actually taught in a lesson. Turner recommends caution in evaluating the quality and appropriateness of the placement and instructional tests accompanying basal reading series.

Informal procedures provide a broad range of information. Not all of this information, however, is needed or desired for instructional planning. The diagnostician must carefully select the device that will yield the specific information required. Information concerning word-attack skills, for example, may require the use of a different set of assessment devices than would the evaluation of reading comprehension skills. By precisely defining the skill to be assessed and then selecting an appropriate assessment procedure, valuable diagnostic and instructional time can be saved.

A number of informal procedures are available for periodic assessment. In the following discussion information will be presented concerning the construction and use of the following procedures: Informal Reading Inventory, graded word lists, error pattern analysis, cloze procedure, checklists, interviews and questionnaires, and teacher observation. As mentioned earlier, not all of these procedures would be used for every child. Selection of procedures should be determined by several factors: background information available, the reading program used in the classroom, and severity of the problem.

INFORMAL READING INVENTORY   The Informal Reading Inventory (IRI) is a widely used method of informal reading assessment. Rupley and Blair (1983) note that it is "the single most valuable tool for evaluating a student's reading progress and diagnosing a student's specific strengths and weaknesses in reading. . . . " (p. 54) IRI is used to determine placement in an appropriate basal and to identify a student's reading strengths and weaknesses. It may also be used to determine the appropriateness of reading material, to note various error patterns during oral reading, and to determine a student's hearing level (Ekwall, 1976). Rupley and Blair (1979) also note that an IRI is helpful in assessing comprehension after silent reading. Schell and Hanna (1981) suggest that informal inventories not be used to reveal strengths and weaknesses in comprehension subskills, however. With older students, an IRI may be useful in determining if a social studies book is at the student's instructional level (Ekwall & Shanker, 1983).

Materials contained in an IRI usually include graded word lists, graded passages, and comprehension questions. In order to determine the proper grade level passage on which to begin reading, the examiner may first administer a graded word list. The results of the graded word list suggest a placement level in the graded reading passage. The highest list on which the student made no errors should be used as the entry level for the oral reading passages. If word lists are not available, the teacher should begin with a passage that the student can read with ease. Proper placement in these passages is confirmed when the student is able to read aloud with little difficulty, decode words efficiently, and answer comprehension questions about the passage.

The reading passages consist of a carefully graded series of 50 to 200 words, usually from preprimer through eighth-grade levels. From the first-grade level on, there is usually a passage to be read orally and another passage to be read silently. While the student is reading the passages aloud, the teacher records the errors. The student continues to read passages until the material becomes too difficult.

After each passage is completed, the teacher asks three to five comprehension questions. The percentage of words read and comprehension questions answered correctly are computed. These percentages are then used to determine the student's reading ability at three levels: independent, instructional, and frustration (Johnson & Kress, 1965). At the independent level, the student can read the material easily and without any assistance; he or she reads 98 to 100% of the words correctly and comprehends with 90 to 100% accuracy. At the instructional level, the material is challenging, yet not too difficult; the student reads 95% of the words correctly and comprehends approximately 75% of the material. Reading instruction should be provided at this level. At the frustration level, reading is quite difficult. The student reads 90% or less of the words correctly with comprehension at 50% or less. A fourth level, hearing comprehension, is also used to indicate the highest level at which pupils are able to understand material read aloud to them. At this level, a student comprehends 75% of the material. These levels are presented in Table 5-2.

Several informal reading inventories are available. Jongsma and Jongsma (1981) note that IRI's may differ with respect to contents of

TABLE 5-2   Scoring Criteria for an Informal Reading Inventory

Reading Level	Word Recognition	Comprehension
Independent	98–100%	90–100%
Instructional	95%	75%
Frustration	90% or below	50% or below
Hearing Comprehension		75%

the tests; content, style, and length of passages; administration; comprehension questions; scoring; and interpretation. The authors recommend choosing an inventory that closely corresponds to the regularly used instructional materials and one that matches your personal philosophy. Examples of IRI's follow:

Analytical Reading Inventory (2nd ed.). (1977). M. L. Woods and A. Moe. Columbus, OH: Charles E. Merrill.
Basic Reading Inventory (1978). J. L. Johns. Dubuque, Iowa: Kendall/Hunt.
Classroom Reading Inventory (4th ed.). (1982). N. Silvaroli. Dubuque, Iowa: Wm. C. Brown.
Informal Reading Inventory (1985). P. C. Burns and B. D. Roe. Boston: Houghton Mifflin.
Sucher-Allred Reading Placement Inventory. (1973). F. Sucher and R. A. Allred. Oklahoma City, OK: Economy.

Teachers can develop their own IRI's also by selecting a basal series with which the student is not familiar. IRI's, however, were originally designed to sample graded materials drawn directly from texts used in the student's instructional program (Otto & Smith, 1980). Rupley and Blair (1979) note that materials that will be used for instruction may be sampled during administration of an I.R.I.

A teacher may use a word list already developed, such as the *Dolch Basic Sight Word List,* to determine an approximate level at which to begin administering the graded passages (Collins-Cheek & Cheek, 1984). Graded word lists may also be developed by randomly selecting words from a series of graded texts. These words can often be found at the back of the book. Ten to twenty words are chosen from each book and typed or printed on cards or a sheet of paper. Each list therefore represents words used at a particular level of difficulty. The highest level at which the student makes no errors is used as the placement level in a graded reading passage.

Selections used as graded passages should be taken from a well-graded series of readers, should be near the beginning of the book, and should be representative of that level in language and vocabulary. Two passages should be obtained from each level, first through eighth grades. One passage is to be read orally and one read silently.

A 50-word selection is usually used for the preprimer level, 100-word passages at primer and first-grade levels, and 200-word passages at second grade and above. For each reading passage, a brief introduction including background information should be prepared (e.g., "Read to find what Sam did on his trip").

A readability formula may be applied as a rough approximation of level of difficulty of the reading material. Carnine and Silbert (1979) recommend the Fry formula for classroom teachers since it is the least time-consuming. An example of this readability formula is provided in Figure 5-2. A computer program may also be used to analyze a text sample to quickly obtain a readability level. The *School Utilities* readability program is designed for the user to select from six different readability methods (School Utilities Volume II, 1982).

After selecting the graded passages, five to ten comprehension questions should be prepared. Many different kinds of questions should be used—such as questions that ask for factual recall, knowledge of vocabulary, main ideas, important details, and the ability to make inferences. Valmont (1972) offers some excellent guidelines for the construction of questions:

- State the questions in the approximate order in which the information was presented in the text.
- Ask the most important questions.
- If possible, state the questions so that they begin with who, what, when, where, how, or why.
- State questions in a positive manner.
- Construct the questions to measure the student's comprehension of written matter, not the accompanying picture.
- Avoid asking yes/no questions.
- Keep questions as short and simple as possible.

A sample reading passage and comprehension questions from an IRI are presented in Figure 5-3.

To administer the IRI, a period free of interruptions should be available. If the passage is at first- or second-grade level, the student should be told the proper names of the characters in the story. The student then begins reading orally. If he pauses five seconds or more on a word, the teacher should tell the student the word. Student errors may be noted on the teacher's copy of the selection and later analyzed. After completing the passage, comprehension is checked. Prepared questions or a free-response method may be used to check comprehension. Some teachers prefer to use the free-response method by having the student tell the

FIGURE 5-2 Graph for Estimating Readability—Extended

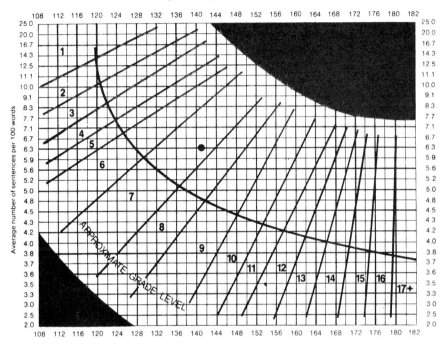

Average number of syllables per 100 words

DIRECTIONS: Randomly select 3 one hundred word passages from a book or an article. Plot average number of syllables and average number of sentences per 100 words on graph to determine the grade level of the material. Choose more passages per book if great variability is observed and conclude that the book has uneven readability. Few books will fall in gray area but when they do grade level scores are invalid.

Count proper nouns, numerals and initializations as words. Count a syllable for each symbol. For example, "1945" is 1 word and 4 syllables and "IRA" is 1 word and 3 syllables.

EXAMPLE:		SYLLABLES	SENTENCES
1st Hundred Words		124	6.6
2nd Hundred Words		141	5.5
3rd Hundred Words		158	6.8
	AVERAGE	141	6.3

READABILITY 7th GRADE (see dot plotted on graph)

Source: Edward Fry, Director, Rutgers University Reading Center, New Brunswick, NJ 08904. For further information and validity data, see the *Journal of Reading,* December 1977.

teacher about the story that was read. However, it is difficult to establish mastery criteria with this method. If story retell is used, the teacher should have an outline of the selections or an additional copy to record the concepts the student was able to comprehend.

If the student is able to read at or above third-grade level, oral and silent reading should both be tested. The teacher may then compare questions answered after an oral and silent reading session. Factors contributing to slow silent reading may be noted.

FIGURE 5-3   Sample Passage and Comprehension Questions from Informal Reading Inventory

FORM B, PART II—*Level 3* (96 words)   W.P.M.

$$\overline{\big)\,5760}$$

MOTIVATION: This story tells some unusual things about some baby birds. Read the story to see how they got their name.

"SILLY BIRDS"

    Even with food all around, turkeys will not eat. Turkeys can really be called "silly birds." Many die from lack of food. Straw is kept in their houses but some never seem to discover what it is used for. We will never understand senseless turkeys.

    The silly young birds don't know enough to come out of the cold, either. So many get sick and die. If they see anything bright, they try to eat it. It may be a pencil, a small nail or even a shovel. You can see how foolish these "silly birds" are.

COMPREHENSION CHECK

(I) 1. __ What kind of a bird does this story tell about?
(Turkeys)

(F) 2. __ What do turkeys do when they see something bright?
(Try to eat it)

(I) 3. __ What is the danger to turkeys when they do silly things?
(They die)

(F) 4. __ Tell at least two things that a baby turkey will try to eat.
(Pencil, nail, shovel or something bright)

(I) 5. __ What do you think is the most important thing this story tells you about turkeys?
(They are very foolish, silly, or dumb)

Scoring Guide: Third

WR Errors		COMP Errors	
IND	2	IND	0–1
INST	5	INST	1½–2
FRUST	10	FRUST	2½ +

    Gillespie-Silver (1979) notes that the IRI is only as good as the teacher who administers it. Although it may be helpful in assigning instructional material to a student, the IRI does not measure all aspects of reading and therefore should not be used as the only assessment measure. As with any other measure, the IRI is a sample of behavior (Jongsma & Jongsma, 1981). If a different set of passages is given on another day, you may get different results.

GRADED WORD LISTS   In addition to using graded word lists as the first step in administering an Informal Reading Inventory, the lists may also be used to assess general sight-word knowledge and reading level based only on word knowledge (Ekwall & Shanker, 1983). Otto, McMenemy, and Smith (1973) note that graded word lists also may reveal basic weaknesses in word-analysis skills.

A graded word list usually samples 20 to 25 words at each grade level. The resulting score is based on the student's ability to pronounce words at different levels of reading difficulty. The list at which all words are pronounced correctly is called the *basal list*. The list at which none of the words are pronounced correctly is called the *ceiling list*. Lerner (1985) defines the student's independent level by the list at which one of ten words is missed. At the instructional level, 2 to 10 words are missed, and at the frustration level, 3 or more of 10 words are missed.

Many commercial word lists are available that can utilize this assessment method. The Dolch list (Dolch, 1948) is widely used and includes 220 sight words, 50 to 65% of which the student encounters in basal readers. *The Word Recognition Inventory of the Mann-Suiter Developmental Reading Inventory* (Mann, Suiter, & McClung, 1979) contains ten word lists, 20 words each at preprimer through eighth-grade levels. Other sources of commercial word lists are the *Botel Reading Inventory* (Botel, 1970), the *Diagnostic Reading Scales* (Spache, 1972), the *Brigance Diagnostic Inventory of Basic Skills* (Brigance, 1977), the *Durrell Analysis of Reading Difficulty* (Durrell, 1955), and Fry instant words (Fry, 1977).

The *New Instant Word List*, developed by Edward Fry, includes 300 words, which, with their common variants, represent 65% of all the words written in English (Fry, 1980). Fry calls these words "instant words" because " . . . a student must learn to recognize them instantly in order to achieve fluency in reading, writing, or spelling." (p. 285) He suggests that they be used as an oral sight-reading test or as a spelling test. This word list is presented in Table 5–3. For an expanded word list, see *3000 Instant Words* by Elizabeth Sakiey and Edward Fry, Jamestown Publishers, 1979.

Graded word lists may also be easily prepared by teachers, constructed from basal readers or from content area textbooks. From glossaries of graded texts, 20 or 25 words should be randomly selected for each level from preprimer through sixth grade. For example, if there are 250 words in the glossary, every tenth word would be chosen. The words should be representative of a wide range of word-attack skills.

Mercer and Mercer (1985) note that the words may be listed on a sheet of paper and presented through a window with the use of a tachistoscope made from oaktag strips. Cohen and Plaskon (1980) suggest two additional ways that word lists can be presented to students. A one-second timed exposure to test sight-word vocabulary may be followed by an untimed presentation of the words on the list that were not recognized. By using this approach, it can be determined if the student is able to use and apply word-attack skills.

TABLE 5-3   The New Instant Word List

FIRST HUNDRED			
First 25	*Second 25*	*Third 25*	*Fourth 25*
Group 1a	*Group 1b*	*Group 1c*	*Group 1d*
the	or	will	number
of	one	up	no
and	had	other	way
a	by	about	could
to	word	out	people
in	but	many	my
is	not	then	than
you	what	them	first
that	all	these	water
it	were	so	been
he	we	some	call
was	when	her	who
for	your	would	oil
on	can	make	now
are	said	like	find
as	there	him	long
with	use	into	down
his	an	time	day
they	each	has	did
I	which	look	get
at	she	two	come
be	do	more	made
this	how	write	may
have	their	go	part
from	if	see	over

Common suffixes: *s, ing, ed*

SECOND HUNDRED			
First 25	*Second 25*	*Third 25*	*Fourth 25*
Group 2a	*Group 2b*	*Group 2c*	*Group 2d*
new	great	put	kind
sound	where	end	hand
take	help	does	picture
only	through	another	again
little	much	well	change
work	before	large	off
know	line	must	play
place	right	big	spell
year	too	even	air
live	mean	such	away
me	old	because	animal
back	any	turn	house
give	same	here	point

(continued)

TABLE 5-3 *(continued)*

SECOND HUNDRED *(continued)*

First 25 Group 2a	*Second 25* Group 2b	*Third 25* Group 2c	*Fourth 25* Group 2d
most	tell	why	page
very	boy	ask	letter
after	follow	went	mother
thing	came	men	answer
our	want	read	found
just	show	need	study
name	also	land	still
good	around	different	learn
sentence	form	home	should
man	three	us	America
think	small	move	world
say	set	try	high

Common suffixes: *s, ing, ed, er, ly, est*

THIRD HUNDRED

First 25 Group 3a	*Second 25* Group 3b	*Third 25* Group 3c	*Fourth 25* Group 3d
every	left	until	idea
near	don't	children	enough
add	few	side	eat
food	while	feet	face
between	along	car	watch
own	might	mile	far
below	close	night	Indian
country	something	walk	real
plant	seem	white	almost
last	next	sea	let
school	hard	began	above
father	open	grow	girl
keep	example	took	sometimes
tree	begin	river	mountain
never	life	four	cut
start	always	carry	young
city	those	state	talk
earth	both	once	soon
eye	paper	book	list
light	together	hear	song
thought	got	stop	leave
head	group	without	family
under	often	second	body
story	run	late	music
saw	important	miss	color

Common suffixes: *s, ing, ed, er, ly, est*

Source: The New Instant Word List. Reprinted by permission of E. Fry, Rutgers University Reading Center, 1980.

Ekwall and Shanker (1983) note two limitations of graded word lists. First, only a small number of words are sampled at each level, so the reading levels obtained may only serve as rough approximations. Second, a student's problem may center around comprehension difficulties, in which case the graded word list would be inaccurate in terms of placement level.

ANALYSIS OF ERROR PATTERNS   The analysis of error patterns involves the careful scrutiny of a student's work. Because this procedure is very time-consuming, it may be used less frequently. Specific error patterns are often noted when administering an Informal Reading Inventory or listening to a student reading a passage orally in a basal text. As the student reads the passage, it is helpful to tape-record the student's reading performance so that any errors may be accurately recorded and analyzed. Pflaum (1979) also recommends verification of errors by having a colleague rate the taped passage.

Before beginning the oral reading session, the teacher must decide which errors are of instructional importance. McLoughlin and Lewis (1981) note that most teachers agree that mispronunciations and non-pronunciations are important to instruction, while the addition of an occasional *s,* a hesitation, or omission of a punctuation mark may not be quite as important.

Various types of errors may be considered when analyzing oral reading performance. Listed below are eight categories of errors and the possible causes of each type (Ekwall, 1976).

1. omissions—carelessness or a deficit in word recognition or analysis skills
2. substitutions—carelessness or a lack of word recognition skills
3. mispronunciations—poor word recognition and analysis skills—particularly in phonics, structural analysis, and use of context clues
4. repetitions—poor word recognition and analysis skills or poor habits
5. insertions—lack of comprehension, carelessness, or oral language ability which surpasses reading ability
6. reversals—possible perceptual immaturity
7. hesitations—deficit in word recognition or analysis skills, or habit of word-by-word reading
8. omission of punctuation marks—unfamiliar with meaning of punctuation mark, lack of comprehension, failure to attend to punctuation because of difficulty of material

Two other categories of errors are unknown or aided words and self-corrected errors. It is helpful to develop an easy system to mark these errors. A notation system is provided in Table 5–4.

TABLE 5–4   Notation System for Indicating Oral Reading Errors

Error Type	Notation	Example
Omissions	Circle the word, words, or part of a word that is omitted	He did not want to go into his friend's house.
Substitutions	Write the substituted word above the correct word	She put the coins in the bag. *box*
Mispronunciations	Write the mispronounced word above the correct word.	The man is a thief. *thife*
Repetitions	Draw a wavy line under the repeated word or words.	He wants a truck for his birthday.
Insertions	Write in the insertion. Indicate with a caret.	The doll has brown hair. *dark*
Reversals	For a letter reversal within a word, write the substituted word above the corrected word.	They were cooking soup in the pot. *Top*
	For reversals of words, draw a line indicating the transposition of words.	He looked quickly for his homework.
Hesitations	Indicate with a slash mark.	The park/was close/to the school.
Unknown or aided	Underline the word(s) after waiting a sufficient time for a response.	The boys were <u>exhausted</u> from their hike.
Omission of punctuation marks	Cross out the punctuation mark that was omitted.	The little girl put on her coat, She went outside.
Self-corrected errors	Write the incorrect word and place a check beside it.	He wants a new bike for his birthday. *bike ✓*

Reading miscue analysis is another method of analyzing a student's oral-reading error patterns (Goodman, 1969). In analyzing oral reading errors, or miscues, the emphasis is placed on the nature of the reading error instead of on the number of errors made. Goodman and Burke (1972) note that reading includes three language systems: 1) semantics, 2) grammar, and 3) graphic-sound symbols. A miscue is involved with one or more of these systems. The *Reading Miscue Inventory* (Goodman & Burke, 1972) includes nine questions used to analyze each miscue:

1. Is a dialect variation involved in the miscue?
2. Is a shift in intonation involved in the miscue?
3. How much does the miscue look like what was expected?
4. How much does the miscue sound like what was expected?
5. Is the grammatical function of the miscue the same as the grammatical function of the word in the text?
6. Is the miscue corrected?
7. Does the miscue occur in a structure which is grammatically acceptable?
8. Does the miscue occur in a structure which is semantically acceptable?
9. Does the miscue result in a change of meaning?

The teacher must examine whether the miscues form a consistent pattern and then develop a plan for remediation. Elaborate procedures for analyzing and interpreting reading miscues have been developed by Goodman (1969) and Goodman and Burke (1972). These procedures are generally very cumbersome and time-consuming for the teacher (Gillet & Temple, 1982). However, by becoming familiar with analysis procedures for reading miscues, teachers may better understand the reading process and therefore become more aware of a student's reading strengths and weaknesses.

CLOZE PROCEDURE The cloze procedure is another technique used primarily for placing students in graded materials and for selecting materials appropriate for a group of students (Ekwall & Shanker, 1983). It may also be used for diagnostic purposes to assess a reader's use of context as a strategy for comprehending what was read (Gillet & Temple, 1982).

In this approach, a passage with every nth word deleted is presented to a student. (In most passages, every fifth or tenth word is deleted.) The student reads the passage silently, filling in the missing words according to context. The teacher then calculates the percentage of correct responses.

In constructing a cloze passage, reading material from a graded basal may be used. Ekwall (1976) offers several construction guidelines. A 250-word passage may be selected. The first and last sentences should be left intact. Beginning with the second sentence, every fifth word is omitted so that there are fifty uniform blanks in the passage. Each blank will then be worth two percentage points. There are no time limits in completing the task. Correct synonyms are not counted as correct because scoring becomes more difficult and interscorer reliability is lost. However, students are not penalized for incorrect spelling. A teacher may use a plastic overlay for easy scoring. The independent level is indicated by 58 to 100% correct responses, the instructional level by 44 to 57%

correct responses, and the frustration level by 43% or less correct responses (Ekwall & Shanker, 1983). An example of the cloze procedure is presented in Figure 5-4.

Pikulski and Pikulski (1977) note that the cloze procedure is easily constructed, may be group administered, and is rapidly and objectively scored. However, some students find it too difficult. A less difficult modification of the cloze technique is called the maze procedure (Guthrie, Seifert, Burnham, & Caplon, 1974). The cloze blank is replaced by word choices and therefore becomes a recognition task rather than a recall task:

<blockquote>
She is driving a car.
        book.
        running.
</blockquote>

Unlike the cloze procedure, the maze technique does not delete a specified number of words. The three alternatives usually provided are: the correct word, an incorrect word from the same grammatical class, and an incorrect word from another grammatical class (Gillet & Temple, 1982).

According to a study of fifth graders by Pikulski and Pikulski (1977), the maze and cloze scores tended to overestimate a student's ability when compared to teacher judgment. Therefore, the cloze technique may be helpful in identifying the reading level of many readers, but should be used in combination with other procedures.

CHECKLISTS Checklists may be used to monitor reading skill development. An entire range of reading skills may be surveyed on a checklist, and they also may be used to note difficulties in reading. In the assessment of reading comprehension, a checklist may be used to indicate individual or group progress on any range of skills (Wallace & Larsen, 1978). The progress of five children in a reading group may be easily recorded on a checklist as illustrated in Figure 5-5. By using a checklist, children needing help with a specific reading behavior may be easily identified and assembled as a special instructional group (Harris & Sipay, 1980).

Another approach to using a reading checklist is for the teacher to call each child to the teacher's desk to read aloud for one or two minutes. Major oral reading problems may be surveyed in this way and recorded on a checklist. Harris and Sipay (1980) suggest eight categories of errors that may be noted during oral reading: 1) general word recognition, 2) use of context, 3) decoding procedures, 4) possible specific decoding difficulties (such as reversal tendency), 5) comprehension, 6) fluency, 7) use of voice, and 8) behaviors (such as motivation).

At the secondary level, teachers may find a checklist useful to determine if students have developed reading necessary to succeed in a

FIGURE 5-4   Reading Selection Illustrating the Cloze Procedure

Let's Go Fishing

Fishing is one of the oldest yet one of the most popular of sports.

If you look at ___1___ map of the world, ___2___ will see that two-thirds ___3___ the earth's surface is ___4___ . There are oceans, bays, ___5___ , gulfs, rivers, streams, lakes, ___6___ ponds. There are also ___7___ the lakes, waterways, reservoirs, ___8___ irrigation ditches that people ___9___ made.

So, no matter ___10___ you live or may ___11___ , there is always a ___12___ nearby to go fishing.

___13___ of the time you ___14___ want to go with ___15___ friend and have the ___16___ of fishing together. Going ___17___ with a group is ___18___ way of keeping your ___19___ friends and also a ___20___ of making new ones.

___21___ you start fishing, you ___22___ meet other people who ___23___ willing to share their ___24___ and fishing secrets, as ___25___ , too, will be.

Fishing ___26___ not a sport in ___27___ there must always be ___28___ winner and a loser. ___29___ do you have to ___30___ a lot of rules ___31___ order to be able ___32___ catch a fish.

All ___33___ have to do is ___34___ your line in the ___35___ where there is a ___36___ fish. Your chance of ___37___ a fish is as ___38___ as the expert's.

You ___39___ not need a lot ___40___ high cost equipment to ___41___ fishing. If you do ___42___ have most of the ___43___ you need around the ___44___ , you can get them ___45___ less than a dollar.

Once you start fishing, you will know why it is so popular.

Correct Answers:

1. a	12. place	23. are	34. get
2. you	13. Most	24. equipment	35. water
3. of	14. will	25. you	36. hungry
4. water	15. a	26. is	37. catching
5. seas	16. fun	27. which	38. good
6. and	17. fishing	28. a	39. do
7. all	18. a	29. Nor	40. of
8. and	19. old	30. remember	41. go
9. have	20. way	31. in	42. not
10. where	21. When	32. to	43. things
11. travel	22. will	33. you	44. house
			45. for

Source: From Catch a Fish, copyright © 1965 by Marie Puccinelli, used with permission of the publisher, The Bobbs-Merrill Company, Inc.

FIGURE 5-5   Group Reading Comprehension Checklist

Students					Skills
Doug	Susie	Jimmy	Billy	Sam	
X	X		X		draws conclusions from given facts
X	X		X		recalls main ideas
X	X	X	X	X	recalls details
X		X		X	able to sequence events
X		X		X	tells whether factual or make-believe

particular content area. Roe, Stoodt, and Burns (1978) discuss skills common to all content areas that could be included in a checklist:

1. Understanding and using parts of textbooks (table of contents, index, list of illustrations, appendices, bibliography, glossary)
2. Interpreting maps, tables, charts, graphs, diagrams, cartoons
3. Knowing specialized vocabulary
4. Using reference materials (encyclopedias, dictionaries, supplemental reference books)
5. Recognizing special symbols, formulas, and abbreviations

Many checklists are available to survey a range of reading skills. Several formal tests include checklists. For example, the *Barbe Reading Skills Check Lists* (Barbe, 1975), included in the *Reading Skills Competency Tests* (Barbe, Allen, & Thorton, 1978, contains seven checklists that assess from readiness level through the sixth-grade level. Four general skill areas are included in each checklist: 1) vocabulary, 2) perceptive skills, 3) comprehension, and 4) oral and silent reading.

Ekwall (1981) has devised a reading diagnosis checklist consisting of twenty-eight reading abilities and related abilities. It is designed to give a teacher the opportunity to assess each of the twenty-eight skills three times during the year. As Ekwall notes, the checklist does not categorize reading difficulties by severity, although some behaviors listed are more serious than others. An example of the checklist is provided in Figure 5-6.

If a commercially developed checklist is not suitable for a teacher's needs, a checklist may be easily constructed by using a skill network such as the one provided in Table 5-1, which covers a broad range of behaviors relevant to the assessment of reading. Individual sections or

FIGURE 5-6 Reading Diagnosis Sheet

Name _____
Grade _____
Teacher _____
School _____

#	1st Check	2nd Check	3rd Check	Description	Category
1				Word-by-word reading	ORAL READING
2				Incorrect phrasing	
3				Poor pronunciation	
4				Omissions	
5				Repetitions	
6				Inversions or reversals	
7				Insertions	
8				Substitutions	
9				Basic sight words not known	
10				Sight vocabulary not up to grade level	
11				Guesses at words	
12				Consonant sounds not known	
13				Vowel sounds not known	
14				Blends, digraphs or diphthongs not known	
15				Lacks desirable structural analysis	
16				Unable to use context clues	
17				Contractions not known	
18				Fails to comprehend	ORAL SILENT DIFFICULTIES
19				Unaided recall scanty	
20				Response poorly organized	
21				Low rate of speed	SILENT READING
22				High rate at expense of accuracy	
23				Voicing—lip movement	
24				Inability to skim	
25				Inability to adjust reading rate to difficulty of material	
26				Written recall limited by spelling ability	OTHER RELATED ABILITIES
27				Undeveloped dictionary skill	
28				Inability to locate information	

The items listed above represent the most common difficulties encountered by pupils in the reading program. Following each numbered item are spaces for notation of that specific difficulty. This may be done at intervals of several months. One might use a check to indicate difficulty recognized or the following letters to represent an even more accurate appraisal: D—difficulty recognized, P—Pupil progressing, N—No longer has difficulty.

Source: Reprinted by permission from E. Ekwall. (1981) *Locating and correcting reading difficulties,* 3rd ed. Columbus, OH.: Charles E. Merrill, p. 5.

the complete skill network may be used to construct a checklist. Local school districts often have a specific curriculum that teachers are required to follow. A basal reading series, generally used as part of this reading program, often includes a detailed scope-and-sequence skill list for each grade level in the teacher's manual. These skill lists may be used to construct a checklist for use with individual students, a small reading group, or a whole class. Commercially produced reading kits such as the *Sound Foundations Program* (Szymandera, 1972), published by Developmental Learning Materials, and *Schoolhouse: A Word Attack Skills Kit* (Clarke & Marsden, 1973), published by Science Research Associates, also provide a hierarchy of reading skills. Both could be used to construct a checklist for a limited number of skills. A description of the elements to include in a teacher-made checklist is provided in chapter 4. An example of a teacher-made checklist for reading is provided in Figure 5–7.

QUESTIONNAIRES AND INTERVIEWS A student's attitude and interests related to reading affect his or her motivation and achievement in school (Rupley & Blair, 1983). Because of this, these areas should be monitored often. To obtain information about a student's attitudes toward reading and reading interests, a teacher may choose to use a questionnaire or interview. The questionnaire differs from an interview in that it is written. McLoughlin and Lewis (1981) note that a questionnaire may be used with older students or better readers while an interview is often used with young students or those with poor reading ability.

Many types of questions may be asked in a questionnaire or interview, such as questions about a student's attitude toward reading in class, recreational reading, and reading in the library. Information may also be obtained about family reading habits, books a student has read, reading strategies, and study habits.

The Incomplete Sentence Projective Technique (Boning & Boning, 1957) is also often very revealing of a child's attitudes and interests toward reading. It is very practical in that it may be used over a wide range of ages, as a questionnaire with a student writing the responses, or in an interview format with an individual student. Examples of the technique are as follows:

When I have to read, I...
I like to read about..
I'd read more if ....
Reading science..
When I don't understand what I'm reading, I ....

The interview may be used as a source of information from students and parents. Though time-consuming to administer, information may be obtained from a parent interview that would seldom become available elsewhere and thus be of considerable value in the development of an

FIGURE 5-7   Reading Problem Checklist

Skill	Date Observed			
Word-Recognition and Analysis Skills				
1. inadequate sight vocabulary				
2. doesn't attempt to decode unknown words				
3. guesses unknown words				
4. unsuccessfully attempts to decode words				
5. overrelies on configuration, size, or shape				
6. tendency to reverse letters or words				
7. has poor sound–symbol relationship skills				
Comprehension Skills				
8. cannot recall main ideas				
9. cannot remember details				
10. cannot draw inferences				
11. cannot draw logical conclusions				
12. relies heavily on context				
13. inadequate use of context				
Oral and Silent Reading Skills				
14. word-by-word reading				
15. hesitations				
16. repetitions				
17. ignores or misinterprets punctuation				
18. inappropriate speed				
19. inappropriate use of voice				
20. inappropriate behaviors that accompany reading (head movements, lip movements, whispering, pointing, poor concentration)				
Directions: Indicate the presence of the behavior with a checkmark.				

educational plan (Ekwall & Shanker, 1983). The authors suggest the following types of information that may be derived from a parent interview:

1. a parent's view of the child's problem
2. the emotional climate of the home
3. related health factors
4. reading material available at home

5. library habits and time spent in reading
6. study habits and study environment
7. parental expectations
8. social adjustment
9. independence and self-concept
10. duties at home
11. sleep habits
12. successful practices with the student
13. previous tutoring and results

Additional information may be derived from interviewing the student about his or her self-concept, perception of his or her reading problem, past experiences with reading, attitudes about reading, reading interests, reading environment, and instruction techniques and materials used in the past.

Interviews may also be used to assess students' perceptions of classroom reading tasks (Wixson, Bosky, Yochum, & Alvermann, 1984). The Reading Comprehension Interview presented in Figure 5–8 is designed to gain insight into a student's reading strategies and areas to be strengthened.

TEACHER OBSERVATION   Observation permeates all other types of informal assessment. Whether using a checklist, giving an Informal Reading Inventory, or questioning a student, the teacher is continuously making observations about reading behavior. Activities such as oral and silent reading sessions, recreational reading, written seatwork, group discussion, and testing sessions offer good opportunities for observation.

Hammill and Bartel (1982) suggest the use of the round robin oral reading approach for quickly identifying children needing immediate attention. Although criticized as a teaching method, this approach may be a useful observational technique. If a student has trouble with more than 5 out of 100 continuous words, reads too slowly, reads in a word-by-word manner, or has other reading difficulties, the material may be too difficult.

Several questions may be kept in mind by the secondary school teacher as he or she observes:

1. Does he or she approach the assignment with enthusiasm?
2. Does he or she apply an appropriate study method?
3. Can he or she find answers to questions of a literal type (main idea, details, sequence, etc.)?
4. Is he or she reading below the surface (answering interpretive and critical level questions)?
5. Can he or she ascertain the meanings of new or unfamiliar words? What word recognition skills are used?

FIGURE 5-8   Reading Comprehension Interview

Name _____   Date _____
Classroom teacher _____   Reading level _____
     Grade _____

Directions: Introduce the procedure by explaining that you are interested in finding out what children think about various reading activities. Tell the student that he or she will be asked questions about his/her reading, that there are no right or wrong answers, and that you are only interested in knowing what s/he thinks. Tell the student that if s/he does not know how to answer a question s/he should say so and you will go on to the next one.

General probes such as "Can you tell me more about that?" or "Anything else?" may be used. Keep in mind that the interview is an informal diagnostic measure and you should feel free to probe to elicit useful information.

1. What hobbies or interests do you have that you like to read about?
2. a. How often do you read in school?
   b. How often do you read at home?
3. What school subjects do you like to read about?

Introduce reading and social studies books.

Directions: For this section use the child's classroom basal reader and a content area textbook (social studies, science, etc.). Place these texts in front of the student. Ask each question twice, once with reference to the basal reader and once with reference to the content area textbook. Randomly vary the order of presentation (basal, content). As each question is asked, open the appropriate text in front of the student to help provide a point of reference for the question.

4. What is the most important reason for this kind of material?
   Why does your teacher want you to read this book?
5. a. Who's the best reader you know in _____ ?
   b. What does he/she do that makes him/her such a good reader?
6. a. How good are *you* at reading this kind of material?
   b. How do you know?
7. What do you have to do to get a good grade in _____ in your class?
8. a. If the teacher told you to remember the information in this story/chapter, what would be the best way to do this?
   b. Have you ever tried _____ ?
9. a. If your teacher told you to find the answers to the questions in this book, what would be the best way to do this? Why?
   b. Have you ever tried _____ ?
10. a. What is the hardest part about answering questions like the ones in this book?
    b. Does that make you do anything differently?

Introduce at least two comprehension worksheets.

Directions: Present the worksheets to the child and ask questions 11 and 12. Ask the child to complete portions of each worksheet. Then ask questions 13 and 14. Next, show the child a worksheet designed to simulate the work of another child. Then ask question 15.

11. Why would your teacher want you to do worksheets like these (for what purpose)?

(continued)

FIGURE 5-8 *(continued)*

12. What would your teacher say you must do to get a good mark on worksheets like these? (What does your teacher look for?)

Ask the child to complete portions of at least two worksheets.

13. Did you do this one differently from the way you did that one? How or in what way?
14. Did you have to work harder on one of these worksheets than the other? (Does one make you think more?)

Present the simulated worksheet.

15. a. Look over this worksheet. If you were the teacher, what kind of mark would you give the worksheet? Why?
    b. If you were the teacher, what would you ask this person to do differently next time?

Source: From K. Wixson, A. Bosky, M. Yochum, and D. Alvermann. (1984). An interview for assessing students' perceptions of classroom reading tasks. *The Reading Teacher, 37,* pp. 346–352. Reprinted by permission of the authors and the International Reading Association.

6. Can he or she use locational skills in the book?
7. Can he or she use reference skills for various reference sources?
8. Is he or she reading at different rates for different materials and purposes? (Roe, Stoodt, & Burns, 1978, p. 355)

The diagnosis of a student's knowledge of study skills is an important area of assessment, particularly for the secondary student who is not performing adequately in school work. Most skills listed in Table 5-5 can be assessed in a group.

As students move through the grades, rate of reading becomes an important issue (Heilman, Blair, & Rupley, 1981). Different rates should be developed for different types of reading material and the thoroughness that the reader desires. When assessing rate of silent reading, the material used should be of the same level of difficulty throughout (Harris & Sipay, 1980). A selection of several hundred words may be used. The time required to finish the selection is recorded and then students are tested on comprehension of the material. Although reading rate varies according to the nature of the material, teachers may refer to reading rate norms for a rough approximation of an adequate rate. Suggested reading rates are provided in Table 5-7 later in this chapter.

By effectively using observational techniques, information can be collected concerning specific skill strengths and weaknesses, error patterns, interests, and attitudes. Wallace and Larsen (1978) note that this information must be recorded systematically to be beneficial—summarized periodically or kept in checklist form. The checklist presented in Figure 5-7 may be used as a guide for teacher observation of reading problems. Interpretations should be based on multiple observations over

TABLE 5-5   Assessment of Study Skills

Skill	*Method of Assessment*
1. Using table of contents	Using students' textbooks, ask questions such as "What chapter contains a discussion of wild animals?" "On what page does Chapter 10 begin?"
2. Using index	Using students' textbooks, ask questions such as "On what page would you find information on the topic of polar bears?"
3. Using glossary	Using students' textbooks, ask questions such as "What does your book say the word *armature* means?"
4. Using encyclopedia	Ask questions such as "On what page of what volume would you find information on the life of Abraham Lincoln?" "What other topics would you look under to find more information on Lincoln?"
5. Using almanac	Ask questions such as "What city has the largest population in the world?"
6. Using telephone directory	Ask questions such as "What is the telephone number for Amos Abrams?" "List the telephone numbers for three companies that sell firewood."
7. Using library card index	Use questions such as "How many cards have a listing for the book, *World War Two Airplanes?*" "What does the Author Card include?" "What does the Subject Card include?" "What does the Title Card include?" "What is the call number of the book, *Hitler?*"
8. Learning to skim	Using a newspaper, give timed exercises for finding such things as an article on atomic energy or auto accidents. Or, using students' textbooks, give timed exercises in finding a certain date, sentence, etc., in a specific chapter.
9-12. Learning to read maps, graphs, tables, and diagrams	Use students' textbooks to derive questions. This will be more meaningful than questions commonly asked on standardized achievement tests.
13. Learning to take notes	Play a short tape recording of a lecture or radio program on a subject in which the students are interested and ask them to take notes.
14. Using time to good advantage	Use a time analysis sheet.

Source: "Diagnosis of study skills." Reprinted by permission from E. Ekwall & J. Shanker (1983). *Diagnosis and Remediation of the Disabled Reader.* Newton, MA.: Allyn and Bacon.

an extended period of time. This provides a more representative sample of the student's behavior and helps to eliminate incorrect diagnostic conclusions that may be made if the student is assessed only one time.

■ Continuous Assessment

The results obtained from previous periodic testing should suggest a student's strengths and weaknesses in reading and an approximate point at which to begin reading instruction. A more precise analysis of the student's instructional needs should be obtained by using continuous criterion-referenced assessment to assess the skills contained in the reading skill network. The results may then be compared to a mastery or proficiency criterion. Periodic testing may indicate, for example, that a student is deficient in word-attack skills. As a result, the teacher may want to determine, by the use of a criterion-referenced test, if a student is able to recognize two-letter consonant blends in a word list, a skill taught in the accompanying basal workbook. If performance does not reach a stated criterion of 90 to 100%, the teacher provides additional instruction, and then continues to assess the skill daily or as often as possible.

☐ *Commercial Criterion-Referenced Tests*
Commercial criterion-referenced tests may be used to measure a wide array or selected number of academic skills on a continuous basis. Tests differ in number of objectives covered, number of items per objective, and mastery criteria. Examples of tests that measure reading skills are provided in Table 5–6.

☐ *Teacher-Made Tests*
Because the particular skills assessed and sequences of skills presented differ between materials, it may be appropriate to develop a criterion-referenced test to measure the specific skills taught in the curriculum. When constructing a criterion-referenced test, special care should be taken to ensure that the device is carefully designed. Instructions and test items should be clearly printed or typed. Ideally, the pages should be laminated and then inserted into a standard ring-binder notebook.

Test items may be obtained from instructional materials similar to that to which the student will be exposed. Textbooks, workbooks, worksheets, flashcards, and manipulative materials may be helpful in designing a test of this type. Care should be taken, however, that enough questions are asked to ensure a thorough examination.

The test should also be constructed so that the student's responses are similar to the ones required during instruction. If, for example, the student is required to read orally a word list in class, then the test should

TABLE 5-6 Commercial Criterion-Referenced Tests

Test	Grade	Reading Skills Measured
Brigance Diagnostic Comprehensive Inventory of Basic Skills (Brigance, 1983)	K–9+	reading readiness, word recognition, oral reading, comprehension, word analysis, and functional word recognition
Brigance Diagnostic Inventory of Basic Skills (Brigance, 1977)	K–6	reading readiness, word recognition, oral reading, comprehension, word analysis, and vocabulary
Brigance Diagnostic Inventory of Early Development (Brigance, 1978)	0–7 yrs.	auditory discrimination, basic phonics, word recognition, and oral reading
Brigance Diagnostic Inventory of Essential Skills (Brigance, 1981)	9–12	word recognition, oral reading, comprehension, functional word recognition, word analysis, and reference skills
Fountain Valley Teacher Support System in Reading (Zweig Associates, 1971)	K–6	phonetic analysis, structural analysis, vocabulary development, comprehension, and study skills
Multilevel Academic Skill Inventory (Howell, Zucker, & Morehead, 1982)	1–8	decoding skills, comprehension, and vocabulary
Regional Resource Center Diagnostic Reading Inventory (1971)	K–6	consonant sounds, vowel sounds, blending, and oral reading
Wisconsin Tests of Reading Development (Kamm, Miles, VanBlaricom, Harris, & Stewart, 1971)	K–6	word attack, comprehension, study skills, self-directed reading, interpretive reading, and creative reading

be prepared in a similar manner. By doing this, a more precise assessment of instructional problems may be obtained.

Some types of criterion-referenced tests should be administered individually. Skills that require an oral response or manipulation of objects may be more suitable for individual administration. For example, a teacher may want to assess an auditory discrimination skill by asking the student if two words are the same or different. The teacher may want to listen to a student read a list of sight words, or watch a student point to pictures that begin with a particular consonant sound.

There are, however, situations that necessitate the testing of a small number of children in a reading group. In this case, a written response may be more appropriate in that a larger number of children may simultaneously participate. Examples of reading tasks of this type are dividing words into syllables, marking the long or short vowels in words, or answering objective test items.

OBJECTIVE TEST ITEMS Various formats for written test questions may be used. As described in chapter 2, multiple choice, matching, completion or short answer, and true–false questions have been traditionally used as test items in teacher-made tests. In the assessment of reading, these types of test questions may be used to assess word-recognition and analysis skills and some comprehension skills on a continuous basis. Examples of objective test items are provided in Figure 5–9.

QUESTIONING TO ASSESS COMPREHENSION Objective test items are useful in assessing word-analysis skills and some areas of comprehen-

FIGURE 5-9 Objective Test Items for Assessing Reading Skills

Matching

Draw a line from the word in the first column to the word in the second column that completes the compound word.

1.	day	a.	ball
2.	snow	b.	coat
3.	home	c.	corn
4.	pop	d.	made
5.	rain	e.	time

Completion/Short Answer

The little girl in the story mixed yellow and blue paint to get _____ .
Then she mixed red and yellow paint and got _____ .
She also mixed red and blue paint to get _____ .

Multiple Choice

Jack and his mother _____ to the store to buy clothes.
    (bent, sent, tent, went)
Do not _____ in that tree.
    (climb, comb, dumb, limb)
Cindy had her broken leg in a _____ .
    (last, fast, past, cast)

---

sion, particularly literal comprehension—such as knowledge of word meanings, recall of main ideas and details, and sequence of story events. However, questioning techniques should be the primary tool in evaluating the development of thinking and comprehension skills. Heilman, Blair, and Rupley (1981) note several important aspects of questioning, including quality, number, and type of questions, and the teacher's response to a student's answer. For example, Rowe (1974) found that students benefit when teachers wait before redirecting a question and when teachers increase the time in which they react to a student response.

Durkin (1983) notes that prereading questions may be designed to encourage children to attend to what is important and to facilitate comprehension. The selection of prereading questions depends on the reading selection and the students' reading needs.

A *DRTA (Directed Reading Thinking Activity)* is an excellent method to use as a guide for prereading and postreading discussion (Gillet & Temple, 1982). Open-ended questions are asked by the teacher to encourage divergent thinking. Two questions commonly asked are: 1) What do you think will happen? and 2) Why do you think so? Students predict story events and outcomes, then read to confirm or disprove their hypotheses. This method has been shown to significantly improve comprehension, and as an assessment method may give information about a student's background concepts or general knowledge about a particular topic.

Roe, Stoodt, and Burns (1978) stress that questioning should be carefully planned so that students learn to identify significant ideas and concepts in the reading selection. The authors suggest a framework for developing thinking at four levels:

1. Literal Thinking. Literal comprehension questions include identification and recall of ideas directly stated in the selection. The main types of literal comprehension are recognizing and recalling main ideas, details, and sequence of events, following directions, and recognizing cause and effect. Examples of questions at this level are the following:

   What did the story say about.............................?
   What events led to.............................?
   Who was.............................?
   What was the effect of ....?

2. Interpretive Thinking. Interpretive or inferential questions require reading between the lines to recognize the author's purpose, draw conclusions, make generalizations, predict outcomes, and understand figurative language. Examples of questions at this level are the following:

   Why do you think this story is called.............................?

What caused .... to happen?

What was the result of ....?

3. Evaluative or critical thinking. Evaluative questions ask the reader to make judgments about the quality, value, and validity of the story's content. Examples of critical reading questions follow:

   How would you have felt if you...?

   What would you have done...?

   Does the story accurately portray ....?

   For what reason would you ....?

4. Creative thinking. Creative reading requires the reader to go beyond the information in the selection to find new ways of viewing ideas, events, or characters. Examples of creative thinking questions follow:

   Can you develop a new way to ....?

   Can you write a new ending in which ....?

   Can you rewrite this story setting in...................................?

PROBES   Another method of criterion-referenced assessment used to assess specific reading curriculum objectives is the probe. (Probes were also discussed in chapter 2.) Because they are often administered for one minute, probes are particularly useful for the daily assessment of word-analysis and comprehension skills. Reading probes may take many forms. Arranging letters in alphabetical order, reading orally, identifying consonant blends on flashcards, and distinguishing between facts and opinions are but some examples of probes. As stated in chapter 2, skills assessed on probe sheets are evaluated in relation to the stimulus presented and the response required of the student. A see–say probe, for example, would require the student to read a letter, word, or selection and then orally respond. A hear–write probe, however, would necessitate listening to the stimulus and writing the response. Structuring probes in this manner allows for an examination of learning channels that might be weak. If a student, for example, always performs poorly on see–write probes while performing adequately on see–say probes, then a closer examination of the student's writing abilities may be indicated. In addition, assessment may be tailored to reflect the stimuli and responses that will be required of students in instructional settings. If the student will be required to complete a see–say reading task, then the assessment procedure should reflect that task. In this way, assessment results can greatly aid instructional planning.

The items on the probe shown in Figure 5–10 assess one specific reading objective. Only those CVC (consonant-vowel-consonant) trigrams with an *a* in the middle are included on this probe. In contrast, a mixed probe may include many related objectives. The items in the probe shown in Figure 5–11 include a mixture of CVC trigrams with *a, e, i, o,*

FIGURE 5-10   Probe on Single Reading Skill: CVC (Consonant-Vowel-Consonant) Trigrams with Short *a*

sat	mat	rat	bat	fat	cap	sap	map	lap	rap	*(10)*
am	ram	ham	jam	rag	tag	bag	wag	hag	can	*(20)*
man	ran	tan	fan	sad	mad	had	lad	pad	sat	*(30)*
sap	sad	map	man	mat	mad	tan	tax	cab	cap	*(40)*
can	bag	bad	ban	hat	ham	had	rap	lad	lap	*(50)*
fan	fat	sat	man	tan	pat	ban	map	rag	cat	*(60)*
lap	ham	bat	tap	jam	fan	dam	had	sat	cap	*(70)*
rag	can	sad	mat	sap	ram	bag	man	mad	rat	*(80)*
map	tag	ran	had	bat	tap	wag	tan	lad	cat	*(90)*
lap	hag	fan	pad	rap	jam	dad	lap	sap	cap	*(100)*

Name _____

Date _____

Time _____

Number Correct _____

Number Incorrect _____

FIGURE 5-11   Mixed Probe on CVC (Consonant-Vowel-Consonant) Trigrams Using All Vowels

mat	met	pit	mop	pup	but	pot	him	pet	map	*(10)*
men	tap	top	bit	hut	pat	ten	hit	nut	fun	*(20)*
hot	nip	net	ham	tub	not	pin	get	hat	peg	*(30)*
cot	fan	tin	bun	nap	beg	rip	rob	cut	fog	*(40)*
bed	rub	fig	pan	run	hog	sip	jet	rag	bug	*(50)*
sod	sit	wet	bag	sob	dip	rug	gap	red	sap	*(60)*
bid	dog	dam	hid	let	pod	sad	mug	leg	did	*(70)*
rod	bus	jot	fed	sun	lot	sat	jam	led	wig	*(80)*
lot	dug	log	yet	sap	yes	mop	hid	jug	jam	*(90)*
mud	hot	did	red	sad	fix	job	fun	zip	mad	*(100)*

Name _____

Date _____

Time _____

Number Correct _____

Number Incorrect _____

or *u* in the middle. A probe sheet with a single skill might be used initially. After the student achieves the goals set for several single skills, the skills may be combined into a mixed probe. Examples of probes used to assess other reading skills on a continuous basis are presented in Figure 5-12 and Figure 5-13.

FIGURE 5-12   Probe: See-Say Consonant Sounds

m	t	d	h	n	s	f	c	r	l	(10)
w	b	g	p	v	j	k	x	qu	y	(20)
z	t	w	g	m	z	c	n	d	s	(30)
l	r	p	b	v	k	j	qu	y	m	(40)
x	w	f	h	d	t	r	l	n	b	(50)
g	v	y	x	k	p	j	c	g	f	(60)
s	h	z	m	d	h	s	f	r	w	(70)
g	p	j	qu	y	t	n	c	l	b	(80)
w	g	p	v	j	k	qu	x	z	y	(90)
m	s	c	g	v	qu	x	y	k	p	(100)

Name _____

Date _____

Time _____

Number Correct _____

Number Incorrect _____

A probe may also be used to sample comprehension skills. Examples of using a probe in this manner are the following: 1) list all the details about a story event, 2) list possible conclusions to a story starter, and 3) circle all the opinions in the story.

Flashcards with letters or words printed on them may also be used as probes. Cards of uniform size are presented one at a time over a one-minute period. The flashcards are placed in either a correct or incorrect pile depending upon the student's response. After analyzing the error patterns, the total number of cards (correct and incorrect) are then recorded on a chart.

Rupley and Blair (1983) note that tachistoscopic devices may be used to assess vocabulary words. The Tach-X (Educational Developmental Laboratories), a 35 mm filmstrip projector, flashes words on a screen at rates ranging from 1/100 second through one and one-half seconds.

Oral reading progress may also be measured with probes by simply recording the number of errors that occur during any one-minute period of a reading session. Recordkeeping may be facilitated by marking, on another copy of the passage, the beginning and end of the timing period and the specific errors (see the notation system for recording errors in Table 5-4). The incorrect words (errors) may then be used for drill or as the basis for further instruction.

Probes provide educationally relevant data by identifying any changes that occur in the student's reading behavior. Because this assessment occurs on a relatively continuous basis, instructional programs may be quickly and easily modified to facilitate student growth.

FIGURE 5-13   Probe: See-Write Prefix Meanings

de-: down, from, away
en-: in, into, put or make into
in-: in, into, within, on, toward
mis-: wrong, bad
re-: back, again

dis-: away, apart, opposite
im-: not, opposite
inter-: between, among
pre-: before
un-: not, lack of, opposite

Write the meaning of each prefix listed below.

un _____   inter _____   en _____

in _____   de _____   pre _____

dis _____   re _____   im _____

mis _____   un _____   mis _____

im _____   in _____   dis _____

re _____   un _____   re _____

pre _____   in _____   pre _____

de _____   dis _____   inter _____

inter _____   mis _____   im _____

en _____   de _____   en _____

Name _____
Date _____
Time _____
Number Correct _____
Number Incorrect _____

RECORDING PERFORMANCE AND SETTING OBJECTIVES

■ ■   All of the assessment data concerning the student's strengths and weaknesses in reading should be organized and recorded. There are a variety of ways in which to do this. Recordkeeping systems may be provided through a basal series or a school district's curriculum guide, but often it will be helpful to use a recordkeeping system to suit individual needs.

■ **Record of Periodic Assessment Data**

The periodic assessment data in reading may be organized and recorded on the Periodic Reading Assessment Record, presented in Figure 5-14.

FIGURE 5-14 Periodic Reading Assessment Record

A. Formal Tests   Scores
   1. _____
      _____
      _____
      _____
      _____
      _____
   2. _____
      _____
      _____
      _____
      _____
      _____

B. Informal Reading Inventory
   _____ Independent Level
   _____ Instructional Level
   _____ Frustration Level

   Word Recognition/Analysis
   Errors _____
   _____
   _____

   Comprehension Errors
   _____
   _____
   _____

C. Graded Word List
   _____ Independent Level
   _____ Instructional Level
   _____ Frustration Level

D. Cloze Procedure
   _____ Independent Level
   _____ Instructional Level
   _____ Frustration Level

E. Error Pattern Analysis
   _____ omissions
   _____ substitutions
   _____ mispronunciations
   _____ repetitions
   _____ insertions
   _____ reversals
   _____ hesitations
   _____ unknown or aided
   _____ omission of punctuation
   _____ self-corrected error
   Other comments _____
   _____

F. Checklist Information
   _____
   _____
   _____
   _____
   _____

G. Interviews and Questionnaires
   _____
   _____
   _____
   _____

H. Observation
   _____
   _____
   _____
   _____
   _____
   _____
   _____
   _____
   _____

Student Name _____
Grade/Teacher _____
Date _____

Sections are provided to record formal and informal assessment results. An analysis can then be conducted to indicate which aspects of the skill network require more extensive and continuous assessment.

■ **Record of Continuous Assessment Data**

When periodic assessment data are analyzed in relation to the skill network, the results suggest various specific reading skills that should be more precisely and continuously assessed for possible daily instruction.

These specific skills, which will serve as the focus for further assessment and instruction, should be listed on the Continuous Assessment Record. (An example is provided in the case study at the end of the chapter.) Continuous assessment procedures may then be used to evaluate student performance more precisely in each of these skill areas. The conditions related to assessment, the target skill or behavior required of the student, current performance results, and the proficiency goal should be listed. After assessment has been completed, student performance should be judged in relation to the stated level of proficiency. If assessment indicates that the student is deficient in a skill, that skill may serve as an instructional objective.

☐ *Charting*
The reading skills established as objectives generally require some form of ongoing or daily measurement such as a chart. Many reading skills are appropriate for charting; for example, correct and incorrect responses on a reading probe, such as see–say sight words. Responses obtained from the reading probes may be entered on an equal-interval or proportional chart in order to achieve a clear visual display of reading growth.

Precise recording of periodic and continuous assessment data greatly facilitates instructional planning by allowing a systematic analysis of student performance in relation to a skill network. This affords a specific focus for instruction and assists in setting objectives.

☐ *Proficiency Aims*
The charted reading probe results may be compared to mastery or proficiency levels established for many reading skills. Skills that fall below these levels may be used to set instructional objectives. Mastery or proficiency goals should represent those levels at which a reading skill may be accurately and fluently used. Although research has not conclusively determined specific proficiencies for reading tasks, enough data are available to indicate trends on some tasks. These data, illustrated in Table 5–7, may be used to provide a goal for instruction. Probes and charting should continue until proficiency is reached, at which time the next more difficult reading skill is introduced.

TABLE 5-7 Reading Proficiency Goals

Source	See–Say Isolated Sounds (Correct/Incorrect per minute)	See–Say Words in a List (Correct/Incorrect per minute)	See–Say Words in Text (Correct/Incorrect per minute)
Alper, Nowlin, Lemoine, Perine, & Bettencourt (1974)	80/2	60–80/2	100–120/3
Haring & Gentry (1976)	61/4	58/7	
Precision Teaching Project	60–80/0	80–100/0	200+/0
Regional Resource Center Diagnostic Reading Inventory	60–80/2	80–100/2	100–120/2
Starlin (1982)		80–250/2	150–250/5
SIMS (1978)		50/2	100/2

Mastery criteria may also be expressed as a percentage of correct responses. Percentage is especially useful in measuring skills such as comprehension and in assessing the accuracy of responses. Smith (1981) notes that teachers often demand three days of 90 to 100% accuracy before introducing a new task.

A very precise analysis of student reading behavior may be obtained by assessing on a daily basis. Recording daily data on a chart supplies a clear visual record of the direction and extent of change in performance. Adding proficiency or mastery goals to this system allows the classroom teacher to know when instructional goals have been met and instructional changes should be made.

☐ *Using Data to Make Instructional Decisions*
Much of the information obtained while assessing a student can be used to assist in preparing effective instructional strategies. Assessment indicates the skills that are deficient and the antecedent and consequent conditions associated with each task, which may provide additional information to aid in instructional planning.

CASE STUDY

An example of how periodic reading assessment results may be organized is provided in Figure 5-15. An analysis of these data indicate that although Jim is in the fifth grade, his instructional level, as measured by the *Woodcock Reading Mastery Tests* and an Informal Reading Inventory, is approximately at the second-grade level. Observations from the Informal Reading Inventory indicate that Jim has difficulty in correctly using vowels and answering recall questions. An error-pattern analysis shows that a high frequency of mispronunciations, repetitions, and hesitations is occurring, while a checklist verifies problems with phonic rule understanding and comprehension. Observations show that vocalizations occur while reading. The results obtained from an interview indicate that little emphasis is placed on reading at home. However, Jim is very interested in anything related to sports. Finally, Jim states that he does not like attending his current reading class.

An example of Jim's continuous assessment data is provided in Figure 5-16. An analysis of these data indicate that Jim has attained proficiency in see–say consonant sounds and see–say consonant blends. However, he is not proficient in saying sight words or phonetically regular words, saying words in context, or in recalling details. These final skills are examples of those that may be selected as instructional objec-

FIGURE 5-15 Case Study: Periodic Reading Assessment Record

A. Formal Tests   Scores
  1. _Woodcock_ _____ 2.4
       letter ID _____ 3.2
       word ID _____ 2.2
       word attack _____ 2.3
       word comprehension _____ 1.8
       passage comprehension ___ 2.1
  2. _____
     _____
     _____
     _____
     _____
     _____

B. Informal Reading Inventory
  __1.0__ Independent Level
  __2.0__ Instructional Level
  __3.0__ Frustration Level

Word Recognition/Analysis
Errors _lacks vowel rule understanding_____
_____
_____

Comprehension Errors
_____
_____
_____

C. Graded Word List
  _____ Independent Level
  _____ Instructional Level
  _____ Frustration Level

D. Cloze Procedure
  _____ Independent Level
  _____ Instructional Level
  _____ Frustration Level

Student Name ____Jim C._____
Grade/Teacher _5th / Smith_____
Date _____9/20_____

E. Error Pattern Analysis
  _____ omissions
  _____ substitutions
  __X__ mispronunciations
  __X__ repetitions
  _____ insertions
  _____ reversals
  __X__ hesitations
  __X__ unknown or aided
  _____ omission punctuation
  _____ self-corrected error
  Other comments _____
  _____

F. Checklist Information
  sight-word vocabulary below grade level;
  word-by-word reading; doesn't know vowel
  rules; poor recall of facts after reading____
  _____

G. Interviews and Questionnaires
  parent expectations poor;_____
  little reading material at home;_____
  dislikes reading class_____
  _____

H. Observation
  vocalizes while reading;_____
  very interested in sports and athletes_____
  _____
  _____
  _____
  _____
  _____
  _____

FIGURE 5-16 Case Study: Continuous Assessment Record

Date	Conditons	Skill/Behavior	Current Performance	Proficiency Criterion/Goal	Date Attained
10/2	probe sheet, praise	says consonant sounds	65/min. corr. 0/min. inc.	60/min. corr. 0/min. inc.	
10/2	probe sheet, praise	says consonant blends	100% correct	100% correct	
10/2	probe sheet, praise	says sight words	20/min. corr. 12/min. inc.	80/min. corr. 0/min. inc.	
10/2	probe sheet, praise	says long-vowel words	15/min. corr. 5/min. inc.	80/min. corr. 0/min. inc.	
10/4	basal text, reading group	reads words orally	50/min. corr. 8/min. inc.	120/min. corr. 0/min. inc.	
10/4	basal text, reading group	answers "detail" ques- tions	50% correct	95% correct	

Student's Name _____ Jim C. _____
Grade/Teacher _____ 5th / Smith _____

tives. A further examination of the data does not clearly indicate that any specific stimulus or response factors are exclusively related to success or failure.

Skills selected as instructional objectives have been charted daily. As seen in Figure 5–17, Jim has had five days of probes on sight-word identification, specifically, words from his basal series. These data indicate that improvement is occurring in correct and incorrect responses. No instructional change is required.

As seen in Figure 5–18, Jim is not progressing as well in the skill of saying phonetically regular long-vowel words (CVCe). Correct responses are not improving and incorrect responses are increasing. An educational change is necessary. This could consist of changing the mode of presentation, dropping back to an easier prerequisite skill, or changing the type of teacher correction or reinforcement.

Based on the periodic and continuous assessment data presented in Jim's case, the following objectives were developed:

1. Given a second-grade basal list of vocabulary words, Jim will say these words at a rate of 80 words per minute correct with two errors or less for three consecutive days.
2. Given a list of five common phonics rules, Jim will be able to apply the appropriate rule to a given example correctly 90% of the time, for three days in a week. (These rules were described in Table 5–1, under the heading Word Recognition and Analysis Skills—Rapid Development Stage.)
3. After having read a story in a second-grade basal reader, Jim will answer 90% of the detail questions correctly for three consecutive days.

In order to accomplish these goals, Jim's progress on the three objectives was monitored daily for one week during his reading class. To help collect the data related to the first objective, a peer individually administered a one-minute timing daily on Jim's basal sight words.

Jim was also assessed three times a week by his teacher on his knowledge of phonics rules. A word was presented to him and he was asked to state the corresponding rule (e.g., *rain*—"when there are two vowels together, the first is long and the second is silent").

Assessment of reading comprehension was completed during Jim's daily reading group session. After taking his turn reading orally, Jim was asked several questions on details related to the story.

The rate of saying sight words, the percentage of correctly identified phonics rules, and reading comprehension questions were charted three to five times a week. These charts served as a visual display so that Jim, his parents, and teachers could review his daily progress.

FIGURE 5-17   Continuous Charting on Sight-Word Identification

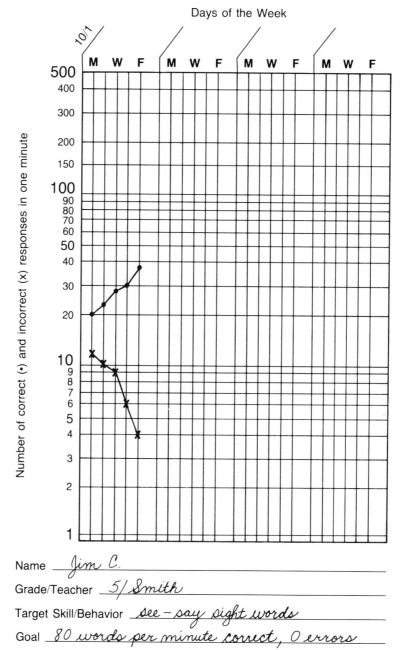

Days of the Week

Number of correct (•) and incorrect (x) responses in one minute

Name _Jim C._

Grade/Teacher _5/ Smith_

Target Skill/Behavior _see – say sight words_

Goal _80 words per minute correct, 0 errors_

FIGURE 5-18   Continuous Charting on Phonetically Regular Long-Vowel Word Identification

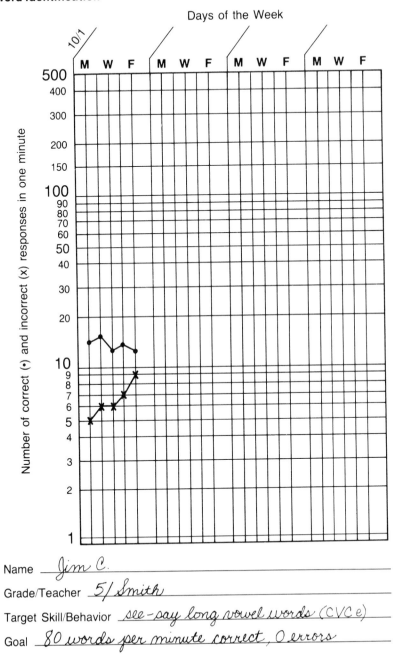

Name _Jim C._

Grade/Teacher _5/ Smith_

Target Skill/Behavior _see–say long vowel words (CVCe)_

Goal _80 words per minute correct, 0 errors_

Because Jim is in the fifth grade but reading at the second-grade level, it may be difficult to get him interested in reading. Many books have been written specifically to combine interest appeal with simplified vocabulary and style. Jim may need the extra incentive of this high interest–low vocabulary reading material, possibly stories about sports. As Jim responds to instruction, assessment should be continued and new goals established.

The ongoing process of assessment, analysis, and teaching may greatly enhance Jim's reading progress and that of other students like him. Reading, instead of being a laborious task, may become an enjoyable, worthwhile activity.

CONCLUSION

Reading instruction is perhaps the most important of academic skills. Virtually every aspect of daily life contains some element of reading. Because of this, it is absolutely essential that reading skills be precisely and accurately assessed. This assessment may take many forms and concentrate on numerous skills. The end goal, however, is to obtain information that assists in the development and implementation of an effective reading program.

ACTIVITIES

1. What are the most essential components of reading?
2. Most reading instruction can be categorized into six general methods of instruction. Name the methods and briefly describe each one.
3. List examples of word-recognition and analysis skills; comprehension skills; and oral and silent reading skills for the readiness stage, beginning reading stage, rapid development stage, and wide reading stage included in the reading skill network in Table 5–1.
4. Four categories of formal tests are commonly used to assess reading. List and describe each one.
5. Describe the following informal procedures and how each is best used in periodic assessment: IRI, graded word lists, error pattern analysis, cloze procedure, checklists, interviews and questionnaires, and teacher observation.
6. Develop a graded word list from a text in a content area such as science or social studies.

7. Develop matching, completion, and multiple-choice test items to assess word-recognition and analysis skills.

8. Using a passage from a graded basal text, develop a comprehension question for the four levels of thinking (literal, interpretive, evaluative, and creative).

9. Using curriculum materials of an elementary classroom, design twelve probes, one for each area and stage of the skill network. (See the format provided in Question 3).

10. Administer three one-minute timings with an elementary student (see–say consonant sounds, see–say words in a list, and see–say words in a text). Compare the results with the reading proficiency goals suggested in Table 5–7.

6

Assessment of Mathematics

■ **Learning Objectives**

After completing this chapter, the reader should be able to:

■ identify the areas included in an essential math skills curriculum
■ list and describe the fundamentals of computation
■ describe the basic levels of learning (concrete, semiconcrete, and abstract)
■ list examples of skills that might be included in a math network
■ describe procedures used to assess math skills
■ describe how to record the data collected in math assessment and set objectives for instruction

Generally, math learning follows a sequence that includes the understanding of concepts, the development of computation skills, and the application of computation skills. Students with learning problems may have difficulty with any one or all of the components of the math learning sequence.

Many students lack an understanding of concepts that are basic to achieving computation proficiency. For example, if a student memorizes 7×3 is 21 but sees 3×7 as a new problem to memorize, he or she does not understand the commutative property of multiplication.

Most math programs do not provide adequate activities for teaching math concepts. They tend to move quickly to abstract levels of instruction and limit the concrete and semiconcrete activities that are best suited for teaching the understanding of math concepts. Many researchers (Copeland, 1979; Reisman, 1982; Underhill, Uprichard, & Heddens, 1980) claim that failure to understand basic concepts in beginning math instruction contributes heavily to later learning problems in arithmetic. Howell and Kaplan (1980) report that the teaching of concepts is essential if the purpose of instruction is to help the student generalize material to new problems.

Although mastery is typically obtained through practice and review, students are often introduced to new concepts or skills before they obtain mastery on lower-level concepts and skills. Silbert, Carnine, and Stein (1981) claim that a major weakness of most basal math programs is the inadequate amount of practice and review activities. For students with poor memory skills, insufficient practice results in failure to learn basic facts and algorithms that are germane to obtaining proficiency in computation. Moreover, since lower-level math skills are prerequisites to learning higher-level skills, students in later grades readily develop extensive deficits in math.

Students may learn basic computation skills but fail to apply these skills to real problems. Problem solving in math is widely recognized as a deficit area for students with learning problems. The application of computation skills to everyday situations has become a major emphasis of recent math programs and is part of the back-to-basics movement in math (Reisman, 1981; Thornton, Tucker, Dossey, & Bazik, 1983). The National Council for Teachers of Mathematics (1980) listed computation as one of their ten basic skill priority areas. Students with learning problems need to apply computation skills to problem solving so they can recognize the functional uses of math as well as practice activities that enhance the generalization of basic computation skills.

Math curriculum typically includes a wide range of skill areas. Generally the regular student is able to learn the content in each math skill area; however, the student with learning problems has difficulty mastering a wide range of skills with the limited practice provided. Thus, it becomes important to identify what skill areas are most essential for students with special needs and provide them with intensive instruction in these areas.

This chapter provides assessment procedures that enable a teacher to determine the appropriate math skills for beginning instruction and for monitoring the progress of students along a continuum of essential math skills presented in the K–6 math curriculum. Most students with math problems have difficulty with the skills included in this grade span.

DETERMINING SKILLS TO BE ASSESSED

Teachers have the responsibility of determining short- and long-range instructional objectives in math. To do this effectively, a teacher must have an understanding of math curriculum and the general sequence in which the concepts and skills are taught. Knowledge of a math skill network provides the teacher with a clear understanding of the skills a student has mastered and those that need to be mastered. To help the teacher assess math skills, this section presents basic information about math curriculum, skill sequencing, and skill mastery.

In working with students with math problems it is very important to focus on the most essential math skills. Basal math programs include content areas (e.g., probability, integers, real numbers, graphing, and statistics) that are important but not germane to effective remedial or corrective instruction. Because students with math problems need more time to acquire basic skills, some of the nonessential skills must be omitted or delayed until the student learns the basic ones. Most researchers agree that computation skills and their application to real-life problems are the most important areas of an essential math skills curriculum. Moreover, inherent in these essential skills are math concepts that must be taught. For example, the concept of each of the four operations (addition, subtraction, multiplication, and division) must be understood before computation skills are mastered. Other concepts are important for applying math skills in such functional areas as time, money, measurement, word problems, and geometry. Thus, *concepts, computation,* and *functional applications* are the areas of an essential math skills curriculum.

■ **Fundamentals of Computation**

Knowledge of five areas is essential to learning addition, subtraction, multiplication, and division: understanding of math operations; basic facts; place value, including regrouping; structures, that is, laws and properties; and algorithms (Underhill, Uprichard, & Heddens, 1980). *Understanding* means comprehending a math operation at the concrete, semiconcrete, and abstract levels. *Basic facts* are the tools of computation that must eventually be memorized. An example of a basic fact is a single-element (one computation) operation involving two one-digit whole numbers and a third whole number that may be one or two digits. Other examples include:

$$
\begin{array}{cccccccc}
5 & 9 & 6 & 14 & 4 & 6 & 4 \div 2 = 2 \\
+3 & +8 & -3 & -8 & \times 2 & \times 3 & 27 \div 3 = 9 \\
\hline
8 & 17 & 3 & 6 & 8 & 18 &
\end{array}
$$

There are 390 basic facts—100 addition, 100 subtraction, 100 multiplication, and 90 division facts. Once understanding and basic facts are mastered, a math operation can be readily expanded by using *place value* and *regrouping* (Mercer & Mercer, 1985). For example, if the student recognizes that 4×2 is 8, the place value concept can be applied to compute a series of problems such as the following:

$$
\begin{array}{cccccc}
4 & 40 & 400 & 4{,}000 & 40 & 400 \\
\times 2 & \times\ 2 & \times\ \ 2 & \times\ \ \ \ 2 & \times 20 & \times\ \ 20 \\
\hline
8 & 80 & 800 & 8{,}000 & 800 & 8{,}000
\end{array}
$$

Regrouping, often referred to as *carrying* and *borrowing*, is essential for solving more complex problems in each of the four operations. *Structures* are mathematical properties (or concepts) that help the student understand computation. If a student memorizes $8 + 6$ is 14 but sees $6 + 8$ as a new problem to memorize, he or she needs to understand a basic structure—in this case, the commutative property of addition—in order to learn addition effectively. Algorithms are fundamental in learning to compute. An *algorithm* refers to the specific steps used to calculate a math problem—the problem-solving pattern used to compute an answer.

■ The Nature of Mathematics

Mathematics content has a logical structure. Students make simple relationships first and then progress to more complex tasks. As the student progresses in this ordering of arithmetic tasks, the learning of skills and content transfers from each step to the next higher step. Researchers (Silbert, Carnine, & Stein, 1981; Underhill, Uprichard, & Heddens, 1980) report that optimal learning occurs when instruction follows a hierarchy of math skills. Since mastery of lower-level skills is necessary to learning higher-order skills, the concept of *preskill development* is important. For example, if a student has not mastered the basic concepts and facts related to addition, he or she is not ready for subtraction.

Once formal arithmetic instruction begins, the student must master operations and basic structures in order to acquire skills in computation and problem solving. Mathematical operations are well known, but basic structures are less familiar. Alley and Deshler (1979) list some basic structures that are especially important for teaching arithmetic skills to students with learning problems: commutative property of addition, commutative property of multiplication, associative property of addition and multiplication, distributive property of multiplication over addition, and inverse operations for addition and multiplication.

The *commutative property of addition* means that in whatever order the same numbers are combined, the sum remains constant:

$$a + b = b + a$$

$$6 + 2 = 2 + 6$$

The *commutative property of multiplication* means that regardless of the order of the numbers being multiplied, the product remains the same:

$$a \times b = b \times a$$
$$9 \times 6 = 6 \times 9$$

The *associative property of addition and multiplication* means that regardless of grouping arrangements, the sum or product is constant:

Addition

$$(a + b) + c = a + (b + c)$$
$$(5 + 4) + 2 = 5 + (4 + 2)$$

Multiplication

$$(a \times b) \times c = a \times (b \times c)$$
$$(6 \times 3) \times 2 = 6 \times (3 \times 2)$$

The *distributive property of multiplication over addition* relates the two operations:

$$a(b + c) = (a \times b) + (a \times c)$$
$$7(3 + 2) = (7 \times 3) + (7 \times 2)$$

Inverse operations relate operations that are opposite in their effects:

Addition and Subtraction

$$a + b = c \qquad 5 + 4 = 9$$
$$c - a = b \qquad 9 - 5 = 4$$
$$c - b = a \qquad 9 - 4 = 5$$

Multiplication and Division

$$a \times b = c \qquad 8 \times 4 = 32$$
$$c \div a = b \qquad 32 \div 8 = 4$$
$$c \div b = a \qquad 32 \div 4 = 8$$

Due to the hierarchical nature of mathematics (and especially of computation skills), it is essential that instruction begin precisely at the student's level. Instruction at levels too difficult or too easy does not result in efficient learning. To avoid this, assessment in math should be based on a skill network or hierarchy. By assessing a student's performance along a continuum of math skills, it is possible to determine the skills that have been mastered and those which need to be taught. In this way, instructional objectives generated through the assessment procedure enable instruction to begin at the appropriate point in the skill hierarchy.

■ Levels of Learning

As noted earlier, understanding the ordering of the basic operations and related concepts (properties) that affect computation and application skills helps the teacher to assess math problems and plan instruction. Also, knowledge of the *levels* of understanding is vital to math assessment and instruction. Underhill, Uprichard, and Heddens (1980) report several basic levels of learning in mathematical learning experiences. These levels are *concrete, semiconcrete,* and *abstract.*

The *concrete level* involves the manipulation of objects, a level at which the student learns to relate manipulative and computational processes. At this level, the learner concentrates on both the manipulated objects and the symbolic processes that describe the manipulations (Underhill et al., 1980). For example, in instruction of addition problems involving sums of 9, a concrete activity would be to have the student group eight blocks into all possible combinations of 9 (6 + 3, 5 + 4, and so on). Some students demonstrate their need for concrete-level activities by counting on their fingers when requested to complete simple addition problems. Concrete experiences are important for learning skills at all levels in the math hierarchy.

The *semiconcrete level* involves working with illustrations of items to perform math tasks. Items may include dots, tallies, pictures, or nonsense items. Some researchers divide this level into semiconcrete and semiabstract (Underhill et al., 1980). Semiconcrete involves the use of pictures of real objects, whereas semiabstract refers to the use of tallies. A worksheet that requires the learner to match sets of the same number of items represents a semiconcrete-level task. Most commercial math programs include worksheets with tasks at this level. Most students with math learning problems need practice at this level to master a concept or fact. Often students show their reliance on this level by making their own graphic representations. For example, they may approach the problems 7 + 5 = _____ and 4 × 2 = _____ in the following manner:

$$7 \;\; ///////$$
$$+5 \;\; /////$$
$$\overline{12}$$

$$4 \;\; \begin{matrix} X X \\ X X \\ X X \\ X X \end{matrix}$$
$$\times 2$$
$$\overline{8}$$

At the semiconcrete level, the focus is on developing associations between visual models and symbolic processes.

The *abstract level* refers to the use of numerals. In computation, for example, this level involves working only with numerals to solve math problems. Students with difficulty in math usually need much experience at the concrete and semiconcrete levels before they can use numerals meaningfully.

Traditionally, assessment has focused on the abstract level. However, authorities in mathematics education (Denmark, 1976; Engelhardt, 1976; Reisman, 1982; Underhill, 1976) maintain that assessment should not be limited to the abstract level. These researchers stress that the goal of assessment is to determine the learner's ability to relate to arithmetic computation in a meaningful way. To do this they suggest using tasks at each of the levels. Unfortunately, commercial instruments for assessing understanding at the three levels are few. Only the *Sequential Assessment of Mathematics Inventory* (Reisman, 1984) includes a concrete materials kit that contains manipulative materials for testing math at the concrete level. Teachers must realize that available tests are primarily limited to items at the abstract level. These tests are useful mainly in helping to determine the student's level of achievement and general area of weakness. Once the problem area is identified, the teacher may use informal assessment techniques at the concrete level to determine the instruction necessary for teaching specific concepts and facts.

■ Organizing a Math Curriculum

A math curriculum for students with learning problems includes the skills and concepts fundamental to computation. These skills typically follow a sequence that begins with number readiness and proceeds with addition, subtraction, multiplication, division, fractions, percent, and decimals. Also, within the area of numeration and place value, the basic math concepts of computation are presented throughout the K–6 period. Paralleling the emphasis on the basic computation areas is the coverage of critical skills in such areas as geometry, time, money, measurement, and estimation. In addition to being important for real-life functioning, these skill areas provide students with meaningful opportunities to apply computational skills.

Silbert, Carnine, and Stein (1981) maintain that maximum student learning occurs when two or more skills from unrelated areas (i.e., areas dissimilar enough to keep from confusing the student) are presented concurrently. For example, instead of presenting all addition, then subtraction, and then multiplication, Silbert et al. suggest teaching addition and another area (e.g., time or geometry) simultaneously. Most basals are organized in this way; however, as mentioned earlier, they present too many areas for the problem learner, so it is necessary to delineate the most essential skills for a corrective or remedial math program. Parallel instruction breaks up the drill-practice routine of computation, and in many instances (e.g., story problems, money, time) it provides the student with the opportunity to generalize his or her computational skills. Thus, concurrent skill instruction can facilitate motivation, increase generalization, and develop functional skills.

■ Sequencing Math Instruction

Designing a math program to ensure efficient learning of essential skills involves the melding of levels of learning, sufficient practice activities, and coverage of concepts, computation, and skill applications. Moreover, this must be accomplished in a manner that fosters student motivation and incorporates concurrent instruction in two or more dissimilar skill areas.

The teaching sequence in Figure 6-1 presents a framework to show how the numerous components of a math program are integrated. The sequence features two strands. The computational/concept strand rep-

FIGURE 6-1 Mathematics Teaching Sequence

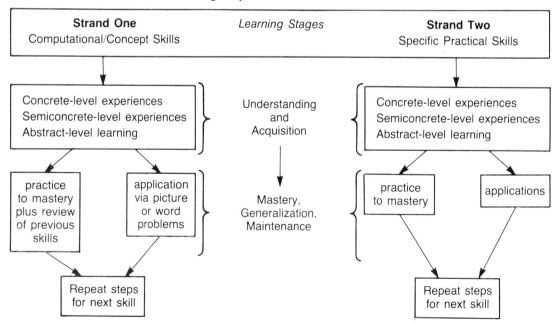

resents that portion of the curriculum that focuses on essential computational skills and concepts, whereas strand two covers skills in the areas of geometry, money, time, and measurement. Strand two skills are dissimilar from strand one in that they do not concurrently involve the computational skill being covered in strand one. Thus computations in strand two are those that have been previously learned and are being applied to new practical skill areas.

Both strands follow the same learning stages. The concrete- and semiconcrete-level experiences focus on teaching students to understand mathematics content. This understanding promotes the acquisition of the skill at the abstract level, the level at which memorization must occur. Much practice is usually needed for students to master skills at the abstract level. This is especially true in the computational skill strand, in which extensive practice is necessary before mastery is obtained.

An understanding of the organization of the math curriculum and sequencing of instruction helps with assessment. It enables the diagnostician to target the learning level and learning stage of a student on a specific skill and generate very specific instructional objectives. Moreover, the concept of parallel instruction provides the diagnostician with a framework for assessing several skills that may need corrective instruction.

■ Skill Mastery

The assessment process focuses on determining which skills have been mastered and locating the skill area in which mastery is lacking. The determination of skill mastery may be accomplished by using percent correct and rate correct and incorrect. If an untimed criterion approach is used, it is a good practice to include three items for each skill and 67% or 100% as a criterion for mastery (Underhill, Uprichard, & Heddens, 1980). Most commercial tests do not adequately sample a specific skill. Including three items per skill helps to control for carelessness and provides an adequate test sample.

For teachers who prefer to use timed probes, a probe for each skill is constructed, and a criterion is established in terms of correct and incorrect responses per minute. To obtain a valid performance, each probe should be administered at least three times. The highest rate from the three samples is used for determining the criterion. From analyzing proficiency rates, it appears that 50 to 60 correct digits per minute with no errors is a useful criterion for most arithmetic skills. Students' increasing use of hand-held calculators needs to be considered in establishing proficiency criteria. Current rates are based on see–write tasks, and proficiency criteria are needed for using hand-held calculators.

■ **Mathematics Skill Network**

A math skill network (scope and sequence) is a comprehensive resource for assessing math progress. This section presents two math skill networks. The first one (Table 6–1) displays the sequencing of math skills across grade levels. Although it does not include all skills covered in a basal math program, it is comprehensive and enables the teacher to examine a sequence of skills taught at each grade level. Moreover, since it combines concepts, computation, and application skills, it serves as an example of the parallel teaching of different skills. The precise ordering of many of the skills varies across basal math programs. Thus, sequencing of some skills is arbitrary and left up to teacher preference.

TABLE 6–1   Mathematics Scope-and-Sequence Skills List by Grade Levels

Kindergarten

Position concepts: above, below, in, out, on, off, left, right, top, bottom, middle, front, back
Classification: identity, color, size, shape, patterns, size
One to One: as many as, using tallies to count events or objects
Comparing: more than, less than, same
Counting: 0 to 5
Ordinal numbers: first, second, third
Geometry: box, ball, square, circle, triangle, rectangle, inside, outside
Measurement: comparing larger, smaller, taller, shorter, longer, same length
Time: daytime, nighttime, sequence, duration, clock, calendar
Money: value of penny, identifying nickel and dime, reading price tags, determining if enough money
Writing numerals: 0 to 10
Combining sets: picture addition stories
Sums to 5: picture addition stories
Separating sets: picture subtraction stories

First Grade

Numeration: numbers and values 1 to 10
Matching and joining sets
Sums to 6
Addition properties: commutative property of addition, zero property
Ordinal numbers: first to fifth
Sums 7 to 10
Families of facts: sum of 1, 2, 3, 4, 5, 6, 7, 8, 9 families: e.g., sum of 7 family is
    $0 + 7, 7 + 0, 6 + 1, 1 + 6, 5 + 2, 2 + 5, 3 + 4, 4 + 3$
Addition sentences: completing, writing, and choosing

TABLE 6-1 *(continued)*

Finding missing addends (e.g., 4 + _ = 7)
Subtracting from sums or minuends to 6
Subtracting from sums or minuends to 10
Subtraction sentences: completing, writing, and choosing
Money: subtracting prices, determining how much money (pennies, nickels, dimes)
Numeration/place value: counting and writing tens and ones, recognizing numbers 10 to 90, order of numbers to 100
Counting: one more than, less than, counting by 2's, 3's, 5's, and 10's, skip-counting
Time: calendar, hour, half hour, quarter hour
Sums 11 to 18
Subtracting from sums or minuends 11 to 18
Families of facts: sum of 11–18 families
Adding three addends
Money: adding and subtracting with money
Geometry: rectangle, square, circle, triangle
Measurement: linear—comparing lengths, arbitrary units, metric units (centimeter, meter), customary units (inch, foot, yard); capacity—metric units (liter), customary units (cup, pint, quart); weight—kilogram; temperature—thermometer scales
Addition of 2d* + 1d without regrouping
Addition of 2d + 2d without regrouping
Subtraction of 2d − 1d without regrouping
Subtraction of 2d − 2d without regrouping
Fractions: recognizing equal parts or shapes, 1/2's, 1/3's, 1/4's, finding 1/2 of set
Story problems: involving addition and subtraction

Second Grade

Numeration/place value: grouping tens and ones, order to 100, hundreds, tens, and ones
Equations with missing numbers (7 + _ = 14, _ + 3 = 13, 6 + 5 = _)
Three or more addends: sums to 18
Addition of 2d numbers with regrouping
Subtraction of 2d numbers with regrouping
Story problems: using addition and subtraction
Fractions: identifying and writing fractional parts, dividing shapes in half
Time: writing times, 15-minute intervals, 5-minute intervals, telling time, calendar—earlier or later
Geometry: solid shapes, polygons, congruent figures, symmetry
Measurement: linear—nearest inch, perimeter in centimeters; area—square units, by counting; capacity—millileter; volume—by counting; weight—customary units (pound, ounce); temperature—Celsius, Fahrenheit
Multiples facts: multiples of 2, 3, 4, 5; factors 2, 3, 4, 5, 0, 1; commutative property of multiplication

(continued)

TABLE 6-1 *(continued)*

Numeration: order of numbers to 1000, 100 more than, 100 less than
Subtraction of 3d − 2d with regrouping
Subtraction of 3d − 3d with regrouping
Story problems: using 3d numbers and two-step problems
Money: half dollar, using ¢ and $, adding and subtracting money, writing
amounts, e.g.,

$$
\begin{array}{cc}
\$4.63 & \$6.74 \\
+\,\$2.12 & -\,\$3.41 \\
\hline
\$6.75 & \$3.33
\end{array}
$$

Third Grade

Adding zero property
Rounding to nearest 10 or 100
Estimating sums: to three digits
Adding larger numbers: multi-digit + multi-digit
Addition as a check for subtraction
Subtraction with regrouping more than once and with zero in minuend
Estimating differences: to 3 digits
Subtraction of 4d numbers with regrouping
Story problems: using addition and subtraction
Multiplication facts: 6–9, zero and one properties, order property
Multiplication of 2d × 1d without regrouping
Division facts: 2d ÷ 1d, division equation, division and sets
Story problems: using multiplication and division
Division in vertical format
Multiplication and division related: division by finding the missing factor
Division with remainders
Fractions of a number
Equivalent fractions
Measurement: linear—kilometer, mile, perimeter of polygons by adding inches;
area—square centimeters by counting, square inches by counting; capacity—
gallon; volume—cubic centimeters, cubic inches; mass weight—gram, kilo-
gram; temperature—below zero
Comparing fractions using < and >
Geometry: areas, rectangular solid, segments, end points, sides, diagonals, sym-
metry, points on a grid
Multiplication of 2d × 1d with tens regrouping
Multiplication of 2d × 1d with hundreds regrouping
Multiplication of 3d × 1d without regrouping
Multiplication of 3d × 1d with regrouping
Division of 2d numbers without regrouping: 36 ÷ 3
Division of 2d numbers with regrouping: 51 ÷ 3
Multiplication with addition, subtraction, and division using symbols: 8 × 4 ÷
2 − 2 = __

TABLE 6-1 *(continued)*

Fourth Grade

Rounding to nearest 1000
Numbers to millions
Addition of numbers to six digits
Place value of decimals
Order and grouping properties of multiplication: $(3 \times 2) \times 4 = 24$, $3 \times (2 \times 4)$
    $= 24$
Multiples and common multiples: 36 is a multiple of 6, 36 is a common multiple
    of 6 and 4
Finding missing factors: $4 \times \_ = 36$
Zero as divisor
Story problems: using addition, subtraction, multiplication, and division
Fractions: fractions and sets, equivalent fractions, fractions of a number, nu-
    merator of 1 and more than 1
Reducing fractions
Adding fractions with like denominators
Adding fractions with unlike denominators
Subtracting fractions with like and unlike denominators
Writing mixed numbers as fractions
Changing fractions to mixed numbers
Adding and subtracting mixed numbers
Story problems: using addition and subtraction of fractions
Measurement: linear—decimal measures, perimeter formulas, area formulas; vol-
    ume—by counting, by multiplying; estimating temperature
Multiplication of 3d $\times$ 1d with regrouping
Multiplication of 4d $\times$ 1d with regrouping
Estimating products
Division of 3d number by 1d number with regrouping: including estimation
Division of 4d number by 1d number with regrouping: including estimation
Multiplication as a check for division
Geometry: segments, lines, rays, angles, parallel lines
Multiplication by 10 and multiples of 10
Multiplication by a 2d number: $\begin{array}{r} 24 \\ \times 13 \\ \hline \end{array}$
Division by a 2d number with regrouping: $12\overline{)53}$, $15\overline{)328}$
Decimals: writing and reading decimals to hundredths, place value of decimal
    numbers, adding and subtracting decimals with regrouping
Applications: catalogs and order forms, computing averages

Fifth Grade

Values to billions
Rounding to nearest millions and billions
Roman numerals: I to X
Story problems: using addition and subtraction with fractions and mixed num-
    bers

(continued)

TABLE 6-1 *(continued)*

Least common multiples
Multiplying by 100 and multiples of 10 and 100
Distributive property: (9 × 4) × 3 = _ , 9 × (4 × 3) = _
Multiplication of 3d × 2d with regrouping
Story problems: using multiplication and division with fractions
Factors and common factors
Geometry: vertex, perpendicular lines, corresponding parts, naming angles, protractor, diagonals, measuring angles
Least common denominators
Multiplication and division of fractions
Decimals to thousandths
Rounding to the nearest whole number
Measurement: linear—millimeter, decimeter, nearest 1/16 of an inch, perimeter formulas, curved figures, circumference, area formulas by multiplying, area of triangles, capacity—fluid ounce; volume—rectangular prisms, by counting, by multiplying
Multiplying decimals
Dividing decimals
Story problems: using multiplication and division with decimals
Applications: discounts, sales tax, profits

Sixth Grade

Base two numerals
Place value in metric system
Multiplication: exponents
Prime factorization
Division with 3d numbers
Rounding divisors
Geometry: intersecting lines; acute, right, obtuse angles; parallelogram, rhombus, dexagon, trapezoid, kite
Decimals: finding decimal between two numbers, decimals and money, rounding decimals, multiplying dollars, changing decimals to fractions, multiplying and dividing decimals, repeating decimals
Measurement: linear—relation of metric units to decimal system, adding metric units, adding customary units, area formulas, parallelograms, surface areas of rectangular prisms, cylinders, circle; capacity—metric cup, kiloliter, half-gallon, comparing measures, adding measures; mass weight—milligram
Estimating: time, volume, weight, bar graph
Decimals and percents: converting dollars and cents, multiplying dollars
Story problems: using percent
Applications: stocks, unit pricing, installment buying, checking account

Note: In this table "d" refers to *digit.*
Source: Adapted from *Teaching Students with Learning Problems* (2nd ed.), pp. 502–508, by C. D. Mercer and A. R. Mercer, 1985, Columbus, OH: Charles E. Merrill Publishing Co. Copyright © 1985 by Bell and Howell Co. Reprinted by permission of Charles E. Merrill Pub. Co.

The second skill network (Table 6–2) is organized by specific skill areas in order to allow the teacher to identify a student's progress on a specific skill. This network was developed from a variety of sources including textbooks (Mercer & Mercer, 1985; Underhill, Uprichard, & Heddens, 1980) and basal math programs. Generally, the first skill network (Table 6–1) enables the teacher to survey math skills and note general areas of strengths and weaknesses. The second skill network enables the teacher to assess within a skill area and precisely locate the student's level of progress in that skill.

TABLE 6-2   Mathematics Scope-and-Sequence Skills List by Skill Areas

Addition Hierarchy

Recognizes inequalities of numbers less than 10
Comprehends seriation of numbers less than 10
Recognizes the words *added* and *sum*
Comprehends the "+" sign
Computes sums less than 10 (memorize)
Solves word problems involving computations of sums less than 10
Comprehends place value of ones and tens
Computes sums 10–18, both addends less than 10 (memorize)
Calculates 2d* + 1d without regrouping and 2d + 2d without regrouping
Solves word problems involving computations of 2d + 1d and 2d + 2d without regrouping
Understands place value concerning regrouping tens and ones
Calculates 2d + 1d with regrouping and 2d + 2d with regrouping
Computes 2d + 2d + 2d with sums of ones greater than 20
Comprehends place value of hundreds, tens, and ones
Calculates 3d + 3d without regrouping
Comprehends place value concerning regrouping hundreds and tens
Calculates 3d + 3d with regrouping
Solves word problems involving computations of 2d + 1d or 2d with regrouping and 3d + 3d with and without regrouping
Estimates sums

Subtraction Hierarchy

Finds missing addends (e.g., 4 + _ = 7)
Understands the "−" sign
Uses set separation as model for subtraction
Expresses a related addition statement in subtraction form (e.g., addend + *addend* = sum ⟷ sum − *addend* = addend)
Relates the words *minuend, subtrahend,* and *difference* to sum, *given addend,* and *missing addend*
Learns basic subtraction facts 0–9

(continued)

TABLE 6-2 *(continued)*

Solves word problems involving subtraction facts 0–9
Understands place value of ones and tens
Memorizes basic subtraction facts 0–18
Computes the difference between a two-place whole number (2d) and a one-place whole number (1d) (not a basic fact and no regrouping)
Computes the difference between 2d and 2d with no regrouping
Solves word problems involving computations of 2d − 2d with no regrouping
Computes the difference between 3d and 2d with no regrouping
Computes the difference between 3d and 3d with no regrouping
Computes the difference between two many-digit whole numbers with no regrouping
Computes the difference between 2d and 1d (not a basic fact) with regrouping
Computes the difference between 2d and 2d with regrouping from tens to ones
Computes the difference between 3d and 2d with regrouping from tens to ones
Computes the difference between 3d and 2d with double regrouping
Computes the difference between 3d and 3d with single regrouping
Computes the difference between two many-place whole numbers with several regroupings
Solves word problems involving computations of 3d − 2d and 3d − 3d with and without regrouping
Computes the difference when a zero appears in a single place in the minuend
Computes the difference when zeros appear in the tens and ones place of the minuend
Estimates differences

Multiplication Hierarchy

Recognizes sets as a model for multiplication (number of sets and number of objects in each set)
Recognizes and uses arrays as a model for multiplication; for example,
3
xxx
xxx3
xxx
Comprehends the words *factor* and *product*
Understands the "x" sign
Understands the commutative property of multiplication; for example, $a \times (b + c) = (a \times b) + (a \times c)$ [$a \le 5$, $b \le a$)
Memorizes basic multiplication facts for $a \times b$ ($a \le 5$, $b \le 5$)
Memorizes basic multiplication facts for $a \times b$ ($5 < a < 10$, $b < 10$)
Solves word problems involving multiplication facts
Names the product if one factor is 10, 100, etc.
Expands basic multiplication facts (e.g., 4×3 to 4×30)
Computes 2d × 1d without regrouping
Understands place value of tens, ones, regrouping
Computes $a \times (b + c) = (a \times b) + (a \times c)$ [$a < 10$, $a \times (b + c) < 100$ with regrouping] (e.g., $6 \times (10 + 3) = \_ + \_ = \_$)

TABLE 6-2 *(continued)*

Calculates 2d × 1d with regrouping, product < 100
Understands place value of hundreds, tens, ones
Calculates 2d × 1d with regrouping, product > 100
Calculates 2d × 2d with regrouping
Calculates 3d × 1d with regrouping
Calculates 3d × 2d with regrouping
Solves word problems involving computations of 2d × 1d, 2d × 2d, 3d × 1d, and 3d × 2d with and without regrouping

Division Hierarchy

Finds missing factor (e.g., 6 × _ = 42)
Uses symbols that indicate division (2)4 , 4 ÷ 2, 4/2)
Expresses a related multiplication sentence as a division sentence (product + factor = factor)
Calculates division facts with one as divisor (e.g., 6 ÷ 1)
Calculates basic division facts (a ÷ b where a ≤ 81, b ≤ 9)
Solves word problems involving division facts
Calculates division of a nonzero number by itself (e.g., 9 ÷ 9)
Calculates 1d ÷ 1d with a remainder
Estimates 2d ÷ 1d and computes 2d ÷ 1d with a remainder
Calculates quotients with expanding dividend (e.g., 6 ÷ 3, 60 ÷ 3, 600 ÷ 3)
Estimates 3d ÷ 1d and computes 3d ÷ 1d (e.g., 347 ÷ 6)
Calculates quotient of many-place dividend with a one-place divisor (e.g., 87348 ÷ 4)
Estimates 3d ÷ 2d and computes 3d ÷ 2d where divisor is multiple of 10 (e.g., 864 ÷ 20)
Calculates quotient with divisors of 100, 1000, etc. (e.g., 8679 ÷ 1000)
Estimates 3d ÷ 2d and computes 3d ÷ 2d (e.g., 489 ÷ 17)
Calculates quotient of many-place dividend and many-place divisor (e.g., 487876 ÷ 3897)
Solves word problems involving computations of 1d ÷ 1d, 2d ÷ 1d, 3d ÷ 1d, and 3d ÷ 2d

Fraction Hierarchy

Readiness Areas

Divides regions into subregions that are equivalent
Expresses 1 in many different ways
Uses the terms *fraction, fraction bar, numerator,* and *denominator*
Models, on the number line, equivalent fractions
Produces sets of equivalent fractions
Renames fractions in simplest form
Converts improper fractions to mixed numerals
Converts mixed numerals to improper fractions

(continued)

TABLE 6-2 *(continued)*

Develops concept of least common denominator using the concept of least common multiple

Compares fractional numbers

Develops concept of least common denominator using the concept of greatest common factor

Addition

Calculates sums less than 1, same denominator

Calculates sums of mixed numerals, no regrouping, same denominator

Calculates sums between 1 and 2, same denominator, regrouping

Calculates sums of mixed numeral and nonunit fraction, regrouping, same denominator (e.g., $4\frac{2}{5} + \frac{4}{5}$)

Calculates sums of mixed numerals with regrouping, same denominator (e.g., $7\frac{3}{5} + 1\frac{4}{5}$)

Calculates sums less than 1, different denominators

Calculates sums of mixed numerals, no regrouping, different denominators

Calculates sums of mixed numerals, regrouping, different denominators

Calculates sums of three nonunit fractions, different denominators

Solves word problems requiring addition of fractions

Subtraction

Calculates differences between two fractions with like denominators without regrouping, then with regrouping

Calculates differences between two fractions with unlike but related denominators without regrouping, then with regrouping

Calculates differences between two fractions with unlike and unrelated denominators without regrouping, then with regrouping

Solves word problems requiring subtraction of fractions

Multiplication

Calculates product of whole number × unit fraction, product < 1 (e.g., $2 \times \frac{1}{4} = \_$)

Computes product of whole number × nonunit fraction, product < 1 (e.g., $3 \times \frac{2}{5} = \_$)

Gives fraction names for one (e.g., $1 = \frac{?}{6}$)

Solves regrouping problem by writing fraction as mixed numeral, $1 < a < 2$ (e.g., $\frac{8}{5} = \_$)

Computes product of whole number × nonunit fraction, $1 < \text{product} < 2$ (e.g., $4 \times \frac{3}{5} = \_$)

Computes product of unit fraction × unit fraction (e.g., $\frac{1}{5} \times \frac{1}{4} = \_$)

Computes product of nonunit fraction × nonunit fraction (e.g., $\frac{1}{3} \times \frac{4}{5} = \_$)

Computes $a \times (b + c) = (a \times b) + (a \times c)$, a and b are whole numbers, c is a unit fraction, no regrouping (e.g., $3 \times (2 + \frac{3}{4}) = \_ + \_$)

Computes $a \times (b + c) = (a \times b) + (a \times c)$, a and b are whole numbers, c is a nonunit fraction, regrouping (e.g., $4 \times \frac{3}{5} = 4 \times (3 + \frac{4}{5}) = \_ + \_ = \_$)

TABLE 6-2 *(continued)*

Computes product of nonunit fraction × mixed numeral using improper fractions—e.g., $\frac{1}{6}$ × $2\frac{2}{3}$ (change to improper fractions)

Computes product of mixed numeral × mixed numeral using improper fractions—e.g., $3\frac{3}{4}$ × $1\frac{5}{8}$ (use improper fractions)

Solves word problems involving computations of fraction × fraction, fraction × mixed numeral, and mixed numeral × mixed numeral

Division

Calculates quotient of 1 ÷ unit fraction (e.g., $1 \div \frac{1}{5}$)

Calculates quotient of whole number ÷ nonunit fraction, 1 < whole number < 10—e.g., $2 - \frac{3}{5}$ (use repeated subtraction and remainder as fractional part)

Calculates $\frac{1}{a} \div \frac{1}{b}$ where a < b (common denominator approach) (e.g., $\frac{1}{2} \div \frac{1}{5}$)

Calculates $\frac{a}{b} \div \frac{c}{d}$ (common denominator approach) (e.g., $\frac{3}{5} \div \frac{2}{6}$)

Calculates quotient of two mixed numerals (common denominator approach) (e.g., $2\frac{1}{3} \div 1\frac{2}{5}$)

Solves word problems involving computations of whole number ÷ fraction, fraction ÷ fraction, and mixed numeral ÷ mixed numeral

Decimal Hierarchy

Readiness Areas

Generates decimal place value by rewriting fractions with denominators of powers of 10

Recognizes decimal place value to millionths place

Reads and writes rational numbers expressed as decimals

Converts fractions to decimals

Models rational numbers expressed as decimals using the number line

Produces equivalent decimals by appending zeros

Addition

Computes the sum of two rational numbers expressed as decimals having the same place value

Computes the sum of two rational numbers expressed as decimals having different place values

Computes the sum of more than two rational numbers expressed as decimals having different place values

Solves word problems requiring addition of rational numbers expressed as decimals

Subtraction

Computes the difference between two rational numbers expressed as decimals having the same place value (without regrouping and with regrouping)

(continued)

TABLE 6-2 *(continued)*

Computes the difference between two rational numbers expressed as decimals having different place values (without regrouping and with regrouping)
Solves word problems requiring subtraction of rational numbers expressed as decimals

Multiplication

Computes the product of two rational numbers expressed as decimals when it is necessary to append zeroes to the left of a nonzero digit as decimal holders
Computes the product of more than two rational numbers expressed as decimals
Solves word problems requiring multiplication of rational numbers expressed as decimals

Division

Computes the quotient of rational numbers expressed as decimals when the divisor is a whole number
Computes the quotient of any two rational numbers expressed as decimals by using the division algorithm
Solves word problems requiring division of rational numbers expressed as decimals

Percents

Recognizes the symbol for percent (%) as a fraction and as a decimal
Rewrites percents as decimals and fractions for percents less than 100% and then for percents equal to or greater than 100%
Rewrites fractions or decimals as percents
Solves word problems requiring percents

Money Hierarchy

Recognizes coins
Identifies relative value of coins
Makes change for amounts up to $1.00
Identifies and uses money notation
Writes amounts of money
Identifies currency and makes change for currency
Computes operations involving money
Solves examples and word problems involving money

Time Hierarchy

Associates the face of the clock with the number line through 12 for hours
Associates the face of the clock with the number line through 60 for minutes
Tells time by the hour
Tells time by the minute
Comprehends the difference between A.M. and P.M.

TABLE 6-2 *(continued)*

Writes times
Computes operations involving time measures
Solves examples and word problems involving time

Measurement Hierarchy

Comparisons

Compares larger, smaller, same length, longer, shorter, taller, tallest, same shape, more, less, heavier

Linear

Compares lengths
Measures with nonstandard units
Measures with metric units (centimeter, meter)
Measures with customary units (inch, foot, yard)
Estimates length
Measures to nearest inch
Understands perimeter
Understands kilometer and mile
Measures perimeter of polygons by counting inches
Uses decimal measures
Uses perimeter formulas
Measures with millimeter and decimeter
Measures to the 1/16th of an inch
Uses perimeter formulas for curved figures, circumference
Understands relation of metric units to decimal system
Adds metric measures
Adds customary measures

Area

Computes square units by counting
Computes metric units, square centimeters, by counting
Computes customary units, square inches, by counting
Solves area formulas for squares and rectangles by multiplying
Solves area formulas for triangles
Solves area formulas for parallelograms
Finds surface area of rectangular prisms, cylinders, and circles

Capacity

Uses metric units (liter)
Uses customary units (cup, pint, quart)
Uses milliliters
Uses gallons

(continued)

TABLE 6-2 *(continued)*

Uses fluid ounces
Measures using metric cup, kiloliter, and half-gallon
Compares capacity measures
Adds metric measures
Adds customary measures

Weight

Uses kilograms
Uses customary units (pounds, ounces)
Finds mass weight using grams
Finds mass weight using milligrams

Temperature

Uses thermometer scale
Understands Celsius degrees
Understands Fahrenheit degrees
Measures below zero
Estimates temperature
Uses temperature chart

Volume

Computes volume by counting
Computes volume in cubic centimeters
Computes volume in cubic inches
Computes volume by multiplying
Computes volume of rectangular prisms by counting and by multiplying

*Note: "d" refers to "digit."

Source: Based on material from Mercer & Mercer (1985), Underhill, Uprichard, & Heddons (1980), and basal math programs.

SELECTING AND ADMINISTERING
AN ASSESSMENT PROCEDURE

■ ■   The selection of assessment procedures and instruments is directly related to the purpose and frequency of the assessment. It is often impractical for teachers to conduct elaborate testing throughout the school year, but it is reasonable to expect an initial assessment, periodic assessments of global progress, and daily/weekly evaluations of student progress on specific skills.

■ Periodic Assessment

Numerous assessment instruments are available for conducting periodic evaluations. One of the major tasks in conducting evaluations is selecting the most appropriate instruments and procedures from among the many available formal and informal tests.

☐ *Formal Tests*

Formal arithmetic assessment refers to the use of published tests. These tests are standardized and norm-referenced and include both survey and diagnostic instruments.

Mercer and Mercer (1985) note that standardized math tests are usually classified into two categories: survey or achievement, and diagnostic. Survey tests cover a range of arithmetic skills and are designed to provide an estimate of the student's general level of achievement. They yield a single score which is compared to standardized norms and converted into a grade- or age-equivalent score. Survey tests are useful in screening students to identify those who need additional assessment. Diagnostic tests, in contrast, usually cover a narrower range of content and are designed to assess the student's performance in specific arithmetic skills. Diagnostic tests focus on determining the student's strengths and weaknesses. Several of the commonly used survey tests and diagnostic tests are listed in the Appendix.

☐ *Informal Procedures*

Informal assessment enables teachers to sample specific skills to determine the student's understanding of arithmetic concepts at the concrete, semiconcrete, and abstract levels. Although most informal tests used for periodic assessment are teacher constructed, they may also include tests from basal math programs and adaptations of basal and criterion-referenced commercial tests. Thus, basal tests and criterion-referenced math tests are often good sources for developing informal measures. The overall best source for constructing informal measures is a comprehensive scope-and-sequence skills network (see tables 6–1 and 6–2).

CRITERION-REFERENCED TESTS Criterion-referenced achievement or inventory tests usually cover several academic areas. Each of these areas is further subdivided into skill categories. Of all available published tests, criterion-referenced diagnostic tests are the most suited for identifying specific arithmetic problems. Several of the most often recommended criterion-referenced diagnostic tests are included in Table 6–3.

TABLE 6-3   Criterion-Referenced Tests in Mathematics

Test	Grade	Math Skills Measured
Brigance Diagnostic Comprehensive Inventory of Basic Skills (Brigance, 1983)	K–9	readiness skills, number facts, computation of whole numbers, fractions and mixed numbers, decimals, percents, word problems, metrics, and math vocabulary
Brigance Diagnostic Inventory of Essential Skills (Brigance, 1981)	4–12	functional and applied math skills
Classroom Learning Screening Manual (Koenig & Kunzelmann, 1980)	K–6	precomputational number skills, addition facts, subtraction facts, multiplication facts, and division facts
Enright Diagnostic Inventory of Basic Arithmetic Skills (Enright, 1983)	K–8	computational ability in a specific skill area, basic facts in addition, subtraction, multiplication, and division, and error patterns in computation
Diagnostic Tests and Self-Helps in Arithmetic (Brueckner, 1955)	3–8	computation of whole numbers, fractions, decimals, percent, and operations in measurement

SURVEY TESTS   To identify specific math problem areas, the teacher may construct a survey test with items at several levels of difficulty across numerous skill areas. A four-step process details how to develop and use this type of test.

1. Select a hierarchy that includes the content areas to be assessed. This hierarchy may come from a basal series, a curriculum guide, or a textbook. (See also tables 6–1 and 6–2, two types of scope-and-sequence skills lists.)
2. Decide on what span of skills needs to be evaluated. Since a hierarchy includes a wide range of skills, the teacher must select which range of skills needs to be evaluated with an individual

student. This is done by examining the student's performance on published tests and by analyzing the arithmetic curriculum by grade level. In deciding on the span, the teacher should begin with items that are easy for the student and proceed to items that are difficult.

3. Construct items for each skill within the range selected. A survey test is designed to assess the student's understanding of concepts and computational skills and their applications. For an untimed test, it is a good practice to use three items and establish 67% as criterion.

4. Score the test and interpret the student's performance. The teacher starts with the easiest skill items and applies the "two out of three" 67% criterion. At the point where the criterion is not achieved, the teacher analyzes the student's performance to determine where further specific skill assessment is needed.

A sample survey test for fourth graders, presented in Figure 6–2, is developed from the comprehensive scope-and-sequence skills list presented earlier in Table 6–1. By using a scope-and-sequence skills list, the teacher can develop a survey test to assess any span of skills within it. The survey test in this chapter features selected skills from the third-grade sequence.

A survey math test primarily includes abstract items. Before skill mastery is obtained a student must demonstrate proficiency at the abstract level. Thus, abstract-level items serve as a good indicator for determining a student's progress. Word problems are used to ascertain if the student understands the application of computational skills. In analyzing word problems, it is also important to consider the student's reading skills. For example, if a student misses all word problems, it is helpful to ask him or her to read the problems aloud to check reading. In the survey format, word problems typically cover a cluster of computational skills that help locate the area of difficulty (e.g., multiplication). However, further assessment may be needed to pinpoint the problem (e.g., two digit times one digit with regrouping)

Much flexibility is needed in designing survey tests. A teacher may wish to omit or include many word problems or limit the survey to computational skills only (e.g., multiplication or division). Silbert, Carnine, and Stein (1981) provide survey tests for each grade level up to sixth grade. Other survey tests include skill items that span across several grade levels. It is often helpful to design survey tests by using a scope-and-sequence skills list from the basal math program that the student is using. Also, survey tests may be administered individually or to groups. Once the survey test results are analyzed (see Figure 6–3), the teacher determines which skill areas need further assessment.

FIGURE 6-2 Survey Test for Beginning Fourth Graders

1.   3167
   +5325

2.   4728
   +3762

3.   6974
   + 367

4.   624
   −338

5.   708
   −259

6.   501
   −238

7.   8143
   −3576

8.   6093
   −5640

9.   4762
   −1683

10. 4632 dogs   How many animals?
    873 cats   _____

11. 402 cookies   How many left?
    237 cookies sold   _____

12. David had $8.16. He spent $3.28 at the store. How much money does he have left?

13. A farmer had 4651 chickens. He sold 1572 of them. How many does he have left?

14.   9
   ×8

15.   9
   ×6

16.   8
   ×7

17. 27 ÷ 3 = ___

18. 8 ÷ 2 = ___

19. 3)9

20. 5)13

21. 4)34

22. 7)64

23. There are 7 oranges in one box. Sam has 4 boxes. How many oranges does Sam have?

24. Rena has 32 oranges. There are 4 oranges in a box. How many boxes does Rena have?

25. $\frac{1}{3}$ of 6 = ___
   ∅∅∅
   ∅

26. $\frac{1}{4}$ of 8 = ___
   ∅∅∅∅
   ∅∅∅∅

27. $\frac{1}{2}$ of 12 = ___
   ∅∅∅∅∅∅
   ∅∅∅∅∅∅

28. $\frac{1}{2} = \frac{}{4}$

29. $\frac{3}{4} = \frac{}{8}$

30. $\frac{3}{5} = \frac{}{15}$

31. Rico had 27¢. He spent 1/3 of it. How much money did Rico spend?

32.   17
   × 4

33.   38
   × 2

34.   14
   × 7

35.   81
   × 3

36.   164
   × 2

37.   141
   × 5

38.   36
   × 4

39.   154
   × 7

40.   173
   × 4

FIGURE 6-2 *(continued)*

41. There are 47 minutes in a period. Cathy goes to school for 6 periods. How many minutes does she go to school?

42. There are 247 dotted lines in one mile of a highway. How many lines are in 6 miles of road?

43. $7 \times 6 \div 2 + 3 =$ ___ **44.** $8 \times 4 + 4 \div 9 =$ ___ **45.** $3 + 2 - 4 =$ ___

46. 3)‾36 **47.** 4)‾48 **48.** 2)‾36

49. 3)‾51 **50.** 4)‾72 **51.** 7)‾84

52. Mike drove 86 miles in 2 hours. How many miles did he average each hour?

53. The teacher had 48 apples and 9 students. She divided the apples evenly among the 9 students. How many apples did each student receive?

54. Round to nearest 1000   **55.** Round to nearest 1000   **56.** Round to nearest 1000
    6784 to ___   4489 to ___   6501 to ___

57.   28 rounds to ___   **58.**   33 rounds to ___   **59.**   376 rounds to ___
    $+53$ rounds to ___ $+47$ rounds to ___ $+133$ rounds to ___
    estimate ___   estimate ___   estimate ___

60.   91 rounds to ___   **61.**   873 rounds to ___   **62.**   439 rounds to ___
    -26 rounds to ___ -279 rounds to ___ -188 rounds to ___
    estimate ___   estimate ___   estimate ___

63. Measure in inches. ___ inches   **64.** Measure in inches. ___ inches

|————————————| |————————|

65. Measure in centimeters. ___ cm   **66.** Measure in centimeters. ___ cm

|————————| |————————————|

67. Give the perimeter.   **68.** Give the perimeter.   **69.** Give the perimeter.

2cm
2cm

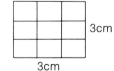
3cm
3cm

<table><tr><td>2in</td></tr><tr><td>4in</td></tr></table>

_____   _____   _____

70. Give the *area* of the figure in #67. _____ square centimeters

71. Give the *area* of the figure in #68. _____ square centimeters

(continued)

FIGURE 6-2 *(continued)*

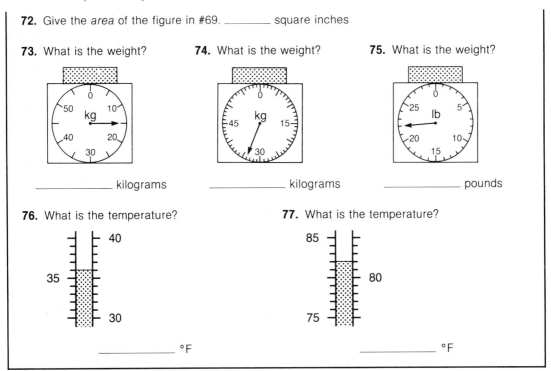

72. Give the *area* of the figure in #69. _____ square inches

73. What is the weight?

_____ kilograms

74. What is the weight?

_____ kilograms

75. What is the weight?

_____ pounds

76. What is the temperature?

_____ °F

77. What is the temperature?

_____ °F

SPECIFIC SKILL ASSESSMENT   Through the survey math assessment the skill area or areas that need further assessment are identified. At this point the scope-and-sequence list by skill areas is useful for designing specific skill tests. These tests may be developed in any one or several areas (e.g., addition, division, measurement, money). Figure 6–4 features a specific skill test in division. By giving a test of this type the teacher is able to determine precisely at what point the student is functioning in the scope and sequence of a specific skill. In Figure 6–5, an analysis form for the specific skill test in Figure 6–4 is presented.

Once the specific problem area is located, it is helpful to determine the student's mastery of the facts in the respective mathematical operation. Since proficiency in facts occurs over a period of time and overlaps or parallels the development of other computational skills, it is a good practice to test fact proficiency through the use of timed probes.

Once the skill problem area is identified, an assessment of the student's understanding of the skill is helpful. This involves determining the student's level of understanding within the concrete, semiconcrete, and abstract sequence of understanding.

FIGURE 6-3 Analysis Form for Survey Test (Figure 6-2)

Name _____ Date _____

	TEST			PERFORMANCE		
Item Number	Area	Skill	Grade Level (semester)	Criterion	Comments	
1–3	addition	multidigit (2d* and 3d) with regrouping	3(1)			
4–6	subtraction	3d − 3d with regrouping and zero in minuend	3(1)			
7–9	subtraction	4d − 4d with regrouping	3(1)			
10–13	word problem	multidigit addition and subtraction with regrouping	3(1)			
14–16	multiplication	facts	3(1)			
17–19	division	facts	3(1)			
20–22	division	2d ÷ 1d with remainder	3(2)			
23–24	word problem	multiplication and division facts	3(2)			
25–27	fractions	fractional part of number—quantity	3(2)			
28–30	fractions	equivalent fractions	3(2)			
31	word problem	fractional part of number	3(2)			
32–34	multiplication	2d × 1d with tens regrouping	3(2)			
35–37	multiplication	2d × 1d with hundreds regrouping	3(2)			

(continued)

FIGURE 6-3 *(continued)*

	TEST			PERFORMANCE	
Item Number	Area	Skill	Grade Level (semester)	Criterion	Comments
38–40	multiplication	2d and 3d × 1d with two regroupings	3(2)		
41–42	word problem	2d and 3d × 1d with regrouping	3(2)		
43–45	mixed opera-tions	mixed operations with symbols	3(2)		
46–48	division	2d ÷ 1d without regrouping (not a fact)	3(2)		
49–51	division	2d ÷ 1d with regrouping	3(2)		
52–53	word problem	2d ÷ 1d with and without regrouping	3(2)		
54–56	numeration	round to nearest 100	3(1)		
57–59	numeration	round and estimate sums to three digits	3(1)		
60–62	numeration	round and estimate differences to three digits	3(1)		
63–66	measurement	measuring in inches and centimeters	3(2)		
67–69	measurement	measuring perimeters	3(2)		
70–72	measurement	computing area by counting	3(2)		
73–75	measurement	readng scale weight in kilograms and pounds	3(2)		
76–77	measurement	reading thermometer in °F	3(2)		

*Note: "d" refers to "digit."

244

FIGURE 6-4   Specific Skill Test: Division with Whole Numbers

1. Identify symbols for division by circling problems that require division.

$$\begin{array}{c}4\\+3\end{array}\qquad\qquad 7\times3\qquad\qquad 6\div2\qquad\qquad 7-4\qquad\qquad \dfrac{6}{2}$$

2. Write related division sentence.
   $6\times4=24\qquad\qquad 6\times6=48\qquad\qquad 6\times3=18$

3. $1\overline{)9}$ $\qquad\qquad$ $1\overline{)1}$ $\qquad\qquad$ $1\overline{)4}$

4. $4\overline{)36}$ $\qquad\qquad$ $7\overline{)42}$ $\qquad\qquad$ $8\overline{)56}$

5. $9\overline{)9}$ $\qquad\qquad$ $27\overline{)27}$ $\qquad\qquad$ $1\overline{)1}$

6. $3\overline{)8}$ $\qquad\qquad$ $5\overline{)6}$ $\qquad\qquad$ $2\overline{)7}$
   $8\overline{)76}$ $\qquad\qquad$ $4\overline{)31}$ $\qquad\qquad$ $3\overline{)17}$

7. $2\overline{)8}$ $\qquad\qquad$ $2\overline{)80}$ $\qquad\qquad$ $2\overline{)800}$
   $3\overline{)6}$ $\qquad\qquad$ $3\overline{)60}$ $\qquad\qquad$ $3\overline{)600}$
   $4\overline{)8}$ $\qquad\qquad$ $4\overline{)80}$ $\qquad\qquad$ $4\overline{)800}$

8. $8\overline{)638}$ $\qquad\qquad$ $4\overline{)341}$ $\qquad\qquad$ $3\overline{)262}$

9. $7\overline{)47,863}$ $\qquad\qquad$ $6\overline{)2749}$ $\qquad\qquad$ $3\overline{)568,287}$

10. $40\overline{)761}$ $\qquad\qquad$ $30\overline{)870}$ $\qquad\qquad$ $10\overline{)964}$

11. $100\overline{)784}$ $\qquad\qquad$ $100\overline{)5370}$ $\qquad\qquad$ $100\overline{)673}$
    $1000\overline{)5486}$ $\qquad\qquad$ $1000\overline{)88,380}$ $\qquad\qquad$ $1000\overline{)7429}$

12. $27\overline{)684}$ $\qquad\qquad$ $39\overline{)971}$ $\qquad\qquad$ $13\overline{)8973}$

13. $648\overline{)78,743}$ $\qquad\qquad$ $3645\overline{)100,087}$ $\qquad\qquad$ $247\overline{)8964}$

SPECIFIC SKILL ASSESSMENT: LEVELS OF UNDERSTANDING   Specific skill assessment is helpful in determining specific instructional objectives that relate to the student's understanding level. It helps teachers avoid the common mistake of having students memorize abstract math operations or facts before they understand the concepts. Since most commercial tests and basal tests do not include concrete-level assessment, the teacher has limited resources for designing items at the concrete level.

FIGURE 6-5   Analysis Form for Specific Skill Test (Figure 6-4)

Item	Skill	Performance (%)	Comments
1	identify symbols for division		
2	express related multiplication sentence as division sentence		
3	division facts involving 1 as divisor		
4	division facts		
5	division of nonzero number by itself		
6	1d* ÷ 1d with regrouping; 2d ÷ 1d with regrouping		
7	quotients with expanding dividend		
8	3d ÷ 1d with regrouping		
9	multidigit ÷ 1d		
10	3d ÷ multiple of 10 divisor		
11	multidigit ÷ multiple of 100 and 1000		
12	3d ÷ 2d		
13	multidigit ÷ multidigit		

*Note: "d" refers to "digit."

The examples that follow should help the teacher develop tests in specific skill areas. The teacher interested in a more detailed discussion of this type of assessment should consult Reisman (1977, 1982) and Underhill et al. (1980).

Skill: Addition Facts (0–18): Example 7 + 5

Concrete level: Redistribute blocks to show tens and ones and then write the sum.

Student work:

Semiconcrete level: Circle tens and write sum.

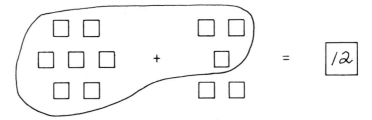

Abstract level: Write sum.

$$\begin{array}{r} 7 \\ +5 \\ \hline \end{array}$$

Skill: Subtraction Operation with Regrouping: Example 32 − 15

Concrete level: Write difference or missing addend by rearranging blocks and use string to show work. (Let [   ] = 1 ten and □ = 1 one.)

Student work:

= /7

(One ten block is broken into 10 unit blocks; then the known addend is circled. The blocks outside the string sum to the missing addend or difference.)

Semiconcrete level: Write difference or missing addend and show work with slashes.

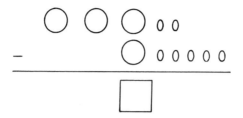

Student work:

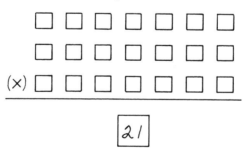

Abstract level: Write difference or missing addend.

$$\begin{array}{r} 32 \\ -15 \\ \hline \end{array}$$

Skill: Basic Multiplication Facts: Example 3 × 7

Concrete level: **a.** Write product.

☐ ☐ ☐ ☐ ☐ ☐ ☐

☐ ☐ ☐ ☐ ☐ ☐ ☐

(×) ☐ ☐ ☐ ☐ ☐ ☐ ☐

$$\boxed{21}$$

b. Use blocks to show 3 × 7 matrix.

Semiconcrete level: Write product.

× × × × × ×

× × × × × ×

(×) × × × × × × ×

$$\boxed{21}$$

Abstract level: Write product.

$$\begin{array}{r} 3 \\ \times 7 \\ \hline \end{array}$$

Skill: Basic Division Facts: Example 16 ÷ 4

Concrete level: Write quotient. Use strings to show work.

Student work:

(tape on table or desk)

Semiconcrete level: Write quotient. Circle sets to show work.

Student work:

Abstract level: Write quotient.

$$4\overline{)16}$$

Skill: Addition of Fractions with like Denominators: Example 1/5 + 1/5

Concrete level: Let [ ] = 1 and [ ] = 1/5. Write sum of 1/5 + 1/5 and show work with blocks.

Student work:

Semiconcrete level: Display the sum of 1/5 + 1/5 by shading in the squares.

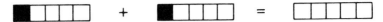

Abstract level: Write sum.

$$1/5 + 1/5 = \underline{\hspace{1cm}}$$

ERROR ANALYSIS   The error patterns of each student must be considered. However, it is also helpful to examine the research on types of errors that many students of different grades make. In a study of the computational errors of third graders, Roberts (1968) identified four error categories:

1. *Wrong operation.* For example, the student adds when he or she should subtract.
2. *Obvious computational error.* The student uses the correct operation but makes an error in recalling a basic number fact.
3. *Defective algorithm.* An *algorithm* includes the specific steps used to compute a math problem. It is defective if it does not deliver the correct answer. For example, if the child adds 26 + 14 by adding each number without regard for place value—that is, "2 + 6 + 1 + 4 = 13"—he or she is using a defective algorithm, because the correct answer is 40. When a defective algorithm is the only error, the pupil is using the correct operation and recalling the basic facts.
4. *Random response.* In a random response, no apparent relationship exists between the problem-solving process and the problem. For example, random responding may include guesses that do not even involve estimates.

Roberts (1968) notes that careless computational errors and poor recall of addition and multiplication facts were found with the same frequency in all levels of ability. Random responses and use of an incorrect operation occurred frequently with students of low ability. While random responses accounted for the most errors in low-ability students, defective algorithm techniques accounted for the most errors of pupils in the other three ability levels. In a study of seventh graders' errors in computation, Lankford (1972) reports that many errors were due to the use of defective algorithms. In a study of subtraction errors of learning-disabled students, Frank, Logan, and Martin (1982) found that systematic error patterns were more common than random errors.

Determining the cause of an error is very important because the remediation procedure (i.e., instructional objective) is influenced by the cause. If a student misses items because of basic fact errors, the teaching plan consists of either providing practice in the respective facts, increasing motivation, and/or determining the level of understanding of the operation. However, if a student misses problems because of a faulty algorithm, instruction consists of reteaching the algorithm.

Howell and Kaplan (1980) provide the following guidelines for conducting an error analysis:

1. Collect an adequate behavior sample by having the student do several problems of each type in which you are interested.
2. Encourage the student to work, but do nothing to influence the responses the student makes.
3. Record all responses the student makes, including comments.
4. Look for patterns in the responses.
5. Look for exceptions to any apparent pattern.
6. List the patterns you have identified as assumed causes for the student's computational difficulties. (pp. 250–251)

In addition to analyzing the student's work, it is very helpful to ask the student how he or she solved a problem. The student's response may give immediate insights into the error pattern and its cause.

Students with learning problems show several common error patterns in addition and subtraction:

1. The sums of the ones and tens are each recorded without regard for place value:

$$
\begin{array}{r} 94 \\ +67 \\ \hline 1511 \end{array}
\qquad
\begin{array}{r} 66 \\ +18 \\ \hline 714 \end{array}
$$

2. All digits are added together (defective algorithm and no regard for place value):

$$
\begin{array}{r} 32 \\ +54 \\ \hline 14 \end{array}
\qquad
\begin{array}{r} 48 \\ +23 \\ \hline 17 \end{array}
$$

3. When the tens column is added, the single-digit number is added to the numeral in the tens column (the lower addend is added twice):

$$
\begin{array}{r} {}^{\prime}58 \\ +\ 9 \\ \hline 157 \end{array}
\qquad
\begin{array}{r} {}^{\prime}29 \\ +\ 6 \\ \hline 95 \end{array}
$$

4. The smaller number is subtracted from the larger number without regard for placement of the number. The upper number (minuend) may be subtracted from the lower number (subtrahend), or vice versa:

$$
\begin{array}{r} 529 \\ -385 \\ \hline 264 \end{array}
\qquad
\begin{array}{r} 865 \\ -689 \\ \hline 224 \end{array}
$$

5. When regrouping is required more than once, the appropriate amount is not subtracted from the column borrowed from in the second regrouping:

$$
\begin{array}{r} {}^{3\,1\,1} \\ \cancel{4}21 \\ -136 \\ \hline 295 \end{array}
\qquad
\begin{array}{r} {}^{6\,1\,1} \\ \cancel{7}32 \\ -487 \\ \hline 255 \end{array}
\qquad
\begin{array}{r} {}^{5\,1} \\ \cancel{6}84 \\ -192 \\ \hline 592 \end{array}
$$

6. The regrouped number is added to the multiplicand in the tens column prior to performing the multiplication operation:

$$
\begin{array}{r} {}^{1} \\ 15 \\ \times\ 3 \\ \hline 65 \end{array}
\qquad
\begin{array}{r} {}^{3} \\ 54 \\ \times\ 8 \\ \hline 642 \end{array}
$$

7. The regrouped number is not added:

$$
\begin{array}{r} 28 \\ \times\ 7 \\ \hline 146 \end{array}
\qquad
\begin{array}{r} 73 \\ \times\ 6 \\ \hline 428 \end{array}
$$

8. The divisor and dividend are reversed. For example, the student thinks $8 \div 4$ and $4 \div 2$ instead of $40 \div 8$ and $20 \div 4$:

$$
8\overline{)40}^{\,2}
\qquad
4\overline{)20}^{\,2}
$$

9. The zero in the quotient is omitted:

$$
\begin{array}{r}
21 \\
8\overline{)1608} \\
\underline{1600} \\
8 \\
\underline{8}
\end{array}
$$

Many computational errors stem from an inadequate understanding of place value. Lepore (1979) analyzed the computational errors of 79 mildly handicapped youngsters aged twelve to fourteen. The type of error they made most frequently involved regrouping, a computation that requires understanding place value. Although place value is introduced in the primary grades, pupils of all ages continue to make mistakes because they cannot comprehend that the same digit expresses different orders of magnitude depending on its *location* in a number. Many of the error patterns presented earlier reflect an inadequate understanding of place value. Ashlock (1982) and Reisman (1982) provide a thorough listing of computational error patterns.

DIAGNOSTIC INTERVIEW TECHNIQUE   The diagnostic interview provides the information that is essential for determining which arithmetic skills to teach the student and how to teach them. In this technique, the student expresses his or her thought processes while solving arithmetic problems. Having students explain what they are doing is a technique often used in administering diagnostic arithmetic tests.

The diagnostic interview enables the teacher to identify specific problems, error patterns, or problem-solving strategies in arithmetic. Mercer and Mercer (1985) provide a sample interview that illustrates how the procedure can yield important information.

> The teacher gave Mary three multiplication problems and said, "Please do these problems and tell me how you figure out the answer." Mary solved the problems in this way:
>
> $$\begin{array}{ccc} \overset{2}{27} & \overset{4}{36} & \overset{3}{44} \\ \times\ 4 & \times\ 7 & \times\ 8 \\ \hline 168 & 492 & 562 \end{array}$$
>
> For the first problem, Jane explained, "7 times 4 equals 28. So I put my 8 here and carry the 2. 2 plus 2 equals 4 and 4 times 4 equals 16. So I put 16 here." Her explanations for the other two problems followed the same logic. (Mercer & Mercer, 1985, p. 187)

The authors note that by listening to Mary and observing her solve the problems, the teacher quickly determines Mary's error pattern: She adds the number associated with the crutch (the number carried to the tens column) *before* multiplying the tens digit. Mary explained that she had been taught to first add the number being carried when regrouping in addition. After identifying Mary's error pattern and its origin, the teacher plans instruction for teaching the correct algorithm and developing an understanding of the multiplication process. Without the interview, the teacher might incorrectly plan instruction in the basic multiplication facts.

The interview session provides an excellent opportunity for the teacher to assess the student's attitude toward arithmetic. In addition to observing the student's attitude during the session, the teacher may examine attitude through oral sentence-completion tasks. In this activity, the teacher starts the sentence and the student completes it:

Arithmetic is very _____.
My favorite subject is _____.
When doing arithmetic problems I feel _____.

The validity of the diagnostic findings depends on the quality of the exchange between teacher and student. The teacher must ensure that rapport exists and that the student feels free to respond honestly. Some general guidelines for conducting an interview include:

- Establish rapport and be alert to the student's attitudes toward arithmetic throughout the session. Begin with items that are easy for the student to do.
- Focus on the student's problem area that is the lowest on the skill sequence. Limit each session to one area of difficulty (e.g., two-column addition with regrouping).
- Allow the student the flexibility to solve the problem in his or her own way.
- Record the student's thinking processes and analyze for error patterns and problem-solving techniques.
- Once an error pattern or faulty problem-solving technique is discovered, introduce diagnostic activities for assessing the student's level of understanding. These activities should include tasks at the semiconcrete and concrete levels.

For more detailed discussions of diagnostic arithmetic interviews, the reader may consult Lankford (1974) and Underhill et al. (1980).

■ Continuous Assessment

Continuous assessment involves the monitoring of a student's progress. It includes daily, weekly, and/or biweekly assessments. Silbert, Carnine, and Stein (1981) discuss the importance of continuous assessment in the following passage:

The importance of careful monitoring cannot be overemphasized. The sooner the teacher detects a student's skill deficit, the easier it will be to remedy. For each day that a student's confusion goes undetected, the student is, in essence, receiving practice in doing something the wrong way. To ameliorate a confusion, the teacher should plan to spend several days reteaching for every day the student's confusion goes undetected. Thus, careful monitoring is a critical component of efficient instruction. (p. 10)

Criterion-referenced assessment is used in continuous assessment. Commercial tests, textbooks, basal tests, and scope-and-sequence skills lists are excellent sources for developing continuous assessment procedures.

☐ *Commercial Criterion-Referenced Tests*
Commercial criterion-referenced tests may be used to measure math skills on a continuous basis. Specific skill tests can be drawn from published tests or subtests. The following commercial criterion-referenced tests are useful in designing continuous assessment measures. (Criterion-referenced tests used for periodic assessment in arithmetic are presented in Table 6–3.)

> *Adston Mathematics Skill Series: Readiness for Operations* (Adams & Sauls, 1979); *Working with Whole Numbers* (Adams & Ellis, 1979); *Common Fractions* (Adams, 1979); *Decimal Numbers* (Beeson & Pellegrin, 1979). These four instruments collectively assess readiness for operations, facts and operations in each area (+, −, ×, ÷), operations with fractions, and decimals. They can be used with students in preschool through secondary level as appropriate for individual needs. Additional materials are available in the areas of operations, problem solving, and prealgebra.
> *Multilevel Academic Skills Inventory* (Howell, Zucker, & Morehead, 1982). This inventory includes criterion-referenced objectives in computation and application. Designed for students in grades 1 through 8, the inventory includes survey tests, placement tests, and specific level tests. Student response booklets are divided into four areas: addition/subtraction; multiplication/division; fractions; and decimals, ratios, and percent/applications.
> *Regional Resource Center Diagnostic Math Inventories* (Regional Resource Center, 1971). These inventories emphasize the use of rate of correct and incorrect responses from one-minute samples of behavior. Each subtest consists of a probe sheet used for the one-minute timings. Each probe sheet assesses a specific arithmetic skill. Subtests are included in the areas of reading numbers 0 to 10,000, writing numbers, addition and subtraction facts, ad-

dition and subtraction equations, addition and subtraction with and without carrying and borrowing, multiplication, and division.

☐ *Teacher-Compiled or -Constructed Tests*

USING BASAL MATH PROGRAMS   Basal math programs usually include a variety of tests (placement tests, chapter tests, specific skill tests, review tests) that may be used to monitor a student's progress. For example, specific skill tests (such as subtraction facts through 18) may be used several times a week to check a student's progress on a selected skill, whereas a unit or review test may be used less often (biweekly to monthly) to check a student's mastery on several skills. Also, the teacher's editions of most basals include a scope-and-sequence skills list for several grade levels and a hierarchical listing of skills with sample items for each skill taught in the respective grade level.

The teacher's task in continuous assessment is a difficult one, and basal tests and skill lists can be viable resources for developing or compiling assessment devices. It is often easier for the teacher to adapt or use existing materials than to create new ones.

USING SCOPE-AND-SEQUENCE SKILLS LISTS   Any continuous assessment procedure is based on mastering a sequence of skills. A scope-and-sequence framework serves as a guide for ordering the skills and enables the teacher to monitor a student's progress along the skill sequence. For daily or frequent monitoring, continuous assessment procedures may involve a measure of a very narrow skill range (e.g., multiplication facts with 6 to 9 as factors), whereas for weekly or biweekly monitoring the skill range is expanded (e.g., multiplication facts plus 4 digits minus 3 digits with regrouping). The comprehensive scope and sequence and the scope and sequence by skill areas in tables 6–1 and 6–2 may be used to develop specific skill assessments or span-of-skill assessments. Likewise, basals serve as an excellent resource for skill sequences and test items.

PROBES   A probe is another criterion-referenced assessment device frequently used to monitor the progress of students. The see–write probe is the most common format used in math. Structuring probes by manipulating the stimulus and response (e.g., hear–say, see–write, see–say) enables the teacher to examine learning channels that might be weak. For example, if a child has very poor fine-motor skills that interfere with his or her writing speed, it would be inappropriate to expect his or her rate of written responses to compare with standard see–write proficiency rates; however, his or her see–say rates might be appropriate for comparing to a proficiency criterion.

Probes may include a variety of items to measure performance in relation to any math objective. Computations of facts and operations are the most commonly used probes. Figures 6-6 and 6-7 present a specific skill probe (multiplication facts) and a mixed probe (addition and subtraction problems with and without regrouping), respectively, and Figure 6-8 shows the first line of a series of probes. These figures are examples of ways in which probes can be used to measure a variety of math skills.

Flash cards with vocabulary, word problems, math facts, or operations may also serve as probes. Cards of uniform size are presented one at a time for one minute. The cards are placed in either a correct or incorrect pile depending on the student's response. The total number of correct and incorrect responses are then recorded on a chart.

Probes provide instructionally relevant data by identifying any changes in the student's math performance. Because this assessment occurs on a continuous basis, instructional programs can be quickly and easily modified to foster student growth.

FIGURE 6-6 Specific Skill Probe: Multiplication Facts

7×6	5×7	1×9	9×8	6×5	6×3	7×9	2×4
7×3	5×3	6×3	7×4	0×8	9×5	3×9	8×6
6×9	4×3	9×2	5×5	3×2	3×8	4×4	8×7
2×5	9×1	8×8	5×8	8×6	9×4	8×1	7×8
7×2	3×1	9×3	7×7	6×8	6×2	9×9	7×5
8×4	6×9	1×7	5×9	9×9	5×2	8×9	3×3

Name _____

Date _____

Number Correct _____

Number Incorrect _____

FIGURE 6-7   Mixed Probe: Addition and Subtraction with and without Regrouping

648 +362	27 −14	4296 −2177	73 −28	3792 +2264	46 +23	378 −188
365 −187	2797 −1454	2746 +2758	56437 −23746	866 + 23	231 +364	854 − 9
156 + 97	60 − 4	2163 4395 +3010	49 +27	33 −22	24 + 8	649 −240
635 + 5	648 −427	43781 −20462	526 + 3	688 − 89	24 + 3	356 292 152 +268
615 − 3	42 +39	951 − 57	291 +308	103 − 20	9696 −2707	39 − 6
496 +374	936 + 2	501 − 24	349 +273	37 +75	47936 −25494	92 −74

Name _____

Date _____

Number Correct _____

Number Incorrect _____

RECORDING PERFORMANCE AND SETTING OBJECTIVES

■ ■ In math, recordkeeping for instructional purposes—that is, the process of collecting and organizing data on student progress—is not simple because students receive instruction in a wide range of skills. Data collection can become cumbersome and awkward, so some teachers find it a negative part of the instructional process (i.e., the teach–test–teach cycle). However, recordkeeping provides the teacher with essential information, and it is helpful to view it as a positive component of the teaching process. When recordkeeping is correctly developed and managed, many benefits are realized:

■ Students enjoy participating in monitoring and recording their progress.

FIGURE 6-8   First Line of a Series of Probes on Various Math Skills

See–Trace

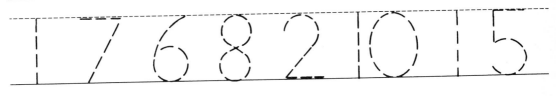

See–Say

| > | < | + | < | = | − |

See–Write Symbol (+, −, ×, ÷)

| TWICE AS | PLUS | TOTAL | SEPARATE INTO | MORE | LESS THAN |

See–Write

1. John has 6 rows of dimes with 7 dimes in each row. How many dimes does John *have altogether*?

2. There are 18 students in Sue's class. If the teacher divides the class into three *equal groups*, how many students will be in *each* group?

See–Say

Feb.   in.   oz.   Sun.   pt.   min.   lb.   yr.   gal.   ft.   yd.   Thurs.

See–Mark

TENTH 0 0 0 0 0 0 0 0 0 0   FOURTH 0 0 0 0 0 0 0 0 0 0

See–Write

_____   _____   _____   _____   _____   _____

- Teachers gain satisfaction from having documented student progress.
- Teachers can pinpoint learning difficulties and make appropriate instructional objectives and timely interventions.
- Teachers can share the progress of students with the parents, principal, and other school personnel.
- The data can be used to make program and placement decisions.

There are a variety of ways for teachers to organize and record assessment data. Teachers must examine the resources (e.g., basal scope-and-sequence skills lists, school district's curriculum guides) available to them that facilitate recordkeeping. It is important for the teacher to adapt, modify, or use recordkeeping systems that suit individual needs and preferences. This section provides some guidelines and suggestions for recording assessment data in math.

■ Recording Periodic Assessment Data

The periodic assessment data in math can be organized and recorded on the Periodic Math Assessment Record presented in Figure 6–9. The record is divided into three major sections: formal test data, informal testing—survey data and informal testing—specific skills data. Each section is designed so initial data and future data can be recorded.

■ Recording of Continuous Assessment Data

Recording of continuous assessment data depends on the math curriculum used, frequency of assessment, and assessment procedures used. Some teachers may be satisfied by using their school district's list of math skills as a format for recording math progress. Others may use a commercial list of skills from a test or curriculum program, while others may prefer charting the rate of correct and incorrect responses. Also, many teachers use a combination of formats for recording continuous data. For example, a probe and the recording of rate correct and incorrect may be used for monitoring progress on facts, whereas a worksheet and percentage correct may be used to monitor progress on word problems. Thus, numerous options are available to the teacher in designing a continuous assessment record. This section presents several types of continous recordkeeping systems. Although instruction follows the concrete-semiconcrete-abstract application sequence, the inclusion of all levels in continuous recordkeeping is unnecessary for most teachers. Because the abstract level is easy to assess and serves as a good indicator of student progress, it is used in a continuous assessment record. Records of levels

FIGURE 6-9 Periodic Math Assessment Record

A. Formal Tests		
FORMAL TEST	SUBTESTS	SCORES

B. Informal Survey Procedures	
SKILL SPAN	CRITERION ACHIEVED

C. Informal Specific Skill Procedures

SKILL	RESULTS (% or rate digits correct/incorrect)	ERROR ANALYSIS	ENTRY LEVEL OF UNDERSTANDING

Student Name _____

Grade/Teacher _____

Date _____

of understanding are more appropriate for frequent measures of student progress needed for daily decision making. (For a sample use of the continuous assessment record and other formats, see the case study section at the end of this chapter.)

☐ *Scope-and-Sequence Checklists*
A simple continuous recordkeeping system can be devised by making a checklist from a scope and sequence of skills. Sample checklists are presented in Figures 6-10 and 6-11.

FIGURE 6-10 Continuous Assessment Record in Math Using a Scope-and-Sequence Skills List

Name ___Alex___   Grade ___3___   Beginning Date ___10/3___

Skill Grade Range ___1st grade, 2nd semester___

Key: ✔ = mastery (mastery in abstract implies mastery at concrete and semiconcrete levels)
   • = currently teaching

Student Performance				Skill
Concrete	Semiconcrete	Abstract	Application	
				Numeration/Place Value
		✔		Counting/writing tens and ones
		✔		Recognizing numbers to 90
		✔		Order of numbers to 100
		✔		Counting one more than, one less than
•				Counting by 2s, 3s, 5s, 10s, and skip-counting
				Time
		✔		Using calendar to locate days and weeks
		✔		Telling time by hour, 1/2 hour, and 1/4 hour
				Addition/Subtraction
		✔		Sums 11 to 18 (facts)
		✔		Subtracting from sums or minuends 11 to 18
		✔		Addition family
		✔		Subtraction family
✔	•			Adding three addends
			•	Adding and subtracting with money (e.g., 4¢ − 2¢ = ___ ¢, 8¢ + 4¢ = ___ ¢)
				Geometry
		✔		Recognizing rectangles, squares, circles, and triangles
				Measurement
				Linear:
		✔		Comparing lengths, arbitrary units
			✔	Using centimeters, meters
✔	✔	•		Using inches, feet, yards

FIGURE 6-10 *(continued)*

Concrete	Semiconcrete	Abstract	Application	
✔	✔	•		Capacity: Using liter, cup, pint, quart Temperature
		✔		Using thermometer scale
				Addition
		✔		2d + 1d without regrouping
		✔		2d + 2d without regrouping
				Subtraction
				2d − 1d without regrouping
				2d − 2d without regrouping
			✔	*Story Problems* Addition problems
✔	•			Subtraction problems

				Fractions
				    Recognizing equal parts, recogniz-
				    ing 1/2, 1/3, and 1/4

•				Finding 1/2 of a set

☐ *Charting*

Charting is used to monitor daily student performance on specific skills. Correct and incorrect responses on a math probe (such as see–write multiplication facts) are especially suitable for charting. Responses obtained from the math probes may be entered on a proportional or equal-interval chart. Recording these data on a chart yields a clear visual record of the direction and extent of change in performance. Adding proficiency or mastery goals to this system allows the classroom teacher to know when instructional objectives are met and when interventions should be modified.

☐ *Proficiency Aims*

The charted data on math probes can be compared to mastery or proficiency levels that exist for many math skills. Mastery or proficiency goals represent those levels at which a math skill is accurately and fluently used. Although research has not conclusively determined exact proficiency rates across math skills, enough data exist to indicate trends. These data, which are presented in Table 6-4, may be used as guidelines

FIGURE 6-11   Continuous Assessment Record in Math Using a Specific Skill Sequence

Name   Sally   Grade   4   Beginning Date   10/12

Skill Area   Subtraction

Key: ✓ = mastery (mastery in abstract implies mastery at concrete and semiconcrete levels)
    • = currently teaching

Concrete	Semiconcrete	Abstract	Application	Skill
		✓		Find missing addend
		✓		Understand ''–'' sign
		✓		Express relationship (addend + addend = sum ←→ sum – addend = addend)
		✓		Subtraction facts 0–9
			✓	Word problems using subtraction facts
		✓		Place value of 10s and 1s
		✓		Subtraction facts 0–18
		✓		2d* – 1d (not a basic fact and no regrouping)
		✓		2d – 2d without regrouping
			✓	Word problems with 2d – 1d and 2d – 2d without regrouping
		✓		3d – 2d without regrouping
		✓		3d – 3d without regrouping multidigit–multidigit without regrouping
		✓		2d – 1d with regrouping
•				2d – 2d with regrouping from tens to ones
				3d – 2d with regrouping from tens to ones
				3d – 2d with double regrouping

Note: ''d'' refers to ''digit.''

for setting instructional goals (that is, rates on skills that fall below these levels may serve as instructional objectives). E. Haughton (personal communication, January 5, 1983) cautions against setting the "rate correct" aims too low. He notes that levels of performance associated with retention, endurance, and application are needed, and these levels are independent of age. Haughton recommends that the rate levels listed in Table 6-4 be achieved as soon as possible. In Table 6-4 the rates provided by Wood, Burke, Kunzelmann, and Koenig (1978) are based on adults who

TABLE 6-4 Suggested Proficiency Rates for Math Skills

	Write Math Facts: Digits in Simple Add. and Sub. Equations		Addition Facts 0-9 Gr. 2-3		Sub. Facts (1-5) and Facts Top Numb. 2-9 Gr. 2-3		Add. Facts Sums 10-18 and Sub. Facts Top Numb. 6-9 Gr. 3-4		Two-column Addition with Regrouping Gr. 4-5		Two-column Subtraction with Regrouping Gr. 4-6		Mult. Facts Through ×9 Gr. 5-6		Division Facts Through Divisor of 9 Gr. 6	
	Cor.	Err.	Cor.	Err.	Cor.	Err.	Cor.	Err.	Cor.	Err.	Cor.	Err.	Cor.	Err.	Cor.	Err.
Koenig & Kunzelmann (1980)			60	—	60	—	90	—	60	—	60	—	90	—	60	—
Precision Teaching Project (Montana)			70–90	—	70–90	—	70–90	—	70–90	—	70–90	—	70–90	—	70–90	—
Regional Resource Center (1971) (not grade-specific)	50	0									50	0	50	0	50	0
Smith & Lovitt (1982)			50+	0	45+	0							50+	0	45+	0
Starlin & Starlin (1973)			20–30	0-2	20–30	0-2	40–60	0-2	40–60	0-2	40–60	0-2	40–60	0-2	40–60	0-2
Wood, Burke, Kunzelmann, & Koenig (1978)	125	0			68	0	60	0	60	0	56	0	80	0	47	0

Source: From Teaching Students with Learning Problems (p. 189), 2nd ed., by C. D. Mercer and A. R. Mercer, 1985, Columbus, OH: Charles E. Merrill Pub. Co. Copyright © 1985 by Bell & Howell Company. Reprinted by permission.

FIGURE 6-12 Proportional Chart Showing Math Progress across Several Skills

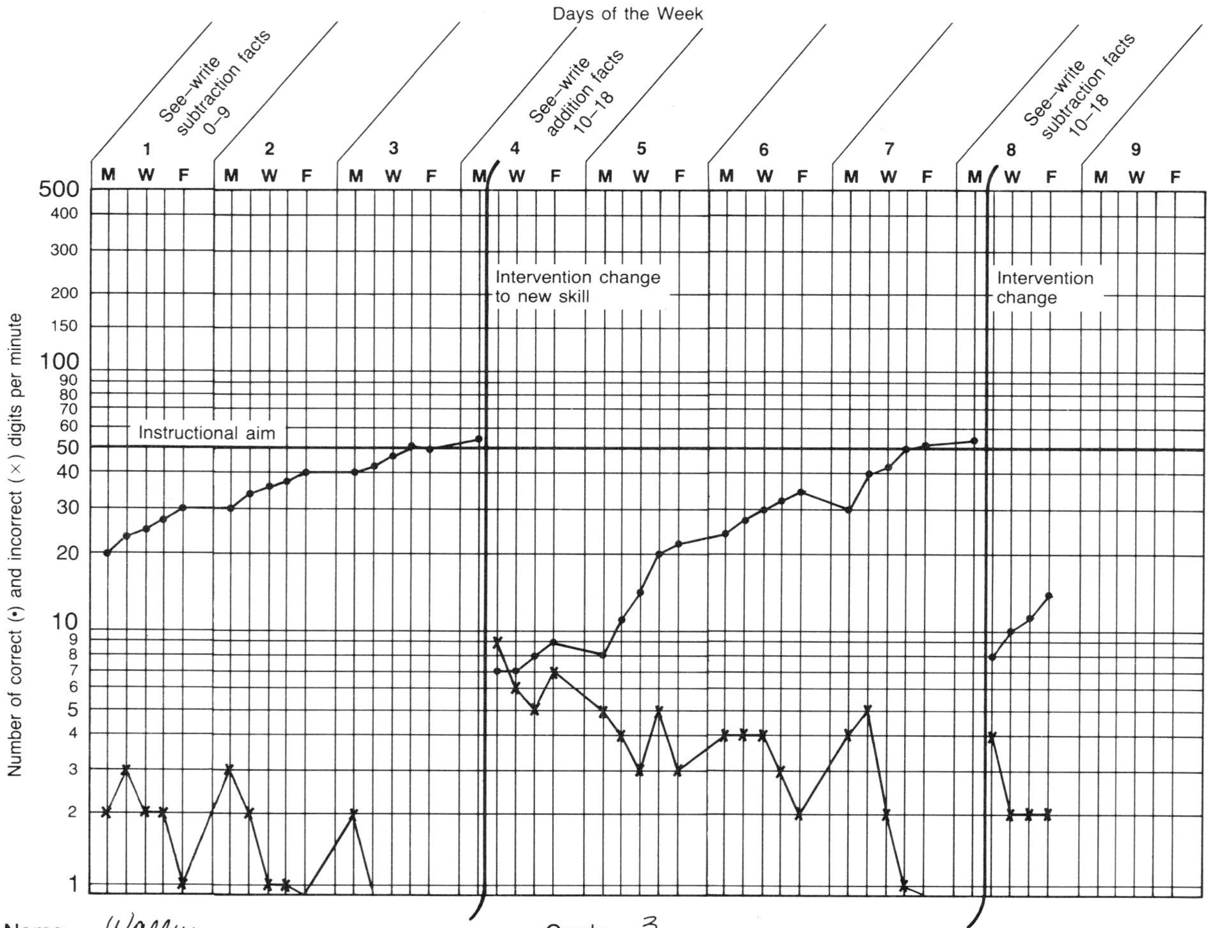

Name _Wally_   Grade _3_

Behavior _Skill #1 – Subtraction facts 0–9; Skill #2 – Addition facts 10–18; Skill #3 – Subtraction facts 10–18_

Goal _50 correct and 0 incorrect digits per minute_

use math in their occupations. Thus, they may be good indicators of application rates. For more information on application rates across a variety of math skills, the reader is referred to the Wood et al. study.

It appears that rate-based proficiencies are most applicable for measuring proficiency on math facts. Figure 6-12 presents a daily record of a student's math progress across several math skills during an eight-week period.

Mastery criteria may also be expressed as a percentage of correct responses. Percentage is especially useful in measuring skills such as word problems and application skills such as measurement or geometry. Smith (1981) notes that teachers often require three days of 90 to 100% accuracy before introducing a new skill. Figure 6-13 presents a daily record of a student's math progress using percent correct as a method of assessment.

☐ *Selected Measures for Monitoring Math Progress*
A matrix may be developed and used to locate arithmetic facts that have not been memorized. The teacher first gives the student a test on selected facts (such as sums: 0-9, 10-18; differences: 0-9, 10-18; products: 0-9). Then the teacher records the student's performance on the matrix. A matrix for subtraction facts 0-18 is presented in Figure 6-14. Inspection of Figure 6-14 suggests that the student is having difficulty with two-digit minus one-digit facts, when the subtrahend is 6, 7, or 8.

FIGURE 6-13 Record of Math Progress Using Percent Correct

Name	Stephanie		Grade	3

Skill #1 Word problems using addition (2d* + 1d without regrouping) and subtraction (2d − 1d without regrouping)

Skill #2 Fractions—recognizing equal parts

Measures	*Date*	*Score*
Skill #1		
Worksheet #1	10/8	33%
Worksheet #2	10/11	50%
Worksheet #3	10/12	90%
Worksheet #4	10/13	100%
Mastery test	10/18	100%
Skill #2		
Worksheet #1	10/19	60%
Worksheet #2	10/20	70%

*Note: "d" refers to "digit."

FIGURE 6-14 A Student's Performance on 0-18 Subtraction Facts

Minuend

Subtrahend \ Minuend	1	2	3	4	5	6	7	8	9	10	11	12	13	14	15	16	17	18
0	√	√	√	√	√	√	√	√	√	√								
1	√	√	√	√	√	√	√	√	√	√								
2		√	√	√	√	√	√	√	√	√	√							
3			√	√	√	√	√	√	√	√	√	√						
4				√	√	√	√	√	√	√	√	√	√					
5					√	√	√	√	√	√	√	√	√	√				
6						√	√	√	√	—	—		—	—	—			
7							√	√	√	—	—	—	—	—	—	—		
8								√	√	—	—	—	—	—	—	—	—	
9									√	√	√	√	√	√	√	√	√	√

√ = basic fact memorized
— = basic fact *not* memorized

Source: Adapted from *Teaching Students with Learning Problems* (2nd. ed.), p. 201, by C. D. Mercer and A. R. Mercer, 1985. Copyright © 1985 by Bell & Howell Co. Reprinted by permission of Charles E. Merrill Pub. Co.

CASE STUDY

This section features a math assessment with the data recorded on the Periodic Math Assessment Record (Figure 6-15) and the Continuous Assessment Records in Math (figures 6-16 and 6-17). After examining the data in these three figures it is apparent that Greg, a fourth grader, was functioning below his age and grade level. The formal test data (Figure 6-15) revealed weaknesses in subtraction, word problems, fractions, and measurement. The informal skill-survey test data (Figure 6-15) confirmed the problems with subtraction and indicated that further assessment was needed in subtraction, time, and multiplication facts. The informal specific-skills testing showed that problems existed in subtraction, and the following instructional objectives in subtraction were generated for continuous assessment: (a) facts 0-9: reach criterion of 50 digits correct per minute with no errors; (b) facts 10-18: reach criterion of 50

FIGURE 6-15 Case Study: Periodic Math Assessment Record

A. Formal Tests

FORMAL TEST	SUBTESTS	SCORES (grade-level scores)
Key Math Diagnostic Arithmetic Test	Numeration	3.8
	Fractions	2.4
	Geometry and Symbols	3.0
	Addition	3.5
	Subtraction	2.7
	Multiplication	3.9
	Division	3.4
	Word Problems	2.4
	Money	3.5
	Measurement	2.6
	Time	3.3

B. Informal Survey Procedures

SKILL SPAN	CRITERION ACHIEVED
1. Second Grade/First Semester Skills:	
Subtraction: 2d*–1d with regrouping	no
Time: 1/2 hour, calendar use	yes
1/4 hour, 5 minutes	no
Measurement: linear—nearest inch, perimeters in cm,	
area by counting weight—pounds, ounce, temperature	yes
2. Second Grade/Second Semester Skills:	
Multiplication: facts (0–5)	yes (used fingers)
Subtraction: 3d – 2d with regrouping	no
3d – 3d with regrouping	no
Money: using and $ in addition and subtraction problems	yes
(no regrouping)	
3. Third Grade/First Semester Skills:	
Numeration: rounding to nearest 100	yes
estimating sums to three digits	yes
Addition: multidigit + multidigit	yes
Multiplication: facts (6 – 9)	no

C. Informal Specific Skill Procedures

SKILL	RESULTS (% or rate digits correct/incorrect)	ERROR ANALYSIS	ENTRY LEVEL OF UNDERSTANDING
1. Subtraction			
facts 0–9	46/3		
facts 10–18	3/12	faulty algorithm (14 – 6 = 12)	concrete

(continued)

FIGURE 6-15 *(continued)*

C. Informal Specific Skill Procedures

SKILL	RESULTS (% or rate digits correct/incorrect)	ERROR ANALYSIS	ENTRY LEVEL OF UNDERSTANDING
2d — 1d no regrouping, 2d — 2d, 3d — 2d, 3d — 3d without regrouping	100%		
word problems	100%		
2d — 1d and 2d — 2d with regrouping	0%	lack of place-value concept in regrouping	concrete
2. *Multiplication*			
facts 0–9	22/6	lack of multiplication concept at abstract level	semiconcrete
2d — 1d without regrouping	100%		
2d — 1d with regrouping	50%		
word problems	60%		
3. *Measurement*			
linear: kilometer, mile	0%		semiconcrete
area: square inches and cm	0%		concrete
capacity: gallon	100%		
volume: cubic inches, cm	0%		concrete
temperature: below 0	50%		concrete
word problems	10%		concrete

Student Name <u>Greg P.</u>

Grade/Teacher <u>4th grade (spring)/Beasley</u>

Note: "d" refers to "digit."

digits correct per minute with no errors; and (c) two-digit minus one-digit with regrouping: reach 100% correct criterion. Specific skill testing (see–write multiplication facts probe) also revealed that multiplication facts were a weak area. Altogether, instructional objectives were generated in multiplication (facts, two-digit times one-digit with regrouping, word problems) and measurement (kilometer, mile, gallon, volume, below zero temperature).

FIGURE 6-16   Case Study: Continuous Assessment Record

Date	Conditions	Skill/Behavior	Abstract level of performance (digits cor./inc. per minute)	Proficiency criterion/ goal	Date attained
3/20	probe sheet, praise	see–write subtraction facts 0–9	46/3	50/0	3/28
3/20	probe sheet, praise	see–write subtraction facts 10–18	3/12	50/0	4/16
3/20	worksheets, praise	see–write answers to subtraction problems 2d – 1d with regrouping	0%	100%	in progress
3/20	probe sheet, praise	see–write multiplication facts 0–9	22/6	50/0	4/8
3/20	worksheet, praise	see–write answers to multiplication problems 2d × 1d with regrouping	50%	100%	4/11
3/20	worksheet, praise	see–write answers to word problems using multiplication	60%	100%	4/10
3/20	worksheet, praise	see–write answers to measurement problems (linear— kilometer and mile)	0%	100%	in progress
3/20	worksheet, praise	see–write answers to time problems (¼ hour, 5 min.)	0%	100%	in progress

Student's Name <u>Greg P.</u>

Grade/Teacher <u>4/Beasley</u>

The Continuous Assessment Record (Figure 6–16) displays the student's progress on eight instructional objectives after four weeks of instruction. The continuous assessment data on the scope-and-sequence skills list in Figure 6–17 (ranging from 1st grade, 2nd semester, to 3rd

FIGURE 6-17   Case Study: Continuous Assessment Record in Math (Using a Scope-and-Sequence Skills List)

Name ___Greg P.___   Grade _____4_____   Beginning Date ___3/21___

Skill Grade Range 1st grade, 2nd semester, to 3rd grade, 2nd semester

Key: • = in progress
  ✓ = mastery (date of mastery at abstract level)

Concrete	Semiconcrete	Abstract	Application	Skill
				Subtraction
		✓ 3/28		facts 0–9
		✓ 4/16		facts 10–18
✓	✓	•		2d* − 1d with regrouping
				2d − 2d with regrouping
				Multiplication
	✓	✓ 4/8		facts 0–9
✓	✓	✓ 4/10		2d × 1d with regrouping
			✓ 4/10	word problems
				Division
				facts 2–9
				relationship of ÷ and × (finding missing factor)
				division with remainders
				Fractions
				fractions of a number
				equivalent fractions
				Time
	✓	•		1/4 hour, 5-minute intervals
				Measurement
	✓	•		linear: kilometer, mile
				area: square inches and cm by counting
				capacity: gallon
				volume: cubic inches and cm
				temperature: below 0°F and 0°C
				word problems

Note: "d" refers to "digit."

272

grade, 2nd semester) display the student's progress on targeted skills and lists skills for future instruction. The data on subtraction and multiplication facts also include see–write probes that are tabulated on the Continuous Assessment Record in Figure 6–16. Overall, it appears that the student is making good progress on the objectives individualized for him.

CONCLUSION

It is important that math assessment complement the curriculum in the classroom. Although a math curriculum is sequential, selected skills are taught concurrently. A student's level of understanding (concrete, semiconcrete, and abstract) of a math process is a necessary component of math assessment. Periodic assessment techniques, including survey tests and specific skill tests are used at major evaluation points in the school year. Continuous assessment using various criterion-referenced tests is important in the daily-to-weekly monitoring of a student's progress.

ACTIVITIES

1. What are the essential areas of a math skills curriculum and in what sequence are these areas usually taught?
2. Explain the importance of assessing a student's level of understanding (concrete, semiconcrete, and abstract) of a math process.
3. Select a span of skills on a comprehensive scope-and-sequence skills list and construct an informal survey skill test.
4. Select a skill area (e.g., addition) on a scope-and-sequence skills list and develop an informal skills test.
5. Develop probes for a set of facts in each of the four mathematical operations.
6. Review a basal series and list the skill ordering in each math skill area for one grade level.
7. Select a span of computational skills and construct a test designed to determine a student's level of understanding.
8. Review a criterion-referenced commercial test and administer it to a student, score it, and interpret it.
9. Develop a mixed probe in multiplication, administer it to a student, and interpret the results.
10. Administer the fourth grade survey test (Figure 6–2) and identify any error patterns and areas needing further assessment.

7

Assessment of Behavior

■ **Learning Objectives**

After completing this chapter, the reader should be able to:

■ describe the ecological approach to the assessment of behavior—the assessment of environmental variables, expectations, and observed behaviors
■ list and describe expectations related to the instructional setting and to behavior that should be included in the assessment of behavior
■ describe the factors involved in precisely analyzing a behavior problem
■ list examples of behaviors that might be included in a behavior network and the appropriate companion behavior that should also be targeted for intervention
■ describe informal procedures used to assess behavior
■ describe different qualities of behavior

The assessment of behavior is an important element of any educational evaluation. It often involves an analysis of the student's behavior in various settings and an examination of the student's environment. By assessing the behaviors, expectations, and interactions of parents, teachers, and peers, effective educational programs may be constructed.

DETERMINING BEHAVIORS TO BE ASSESSED

■ ■ Traditionally, the focus of behavioral assessment was upon the child (Wallace & Larsen, 1978). As a result, a great amount of time and effort was spent in trying to identify and label the student's behavior problem. Often behavior was viewed as symptomatic of a serious underlying psychological disorder. Interventions were largely designed to ameliorate the problem that was thought to reside within the child. More contemporary approaches to the assessment of behavior, however, recognize that behavior affects and is affected by the environment.

An ecological assessment is designed to analyze this interaction and identify those elements of the student's environment that contribute to the behavior problem. As illustrated in Figure 7–1, the focus of assessment is upon an analysis of the environment (both physical-social and physiological-psychological), of the behaviors, and of the expectations of parents, teachers, members of the community, peers, and the student. By sampling all of these areas of the student's life, there is an increased probability of obtaining a comprehensive and accurate view of the behavior problem.

■ **Physical and Social Environment**

The assessment of the physical and social environment should provide an analysis of those events and conditions that may affect student behavior. Additionally, this assessment should identify the resources that are present and needed in each setting.

☐ *Home and Community Environment*
Student behavior may be greatly affected by events or conditions in the home and community. In the home, a lack of physical resources such as

FIGURE 7–1   Focus of Ecological Assessment

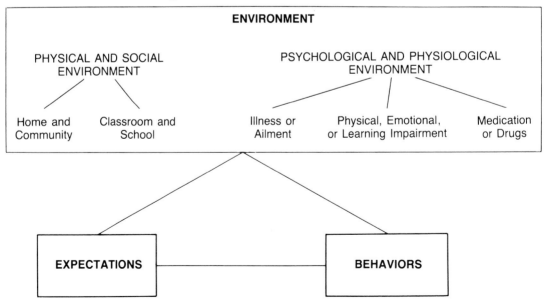

clothing or food, a death of a relative, birth of a sibling, divorce or arguments in the family, viewing real or ficticious portrayals of violence, and abuse or neglect can have an effect on the behavior of a student. Behavior problems may also reflect a code of conduct that is enforced by a peer group.

The activities in which the student engages as well as the student's likes and dislikes may also be sampled. This information may be useful in identifying events that are reinforcing and those that should be avoided.

☐ *Classroom and School Environment*
As stated in chapter 3, the physical conditions in the classroom and school may affect the behavior of a student. The physical arrangement, temperature of the classroom, adequacy of materials, and pupil–teacher ratio are important elements of the educational environment and may have a substantial affect on behavior.

The appropriateness of the instructional program and individual lessons must also be assessed. The objectives should be clearly stated, the material at an appropriate level of difficulty, and the instructional methods designed to meet the needs of the learner.

Assessment should also address how the teacher and students use time in the classroom. The classroom schedule should be well organized so that there is a smooth transition between tasks. The schedule should allow for a maximum amount of time for learning-related activities and should provide an adequate amount of structured free time for the student.

Any evaluation of the school and classroom should identify events and activities that the student likes and dislikes. The student may have a special interest or hobby, for example, or may prefer certain instructional activities or arrangements. This information can be used in instructional planning to increase motivation. Additionally, the student may dislike certain events or conditions and seek to avoid them. Knowledge of this could assist in explaining inappropriate student behavior as well as in identifying activities that should be avoided in the instructional program.

■ Psychological and Physiological Environment

The psychological and physiological environment of the student must also be assessed. This assessment will assist in determining if the student's inappropriate behavior is caused by an illness or disorder, a physical impairment, a learning or severe emotional problem, or as a result of medication or drugs. This information may greatly assist in obtaining services that could be used to effectively intervene with the behavior problem.

☐ *Illness or Ailment*
An illness, such as an upper respiratory infection or an allergy, may greatly affect a student's ability to behave appropriately, attend to tasks, and interact with peers (Heron & Heward, 1982). If the ailment is persistent, assessment conducted in conjunction with medical personnel, parents, and school personnel may seek to identify factors contributing to inappropriate behavior.

☐ *Physical, Learning, or Emotional Impairments*
Assessment should also seek to determine if a student's inappropriate behavior is related to a physical impairment (such as a vision or hearing loss), an inadequate diet, a lack of sleep, a learning problem, or a severe emotional problem. These problems and impairments may cause the student a great deal of frustration, anxiety, or embarrassment. Left untreated, they may continually thwart even the very best attempts at modifying the problem behavior.

☐ *Medication and Drugs*
Inappropriate behavior such as lethargy and restlessness may be unanticipated side effects of medications or drugs prescribed for a student or the result of alcohol or illicit drug use. Any investigation into student use of licit and illicit drugs should be carefully conducted. School and medical personnel, parents, and the student should all be fully informed and participate in this inquiry.

■ Expectations

Of particular interest in the assessment of behavior is an examination of how closely the student's behavior matches the expectations held by others. Algozzine (1981) defines an *expectation* as "the predicted probability of a future event." (p. 170) Expectations determine the reaction the behavior will receive. Behaviors that match the expectations are viewed as appropriate while those that do not are said to be inappropriate for the setting. Parents, teachers, and students all have expectations of what should and will happen. Expectations, in part, grow out of past experiences and what has been learned in the home and school. In a school setting, for example, a student's behavior is judged to be a problem if it stands in contrast to what is expected of students by school officials. Likewise, a student's peers judge behavior to be inappropriate if it violates the rules or expectations of the peer group.

In a classroom setting, much of the instructional program is affected by expectations. A teacher, for example, who expects a student with a low IQ score to be less than competent may alter the instructional program to reflect these perceptions. This has been termed a self-fulfilling prophecy. Additionally, expectations determine the extent and type of verbal and social interactions as well as with whom these will occur. As a result, students whose attributes and behavior match the expectations of teachers or peers may be more socially acceptable.

There are some general expectations that must be addressed in the assessment of behavior in an educational setting. These expectations are related to the instructional program and to behaviors that may occur in the classroom. In the assessment, these expectations should address the unique properties of the particular setting. By doing so, the assessment is relevant and thus helpful in planning an instructional program.

☐ *Expectations Related to Instruction*

Expectations concerning the instructional setting may be assessed by examining the skills that the student is expected to master, the extent to which learning should occur, and the conditons under which learning should occur.

THE SKILLS THE STUDENT IS EXPECTED TO MASTER Students spend much of the school day engaged in academic endeavors. Behavior problems can result if these activities are perceived as being irrelevant or inappropriate in content and level of difficulty. Therefore, it may be necessary to examine if student expectations about the skills to be learned differ from those expectations held by the teacher or school officials. It is important that careful consideration be given to the development and implementation of an instructional program that meets the needs of the student. Wood (1975) suggests that an instructional program consist of carefully sequenced experiences that stimulate student growth and utilization of newly acquired skills. The curriculum should reflect the unique abilities and maturational level of each learner and provide meaningful educational experiences.

THE EXTENT TO WHICH LEARNING SHOULD OCCUR Problems can arise when students, teachers, and parents have different expectations about the standards or criteria used to evaluate student progress. A student, for example, who is very accurate, but slow in word recognition, may believe that it is unfair for a teacher to insist upon accuracy and speed of response. This may result in a difference in opinion as to what should constitute the mastery criteria associated with skill advancement in basic academic subjects such as reading and math.

If the criteria for skill advancement are inappropriate, students may progress without the knowledge necessary to support more advanced and complex skills. For example, students who are passed through a math curriculum with only a cursory knowledge of basic skills may become frustrated when presented with higher level math tasks.

THE CONDITIONS UNDER WHICH LEARNING SHOULD OCCUR Serious problems may also result if there is a discrepancy between the attitudes and behaviors of a teacher and the conditions necessary for student growth. The teacher who believes it necessary to be overly stern, for example, may do little to foster academic achievement with those students who require a more pleasant demeanor. Smith, Neisworth, and Greer (1978) state that a good learning climate results when praise and encouragement are the rule rather than the exception. The teacher who sees his or her role as one of being a motivator who actively involves students in problem solving creates a classroom environment that is conducive for learning and behaving appropriately (Lovitt, 1977).

Teachers who recognize the importance of careful program planning and implementation can do much to alleviate inappropriate behaviors. Gallagher (1979) states that learning may be enhanced and behavior problems avoided by having a dependable and consistent routine and an organized instructional program with materials appropriate to the needs of the individual student. Moreover, teachers who understand the importance of careful planning create learning environments that have a rich diversity of relevant activities that actively involve all students. This is the type of classroom climate that fosters appropriate behavior.

☐ *Expectations Related to Behavior*

Any assessment must examine the expectations that parents, teachers, and students have concerning behavior. Many of these expectations can be evaluated by examining the behaviors considered to be inappropriate, the degree of inappropriate behavior that is tolerable, the methods of discipline used in the classroom, and the characteristics of the student, teacher, or parent that are believed to affect behavior.

BEHAVIORS THAT ARE CONSIDERED TO BE INAPPROPRIATE Each individual has a unique reaction to behavior. While one individual or group may view a behavior as inappropriate, another may not. Rhodes and Paul (1978) and Algozzine (1981) state that the inappropriateness of behavior is a function of not only the behavior, but also a function of with whom and where the behavior occurs. It is in this interaction that behavior is judged to be appropriate or inappropriate.

Hewett and Taylor (1980) note that teachers may differ significantly in their tolerance of behaviors. Additionally, they report that teachers may be more tolerant of academic differences than of behavioral differences.

Studies by Brophy and Good (1974) and Algozzine (1976, 1977) indicate that teachers respond differently to certain behavioral differences. This is illustrated by Schlosser and Algozzine (1979) who report that behaviors thought to be more typical of boys, such as disruptiveness, appear to be more bothersome and disturbing to teachers than those behaviors considered more typical of girls, such as shyness.

Behaviors must also be evaluated for appropriateness to the setting. A student's loud, boisterous behavior on a playground, for example, may be quite appropriate. The same behavior in a quiet class setting may be judged to be very inappropriate.

THE DEGREE OF INAPPROPRIATE BEHAVIOR THAT IS TOLERABLE Individuals respond differently not only to the type of behavior, but also to the quantity of behavior. A teacher may, for example, tolerate or even expect a certain amount of talking out in class. This behavior may be viewed as inappropriate, however, if it occurs too often or in the wrong settings. Likewise, a certain amount of withdrawal from others may not be judged as bothersome. If, however, a student continually withdraws from contact with others, the teacher may become concerned. Reinert (1980) and Apter and Conoley (1984) note that many of the troublesome behaviors emitted by emotionally handicapped students differ from those of their more normal peers in terms of the frequency of occurrence.

METHODS OF DISCIPLINE Major problems can arise in a classroom when student and teacher expectations and perceptions about discipline differ. Learning and behavior problems and a lack of learning may result if students believe that the rules and consequences in a classroom are arbitrary and inconsistently applied. Smith, Neisworth, and Greer (1978) state that student–teacher misunderstandings can be avoided if discipline standards are clearly communicated to students and consistently applied.

There may also be differences in the expectations of students, teachers, and parents concerning the nature or extent of discipline. These differences, if not resolved, can result in major disagreements between all individuals involved. Hewett and Taylor (1980), while acknowledging the efficacy of punishment, state that careful consideration must be given before using any discipline procedure. They assert that the teacher must be comfortable in the use of behavior-change procedures, and all individuals involved should understand the use of such techniques.

THE CHARACTERISTICS OF THE STUDENT, TEACHER, OR PARENT THAT ARE BELIEVED TO AFFECT BEHAVIOR There is a great deal of evidence that teachers' perceptions of a student's behavior are affected by the student's characteristics and attributes (Dusek, 1975). Among these are race (Coates, 1972), sex (Jackson & Lahaderne, 1967), attractiveness (Algozzine, 1976), and achievement (Brophy & Good, 1974). Additionally, there is ample evidence that teachers' perceptions of students are affected by program labels, such as emotionally handicapped or learning disabled, which have been applied to the student (Foster, Ysseldyke, & Reese, 1975). The expectations concerning these labels and attributes appear to affect what teachers expect of students and the reaction student behavior will receive—another example of a self-fulfilling prophecy.

There is also evidence that bias affects the behavior of students toward teachers. Gottfredson (1984) states that teacher assaults were much more likely in schools in which the teacher was of a different race than that of the majority of the student population.

Expectations concerning the labels and characteristics of students and teachers exert a dramatic influence on the way in which behavior is evaluated. As a result, these expectations must be very carefully examined in any assessment of behavior.

■ Behavior

The assessment of expectations addresses the perception of events and the characteristics of the individual. The assessment of behavior, on the other hand, provides an analysis of the specific observable and measureable responses made by an individual.

Prieto and Rutherford (1977) state that in order to adequately analyze a behavior problem, teachers must have three skills. They must be able to:

- ■ specifically describe the behavior without making judgments as to the cause of the problem
- ■ critically observe the behavior in order to identify the environmental or ecological variables related to the behavior
- ■ precisely record the magnitude, frequency, and duration of the behavior

☐ *Defining the Behavior and the Conditions That Influence Behavior*

Rather than referring to a behavior in vague, general terms such as hyperactive, for example, it is better to describe the specific behavior of concern, such as hitting, running around the room, or talking without permission. Additionally, caution should be taken in interpreting behavior. Labels such as "unhappy," "immature," or "impulsive" have certain connotations and may inaccurately interpret behavior (Stephens, Hartman, & Lucas, 1978).

Once the behavior of interest is precisely defined, the setting or conditions associated with the behavior must be carefully analyzed. These conditions consist of antecedent events, or those events that occur before the behavior, and consequent events, which occur after the behavior. By analyzing these events, it may be possible to determine how the occurrence of the behavior is related to the existing conditions. As illustrated in Table 7–1, in the first case, the behavior of tearing up a math worksheet was preceded by the antecedent event of the teacher returning a worksheet with errors marked in red to the student. The behavior was followed by a reprimand by the teacher to the student. If this pattern occurred consistently, there would be good reason to suspect that the red marks on the worksheet or the behavior of the teacher were related to the behavior of the student. In the second case, however, the same behavior, tearing up the worksheet, was accompanied by a different set of circumstances. While these behaviors are similar, the antecedent and consequent conditions associated with each are different and therefore should be individually assessed.

It is important to remember that no two behaviors are exactly the same. They may differ in rate, duration, topography (physical shape or form of an action), and magnitude. While two students may exhibit the behavior of hitting, one of those students may hit other students frequently, forcefully, and without provocation. The other student may rarely hit others and only after a great deal of provocation. In both situations, hitting occurred. The behaviors, however, were substantially different in a number of ways. The description and any accompanying interventions should reflect the unique nature of each behavior.

☐ *Categorizing Behavior*

There have been numerous attempts to categorize behavior problems. The American Psychiatric Association's *Diagnostic and Statistical Manual of Mental Disorders of 1980* (DSM III) presents five major types of disorders: intellectual, behavioral, emotional, physical, and developmental. Within each of these categories are numerous specific disorders

TABLE 7–1 Antecedent and Consequent Conditions that Influence Behavior

Antecedent Conditions	*Behavior*	*Consequent Conditions*
CASE #1		
Teacher returns math worksheet with many errors marked in red.	Student tears worksheet in pieces and throws it on the floor.	Teacher says, "Stop that, and pick that paper up."
CASE #2		
Teacher returns math worksheet after scolding student for talking.	Students tears worksheet in pieces and throws it on the floor.	Teacher ignores the student's behavior.

related to childhood disorders. Apter and Conoley (1984) state that while the DSM III categories are an improvement over previous efforts, many of the behaviors listed cannot be observed or measured in educational settings.

Various authors have proposed behavior classification systems that are more directly related to the school environment (Reinert, 1980; Kauffman, 1981; Morse, Cutler, & Fink, 1964). The system proposed by Quay (1979) allows behavior problem students to be classified into four categories on the basis of observed behaviors:

1. Conduct disorders (fighting, disruptive behavior)
2. Anxiety-withdrawal (feelings of inferiority, depression)
3. Socialized aggression (gang membership, stealing)
4. Immaturity (sloppy work habits, inattentive)

This classification has been found to reflect many of the problems found in students with behavior problems. Students with behavior problems may exhibit not just one discrete type but also a diverse range of inappropriate behaviors. When this happens, it may become quite difficult to classify a student according to a specific category or to use such information for instructional planning.

The categorization scheme suggested by Hewett and Taylor (1980) classifies behavior according to six levels of learning competence. The *attention level* deals with students making contact with their environment by attending to stimuli and using concrete objects. At the *response level*, there is an increased emphasis on verbal and motor activities. The *order level* concerns assisting students in following routines, while activities at the *exploratory level* are designed to help students learn to accurately and thoroughly explore their environment. At the *social level*, students are taught how to gain social approval and interact with others. The mastery level concerns academic, vocational, and self-help skills. As illustrated in Table 7–2, behaviors are classified in relation to these levels of learning and are judged as being inappropriate when they are exhibited too little or too often. Inappropriate behavior, therefore, is viewed as not being qualitatively different from appropriate behavior, but rather as being quantitatively different.

This system is used to categorize behaviors in relation to the educational environment and is designed to identify behaviors that are necessary for learning at each stage. As a result, the behaviors are closely related to the requirements of the curriculum and social setting.

The network presented in Figure 7–2 lists behaviors noted as bothersome by authors such as Reinert (1980), Hewett and Taylor (1980), Quay, Morse, and Cutler (1966), and Campbell, Dobson, and Bost (1985). Some of these behaviors cause problems when they occur excessively.

TABLE 7-2 Common Characteristics of Disturbed Children Viewed as Negative Variants of Six Levels of Learning Competence

Too Little ⟶	Optimal ⟷	Too Much
Disturbances in sensory perception (sed)	Attention	Selective attention (a)	Fixation on particular stimuli (a)
Excessive daydreaming (ii) Poor memory (a) Short attention span (ii) In a world all his or her own (ii)			
Immobilization (a)	Response (motor)	Hyperactivity (cp) Restlessness (cp)	Self-stimulation (sed)
Sluggishness (ii) Passivity (ii) Drowsiness (ii) Clumsiness Depression (pp)			
Failure to develop speech (sed)	Response (verbal)	Extremely talkative (a)	Uses profanity (cp) Verbally abusive (a)
Failure to use language for communication (sed)			
Self-injurious (sed) Lawlessness (a) Destructiveness (cp)	Order	Overly conforming (a)	Resistance to change (sed) Compulsive (a)
Disruptiveness (cp) Attention seeking (cp) Irresponsibility (cp) Disobedience (cp)			
Bizarre or stereotyped behavior (sed) Bizarre interests (sed)	Exploratory	Plunges into activities (a)	Tries to do everything at once (a)
Anxiety (pp) Preoccupation (pp) Doesn't know how to have fun (pp)			

(continued)

TABLE 7-2 *(continued)*

Too Little	→	Optimal	→	Too Much
	Behaves like adult (pp) Shyness (pp)			
Preoccupation with inanimate objects (sed) Extreme self-isolation (sed) Inability to relate to people (sed)	Social withdrawal (pp) Alienates others (a) Aloofness (pp) Prefers younger playmates (ii) Acts bossy (cp) Secretiveness (pp) Fighting (cp) Temper tantrums (cp)	Social	Hypersensitivity (pp) Jealousy (cp) Overly dependent (a)	Inability to function alone (a)
Blunted, uneven or fragmented intellectual development (sed)	Lacks self-care skills (a) Lacks basic school skills (a) Laziness in school (ii) Dislike for school (cp) Lacks vocational skills (a)	Mastery	Preoccupation with academics (a)	Overintellectualizing (a)

KEY: cp conduct problem (Quay, 1972)
ii inadequacy-immaturity (Quay, 1972)
pp personality problem (Quay, 1972)
sed severely emotionally disturbed (GAP, 1966; Eisenberg & Kanner, 1956)
a authors

Source: "Common characteristics of disturbed children viewed as negative variants of six levels of learning competence." Reprinted by permission from F. M. Hewett & F. D. Taylor. (1980). *The emotionally disturbed child in the classroom: The orchestration of success* (2nd ed.). Boston: Allyn and Bacon.

FIGURE 7-2   Behavior Network

Inappropriate Amounts of Behavior	Conditions Influencing the Behavior (task, teachers, peers, parents, community, etc.)	Appropriate Amounts of Behavior
Fails to begin tasks		Begins task promptly
Does not attend to task		Attends to task
Fails to complete tasks		Completes task
Does not follow directions		Follows directions
Does careless or sloppy work		Completes neat work
Is often out of seat		Remains in seat
Interrupts others		Speaks when appropriate
Talks out		Talks with permission
Lies		Tells the truth
Uses abusive language		Speaks appropriately
Tattles		Does not reveal information
Appears to be shy		Interacts with others
Is hypersensitive		Accepts criticism
Needs constant reassurance		Participates without constant re-assurance
Makes self-deprecating statements		Does not make self-deprecating statements
Cries when inappropriate		Cries when appropriate
Engages in inappropriate age play		Engages in appropriate age play
Fails to initiate contact with others		Initiates contact with others
Fails to engage in group activities		Initiates contact with group

(continued)

FIGURE 7-2 *(continued)*

Inappropriate Amounts of Behavior	Conditions Influencing the Behavior (task, teachers, peers, parents, community, etc.)	Appropriate Amounts of Behavior
Has few friends		Has friends
Refuses to share with others		Shares with others
Appearance of mood does not fit setting		Appearance of mood fits setting
Claims illness without apparent physical cause		Is ill with apparent cause
Runs away		Accepts consequences of behavior
Is uncooperative		Cooperates with others
Is disorderly in class		Follows class rules
Is disorderly in school		Follows school rules
Is assaultive		Resolves problems without violence
Destroys property		Respects property
Exhibits temper tantrums		Responds appropriately
Steals		Takes things with permission
Cheats		Completes work on own

Source: Based on information from Reinert (1980), Hewett & Taylor (1980), Quay, Morse, & Cutler (1966), and Campbell, Dobson, & Bost (1985).

Others, such as nonparticipation, are problems because of their nonoccurrence.

The list of behaviors in Figure 7-2 is intended to be very general in nature. Due to differences in teacher tolerance, it is very difficult to state that a particular behavior is inappropriate and in need of remediation. Additionally, a behavior may take many forms. Some students, for example, will be assaultive by hitting, others by throwing things, and yet others will be assaultive in a completely unanticipated manner. Therefore, once a general behavior has been identified, the observer should seek to precisely describe and define the specific behavior that is troublesome.

Behaviors in this skill network should also be described in relation to the surrounding environmental conditions. In evaluating a behavior such as stealing, for example, it is important to know from whom the student steals and if the student only steals specific items in specific settings. It also may be important to know if the stealing was precipitated by an event such as a dare from peers, a demand from a delinquent peer group, or a need for money or food.

It must also be determined if the inappropriate behavior was due to a student's lack of ability, skills, or knowledge. A kindergarten student, for example, may not have the ability to stay in his or her seat and complete long written assignments. Likewise, an older student may not interact appropriately with peers simply because of a lack of knowledge of social skills. If the behavior problem is due to a lack of skills, assessment must focus on what and how new and more appropriate behaviors should be taught.

Many of these appropriate companion behaviors are listed in this skill network. When attempting to decrease an inappropriate behavior, an appropriate companion behavior should be targeted. An applied intervention will hopefully move the behavior toward the more appropriate dimension.

■ Severity of Behavior Problems

Not all behaviors presented in the network displayed in Figure 7–2 can be assessed at any one time. It therefore becomes necessary to decide which behaviors should receive a comprehensive evaluation. One way of analyzing problem behaviors is presented in the matrix in Figure 7–3. Problem behaviors, in this scheme, are evaluated along two different continua. On the vertical axis, behavior can be evaluated by devices such as checklists and direct observation. This analysis allows a determination of the relative frequency or duration of the behavior.

Along the horizontal axis, problem behavior is assessed as to its severity. This examination may address factors such as the extent to which a behavior is at variance with the expectations of others, the intent of the behavior, and the magnitude of the behavior. These elements are difficult, if not impossible, to objectively measure. They therefore must be analyzed subjectively in a cautious and thoughtful manner.

Where a behavior lies on these continua is a matter of individual opinion. As illustrated in Panel 1 of Figure 7–3, Teacher A has a high tolerance for student whispering and may not view this behavior as a

FIGURE 7-3 Problem Behavior Matrix

Panel 1

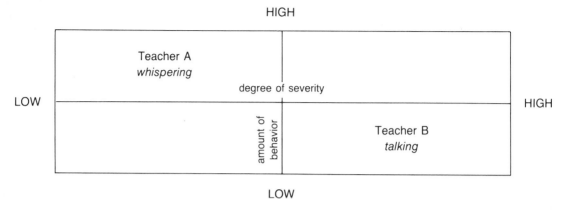

Panel 2

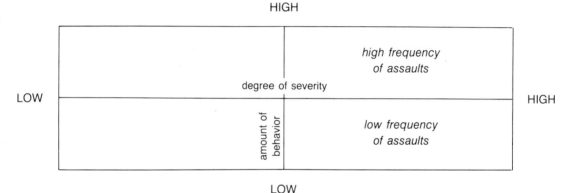

serious infraction even when it occurs frequently. Teacher B, on the other hand, has a very low tolerance for student talking and views this behavior as being extremely inappropriate even when it occurs at a very low frequency. As illustrated in Panel 2 of Figure 7-3, the student who, for no apparent reason, severely assaults a peer may be judged to have a problem of extreme severity even if the behavior occurs infrequently. If this problem occurs quite often, it may be judged to be of monumental proportions.

A comprehensive assessment may be warranted if a behavior is thought to be of even moderate severity. Behavior of extreme severity and frequency, however, must be assessed as quickly as possible. This assessment should address the behavior, the demands of the environ-

TABLE 7-3   **Guidelines for Selecting Behaviors to Assess**

1. Is the behavior related to conditions in the home, community, school, or classroom?
2. Is the behavior symptomatic or related to an illness, physical or emotional disability, drug, or medicine?
3. Is the behavior related to a lack of skill, ability, or knowledge?
4. Is the behavior described in words that indicate what the student does?
5. Can the behavior be observed and measured?
6. How bothersome is the behavior?
7. How extensive is the problem?
8. Is the amount of behavior to be increased or decreased?
9. Have the environmental variables and the settings in which the behavior occurs been adequately assessed?

ment, expectations, and other factors that caused the behavior to be viewed as troublesome. If this assessment is conducted in a careful and comprehensive manner, there is an increased probability that any accompanying interventions will more fully meet the needs of the student.

When assessing behavior, care must be taken to examine the environment, expectations, and the observed behavior. The guidelines presented in Table 7-3 assist in identifying behavior and conditions that may be selected for assessment. By addressing the questions in Table 7-3, behavior problems can be precisely described and then assessed by using appropriate evaluative devices.

SELECTING AND ADMINISTERING AN ASSESSMENT PROCEDURE

Assessment procedures may be used to collect information about the environment, expectations, and behaviors present in settings in which the behavior problem exists and does not exist. Several questions should be addressed related to the assessment of behavior:

ENVIRONMENT

1. What and how do conditions in the home, community, school, and classroom influence the student's behavior?
2. Are there any physiological or psychological conditions or problems that may influence the student's behavior?

EXPECTATIONS

1. What and how do expectations about the instructional program influence student and teacher behavior?
2. What and how do expectations about behavior and student characteristics influence student and teacher behavior?

BEHAVIOR

1. What appropriate and inappropriate behaviors are exhibited across settings?
2. What and how do antecedent and consequent events influence the student's behavior?

Data from these questions aid in further defining the specific type and extent of the problem and in developing interventions. These questions provide a focus for the periodic and continuous assessment procedures that may be used for instructional planning. Assessment data may aid in further defining the specific type and extent of the problem and in identifying variables that may be useful in developing interventions.

Periodic assessment procedures may be either formal or informal. They yield global information that may be used for developing long-term objectives or identifying general skills/behaviors that are in need of a more precise evaluation. In the assessment of behavior, periodic procedures can be used to evaluate the extent of change in a specific behavior—for example, talk-outs, which may occur over a period of time such as a school year. Additionally, these procedures may be used to evaluate a general class of behaviors, such as aggressive responses, which would include specific behaviors such as hitting, kicking, and biting.

■ Formal Procedures

Several types of formal devices may be used to assess behavior and factors that may be related to behavior. Personality tests, many of which are standardized, are generally used in clinical settings by mental health professionals and are thought to assess psychological variables that underlie and affect behavior. Use of these tests in instructional planning is limited and has been called into question by authors such as Kauffman (1981), and O'Leary and Johnson (1979).

Some norm-referenced behavior rating scales are commonly used in school settings. Typically, the teacher, parent, or other individual completing the form answers a series of questions with either a yes or no response or a response that indicates the frequency of occurrence of the behavior. These answers are then tabulated and the results compared to scores obtained by similar students. The results of this assessment indicate how different an individual student's behavior may be from that of his or her peers. A list of the most commonly used formal assessment procedures related to behavior is provided in the Appendix.

■ Informal Procedures

Informal procedures may also be used to periodically assess the behavior of students. They may be used alone or to supplement previously acquired information. These devices may be commercially produced or teacher-made. If teacher constructed, they may be adapted to address the particular behaviors or elements of the setting to be assessed. In the next section, several informal procedures will be described including checklists and rating instruments, interviews, and direct observation.

Each of these assessment procedures can be used in some degree to assess environmental variables, expectations, and behaviors. As illustrated in Table 7–4, checklists, rating scales, and interviews can be used to measure an opinion or perception about environmental variables, expectations, and behavior. Interviews also provide a direct measure of in-

TABLE 7-4   Assessment Procedures and the Areas Assessed

AREAS TO BE ASSESSED	*ASSESSMENT PROCEDURES*		
	Checklists and Rating Scales	*Interviews*	*Direct Observation*
Environmental Variables	provides a measure of the rater's perception of environmental variables	provides a measure of the interviewer's perception of environmental variables	provides a measure of the effect of the environmental variables
Expectations	provides a measure of the rater's perception of expectations	provides a measure of the interviewer's perception of expectations	provides a measure of the observer's perception of expectations
Behavior	provides a measure of the rater's perception of behavior	provides a measure of the interviewer's perception of behavior	provides a direct measure of the amount of behavior

teraction and social skills of the person being interviewed. Observation can be used to directly measure the effect of environmental variables and the amount of behavior. Observation may also provide a measure of the observer's perception of the expectations present in any setting.

☐ *Checklists and Rating Instruments*
Checklists and rating instruments may be used to sample many elements of the environment. Checklists assist in determining whether or not a behavior has occurred. Rating scales are designed to illustrate the perceived degree to which a behavior or characteristic is present. These instruments may be given periodically throughout the school year to estimate any changes that may have occurred in student behavior. They may also be used to identify expectations, student likes, dislikes, and behaviors in need of more extensive and continuous assessment.

CHECKLISTS   Checklists are easy to use and typically consist of items or questions that address the most important concerns of the individual conducting the assessment. They should provide an examination of a wide range of variables that may affect behavior. Wiederholt, Hammill, and Brown (1978) suggest that a checklist should evaluate the student's behavior, interaction with peers, and teacher–student interaction. Additionally, they suggest that because checklists are considered to be a quick screening device, the checklist should rarely exceed thirty items. An example of such a checklist is presented in Figure 7–4.

FIGURE 7-4   Problems in Social and Emotional Development

Teacher Checklist: This measure was designed to be used by teachers in any classroom to make them more aware of their students' behavior. This list might help identify behavior that otherwise might be overlooked or misunderstood. From here the teacher might want to take frequency counts of identified behavior, or in some other way further analyze the situation.

	FREQUENTLY	NOT FREQUENTLY
I. Self Image		
A. Makes "I can't" statements		
B. Reacts negatively to correction		

(continued)

FIGURE 7-4 *(continued)*

	FREQUENTLY	NOT FREQUENTLY

C. Gets frustrated easily
D. Makes self-critical statements
E. Integrity:
    1. Cheats
    2. Tattles
    3. Steals
    4. Destroys property
F. Makes excessive physical complaints
G. Takes responsibility for actions
H. Reacts appropriately to praise
II. Social Interaction
    A. Seeks attention by acting immaturely: thumbsucking, babytalking, etc.
    B. Interacts negatively
    C. Fails to interact
    D. Initiates positive interaction
    E. Initiates negative interaction
    F. Reacts with anger, verbally
    G. Reacts with anger, physically
III. Adult/Teacher Relationships
    A. Seeks attention by acting immaturely
    B. Excessively demands attention
    C. Reacts appropriately to teacher requests
    D. Inappropriately reacts to authority figures
IV. School Related Activities
    A. Attends to task
    B. Exhibits off-task behavior
    C. Interferes with the other students' learning
    D. Shows inflexibility to routine changes

Source: Developed by the following teachers and used with their permission: Lee Person, Becky Beck Browning, Mary Hughes Hiatt, and Margaret Morey-Brown. From ''Problems in Social and Emotional Development.'' Reprinted by permission from J. L. Wiederholt, D. D. Hammill, & V. Brown. (1978). *The Resource Teacher: A Guide to Effective Practices.* Boston: Allyn and Bacon.

To the Teacher: Date the checklist and complete one for each child. When the checklist has been completed and reviewed, write a narrative report with explanations and suggestions for the future. To be effective, the teacher must use the results to make changes in his/her classroom.

While checklists provide a relatively rapid analysis of behavior and the environment, they fail to distinguish between one occurrence of an inappropriate behavior and many occurrences of an inappropriate behavior (Wallace & Larsen, 1978). McMahon (1984) notes that checklists may not provide as accurate an assessment of behavior as other instruments and therefore should be used with caution.

BEHAVIOR RATING INSTRUMENTS Rating scales are similar to checklists. They differ in that behavior is rated in terms of frequency or intensity. They can be used, for example, to determine the perceived severity or frequency of occurrence of a behavior. Rating scales, therefore, provide a more comprehensive analysis of behavior than do checklists.

Rating scales can be quite useful in that they have been shown to accurately identify students who have behavior problems (Kerr & Nelson, 1983). Special care should be taken to select specific items or behaviors that are easily and clearly observed such as "out of seat" or "raises hand" (Siegel, Dragovich, & Marholin, 1976).

Items should be unambiguous and relevant to the age of the student being evaluated. One method of ensuring these criteria is to use or develop items directly related to the behavior network used in the classroom. This network, which is specific to the setting, provides a comprehensive list of the behaviors and expectations related to the classroom environment. Shuller and McNamara (1976) suggest that by increasing the specificity of the items, the reliability of the rating scale also increases.

Rating instruments must also have some means of ranking the behavior along a dimension such as frequency of occurrence or intensity. McMahon (1984) suggests that this measurement scale be fairly specific and offer illustrations. For example, rather than asking the rater to determine if a behavior occurs "occasionally" and "frequently," it would be more helpful to ask if the behavior occurred a certain number of times during a period of time such as a week.

Scales of measurement may be descriptive, numeric, or graphic (Wallace & Larsen, 1978). In *descriptive scales*, the rater is asked to choose from a series of descriptive answers that illustrates the existence or degree of a certain trait or characteristic. In a *numeric scale*, the rater is required to choose the number of an answer that indicates the degree of presence of the trait or characteristic. *Graphic scales*, which are probably the most appropriate scales for use in school settings, allow behaviors or traits to be measured along a horizontal continuum. This type of scale has the advantage of allowing behavior to be rated at any point along this line. An example of each type of scale is provided in Figure 7–5. The three types of scales can be used with teacher-made questions or instruments such as the one in Figure 7–4.

FIGURE 7-5 Scales of Measurement

Check or circle the answer that most accurately represents your perception of the student.

Descriptive Scale

Is the student aggressive when playing with peers?

_____ Always (in all play settings)
_____ Often (in many settings)
_____ Sometimes
_____ Usually plays appropriately, rarely is aggressive
_____ Always plays appropriately, never is aggressive

Numerical Scale

How dependent is the student on others?

1. always dependent on others
2. usually dependent on others
3. sometimes dependent on others
4. rarely dependent on others
5. never dependent on others

Graphic Scale

How would you rate the student's skill in working with others?

1	2	3	4	5
lacking	poor	fair	good	excellent

Another procedure, suggested by Hops and Greenwood (1981), allows raters to rank individuals in order of the frequency or severity of behavior. To do this, three steps must be followed:

1. List all class members.
2. Divide the list into two groups in relation to the frequency of occurrence or severity of the behavior.
3. Rank each member of both groups in relation to the frequency of occurrence or severity of the behavior.

This procedure is illustrated in Figure 7-6.

Rating instruments are not designed to directly measure behavior. They do, however, allow for a relatively quick evaluation of the rater's perception of behavior and of the environment. These data can be quite useful in identifying areas in need of further assessment as well as the expectations and perceptions present in the setting (Mash & Terdal,

---

FIGURE 7-6   Class Behavior Ranking

Step 1

Class Members:
  Student A
  Student B
  Student C
  Student D
  Student E
  Student F

Step 2

Group 1: Those who most often participate in group activities
  Student A
  Student B
  Student F

Group 3: Those who least often participate in group activities
  Student C
  Student D
  Student E

Step 3

Amount of participation in group activities
  Student B (most often)
  Student F
  Student A
  Student C
  Student E
  Student D (least often)

1976). Hewett and Taylor (1980) state that the data from rating instruments provide a general picture of student performance in educational settings. This information, however, may often be of limited use in instructional planning due to its lack of specificity.

The data obtained from rating scales may show a great deal of variability. Caution should be taken to ensure that this variable is not caused by poorly stated or ambiguous questions. Additionally, the rating instrument and its use should be fully explained to the individual who will be completing the instrument.

If the rating instrument is reliable and valid, however, the variability may be influenced by environmental factors that affect student behavior. This is illustrated, for example, by a case in which a student receives uniformly low ratings related to conduct in classes in which there are few rules and little structure, while in structured classes with specific rules and consequences, the student's ratings are considerably higher.

Authors such as Wiggins (1973) and Algozzine and Schmid (1981) note that a number of factors may adversely affect the reliability and validity of rating instruments. The accuracy of responses, for example, may be affected by asking raters to judge behavior in retrospect. Data from rating scales may also be affected by biases (such as race, sex, and assigned label) that the rater may have towards the characteristics of the individual being rated. This information can be useful in identifying perceptions held by the rater towards the student. If the data are biased, however, they may not provide an accurate analysis of the behavior of the person being rated.

Data from rating instruments can provide a great deal of insight into the behaviors, expectations, and environmental variables present in an educational setting. If used appropriately, this information can be useful in instructional planning.

SOCIOMETRIC RATING INSTRUMENTS   Sociometric techniques yield information concerning students' social relationships and status within peer groups. These instruments can be used to assess social interaction by identifying those who are perceived as being isolated and those who are viewed most positively by peers.

To conduct the assessment, each student is asked to list, in order, one or several peers with whom they would like to engage in activities such as schoolwork, playing, or eating lunch. McCandless and Marshall (1957) suggest that this procedure be modified for students who cannot read or write by allowing them to place in order the pictures of their classmates with whom they would like to participate in activities.

Questions to use in conducting this procedure may consist of items such as:

1. With whom would you most enjoy playing?
2. With whom would you most enjoy working with on a science project?
3. Of all your classmates, with whom would you most enjoy going on a vacation?

The most popular students associated with particular activities can be identified if responses are kept secret and the questions are stated in a positive manner. Coie, Dodge, and Coppotelli (1982) note that students who are experiencing problems with peers may be more easily and accurately identified by asking questions in negative terms, such as "With whom would you least enjoy working with on a science project?" Caution must be taken in using negative items, however, in that such questions may cause students to act even more negatively toward the identified individual.

Responses to these items may provide some insight as to who is most and least popular, and who should be the target for activities that foster social relationships. Moreover, this information may suggest who should be grouped together for class activities.

A sociogram, which is a visual representation of the social structure of the peer group, may be developed by identifying the classmates each student most and least prefers to participate with in an activity. The sociogram displayed in Figure 7–7 illustrates, for example, with whom

FIGURE 7–7 Sociogram

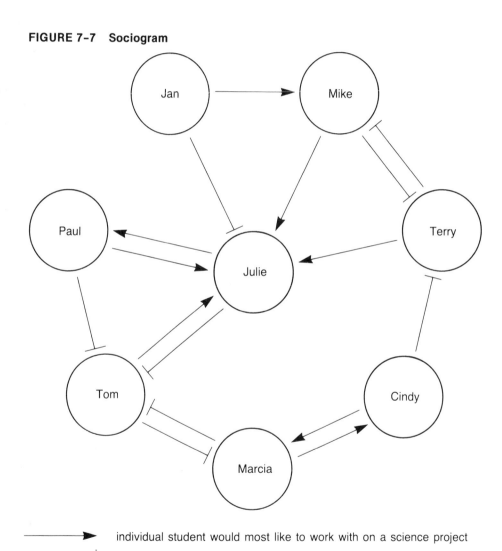

individual student would most like to work with on a science project

individual student would least like to work with on a science project

a group of eight students would most and least like to work with on a science project.

Kerr and Nelson (1983) suggest that three questions must be answered in order to analyze a sociogram:

1. Which students were entirely left out of the rankings, if you use a sociometric that permits exclusion?
2. Who was clearly rated negatively by his peers?
3. Which students are popular and might serve as good peer models? (pp. 178–179)

Hymel and Asher (1977) suggest that peer relationships can also be measured by providing students with a list of their classmates and asking them to rate each peer according to the degree to which they preferred to work with each classmate on an activity. This is illustrated in Figure 7–8.

The data from sociometric rating instruments must be cautiously used. Greenwood, Walker, Todd, and Hops (1979) and Gottman (1977) suggest that actual peer interactions may differ significantly from that indicated by sociometric procedures. Additionally, as Hops and Lewin (1984) indicate, there are continuing questions as to the reliability and validity of sociometric rating instruments. They conclude that such devices may not accurately identify students who are experiencing problems in social relationships. If carefully used and constructed, however, sociometric rating instruments may at least suggest which students or situations should receive further and more extensive assessment.

SELF-REPORT RATING INSTRUMENTS Self-report rating instruments may be useful in obtaining insight into the nature and intensity of a student's behavior, feelings, and thoughts (Watson & Tharp, 1985). More-

FIGURE 7–8 **Sociometric Rating Instrument**

Directions: Indicate to what degree you would like to work with each classmate on an art project.

	Not at all 1	Maybe 2	Very much 3
Kyle	X		
Eddie	X		
Lindsey		X	
Janet	X		
Elaine			X

over, they may assist students in understanding and labeling many of their problems, fears, and feelings.

The Q-sort technique, suggested by Stephenson (1953) and Kroth (1975), allows students to identify discrepancies between their "real" and "ideal" selves. To do this, the student must sort a deck of twenty-five cards, each of which contains a statement related to the setting, onto a pyramid formboard. The formboard, displayed in Figure 7-9, contains nine categories with numerical values ranging from "most like me" (value of 1), to "most unlike me" (value of 8). An example of the statements used with elementary-age students is provided in Table 7-5.

In the first or "real" self sort, the student places a card on each square of the formboard so that the responses most accurately represent his or her current behavior. After recording the answers, a second or "ideal" self sort is conducted in which the student indicates how he or she would like to be perceived. Teachers must then analyze each item for discrepancies that may exist between the "real" and "ideal" self sorts. This is illustrated, for example, when a student rates "follows directions" on the "real" self sort as "very much unlike me" (a value of B) and "most like me" (a value of 1) on the "ideal" self sort. If large dif-

FIGURE 7-9   Behavior Formboard

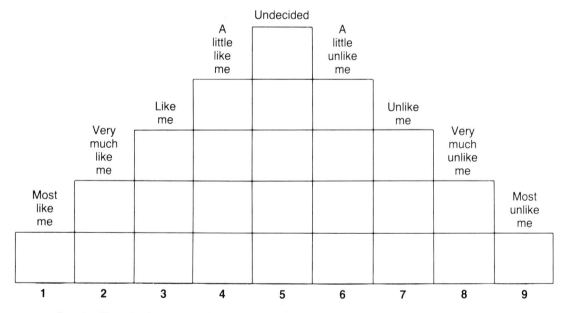

Source: "Behavior Formboard." Reprinted by permission from R. L. Kroth. (1975). *Communicating with Parents of Exceptional Children: Improving Parent-Teacher Relationships.* Denver: Love Publishing Co.

TABLE 7-5   Elementary-level School Items on the Behavioral Q-sort

1. Gets work done on time
2. Pokes or hits classmates
3. Out of seat without permission
4. Scores high in spelling
5. Plays with objects while working
6. Scores high in reading
7. Disturbs neighbors by making noise
8. Is quiet during class time
9. Tips chair often
10. Follows directions
11. Smiles frequently
12. Often taps foot, fingers, or pencil
13. Pays attention to work
14. Works slowly
15. Throws objects in class
16. Reads well orally
17. Talks to classmates often
18. Scores high in English
19. Talks out without permission
20. Rocks in chair
21. Scores high in arithmetic
22. Asks teacher questions
23. Uses free time to read or study
24. Works until the job is finished
25. Walks around room during study time

Source: "Elementary-level school items on the behavioral Q-sort." Reprinted by permission from R. L. Kroth. (1975). *Communicating with parents of exceptional children: Improving parent-teacher relationships.* Denver: Love Publishing Co.

ferences of four points or more appear, the area may be targeted for further assessment or intervention.

Students may also report their feelings and behavior by completing teacher-made checklists and rating instruments. To do this, students may select from a list those items that they believe accurately reflect their behavior or feelings. The items may be related to specific behaviors, such as "fights with playmates," or may be descriptive adjectives such as "sad," "hard working," or "friendly" (Mercer & Mercer, 1985). Additionally, teachers may ask students to rate the degree to which they are like or unlike each item. This is illustrated by what Safran and Safran (1984) refer to as a mood chart. On this rating instrument, the students circle a number on a five-point scale that indicates their current mood concerning four common feelings: sad–happy, withdrawn–friendly, bored–interested, mean–nice.

Rating scales can also be constructed to allow students to report the intensity of their feelings or behaviors (Watson & Tharp, 1985). To do this, the student must develop a scale that graphically illustrates a range of feelings. This is illustrated with the following five-point scale: 1) not angry, 2) slightly angry, 3) moderately angry, 4) very angry, and 5) extremely angry. Students can then use this scale to rate their feelings associated with specific situations that occur throughout the school day. This may assist students in developing a certain amount of self-understanding and identifying the intensity of feelings. When developing a scale of this type, however, great care should be taken to ensure that the student has the skill to label feelings and that there are enough points on the scale to allow an accurate discrimination to be made.

Self-report instruments are dependent upon the student's ability and willingness to accurately report his or her perceptions of behavior or feelings. Self-report rating-scale data, if accurate, may indicate elements of the environment that are particularly troublesome to the student. Once identified, interventions can then be applied to the environment that may reduce the problem.

It may be far beyond the expertise of the classroom teacher, however, to use these data for intensive counseling. Therefore, teachers must very carefully determine why and for what use these type of data are being collected.

☐ *Interviews*

Interviews can be used to obtain information about environmental variables, student behavior, and the expectations of others. Wahler and Cormier (1970) state that interviews allow for an assessment of situations that may otherwise be impossible to observe such as past events or events that occur in the home. Additionally, interviews allow for the direct observation of the social behavior of the individual being interviewed. Interviews may also be quite useful with students who cannot read, write, or respond to checklists or rating scales.

The purpose of the interview must be carefully delineated before being conducted. Gross (1984) suggests that interviews should assist in specifically describing the behavior problem of interest. Of special concern should be a determination of the perceived severity and generality of the problem. Additionally, interviews should assist in identifying the variables that may influence the behavior, such as antecedent and consequent conditions, environmental variables, social relationships, and the expectations of others. Kanfer and Saslow (1969) add to this list by stating that interviews should also determine the student's motives for engaging in the behavior and skill in controlling his or her behavior.

In addition to interviewing the student, it is generally helpful to interview parents, teachers, and other significant adults. This is especially true if the student is unwilling or unable to be interviewed.

Interviews should always be conducted in a private setting in which rapport is quickly established. Great care should be taken to encourage and support the participation of the individual being interviewed. Interviews may be unstructured, in which there is no set format, or structured, in which the interviewer follows a prearranged list of questions. Regardless of the type of interview, however, the goal is to clarify and identify the extent of the behavior problem and identify any variables that may be associated with the behavior.

Maloney and Ward (1976) suggest that interviews should start with general, open-ended questions that require, and even encourage, extended answers on the part of the individual being interviewed. Questions such as "what happens when Betty gets mad at home," or "what do you do when Betty has a temper tantrum?" may foster a great deal of valuable and possibly unanticipated information. If the conversation begins to stray, a statement such as "Yes, I understand what you're saying, but describe Betty's behavior at home to me a little more," will often be enough to focus attention on the behavior of interest.

The interviewer may want to more precisely identify areas of interest by asking the person being interviewed to specifically address the problems and conditions associated with the behavior. To do this, the interviewer may have to be quite persistent by asking questions that require answers of increasing detail, such as "When does Sally have temper tantrums?" and "What was she doing immediately before the temper tantrum?"

Interviews should also examine the perceptions of all individuals related to the behavior problem. The student should be asked if he or she believes that the behavior that was exhibited was appropriate. Additionally, parents, teachers, and students must be asked what behaviors should be expected. By addressing these questions, numerous other elements related to the behavior can be examined so that discrepancies in what is expected and what actually occurs can be reduced.

Interviews may also be accomplished in a written format. Open-ended statements that require written responses may be used to assess the student's feelings and perceptions. The student may be asked to respond to statements such as:

I become angry when _____

I'm happiest when _____

I work best when _____

This type of assessment is dependent upon the teacher developing questions that stimulate the student in identifying elements of the environment that affect behavior.

Essays or written reports on feelings, interests, or recent activities can be used to gain insight into the perceptions and expectations of students. Mercer and Mercer (1985) suggest that students may provide an insight into their behavior by writing an autobiography that addresses a particular event or a broad spectrum of topics. For those students who have difficulty writing, the report could be taped or written as a language experience story. Norris (1985) indicates that students' problem solving and reasoning can be assessed by using essay tests. These tests may require students to solve relatively complex problems by using clues and logic.

Before using written reports with students, teachers and school personnel must determine for what purpose the information is being collected. It may be more appropriate for mental health professionals to collect this information if intensive psychotherapy is planned. Information from these reports can be used, however, to identify environmental variables or events that precipitate or are related to the occurrence of inappropriate behavior. Once identified, many of these variables can be altered by using appropriate school-based interventions.

The information obtained from interviews may be inaccurate if the person being interviewed or the inteviewer is biased. If the questions are poorly stated, the person being interviewed is led to answer in a certain manner, or if respondents are asked to recall in detail events that occurred long ago, the information given may be inaccurate. Interviews can be helpful, however, if they are used for a specific purpose and in conjunction with other assessment data.

☐ *Direct Observation*

Observation can provide accurate and useful data about the student's behavior and environment. It can also be used to measure academic performance and the amount of interaction that occurs between the student and peer and the student and teacher. Before any observation is conducted, however, the target behavior must be precisely described. This description should allow the observer to identify the occurrence of the behavior and eliminate any inference or conclusions about the source or cause of the behavior. Statements like "Johnny throws things" and "Mary talks out in class without teacher permission" are more useful and accurate than those such as "Larry gets angry with himself."

All behavior has several qualities that may be measured: frequency, duration, latency, topography, and magnitude. The description and definition of the behavior often determines which of these qualities will be selected for observation.

Frequency refers to the number of times a behavior occurs within a period of time. Frequency is expressed, for example, by stating that a student "hits others seven times per hour" or "talks out in class without permission two times per minute." In order to determine frequency, the observer must accurately record the number of times the behavior being assessed occurred and the total length of time of the observation. The frequency of discrete behaviors such as hitting, talk-outs, or hand-raises may be measured. It sometimes is desirable to convert these numbers to a rate per minute or hour. This is necessary when the length of the observation time is not constant, as illustrated in the example in Figure 7–10. These data indicate that there has been a change in the number of talk-outs. It is very difficult, however, to determine if there has been a change in the rate of the behavior because of the daily change in the length of the observation. By dividing the number of behaviors (talk-outs) by the length of the observation time, however, these numbers can be converted to a rate per minute. This allows an accurate comparison to be made across days.

Duration refers to the total length of time from the beginning to the end of the behavior. Behaviors such out-of-seat or on-task may be measured in terms of time or duration.

Latency is the length of time it takes for the student to begin a response after being given instructions or told to begin a task. After telling a student to begin a math assignment, the teacher may, for example, measure how long it takes after being given the instruction for the student to actually begin the math assignment.

Behavior may also be described in terms of its shape, form, or *topography*. This usually is accomplished by a precise description of the behavior, such as "Frankie turns to his right and throws his pencil on the floor when given a direction by Mr. Smith."

Magnitude, or the force or intensity of the behavior, is generally measured in a subjective manner. As previously stated, this may be measured by using a rating scale in which the observer indicates his or her perception of the strength of the response. The loudness of talking, the force of a hit, and the severity of a temper tantrum may be measured in this manner.

Observation should focus on a specific quality of behavior such as frequency or duration. The observation sessions should be as long as possible so as to ensure the representativeness of the data. This allows for

FIGURE 7–10 Converting Observational Data to Frequency

Student: John

Day	Number of Talk-Outs	Time Observed	Frequency
1	4	2 minutes	2/minute
2	8	5 minutes	1.6/minute
3	23	17 minutes	1.35/minute
4	39	28 minutes	1.39/minute

the accurate measurement of behaviors that only occur infrequently or in particular settings.

The observational data collected should be quickly recorded. Trusting data to memory is generally not a good strategy. Additionally, care should be taken to ensure that students do not know they are being observed. Students who know they are the objects of examination may behave in a very untypical fashion. To prevent this, the observer must be as unobtrusive as possible and should refrain from looking at the student of interest for too long a period of time.

It also is essential to accurately observe and record the environmental conditions associated with the behavior of interest. By precisely describing these antecedent and consequent events, any variables that may affect behavior can be identified.

RECORDING OF BEHAVIOR   Behavior may be recorded by using one of several types of recording procedures: event, interval or time sample, duration and latency, anecdotal report, and permanent product. The recording procedure selected will depend upon the type of behavior, classroom constraints, and the planned use of the information.

Regardless of the procedure used, it is important that the observational data be accurate, reliable, and valid. Procedures for determining reliability and validity are presented in chapter 1. Effective and appropriate instructional plans cannot be developed unless there is a great deal of assurance that the data are accurate. This necessitates that the behavior be precisely defined, that a sensitive and appropriate measurement strategy be selected, that the observer be well trained, and that the observational data be verified by an independent observer.

In periodic assessment, observations may be conducted at various times during the school year. The data from these observations could then be compared to illustrate change in performance. Additionally, the data from observations could be averaged over a period of time to show the general amount of gain that has occurred. This is illustrated when a teacher compares the average number of out-of-seat behaviors per week (during the first week a particular intervention is introduced) to the number of out-of-seat behaviors from the final week of the grading period. This periodic assessment would provide a very general analysis of student growth.

Event recording may be used to measure the frequency or rate of behavior. To record events, the observer must place a mark in the appropriate spot on an observation form each time the behavior occurs. As illustrated in Figure 7–11, the behavior, throwing items, occurred 7 times in 30 minutes on October 1, 5 times in 30 minutes on October 2, and 10 times in 30 minutes on October 3. If necessary, these data may be converted to rate per minute.

FIGURE 7-11   Event Recording Sample

Name: Jan
Behavior: throws things

Date	Time Period (start–stop)	Number of Behaviors (tallies)	Total Number of Behaviors
10/1	9:20–9:50	卌 //	7
10/2	9:20–9:50	卌	5
10/3	9:20–9:50	卌 卌	10

This method of recording is well suited for easily observed, discrete behaviors that have a clearly identifiable beginning and end (Alberto & Troutman, 1982). Event recording is particularly well suited for use in measuring specific behaviors that a teacher may wish to increase (such as hand raising, words read correctly, and appropriate verbal remarks) or to decrease (such as inappropriate talk-outs, words read incorrectly, and hitting). Event recording may also be used to measure teacher behavior by recording the way in which the teacher responds to appropriate and inappropriate student behavior.

Event recording may not be useful, however, if the behavior occurs at such a high frequency that it is impossible to accurately record the occurrences of the behavior. This procedure also may not be suitable for measuring the duration of a behavior. While it may be helpful to know, for example, the frequency of temper tantrums, it may be more useful to know the total length of time of each occurrence.

In *interval and time-sample recording*, a period of time is selected and divided into equal observation periods. With interval recording these periods are generally no longer than 30 seconds each, while in time-sample recording, the intervals may be several minutes in length. When using an interval-recording procedure the observer notes whether or not the behavior occurred in each time interval. As illustrated in Figure 7–12

FIGURE 7-12   Interval Recording Sample

+ = behavior occurred			0 = behavior did not occur		
30 sec.	30 sec.	30 sec.	30 sec.	30 sec.	30 sec.
+	+	0	+	+	0

each interval is 30 seconds and the behavior occurred in four of the 30-second time blocks.

With time-sample recording, the observer notes whether or not the behavior was occurring at the end of the time period. In Figure 7–13, for example, the behavior was occurring at the end of two of the six time intervals.

Data from interval and time-sampling procedures are reported as the percentage of time intervals in which the behavior occurred. This is calculated by using the following formula:

$$\frac{\text{\# of time intervals in which the behavior occurred}}{\text{total \# of observation intervals}} \times 100$$

Therefore, for the data in Figure 7–13, the following calculation could be made: $2/6 \times 100 = 33.33\%$.

Interval and time-sample recording may be useful in measuring behaviors that occur at such a high frequency that they cannot accurately be recorded (Barton & Ascione, 1984). This may be the case with self-injurious or highly repetitive behaviors.

These recording procedures may also be used to simultaneously observe numerous behaviors in one or more students. To do this, the observation form must allow for a quick recording of several behaviors. This may be done by using a code for behaviors such as the one illustrated in Figure 7–14. To use this form, the observer must write the appropriate letter code of the behavior that was observed in the time-interval block in which the behavior occurred. Swanson and Watson (1982) suggest that a behavior code must precisely identify behaviors that can be clearly observed and that have an identifiable beginning and end.

When used for group observation, each individual to be observed must be assigned a time interval within the observation period. In Figure 7–14, for example, student A would be observed during the first 15-second interval of each observation period, student B during the second 15-second interval, student C during the third 15-second interval, and student D during the fourth 15-second interval.

Interval and time-sample recording systems require the undivided

FIGURE 7-13   Time-Sample Recording

+ = behavior occurred				0 = behavior did not occur	
2 min.	2 min.	2 min.	2 min.	2 min.	2 min.
+	0	0	+	0	0

FIGURE 7-14   Behavior Coding Form for Interval and Time-Sample Recording

Code:
T = talk-out
O = out-of-seat
H = hits others
K = kicks others

1 minute					2 minutes					3 minutes			
15″	15″	15″	15″		15″	15″	15″	15″		15″	15″	15″	15″

4 minutes					5 minutes					6 minutes			
15″	15″	15″	15″		15″	15″	15″	15″		15″	15″	15″	15″

7 minutes					8 minutes					9 minutes			
15″	15″	15″	15″		15″	15″	15″	15″		15″	15″	15″	15″

10 minutes					11 minutes					12 minutes			
15″	15″	15″	15″		15″	15″	15″	15″		15″	15″	15″	15″

13 minutes					14 minutes					15 minutes			
15″	15″	15″	15″		15″	15″	15″	15″		15″	15″	15″	15″

Name of student or students _____

Date _____

attention of the observer who must observe and record the student's behavior, while at the same time watch a clock to ensure the behavior is recorded in the appropriate time interval. This process may become even more difficult when several students are being observed. A signaling device may assist the observer by emitting beeps at observation intervals. In the example provided in Figure 7-14, the beeps would occur every thirty seconds.

Interval and time-sample recording procedures only provide a very general estimation of the frequency and duration of behavior. Hitting, for example, may occur ten times during a particular interval, yet it would be recorded as if one hit had occurred. Likewise, with time sampling a student could be out of his or her seat for four minutes of the 5-minute time interval, yet because he or she was in seat at the end of the observation period, the out-of-seat behavior would not be recorded.

With latency and duration recording, time is recorded. *Latency recording* measures the length of time from the end of the stimulus, such as a request by a teacher or parent, to the beginning of a student's response, such as beginning an assignment. In *duration recording*, the time from the beginning to the end of the behavior is recorded. Duration and latency may be recorded by using forms such as those presented in Figure 7–15.

Duration may be reported as total length of time or as a percentage of the observation period. This is illustrated, for example, by stating that a student was off-task a total of 15 minutes, or 50% of the 30-minute observation period.

Latency is generally reported as the average time lapse between stimulus and response. In three instances, for example, a student may

FIGURE 7–15 Latency and Duration Recording Form

Latency Recording		
Name ___Sally___		
Date ___11/3___		
Behavior ___begins assignment___		
Time Request Given	*Time Behavior Starts*	*Latency Time*
9:10	9:15	5 minutes
10:25	10:35	10 minutes
10:50	10:58	8 minutes
11:30	11:42	12 minutes
Duration Recording		
Name ___Joe___		
Date ___11/3___		
Behavior ___out-of-seat___		
Time Behavior Starts	*Time Behavior Stops*	*Duration*
9:30	9:45	15 minutes
10:15	10:35	20 minutes
11:30	11:35	5 minutes
1:00	1:20	20 minutes

have taken two minutes, four minutes, and three minutes to begin a task. This may be reported as an average latency of three minutes.

Duration and latency are useful measures when length of time must be measured. The observer, however, must focus his or her complete attention on the subject. As Wallace and Larsen (1978) note, this may be quite difficult for the classroom teacher to do and still deliver the instructional program.

Teachers may also keep written or *anecdotal reports* reports of student behavior. Cartwright and Cartwright (1974) state that these records must provide a clear, factual description of behavior rather than a subjective analysis that necessitates interpretation. The following are examples of such statements:

> *Factual:* Johnny walked to Mary's desk and took her reading book. When she asked him to return it, he said, "No, it's mine now and I'm going to keep it."

> *Subjective:* Johnny maliciously stole Mary's reading book. Mary, ever so politely, asked him to please return it. Johnny rudely shouted, "No, it's mine now and I'm going to keep it."

All written records of student behavior should clearly and precisely identify the following information: who was involved, when the behavior occurred, where the behavior occurred, who saw the behavior occur, and what specifically happened.

Anecdotal reports may be kept in a log book and reviewed periodically to determine what conditions are associated with the behavior and if any change has been noted in the frequency of occurrence. Anecdotal reports may also be used to determine what antecedent and consequent events may be associated with behavior. To do this, the observer must record, as precisely as possible, a description of those events and conditions that occurred before the behavior, the behavior itself, and all reactions to the behavior. This may be done in the antecedent/behavior/consequent format in Table 7-1.

Perhaps the easiest way to observe behavior is to record the *permanent product*, or result of behavior. *Permanent product recording* allows the teacher to count such things as problems correct or incorrect after the behavior has occurred. The teacher does not have to spend valuable instructional time observing the behavior. Instead, the data, because it is durable, can be recorded later at a more convenient time as number or percent of problems correct or rate correct or incorrect.

Permanent product recording, however, will not provide an accurate assessment if someone other than the student completed the assignment or product. For this reason, teachers must be sure that the student is, in fact, the author of the behavior.

A large amount of classroom activity and homework results in a product. Permanent product recording allows these data to be collected and recorded in a very easy and manageable manner. Additionally, it is quite easy using this method to simultaneously measure the behavior products of a group or class of students.

☐ *Summary of Informal Periodic Assessment of Behavior*

Each of the assessment procedures described has a specific purpose and is designed to measure specific variables associated with behavior. A summary of these procedures is presented in Figure 7–16. These periodic assessment procedures should be used in an organized manner so that a precise analysis of behavior is accompanied by an examination of expectations and environmental variables that may affect behavior. Only with all of this information can effective educational programs be designed.

■ Continuous Assessment

The data from periodic assessment should indicate the behaviors and elements of the environment that are related to behavior problems. Moreover, this assessment should identify any discrepancies in expectations and behavior that exist in the setting. Once this information has been collected, it can be determined if an intervention should be instituted, and who or what it will involve.

If an intervention is instituted, data should be collected on a frequent basis. This allows for a continuous assessment of the effectiveness of the intervention by noting any discrete changes in behavior.

Most of the assessment used for periodic assessment can be used for continuous assessment. When used continuously, however, the focus is not upon condensing or generally describing the data, as is often the case with periodic assessment. Instead, the goal is to precisely measure variability in performance. This enables the observer to identify specific elements of the environment that are related to changes in the student's behavior. This information is absolutely essential if interventions are to meet the almost continuously changing needs of the student.

☐ *Rating Instruments*

It is often necessary to continuously measure student performance in numerous settings. This is often the case in middle and high schools in which students may frequently change classes and have several teachers. It is impossible for the teacher or observer to follow each student throughout the day and observe him or her in all classes. To solve this problem, teachers in each of the classes may be asked to complete a daily rating instrument. This provides a very general analysis of the observer's perception of the student's behavior. Rating instruments can be quickly completed after class activities so the teacher is not required to

FIGURE 7-16 Summary of Informal Periodic Assessment Procedures

Variables to be assessed	Rating Scales — Behavior	Sociometric	Self-report	Interviews	Event recording	Duration–latency recording	Interval–time-sample recording	Permanent product	Anecdotal reports
Environmental variables that may affect behavior	✓	✓	✓	✓	✓	✓		✓	✓
Expectations of student, behavior, environment	✓	✓	✓	✓					
General frequency or duration of behavior	✓	✓	✓	✓	✓	✓	✓	✓	✓
Specific frequency or duration of behavior					✓	✓	✓	✓	

continuously focus his or her attention upon the student while trying to instruct others.

The rating instrument should be fully explained to all individuals involved. The behavior should be precisely identified and positively stated so that the teacher is encouraged to look for appropriate behaviors. Additionally, the scale should allow for relatively fine discriminations to be made. An example is provided in Figure 7–17.

Before rating instruments are used on a continuous basis, the following questions should be addressed:

■ When during the class period should the rating instrument be completed?
■ Who is primarily responsible for remembering to complete the rating instrument?
■ Is the teacher to return the instrument to the student or return it to the special education teacher?
■ What will be done if the form is lost or destroyed?

FIGURE 7-17   Daily Rating Scale

Student's Name ___Robbie___
Behavior ___Talks out without permission___
Observer or observers name(s) ___Mrs. Smith___

Directions: Indicate, by using the accompanying rating scale, to what degree you observed the identified behavior.

Scale:
   1 (not at all)
   2 (rarely)
   3 (some of the time)
   4 (most of the time)
   5 (all of the time)

Day	Monday	Tuesday	Wednesday	Thursday	Friday
Class Period					
1	4	4	4	4	5
2	2	3	3	2	3
3	1	1	1	1	1
4	1	1	1	1	1
5	3	3	3	3	3
6	2	2	2	2	2

Once collected, these data can be used to assess teacher perceptions, general trends in student behavior, and conditions or classes related to an increased incidence of behavior problems.

Self-rating instruments can also be used so that students can rate their performance or interaction on a daily basis. This information can then be used to assist the student in identifying behaviors or environments that are troublesome.

Rating instruments do not provide a direct measure of behavior, but rather of the perception of behavior. This perception, in many cases, may be as important as the behavior itself.

☐ *Interviews*

Oral and written interviews may also be completed on a continuous basis. These interviews may be designed to assist the student in identifying how he or she dealt with problems during the school day. To do this, the student may be asked to state what happened and how the problem was resolved. If the problem was resolved inappropriately, it may be beneficial for the student to state appropriate ways for dealing with the problem or to identify how the problem could be rectified. This information can assist students in developing strategies for resolving problems and allow teachers to identify and reinforce those instances in which appropriate problem resolution occurred.

☐ *Direct Observation*

Continuous observations can provide a wealth of information to assist in instructional planning. As previously indicated, this information may be collected in a variety of ways that best fit the qualities of the behavior being measured and constraints of the setting.

It is essential that the behavior be identified so that all individuals involved know what is being measured. If temper tantrums are to be measured, the teacher must specifically describe the conditions and behaviors that will define a temper tantrum. For example: "A temper tantrum will be said to occur when the student begins shouting and stomping her feet on the floor." It must then be decided what quality of the behavior will be assessed. If it is most important to know the number of temper tantrums, then an event recording system might be used. It may be more important, however, to measure the total length of time of each occurrence. This means that a duration recording system must be used. After deciding what recording system will be used, the teacher should collect only the data that will be used in planning and implementing an instructional or behavior-management program. This allows the teacher to focus all data-collection efforts on the target behavior.

Data should be collected in an organized and efficient manner on uncomplicated forms that allow data to be quickly recorded. Additionally, the observations should be as long and frequent as possible and conducted in the setting in which the behavior occurs.

Observational data can be collected by teachers, independent observers, or the student. If the student is to observe himself or herself, he or she should be rewarded for simply collecting the data. If this is not done, the student may produce falsified data that is more to the teacher's liking.

All data should be verified periodically by independent observation. This often necessitates that an independent observer be used to judge the reliability of the observation.

Observations can also be verified by evaluating the product of the behavior. If, for example, time-on-task were being measured, the number of problems completed could be counted and used to indirectly verify if time-on-task was being accurately measured. There would be some reason to believe the accuracy of the observations if the length of time-on-task was accompanied by a corresponding increase in the number of problems completed.

RECORDING PERFORMANCE AND SETTING OBJECTIVES

All of the assessment information that has been collected concerning the environment and the student's behavior should be organized and recorded in a systematic manner. These data may be compiled by using record-keeping forms provided by the school district. It is often necessary, however, to organize assessment data to meet the individual requirements of the teacher or setting.

Record of Periodic Assessment Data

Periodic assessment data may be recorded on the Periodic Behavior Assessment Record presented in Figure 7–18. On this form are sections to record formal and informal assessment data related to behavior or environmental conditions. This information may be provided by the student and significant people in the student's life, such as a parent, teacher, or peer. After compiling these data, conclusions are made as to the student's strengths, problems, and the desired appropriate behavior.

Record of Continuous Assessment Data

Specific behaviors that need a more precise and continuous assessment can be identified by analyzing periodic assessment data in relation to the

FIGURE 7-18   Periodic Behavior Assessment Record

A. Formal Assessment Results

B. Informal Rating Instruments

C. Interview

D. Observation
(antecedents)   (behavior)   (consequences)

E. Conclusions
Strengths: _____

_____

Deficits: _____

_____

Appropriate behavior/conditions: _____

_____

Student's Name _____
Grade/Teacher _____
Date _____

behavior network. These behaviors may serve as the focus for further assessment and instruction and should be listed on the Continuous Assessment Record. This record, presented in the case study at the end of this chapter, lists the conditions related to assessment, the target behavior, current performance results, and the behavioral goal. The assessment data should indicate which behaviors differ significantly in terms of type or amount from the expectations of others. These behaviors and the related conditions may then be targeted for intervention.

The form displayed in Figure 7–19 allows an independent examiner, such as a counselor or teacher, to use all previously obtained data from periodic and continuous procedures to examine behavior. This is not in-

FIGURE 7-19 Summary of Observational Data

Observed Antecedents	Student Behavior	Observed Teacher or Peer Reactions (Consequences) to Student's Behavior		
		Reinforcing (positive)	Punishing (negative)	No Response
Teacher identified (not directly observed)				
Directly observed				

Conclusions about student behavior
1. How did he or she behave?
2. Did the behavior consistently occur?
3. Was the behavior significantly different from that of his or her classmates?
4. Was the behavior expected?
5. How was the behavior influenced by the behavior of others? By environmental variables?

Conclusions about teacher or peer reactions
1. How did the teacher or peer respond to various behaviors?
2. Were teacher or peer responses appropriate and consistent?
3. What was the effect of the teacher's or peer's responses?

Student's Name _____
Date _____ Grade _____
Teacher _____

tended to serve as an observation form; rather, it is to be used to compile and analyze data. On this form, anecdotal reports and other assessment formats may be used to describe antecedent conditions. The results from rating instruments, checklists, and interviews may also help to identify behaviors that the teacher perceives as troublesome. Observation is then used to analyze any discrepancies as well as to report the incidence and teacher reaction to student behavior. In using this form, the observer refers to a variety of instruments in order to systematically and thoroughly analyze conditions associated with behavior problems. After all of these data are collected, a number of crucial questions concerning student and teacher behavior should be addressed. These questions are detailed in Figure 7–19. The answers to these questions will dictate if an intervention should be instituted, and if so with whom and what it should be. Once these questions are answered, an instructional program can be effectively designed and implemented.

☐ *Charting*
The data obtained from continuous assessment procedures may be displayed on some form of daily chart or graph. This provides a specific focus for instruction and offers a clear visual display of changes in student behavior.

In order to develop effective instuctional interventions, it is important to know not only what and how much behavior has changed, but also what variables caused or influenced the change. Many of these variables can be identified by using single-subject designs to study what effect the systematic manipulation of interventions has on behavior.

The reversal design is one of the easiest for the classroom teacher to use. To do this, the observer must first collect data during a baseline phase (A) in which no intervention is present. This is followed by an intervention phase (B), a return to baseline conditions (A), and a reimposition of the intervention (B). The effectiveness of the intervention (B phase) may be illustrated if the target behavior changes only when the intervention phase is instituted. In Figure 7–20, for example, the effectiveness of a time-out intervention for throwing things is illustrated. The behavior is at a relatively high rate during both baseline phases. A significant decrease is noted, however, only when time-out is imposed (the B phase in Figure 7–20).

There are some behaviors, however, such as reading or hitting a baseball that do not return to their baseline rates after learning occurs or an intervention is imposed. Also, there are some cases, such as with self-mutilating behavior, when it would be unethical to use the return to baseline design. For these types of behaviors it is more appropriate to use a multiple baseline design. With this design, a baseline (A) is followed only by an intervention phase (B). This sequence is systematically and sequentially applied across subjects, behaviors, or settings. If change

FIGURE 7-20 Reversal Design

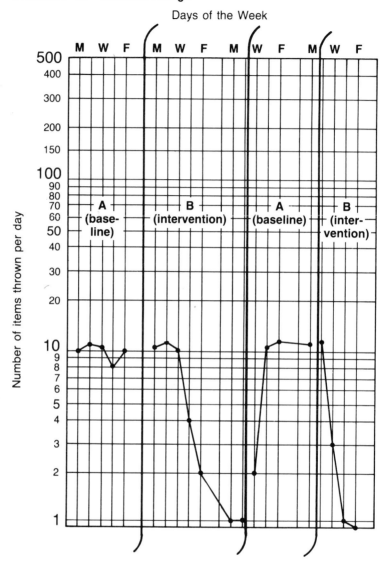

occurs when the intervention is applied, then there is reason to believe that the intervention is effective. In Figure 7–21, time-out is used sequentially with hitting and talk-outs. The data illustrate that the rate of occurrence for both behaviors decreased only when the intervention was applied.

Data from single-subject designs can be used to present compelling

FIGURE 7-21   Multiple Baseline Design

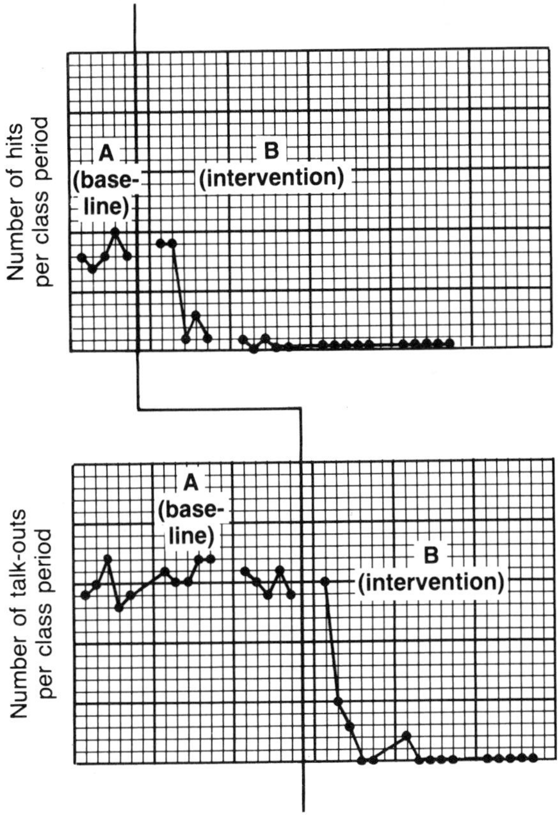

evidence of the effectiveness of interventions. These interventions can then be used with confidence in the educational program.

☐ *Behavior Goals*

The rate or even existence of certain behaviors is dictated by the demands and expectations of the setting. In one class, for example, any student talk-outs would be considered inappropriate, while in another class, the teacher may tolerate a high rate of talk-outs. As a result, goals must reflect the skills and abilities of the student and the requirements of each setting.

Kerr and Nelson (1983) suggest that clear and specific goals should be established in relation to baseline data. The goal could require, for example, a certain percentage of increase or decrease in behavior per week. Additionally, goals can be established by selecting a student, whose behavior is considered to be appropriate, observing the student, and establishing that rate of behavior as a terminal goal.

Goals should be established for both appropriate and inappropriate behavior and should reflect the unique nature of the child and setting. All terminal goals should be realistic and carefully considered. Moreover, by communicating these goals to the student, there is an increased likelihood that they will be reached.

After collecting baseline data and deciding on a terminal goal, it may be beneficial to establish short-term or intermediate goals. This enables the student and teacher to have a daily objective that, if met, will lead to the accomplishment of the final goal. This may be done on an equal-ratio chart by drawing a line from the approximate median of the baseline data to the terminal objective. Above and below this line, additional parallel lines are drawn that form an envelope or a daily goal. The size of this envelope can be altered to reflect the skills of the student or needs of the teacher. This is illustrated in Figure 7–22.

The teacher may judge student performance in relation to these lines. There may be no need to make a change in the intervention if the daily data are within the envelope. The teacher may decide, however, to institute a change if the data fall outside of the envelope for a predetermined number of consecutive days.

This procedure has the advantage of giving the student and teacher a realistic daily goal or objective. It does not require the potentially improbable goal of continuous daily improvement. Rather, it allows for a certain amount of variability in student performance while still requiring growth.

CASE STUDY

An example of how periodic assessment results may be organized is provided in Figure 7–23. Bernard, an eighth grader, often talks out without permission and frequently fights with peers. As indicated on a teacher rating scale, Mrs. Jones, Bernard's teacher, believes that Bernard is a cooperative student, but talks out too frequently in both reading and math class. However, Bernard reports that talking out is only a problem in reading class. Mrs. Jones and Bernard agree that Bernard's fighting with peers is a significant problem. An interview with Bernard revealed that in reading class, he preferred to work in a quiet area and that the close proximity of Dan, another student, was distracting. He also reported that the fights occurred because he was teased by his peers.

Observations conducted by Mr. Blackwell, the special education

FIGURE 7-22   Envelope Used to Establish Short-Term Goals

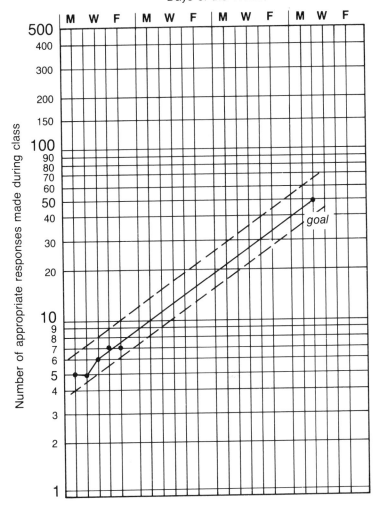

Days of the Week

teacher, indicated that the number and percentage of talk-outs without permission were excessive in reading, but not in math class, and that in-school time-out did not seem to reduce the number of fights per week. These data were shared with Mrs. Jones and Bernard. It was decided that talk-outs in reading class and fighting on the playground would be targeted for continuous assessment and intervention. It was agreed that the talk-outs in math class were not excessive.

FIGURE 7-23   Case Study: Periodic Behavior Assessment Record

A. Formal Assessment Results

B. Informal Rating Instruments
Teacher rating: Mrs. Jones reports that Bernard talks out in reading and math class, fights with peers, but is cooperative with teachers.
Student self-rating: Bernard reports that he talks out in reading class and fights with peers.

C. Interview
Mr. Blackwell, Bernard's resource room teacher, interviews Mrs. Jones:
Mrs. Jones indicates that Bernard talks out in reading and math class, fights with his peers, but is cooperative with teachers.
Mr. Blackwell interviews Bernard: Bernard indicates that in reading class Dan distracts him by talking. He also reports that he likes to work in a quiet area and becomes angry when peers tease him.

D. Observation
(completed by Mr. Blackwell)

(antecedents)	(behavior)	(consequences)
Reading class: Dan sits next to Bernard. Talk-outs seem to occur when teacher is working with another group.	Mean # of talk-outs in 50-minute period = 17 # instances of talking with permission = 3	Mrs. Jones rarely reprimands Bernard.
Math class: Bernard works in a quiet area completing variety of tasks	Mean # of talk-outs in 50-minute period = 2 # instances of talking with permission = 12	Mrs. Jones was in close proximity to Bernard and reprimanded him when he talked without permission.
Playground: Other students tease Bernard.	4 fights per week	In-school time out.

E. Conclusions
Strengths: Bernard is cooperative with teacher.

Deficits: Bernard talks out in reading without permission and fights with peers.
Appropriate Behavior/Conditions: Bernard will talk only with permission and will interact appropriately with peers.

Student's Name Bernard
Grade/Teacher 8th/Jones

Mrs. Jones wanted to increase appropriate talking behavior by Bernard while at the same time reducing inappropriate talk-outs. Therefore, as indicated on the Continuous Assessment Record in Figure 7–24, Bernard would self-record the number of times in which he talked with and without permission in reading class. Instances of talking with permission would then be expressed as a percentage of occurrences of talking.

It was also decided that Bernard would engage in social and verbal skills training with the counselor in order to reduce fights and increase appropriate verbal remarks with peers. While no baseline data were taken on verbal remarks, all individuals involved believed it was important to increase the frequency of occurrence of that behavior. It was unanimously agreed to establish a terminal objective of seven appropriate verbal remarks per day to peers.

Talk-outs, fighting, and appropriate verbal remarks were charted for ten days. As illustrated in Figure 7–25, the number of talk-outs without permission in reading class decreased to zero while the percentage of instances of talking with permission increased. Bernard will continue to self-monitor these behaviors with an occasional check by Mrs. Jones.

As displayed in Figure 7–26, the number of appropriate verbal remarks to peers did not increase while the incidence of fighting did. As a result, a change in intervention is needed. This may necessitate gathering additional data about the behavior and any environmental variables that may be affecting this behavior.

Based on the periodic and continuous assessment data presented in Bernard's case, the following objectives were developed:

1. In reading class, Bernard will talk out without permission no more than one time per class period for ten consecutive days.
2. In reading class, Bernard will receive permission before talking 95% of the time for ten consecutive days.
3. Bernard will reduce the incidence of fighting with peers to 0 times per week for five consecutive weeks.
4. Bernard will increase the number of appropriate verbal remarks made to peers to seven per day.

Self-reporting, with occasional monitoring by the teacher, appeared to be an effective means of continuously assessing Bernard's behavior. These data indicate that Bernard is making adequate progress in reducing talk-outs and increasing instances of talking with permission. Therefore, no program change is necessary.

Fighting, however, requires additional assessment. This may involve a comprehensive analysis of all elements of Bernard's environment such as parents, peer groups, and skills in social interaction and problem solving.

FIGURE 7-24 Case Study: Continuous Behavior Assessment Record

Date	Conditions	Skill/Behavior	Current Performance	Proficiency criterion/ goal	Date attained
10/2	Reading class: Bernard is moved to a quiet area, and receives verbal praise from teacher for talking with permission. Bernard will self-monitor with periodic checks by teacher.	Talks out without permission Talks with permission	17 times in 50-min. period 3 times in period (15% of total instances of talking)	no more than 1 per period for 10 consecutive days; 95% for 10 consecutive days	
10/2	Social and verbal skill training with counselor. Bernard will self-monitor for appropriate verbal remarks to peers.	Fights with peers on the playground Makes appropriate verbal remarks to peers	4 per week	0 per week for 5 consecutive weeks	

Student's Name ___ Bernard ___
Grade/Teacher ___ 8th/Jones ___

328

FIGURE 7-25   Data on Appropriate and Inappropriate Talking

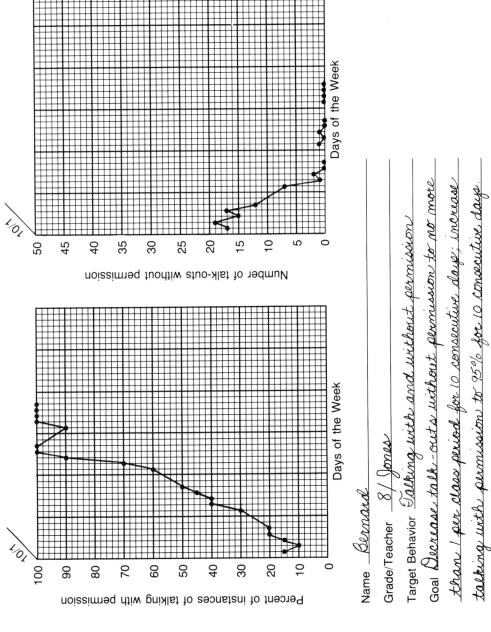

Name _Bernard_

Grade/Teacher _8/ Jones_

Target Behavior _Talking with and without permission_

Goal _Decrease talk-outs without permission to not more_
than 1 per class period for 10 consecutive days; increase
talking with permission to 95% for 10 consecutive days.

FIGURE 7-26   Data on Fighting and Appropriate Verbal Remarks

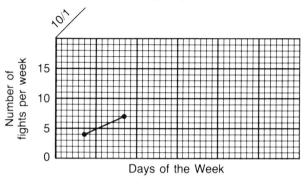

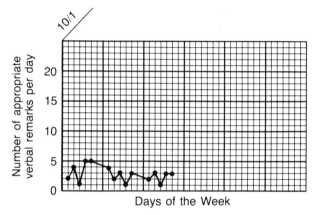

Name _Bernard_

Grade/Teacher _8/Jones_

Target Behavior _fighting with peers, appropriate verbal remarks_

Goal _Decrease number of fights to 0 per week for 5 consecutive weeks; increase number of appropriate verbal remarks per day to seven or more for 3 consecutive weeks._

CONCLUSION

Behavior permeates all elements of the school program. Therefore, it is essential that behavior and the environmental factors and expectations related to behavior be assessed. This process can be difficult and time-consuming. If, however, the assessment is well organized and the results are clearly demonstrated and appropriately used, effective interventions can be developed that will aid the teacher and the student.

ACTIVITIES

1. What does an ecological assessment of behavior examine?
2. List and describe three general expectations related to the instructional setting that must be assessed.
3. List and describe four general expectations related to behavior that must be assessed.
4. Name and describe the four scales of measurement.
5. Name and describe the five qualities of behavior that may be measured.
6. Describe how checklists, rating instruments, and interviews are used to assess environmental variables, expectations, and behavior.
7. Describe and give examples of behaviors that could be measured by using the following procedures: event; interval and time sample; duration; frequency; anecdotal; and permanent product.
8. Observe and record the behavior of an elementary or middle school student.
9. Evaluate the problem behavior, environmental variables, and expectations associated with a particular student. Summarize these data and indicate what behaviors or variables should be continually assessed.
10. Generate behavioral objectives based on the data collected in the previous question.

8

Managing the Assessment Process

■ **Learning Objectives**

After completing this chapter, the reader should be able to:

■ describe the test-teach–test-teach model
■ describe how to summarize and select the assessment procedures to be used for a group of students
■ discuss four factors that influence the implementation of an assessment plan with a group of students
■ describe how to efficiently manage the continuous assessment of a group of students
■ discuss methods of organizing the assessment data that has been collected

All of the major decisions that influence a student's progress at school are based on assessment information. Assessment assists in determining what academic and social behaviors to teach and how they should be taught. A three-step model, which has also served to structure each chapter in this book, provides the framework for the assessment process:

Step 1: Determine the skills, behaviors, or learning variables to be assessed.
Step 2: Select and administer an assessment procedure.
Step 3: Record performance and set objectives.

To effectively use the assessment data to make instructional decisions, a test-teach–test-teach model (see Figure 8–1) is suggested:

1. After initial periodic assessment is collected, state the long- and short-term instructional objectives.

333

FIGURE 8-1 Test-Teach–Test-Teach Model

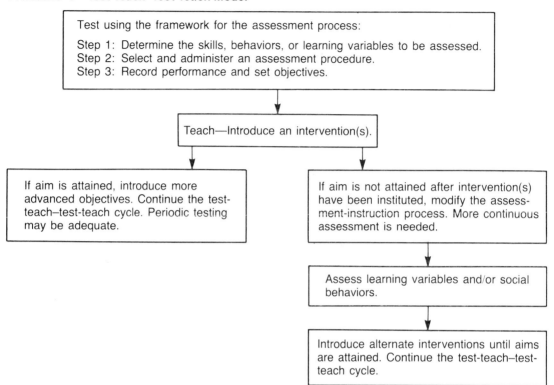

Test using the framework for the assessment process:

Step 1: Determine the skills, behaviors, or learning variables to be assessed.
Step 2: Select and administer an assessment procedure.
Step 3: Record performance and set objectives.

Teach—Introduce an intervention(s).

If aim is attained, introduce more advanced objectives. Continue the test-teach–test-teach cycle. Periodic testing may be adequate.

If aim is not attained after intervention(s) have been instituted, modify the assessment-instruction process. More continuous assessment is needed.

Assess learning variables and/or social behaviors.

Introduce alternate interventions until aims are attained. Continue the test-teach–test-teach cycle.

2. Collect baseline data on the short-term objectives. If the data are moving in the direction of the desired aim, continue collecting data until the aim is attained or stability in the data is noted.
3. Institute an intervention. Continue to collect data and record performance.
4. Evaluate progress. Introduce other interventions if the student has not made progress in three to five days.
5. When the aim is attained, maintain that level of performance for one to three days. Assess that objective on a variable schedule after the aim is achieved.
6. Return to step 1. Proceed with more advanced objectives or aims.

When instruction fails to produce the desired results, assessment for how to teach and/or assess behavior becomes important. Learning-related variables such as motivation factors, instructional arrangements, response factors, and consequent factors may need to be modified. Inappropriate social behaviors may also need to be targeted for change.

To accomplish this process for a group of students, the teacher needs to know how to efficiently organize and manage the entire assessment process. It is necessary to summarize the academic and social behaviors that need to be assessed for each student, to select the assessment procedures to be used, to plan a schedule to efficiently and thoroughly implement the assessment plan, and to organize the resulting data.

SUMMARIZE ASSESSMENT NEEDS FOR EACH STUDENT

The first step in the assessment process is to identify the skills or behaviors that will be examined. The academic and social behaviors that are selected depend upon the student's level of development, the instructional level of development, the instructional methods used by the teacher, and the teacher's instructional responsibilities. Data from the following sources may assist in determining areas that should be more extensively assessed: current standardized test scores, basal test scores, information included on an I.E.P., teacher or parent reports, and other information contained in a student's cumulative folder. Scope-and-sequence networks or school curriculum guides will provide structure to the assessment process by assisting in further identifying specific skills or behaviors to be evaluated.

In most classrooms, there is a wide range of abilities, behaviors, and achievement. Some students will have numerous academic and/or behavior problems and will require extensive assessment. Other students will have few or no problems and will require less assessment. As discussed in chapter 2, the extent and frequency of assessment increases corresponding to the severity of the learning and behavior deficits. Periodic assessment may serve the needs of the student who is progressing adequately. Continuous assessment is important for students who are not making adequate progress.

SELECT THE ASSESSMENT PROCEDURES

After summarizing the assessment needs of each student, the appropriate assessment procedures must be selected. A variety of periodic and continuous devices used to assess academic and behavior problems are presented in previous chapters. The periodic assessment procedure may be either formal or informal and usually yields global information that may assist in surveying a student's general level of performance and in establishing long-range objectives or goals for an I.E.P. The continuous assessment procedures are used to supplement and expand the information obtained using periodic assessment procedures. Data from continuous assessment are helpful in noting discrete changes that occur in student performance and in making more accurate and appropriate educational decisions.

Displayed in Figure 8-2 is an assessment plan for two students. This form may be used to summarize the needs of several students and the procedures to be used for assessment. The assessment plan includes the preassessment information that is available and suggestions for periodic and continuous evaluation. Scores from a current achievement test are available for Ann, a sixth grader. Because she is 2 to 2 1/2 years below grade level in reading, spelling, and math, several periodic and continuous assessment procedures are planned. No records are available for Bill, a third-grader and a new student who will not complete tasks assigned to him. To survey Bill's general level of performance, a formal achievement test is planned. Depending on the results of that test, it may be necessary to do further assessment on a periodic and/or continuous basis. Both students will be observed in their classrooms and parents will be interviewed. This information should assist in determining environmental variables that are contributing to academic and/or behavior problems.

FIGURE 8-2   Assessment Plan Summary

Preassessment Information	Language Arts	Reading	Math	Behavior and Learning Variables
Ann: 6th grade reading—4.0 spelling—3.5 math—3.5	informal spelling inventory, error pattern analysis, written work sample	I.R.I., error pattern analysis, probes	curriculum-based survey test, error analysis, diagnostic interview	observe in class, interview parents
	administer curriculum-based language arts and reading criterion-referenced test			
Bill: 3rd grade, new student, no records, refuses to complete any task assigned	administer Peabody Individual Achievement Test			obtain records, interview parents, observe in a variety of settings

IMPLEMENT THE ASSESSMENT PLAN

■ ■ Assessment is an integral part of the instructional program. It is conducted throughout the school year, uses materials closely related to the educational program, and allows an evaluation of the student in the instructional setting. Assessment continuously guides and directs the teacher in implementing the instructional program (the test-teach–test teach cycle).

Effective implementation of assessment with a group of students is dependent upon: 1) carefully engineering the physical environment, 2) planning detailed student and class schedules, 3) developing classroom rules and a behavior management system, and 4) encouraging student understanding and participation in the assessment and learning process.

■ The Physical Environment

The physical plan of the classroom directly affects the assessment process and the instructional program. In most classrooms, several activities are going on at the same time. Selected areas should be designated for specific activities and for material display and storage. Examples of areas that may be included in a classroom are the following: independent work area with individual desks or study carrels; small group instruction or work area; audio-visual area; learning centers; free-time area; assessment area; and teacher area.

The physical plan should be structured so that these activities will not interfere with each other. For example, it is a good idea to arrange for the assessment area to be in a quiet part of the room away from the free-time activity area. Room arrangements will vary, depending upon resources and space available and teacher preferences, but two factors are important in engineering the physical environment: the "teacher's eye view" and separation of space. The teacher should be able to observe every student at all times from the teacher's desk and from the teacher's seat in group areas (Morsink, 1984). Additionally, adequate personal space should be provided for each student. Morsink also notes that the arrangement of the environment provides cues to students about expected behavior. Straight rows of desks signal quiet, individual tasks, whereas less formal groupings of seats indicate collaborative work or group discussion. A sample room plan is provided in Figure 8–3.

■ Student and Class Schedules

To efficiently implement an assessment plan and an instructional program for a group of students, individual activities should be carefully

FIGURE 8-3 Physical Plan of a Classroom

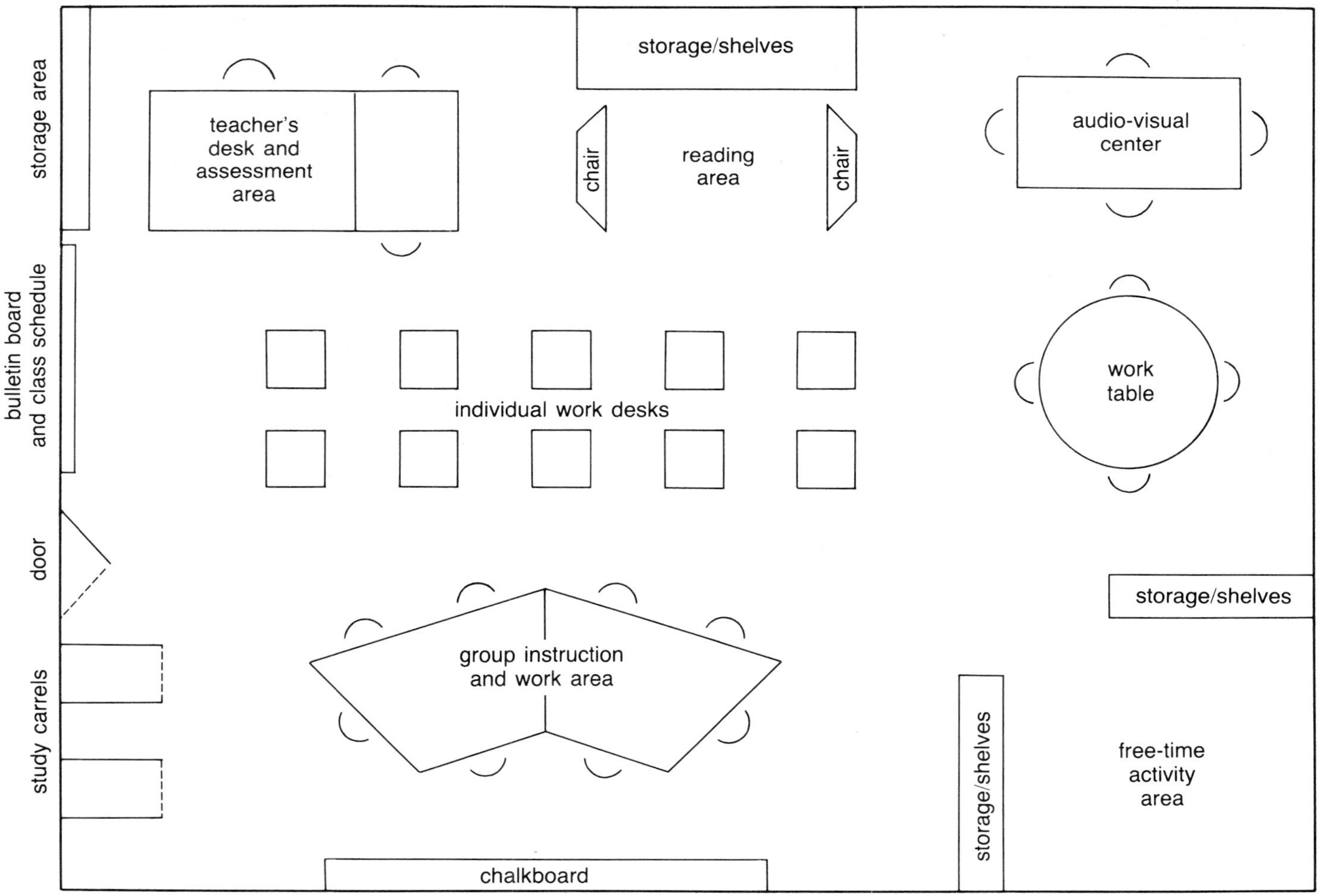

organized. Class schedules usually include opening exercises, closing activities, individual and group academic instruction, nonacademic activities, and transition times. Intensive learning activities, particularly reading, language arts, and math instruction, are usually planned for the morning.

At the intermediate and high school levels, Mercer and Mercer (1985) note that lesson planning must be organized to fit into 50-minute segments. A mini-schedule with various activities must be developed for each class period. Resource room teachers are faced with other scheduling problems. The time scheduled for a student is dependent on the needs of the student, the regular class activity that he or she will miss, and the regular class teacher's preference.

In planning the classroom schedule, Morsink (1984) suggests that quiet periods be alternated with more active periods. Teachers must also organize student activities to allow time for individual assistance. To accomplish this, it is usually wise to schedule activities in a complementary manner (Mercer & Mercer, 1985). In this way, all the students in a class are not working on the same activity at the same time. It is helpful to post this schedule on the blackboard or bulletin board to provide a structured routine for a group of students.

Periodic and continuous assessment procedures may be easily incorporated into the schedule. Because students are generally more alert and motivated in the morning, assessment should be planned for that time of day if possible. Some of the assessment procedures that will be used are teacher-directed and others may be completed independently by the student. The teacher-directed procedures may be suitable for individual or group administration. Therefore, the teacher must schedule activities carefully so that the majority of students are working independently on meaningful tasks requiring little teacher assistance, while an individual or a small group of students are being assessed. An example of a class schedule is provided in Figure 8–4.

After the class schedule is developed, a daily schedule should be provided for each student. To individualize each student's instructional program, it is helpful to use a task sheet that indicates the specific activities to be completed in a class period, in a day, or in a week. Many of the tasks listed on the task sheet will yield assessment information if the tasks are carefully planned. Examples of activities to include on a task sheet are:

1. individual work in a folder (skill sheets, probe sheets, etc.)
2. reading activities (stories from a basal and skill worksheets from an accompanying workbook, basal mastery tests)
3. math activities (skill practice and mastery tests)
4. classroom skill-kit assignments

FIGURE 8-4 Daily Class Schedule

8:30 Opening activities

8:45 Individual assessment and independent work assigned on task sheets

9:15 Reading assessment and instruction period

	Group A	Group B	Group C
9:15	Group with teacher (individual and group assessment and instruction)	Independent work	Audio-visual or group activity
9:35	Independent work	Audio-visual or group activity	Group with teacher (individual and group assessment and instruction)
9:55	Audio-visual or group activity	Group with teacher (individual and group assessment and instruction)	Independent work

10:15 Restroom break and recess OR P.E., music, or art class

10:45 Math assessment and instruction period

	Group A	Group B	Group C
10:45	Independent work	Group with teacher (individual and group assessment and instruction)	Self-correcting activity
11:00	Self-correcting activity	Independent work	Group with teacher (individual and group assessment and instruction)
11:15	Group with teacher (individual and group assessment and instruction)	Self-correcting activity	Independent work

11:30 Open time (assessment, story time, instruction, free time, etc.)

11:50 Lunch

12:15 Language arts (handwriting, spelling, and written composition—individual and group assessment and instruction)

1:00 Open time

1:15 Science or social studies

1:45 Individual activities assigned on task sheet; teacher conferences with individual students

2:15 Closing activities

2:30 Dismissal

5. audio-visual activities (tasks using language master, tape recorder, etc.)
6. self-correcting materials
7. learning games
8. individual assessment or instruction
9. group assessment or instruction
10. timings (teacher- or peer-assisted or self-timing)
11. free-time activities

Task sheets may use picture cues and may also indicate the order of tasks to be completed, the estimated time for completing each activity, and feedback or points earned for successful task completion and/or for following classroom rules. Mercer and Mercer (1985) note that it is usually a good idea to alternate highly preferred tasks with less preferred tasks, to move from a very structured schedule to a less structured schedule, and to move from short assignments to longer ones. An example of a task sheet for a student in a resource room is included in Figure 8–5.

■ Developing Classroom Rules and a Behavior Management System

The implementation of an instructional program can be significantly improved by developing a set of classroom rules and a system for managing behavior. A set of three to seven rules should state clearly, concisely, and positively the expected student behaviors. The rules should be enforce-

FIGURE 8-5 Student Task Sheet

Order	Task	Assignment	Time	Feedback
1.	Folder	Follow directions for completing written work sample.	20 min.	
2.	A-V	Practice words from Box B on language master.	10 min.	
3.	Individual Assessment	Work with teacher on reading test.	20–30 min.	
4.	S-C	Self-correcting area C— Folder 21	15 min.	
5.	Reading Area	Free choice	15 min.	

able, reasonable, and include consequences for infractions. The presentation of the rules may include picture cues and should be posted in the classroom and/or on each student's task sheet. Examples of rules that may be used in a classroom are the following:

1. Start work quickly and quietly.
2. Complete each task.
3. Work quietly.
4. Raise your hand for help.
5. Be helpful to others.
6. Keep your work and work area neat.

A system for managing behavior should include a plan for responding to appropriate and inappropriate behavior. Strategies should be planned in advance for dealing with problems that may occur in the classroom. Social reinforcement including feedback, attention, and approval can be effectively used by teachers to respond to behavior (Kerr & Nelson, 1983). Mercer and Mercer (1985) suggest involving students in self-management by having them develop techniques for modifying their own behavior, by having them model appropriate learning and social behavior for each other, and by asking them to find solutions to social conflicts without teacher intervention. However, in some classrooms, a group-management plan may be necessary. A token economy is an example of a widely used classroom management system.

■ Encouraging Student Participation

A well-organized physical plan, class and student schedules, and a behavior management system all contribute to an effective instructional program. It is also important that students understand the class and individual schedules or task sheets, the location of materials in the classroom, and how to use materials and equipment. This will allow students to participate fully in their own instructional program and will enable them to move independently and efficiently through the daily schedule.

To help students in learning the location of materials and equipment in the classroom, a system of organizing and labeling materials for student use is needed. Selected areas may be designated for storage or display of materials and audio-visual equipment. Areas of the room and individual materials or pieces of equipment may be labeled with signs and/or picture cues.

Reading Area
A-V

S-C (self-correcting materials)
MK-3 (math skill kit—level 3)
F (individual student folder)

These labels should correspond with the task descriptions on each student's task sheet. Clear and concise directions for using materials and equipment should be included.

Another area of the room may be designated for storing materials to be used for continuous assessment. The following materials may be needed to use probe-sheet timings on a continuous basis:

- storage area for probe sheets and answer sheets (e.g., Pendaflex files in cardboard boxes)
- timing devices (a stopwatch or timing tape)
- sheets of acetate
- grease pencils or felt-tip markers
- paper towels or sponges (to erase the acetate)
- raw data sheets
- charts

If the same probe sheet is to be used several times until proficiency is met on a skill, a student can cover the sheet with a sheet of clear acetate and write his or her responses to the probe using a grease pencil or felt-tip marker. The responses can then be erased with a sponge or paper towel, and the probe sheet used over and over again.

Students may be taught to secure and return materials needed for timings, complete timings independently, check performance using an answer sheet, record the raw data, and chart data daily. Students may complete timings individually, work with a peer on timings, be timed individually by the teacher, or be timed in a group. Group timings may be completed at the beginning of a class period, and individual timings completed at different times throughout a period or day. A daily or weekly routine should be established by the teacher to monitor or spot-check the student's progress, check charts, and make instructional decisions.

Another way in which students can participate in their instructional program is to be involved in decision making. Morsink (1984) suggests that students participate in decisions about what they personally want to do and in classroom decisions, such as formulating classroom rules and solving group problems. She notes that students can learn from peer tutors and can be peer tutors in something they do well.

Students should be encouraged to understand and participate in the assessment and instructional process. This will not only enable them to move independently and efficiently through the daily schedule, but will create a positive learning environment in the classroom.

ORGANIZING THE ASSESSMENT DATA

■ ■ After student assessment needs have been determined and the assessment procedures selected and implemented, the data must be organized. The results from periodic assessment procedures may be noted on a Periodic Assessment Record described in previous chapters. This record indicates which aspects of the skill, behavior, or learning-variable network require more extensive and continuous assessment. It also can be easily used as an aid in generating instructional plans or teaching objectives and in developing and updating I.E.P.'s.

Continuous assessment records serve to summarize data collected on a continuous basis. Since the Continuous Assessment Record provides space to indicate academic or behavior goals, it can be used as an aid in identifying short-term objectives. Raw data sheets and charts should be used on a daily or frequent basis to record data from probes, direct observation, and other criterion-referenced assessment procedures.

CONCLUSION

Assessment is necessary in making many decisions that influence a student's progress in school. Assessment data assist the teacher in determining the goals and means of instruction in academic and social skills. In the three-step model presented in this text, a systematic, integrated approach to assessment is provided. Academic skills, learning variables, and behaviors to be assessed are first determined. Then, assessment procedures appropriate for periodic and continuous assessment are selected and administered. For instructional planning purposes, the assessment procedures selected should reflect the skills that will be taught in the curriculum. The extent and frequency of assessment is determined by the severity of the student's problem. Finally, performance is recorded and long- and short-term objectives are developed. To effectively use the assessment data to make instructional decisions, a test-teach–test-teach model is applied. This ensures that the instructional program is precisely directed to meet the needs of each student.

_____ Appendix _____

Formal Tests

Formal Tests Used in Determining How to Teach

Test	Age or Grade Level	Skills/Behaviors Measured
Classroom Learning Screening (Koenig & Kunzelman, 1980)	Preschool–grade 6	probes in readiness, math and reading, learning channel preferences
Detroit Tests of Learning Aptitude (Hammill, 1985)	Ages 6–17	individual strengths and weaknesses
Developmental Test of Visual-Motor Integration (Beery, 1982)	Ages 2–19	learning channel preferences
Learning Methods Test (Mills, 1956)	Grades 1–12	learning channel preferences
Learning Style Inventory (Kolb, 1978)	Grades 3–12	individual preferences in immediate environment, emotionality, sociological needs, and physical needs
Woodcock-Johnson Psycho-Educational Battery (Woodcock & Johnson, 1977)	Ages 3–80	cognitive ability, achievement, and interests

Formal Tests Used to Assess Language Arts

Oral Language Measures

Test	Age or Grade Level	Skills Measured
Clinical Evaluation of Language Functions (Semel-Mintz & Wiig, 1980) *individual administration*	K-12	phonology, syntax, semantics, memory, word finding and retrieval
Houston Test of Language Development (Crabtree, 1963) *individual administration*	Age 6 months to 6 years	accent, melody of speech, gesture, vocabulary, sound articulation, content, grammatical usage, vocabulary
Illinois Test of Psycholinguistic Abilities (Kirk, McCarthy, & Kirk, 1968) *individual administration*	Age 2-4 to 10-3	auditory and visual reception, auditory and visual association, verbal expression, closure, sequential memory, sound blending, manual expression
Test of Adolescent Language (Hammill, Brown, Larson, & Wiederholt, 1980) *group & individual administration*	Age 11-0 to 18-5	listening/vocabulary, listening/grammar, speaking/vocabulary, speaking/grammar, reading/vocabulary, reading/grammar
Test of Auditory Comprehension of Language (Carrow, 1973) *individual administration*	Age 3-0 to 6-11	oral language comprehension, form classes and function words, morphological constructions, grammatical categories, and syntactical structures
Test of Language Development—Primary (Newcomer & Hammill, 1982) *individual administration*	Age 4-0 to 8-11	picture vocabulary, oral vocabulary, grammatic understanding, sentence imitation, grammatic completion, word discrimination, word articulation
Utah Test of Language Development (Mecham, Jex, & Jones, 1967) *individual administration*	Age 1-15	repetition of digits, naming colors and pictures, length of sentences, vocabulary, responding to commands and reading

Measures of Phonology
(individual administration)

Test	Age or Grade Level	Skills Measured
Auditory Discrimination Test (Wepman, 1973)	Age 5-8	receptive phonology, likenesses and differences in word pairs

Formal Tests Used to Assess Language Arts (*continued*)

Measures of Phonology (continued)
(individual administration)

Test	Age or Grade Level	Skills Measured
Goldman-Fristoe Test of Articulation (Goldman & Fristoe, 1972)	Age 6–16 +	expressive phonology, sounds in words, sounds in sentences, stimulability
Goldman-Fristoe-Woodcock Test of Auditory Discrimination (Goldman, Fristoe, & Woodcock, 1976)	Age 5–0	receptive vocabulary, distinguishing speech sounds under different background conditions
Templin-Darley Tests of Articulation (Templin & Darley, 1960)	Age 3–8	expressive phonology, production of vowels, diphthongs, single consonants, and consonant blends

Measures of Morphology and Syntax

Test	Age or Grade Level	Skills Measured
Assessment of Children's Language Comprehension (Foster, Giddan, & Stark, 1973) *group & individual administration*	Age 3–0 to 6–6	receptive language, comprehension of words and utterances through picture identification
Carrow Elicited Language Inventory (Carrow, 1974) *individual administration*	Age 3–8	expressive language, phrase and sentence imitation
Developmental Sentence Scoring (Lee & Koenigsknecht, 1974) *individual administration*	Age 2–0 to 6–11	expressive syntax in spontaneous speech
Northwestern Syntax Screening Test (Lee, 1971) *individual administration*	Age 3–7	syntactical comprehension and use, structures of prepositional phrases, negation, subject–verb agreement

Measures of Semantics

Test	Age or Grade Level	Skills Measured
Boehm Test of Basic Concepts (Boehm, 1971) *group administration*	Grade K–2	receptive understanding of concepts of space, quantity, time
Peabody Picture Vocabulary Test	Age 2–18	receptive language, word comprehension

(*continued*)

Formal Tests Used to Assess Language Arts (continued)

Written Language Measures
(group or individual administration)

Test	Age or Grade Level	Skills Measured
Picture Story Language Test (Myklebust, 1965)	Age 7–17	writing sample measures, productivity, correctness, and meaning
Test of Adolescent Language (Hammill, Brown, Larson, & Wiederholt, 1980)	Age 11–0 to 18–5	writing/vocabulary, writing/grammar
Test of Written Language (Hammill & Larson, 1983)	Age 8–6 to 14–5	vocabulary, thematic maturity, thought units, handwriting, spelling, word usage, style

Spelling and Handwriting Measures

Test	Age or Grade Level	Skills Measured
Basic School Skills Inventory (Goodman & Hamill, 1975) *individual administration*	Age 4–0 to 6–11	writing from left to right, grasping a pencil, writing first name, last name, and letters, proper writing position, copying words, copying from chalkboard, staying on line
Test of Written Spelling (Larson & Hammill, 1976) *group & individual administration*	Age 5–0 to 15	thirty-five predictable words and twenty-five unpredictable words

Selected Standardized Tests with Language Arts Subtests

California Achievement Tests (Tiegs & Clark, 1970, *a*)

Diagnostic Reading Scales (Spache, 1972)

Peabody Individual Achievement Test (Dunn & Markwardt, 1970)

Stanford Achievement Test (Madden, Gardner, Rudman, Karlsen, & Merwin, 1973)

Wechsler Intelligence Scale for Children—Revised (Wechsler, 1974)

Wide Range Achievement Test (Jastak & Jastak, 1978)

Woodcock-Johnson Psycho-Educational Battery (Woodcock & Johnson, 1977)

Formal Tests Used to Assess Reading

General Achievement Tests with Reading Subtests

Test	Grade Level	Skills Measured
California Achievement Test (Tiegs & Clark, 1970*a*)	K–14	vocabulary, comprehension
Comprehensive Tests of Basic Skills (CTB/McGraw HIll, 1968)	K–12	vocabulary, comprehension
Iowa Tests of Basic Skills (Hieronymus & Linquist, 1974)	1.7–9	comprehension, vocabulary, word analysis, word study skills
Metropolitan Achievement Tests (Durost, Bixler, Wrightstone, Prescott, & Balow, 1971)	K–9.5	word knowledge, word analysis, comprehension
SRA Achievement Series (Thorpe, Lefever, & Naslund, 1968)	1–9	vocabulary, comprehension
Stanford Achievement Test (Madden, Gardner, Rudman, Karlsen, & Merwin, 1973)	1.5–9.5	vocabulary, comprehension, word study skills, listening comprehension
Peabody Individual Achievement Test (Dunn & Markwardt, 1970) *individual administration*	K–12	reading recognition, comprehension
Wide Range Achievement Test (Jastak & Jastak, 1978) *individual administration*	preschool– adult	letter recognition, word recognition

Group Reading Survey Tests

Test	Grade Level	Skills Measured
Gates-MacGinitie Reading Tests (Gates & MacGinitie, 1972)	1–12	vocabulary, comprehension, speed, accuracy
California Reading Tests (Tiegs & Clark, 1970*b*)	1–14	vocabulary, comprehension
Iowa Silent Reading Tests (Farr, 1973)	4–14	rate, comprehension, directed reading, word meaning, sentence meaning, paragraph comprehension, location of information

(*continued*)

Formal Tests Used to Assess Reading (*continued*)

Group Reading Survey Tests (continued)

Test	*Grade Level*	*Skills Measured*
Silent Reading Diagnostic Tests (Bond, Clymer, & Hoyt, 1955)	3–6	word recognition, syllabication, root words, word elements, beginning sounds, letter sounds, rhyming
Stanford Diagnostic Reading Tests (Karlsen, Madden, & Gardner, 1976)	2.5–8.5	comprehension, vocabulary, auditory discrimination, syllabication, beginning and ending sounds, blending, sound discrimination

Individual Diagnostic Reading Tests

Test	*Grade Level*	*Skills Measured*
Diagnostic Reading Scales (Spache, 1972)	1–8	word recognition, word analysis, comprehension
Durrell Analysis of Reading Difficulty (Durrell, 1955)	1–6	oral and silent reading, listening comprehension, word analysis, phonics, faulty pronunciation, writing, spelling
Gates McKillop Reading Diagnostic Tests (Gates & McKillop, 1962)	nonreader–up	oral reading, word perception, phrase, perception, syllabication, letter names and sounds, visual and auditory blending, spelling
Woodcock Reading Mastery Tests (Woodcock, 1973)	K–12	letter identification, word identification, word comprehension, word attack, passage comprehension

Specialized Word Analysis Tests

Test	*Grade Level*	*Skills Measured*
Botel Reading Inventory (Botel, 1970) *group administration*	1–12	phonics, word recognition, word opposites, listening
Doren Diagnostic Reading Test of Word Recognition Skills (Doren, 1973) *group administration*	2–8	beginning sounds, sight words, rhyming, whole-word recognition, words within words, speech consonants, blending, vowels, ending sounds, discriminate guessing, letter recognition, spelling

Formal Tests Used to Assess Reading (*continued*)

Specialized Word Analysis Tests (continued)

Test	Grade Level	Skills Measured
Gilmore Oral Reading Test (Gilmore & Gilmore, 1968) *individual administration*	1–8	accuracy, comprehension, rate
Gray Oral Reading Test (Gray & Robinson, 1967) *individual administration*	1–12	accuracy, rate
McCullough Word Analysis Tests (McCullough, 1963) *group administration*	4–6	initial blends & digraphs, phonetic discrimination, matching letters to vowel sounds, sounding whole words, interpreting phonetic symbols, root words, syllabication
Test of Reading Comprehension (Brown, Hammill, & Wiederholt, 1978) *individual or group administration*	1–8	general vocabulary, syntactic similarities, paragraph reading, sentence sequencing, specific knowledge in content areas
Slosson Oral Reading Test (Slosson, 1963)	1–12	word recognition

Formal Tests Used to Assess Arithmetic

Survey Tests of Arithmetic Achievement

Test	Age or Grade Level	Skills Measured
California Achievement Test (California Test Bureau, 1978)	Grades 1–12	computation, concepts, applications
Diagnostic Achievement Battery (Newcomer & Curtis, 1984)	Grades 1–9	mathematics reasoning and calculation
Kaufman Test of Educational Achievement (Kaufman & Kaufman, 1985)	Grades 1–12	mathematics applications and computation

(*continued*)

Formal Tests Used to Assess Arithmetic *(continued)*

Survey Tests of Arithmetic Achievement (continued)

Test	Age or Grade Level	Skills Measured
Metropolitan Achievement Tests: Survey Battery (Prescott, Balow, Hogan, & Farr, 1978)	Grades K–12	numeration, geometry and measurement, problem solving, and operations
SRA Achievement Series (Naslund, Thorpe, & Lefever, 1978)	Grades K–12	concepts, computation, and problem solving
Stanford Achievement Test (Madden, Gardner, Rudman, Karlsen, & Merwin, 1973)	Grades 1.5–9.5	concepts, computation, and applications

Diagnostic Tests of Arithmetic Achievement

Test	Age or Grade Level	Skills Measured
Key Math Diagnostic Arithmetic Test (Connolly, Nachtman, & Pritchett, 1976)	Grades K–6	14 subtests divided into content, operations, and application
Sequential Assessment of Mathematics Inventory (Reisman, 1984)	Grades K–8	mathematics language, ordinality, number/notation, measurement, geometry, computation, word problems, and mathematical applications
Stanford Diagnostic Mathematics Test (Beatty, Madden, Gardner, & Karlsen, 1976)	Grades K–12	number system and numeration, computation, and applications

Formal Tests Used to Assess Behavior

Behavior Rating Instruments

Test	Age or Grade Level	Behaviors/Skills Measured
A Process for In-School Screening of Children with Emotional Handicaps (Bower & Lambert, 1962)	Grades K–12	perception of child's behavior by teachers, peers, and self
Adaptive Behavior Scale (Nihira, Foster, Shellhaas, & Leland, 1974)	3 yrs.–adult	behavior domains important to daily living, maladaptive behavior, social and personal behavior
Behavior Problem Checklist (Quay & Peterson, 1967)	Grades K–8	student maladaptive behavior

Formal Tests Used to Assess Behavior *(continued)*

Behavior Rating Instruments (continued)

Test	*Age or Grade Level*	*Behaviors/Skills Measured*
Behavior Rating Profile (Brown & Hammill, 1978)	Grades 1–7	behavior and attitudes at home, school, and with peers
Burks' Behavior Rating Scales (Burks, 1977)	Grades 1–9	student maladaptive behavior and personality variables
Child Behavior Rating Scale (Cassel, 1978)	Grades K–3	self, home, school, social, and physical adjustment
Conners Abbreviated Teacher Rating Scale (Conners, 1969)	Elementary Grades	behavior problems, attention, anxiety, activity level, sociability
Devereux Adolescent Behavior Rating Scale (Spivack, Haimes, Spotts, 1967)	Ages 13–18	student maladaptive behaviors rated by parents
Devereux Child Behavior Rating Scale (Spivack & Spotts, 1966)	Ages 8–12	student maladaptive behaviors rated by parents
Devereux Elementary School Behavior Rating Scale (Spivack & Swift, 1967)	Grades 1–6	maladaptive classroom behavior rated by teachers
Hahnemann High School Behavior Rating Scale (Swift & Spivack, 1972)	Grades 7–12	academic and social adjustment to social demands
Mooney Problem Check Lists (Mooney & Gordon, 1950)	Junior High, High School, and College	behavior and attitudes important for daily living
Pupil Behavior Inventory (Vinter, Scarri, Vorwaller, & Schafer, 1966)	Ages 4–13	interpersonal skills and behaviors necessary for academic achievement
Vineland Adaptive Behavior Scale (Sparrow, Balla, & Cicchetti, 1984)	Birth to Adulthood	daily living, socialization, motor skills, and adaptive behavior
Vineland Social Maturity Scale (Doll, 1965)	Birth to 30 yrs.	adaptive behavior, self-help skills, communication, social relations
Walker Problem Behavior Identification Checklist (Walker, 1976)	Grades 4–6	inappropriate school behaviors

(continued)

Formal Tests Used to Assess Behavior (*continued*)

Measures of Self-Concept		
Coopersmith Self-Esteem Inventories (Coopersmith, 1981)	Elementary Grades	attitudes toward self in social, academic, and personal contexts
Draw-a-Person (Urban, 1963)	Age 5 or older	self-image
Perceived Competence Scale for Children (Harter, 1979)	Grades 3–6	cognitive and intellectual skills, social skills, physical skills, and self-esteem
Piers-Harris Children's Self Concept Scale (Piers & Harris, 1969)	Grades 3–12	self-concept
Tennessee Self Concept Inventory (Fitts, 1965)	Ages 12 and older	self-concept

References

Adams, S. (1979). *Adston mathematics skill series: Common fractions.* Baton Rouge, LA.: Adston Educational Enterprises.

Adams, S., & Ellis, L. (1979). *Adston mathematics skill series: Working with whole numbers.* Baton Rouge, LA: Adston Educational Enterprises.

Adams, S., & Sauls, C. (1979). *Adston mathematics skill series: Readiness for operations.* Baton Rouge, LA: Adston Educational Enterprises.

Adelman, H. S., & Taylor, L. (1983). Enhancing motivation for overcoming learning and behavior problems. *Journal of Learning Disabilities, 16,* 384–392.

Alberto, P., & Troutman, A. C. (1982). *Applied behavior analysis for teachers.* Columbus, OH: Charles E. Merrill.

Algozzine, B. (1976). The disturbing child: What you see is what you get? *The Alberta Journal of Educational Research, 22,* 330–333.

Algozzine, B. (1977). The emotionally disturbed child: Disturbed or disturbing? *Journal of Abnormal Child Psychology, 5,* 205–211.

Algozzine, R. (1981). Ecological perspective of emotional disturbance. In R. Algozzine, R. Schmid, & C. Mercer (Eds.), *Childhood behavior disorders.* Rockville, MD: Aspen Systems Corporation.

Algozzine, R., & Schmid, R. (1981). Identification and characteristics. In R. Algozzine, R. Schmid, & C. Mercer (Eds.), *Childhood behavior disorders.* Rockville, MD: Aspen Systems Corporation.

Alley, G., & Deshler, D. (1979). *Teaching the disabled adolescent: Strategies and methods..* Denver: Love Publishing Co.

Alley, G., & Foster, C. (1978). Nondiscriminatory testing of minority and exceptional children. *Focus on Exceptional Children, 9,* 1–14.

Allington, R. (1984). So what is the problem? Whose problem is it? *Topics in Learning and Learning Disabilities, 3*(4), 91–98.

Alper, T., Nowlin, L., Lemoine, K., Perine, M., & Bettencourt, B. (1974). The rated assessment of academic skills. *Academic Therapy, 9,* 151–164.

Apter, S. J., & Conoley, J. C. (1984). *Childhood behavior disorders and emotional disturbance.* Englewood Cliffs, NJ: Prentice-Hall.

Archer, A., & Edgar, E. (1976). Teaching academic skills to mildly handicapped children. In S. Lowenbraun & J. Q. Affleck (Eds.), *Teaching mildly handicapped children in regular classes.* Columbus, OH: Charles E. Merrill.

Arter, J. A., & Jenkins, J. R. (1977). Examining the benefits and prevalence of modality considerations in special education. *Journal of Special Education, 11*(3), 281–297.

Ashlock, R. B. (1982). *Error patterns in computation: A semi-programmed approach* (3rd ed.). Columbus, OH.: Charles E. Merrill.

Bailey, J., & Bostow, D. (1979). *Research methods in applied behavior analysis.* Tallahassee, FL.: Copy Graphix.

Barbe, W. B. (1975). *Barbe reading skills check list.* Honesdale, PA.

Barbe, W. B., Allen, H. L., & Thorton, W. C. (1978). *Reading skills competency tests.* West Nyack, N.Y.: The Center for Applied Research in Education.

Barbe, W. B., Lucas, V. H., Hackney, C. S., & McAllister, C. (1975). *Creative growth in handwriting.* Columbus, OH.: Zaner-Bloser.

Bartel, N. R., & Bryan, D. N. (1982). Problems in language development. In D. D. Hammill & N. R. Bartel, *Teaching children with learning and behavior problems* (3rd ed.). Boston: Allyn and Bacon.

Barton, E. J., & Ascione, F. R. (1984). Direct observation. In T. H. Ollendick & M. Hersen (Eds.), *Child behavioral assessment.* New York: Pergamon Press.

Beattie, J., & Algozzine, B. (1982). Improving basic academic skills of educable mentally retarded adolescents. *Education and Training of the Mentally Retarded, 17,* 255–258.

Beatty, L. S., Madden, R., Gardner, E. F., & Karlsen, B. (1976). *Stanford diagnostic arithmetic test.* New York: Harcourt Brace Jovanovich.

Beery, K. E. (1982). *Developmental test of visual motor integration.* Cleveland, OH.: Modern Curriculum Press.

Beeson, B. F., & Pellegrin, L. O. (1979). *Adston mathematics skill series: Decimal numbers.* Baton Rouge, LA.: Adston Educational Enterprises.

Bennett, R. E. (1982). Applications of microcomputer technology to special education. *Exceptional Children, 49,* 106–114.

Berger, N. (1978). Why can't Johnny read? Perhaps he's not a good listener. *Journal of Learning Disabilities, 11,* 633–638.

Berko, J. (1958). The child's learning of English morphology. *Word, 14,* 150–177.

Blankenship, C., & Lilly, M. S. (1981). *Mainstreaming students with learning and behavior problems.* New York: Holt, Rinehart and Winston.

Bloom, L., & Lahey, M. (1978). *Language development and language disorders.* New York: John Wiley & Sons.

Bloomfield, L., & Barnhart, C. (1961). *Let's read: A linguistic approach.* Detroit: Wayne State University Press.

Boehm, A. E. (1971). *Boehm test of basic concepts.* Middleburg Heights, OH.: The Psychological Corporation.

Bond, G. L., Clymer T., & Hoyt, C. J. (1955). *Silent reading diagnostic tests.* Chicago: Lyons and Carnahan.

Bond, G. L., Tinker, M. A., & Wasson, B. B. (1979). *Reading difficulties: Their diagnosis and correction* (4th ed.). Englewood Cliffs, NJ.: Prentice-Hall.

Boning, T., & Boning, R. (1957). I'd rather read than . . . *The Reading Teacher, 10,* 197.

Botel, M. (1970). *Botel reading inventory.* Chicago: Follett.

Bower, E. M., & Lambert, N. M. (1962). *A process for in-school screening of children with emotional handicaps.* Princeton, NJ.: Educational Testing Service.

Breen, L. (1979). Additional approaches and materials. In J. Alexander (Ed.), *Teaching reading.* Boston: Little, Brown, and Co.

Brigance, A. H. (1977). *Brigance diagnostic inventory of basic skills.* North Billerica, MA.: Curriculum Associates.

Brigance, A. H. (1978). *Brigance diagnostic inventory of early development.* North Billerica, MA.: Curriculum Associates.

Brigance, A. H. (1981). *Brigance diagnostic inventory of essential skills.* North Billerica, MA.: Curriculum Associates.

Brigance, A. H. (1983). *Brigance diagnostic comprehensive inventory of basic skills.* North Billerica, MA.: Curriculum Associates.

Brophy, J. E., & Good, T. L. (1974). *Teacher-student relationships: Causes and consequences.* New York: Holt, Rinehart, and Winston.

Brown, A. L. (1979). Metacognitive development and reading. In R. J. Spiro, B. Bruce, & W. F. Brewer (Eds.), *Theoretical issues in reading comprehension.* Hillsdale, NJ.: Lawrence Erlbaum Associates.

Brown, L. L., & Hammill, D. D. (1978). *Behavior rating profile.* Austin, TX: Pro-Ed.

Brown, V. L., & Hammill, D. D., & Wiederholt, J. L. (1978). *The test of reading comprehension: A method for assessing the understanding of written language.* Austin: Pro-Ed.

Brueckner, L. J. (1955). *Diagnostic tests and self-helps in arithmetic.* Monterey, CA.: California Test Bureau/McGraw-Hill.

Bryen, D. (1982). *Inquiries into child language.* Boston: Allyn and Bacon.

Buchannon, C. D., & Sullivan Associates. (1963). *Sullivan programmed readers.* New York: McGraw-Hill.

Burks, H. F. (1977). *Burks' behavior rating scales* (Rev. ed.). Los Angeles: Western Psychological Services.

Burns, P. C., & Broman, B. L. (1983) *The language arts in childhood education* (5th ed.). Chicago: Rand McNally.

Burns, P., & Roe, B. (1985). *Informal reading inventory*. (2nd ed.) Boston: Houghton Mifflin.

California Achievement Tests. (1978). Monterey, CA.: California Test Bureau/McGraw-Hill.

Campbell, N. J., Dobson, J. E., & Bost, J. M. (1985). Educator perceptions of behavior problems of mainstreamed students. *Exceptional Children, 51* (4), 298–306.

Carnine, D., & Silbert, J. (1979). *Direct instruction reading*. Columbus, OH.: Charles E. Merrill.

Carroll, J. B. (1938). Diversity of vocabulary and the harmonic series law of word-frequency distributions. *The Psychological Record, 2.*

Carrow, E. (1973). *Test of auditory comprehension of language*. Austin, TX.: Learning Concepts, Inc.

Carrow, E. (1974). *Carrow elicited language inventory*. Austin, TX.: Learning Concepts, Inc.

Cartwright, G. P. (1969). Written expression and spelling. In R. Smith (Ed.), *Teacher diagnosis of educational difficulties*. Columbus, OH.: Charles E. Merrill.

Cartwright, C., & Cartwright, G. (1974). *Developing observation skills*. New York: McGraw-Hill.

Cassel, R. H. (1978). *Child behavior rating scale*. Los Angeles: Western Psychological Services.

Chadwick, B., & Day, R. (1970). *Systematic reinforcement: Academic performance of Mexican-American and black students*. Unpublished manuscript, University of Washington, Seattle.

Chall, J. (1967). *Learning to read: The great debate*. New York: McGraw-Hill.

Chall, J. (1979). The great debate: Ten years later with a modest proposal for reading stages. In L. Resnick & P. Weaver (Eds.), *Theory and practice of early reading* (Vol. I). Hillsdale, NJ.: Erlbaum.

Clarke, M., & Marsden, F. (1973). *Schoolhouse: A word attack skills kit*. Chicago: Science Research Associates.

Coates, B. (1972). White adult behavior toward black and white children. *Child Development, 43*, 143–154.

Cohen, C., & Abrams, R. (1974). *Spellmaster*. Exeter, NH.: Learnco.

Cohen, S., & Plaskon, S. (1980). *Language arts for the mildly handicapped*. Columbus, OH.: Charles E. Merrill.

Coie, J. D., Dodge, K. A., & Coppotelli, H. (1982). Dimensions and types of social status: A cross-age perspective. *Developmental Psychology, 18*(4), 557–570.

Coleman, M., & Harmer, W. R. (1982). A comparison of standardized reading tests and informal placement procedures. *Journal of Learning Disabilities, 15*, 396–398.

Collins-Cheek, M., & Cheek, E. (1984). *Diagnostic-prescriptive reading instruction* (2nd ed.). Dubuque, IA: Wm. C. Brown.

Comprehensive tests of basic skills. (1968). Monterey, CA.: CTB/McGraw-Hill.

Conners, C. K. (1969). Conners abbreviated teacher rating scale. *American Journal of Psychiatry, 126*, 884–888.

Connolly, A. J., Nachtman, W., & Pritchett, E. M. (1976). *Key math diagnostic arithmetic test*. Circle Pines, MN.: American Guidance Service.

Coopersmith, S. (1981). *Coopersmith Self-Esteem Inventories*. Monterey, CA.: Publishers Test Service.

Copeland, R. W. (1979). *Math activities for children: A diagnostic and development approach*. Columbus, OH.: Charles E. Merrill.

Crabtree, M. (1963). *Houston test of language development*. Houston: Houston Press.

Cronin, M. E., & Currie, P. S. (1984). Study skills: A resource guide for practitioners. *Remedial and Special Education, 5*(2), 61–69.

Cullinan, D., & Epstein, M. H. (Eds.). (1979). *Special education for adolescents: Issues and perspectives*. Columbus, OH.: Charles E. Merrill.

Denmark, T. (1976). Reaction paper classroom diagnosis. In J. L. Higgins & J. W. Heddens (Eds.), *Remedial mathematics: Diagnostic and prescriptive approaches*. Columbus, OH.: ERIC Center for Science, Mathematics, and Environmental Education.

Deshler, D. D., Schumaker, J. B., & Lenz, B. K. (1984). Academic and cognitive interventions for LD adolescents: Part I. *Journal of Learning Disabilities, 17*, 108–117.

Diagnostic and statistical manual of mental dis-

orders (3rd ed.). (1980). Washington, DC.: American Psychiatric Association.

Dickinson, D. J. (1980). The direct assessment: An alternative to psychometric testing. *Journal of Learning Disabilities, 13,* 8–12.

Dixon, R., & Engelmann, S. (1979). *Corrective spelling through morphographs.* Chicago, IL.: Science Research Associates.

Dolch, E. W. (1948). *Graded reading difficulty worksheet.* Champaign, IL.: Garrard Press.

Doll, E. A. (1965). *Vineland Social Maturity Scale: Condensed Manual of Directions.* Minneapolis, MN.: American Guidance.

Doren, M. (1973). *Doren diagnostic reading test of word recognition skills* (2nd ed.). Circle Pines, MN.: American Guidance Service.

Dudley-Marling, C. C. (1985). Microcomputers, reading, and writing: Alternatives to drill and practice. *The Reading Teacher, 38,* 388–391.

Dunlap, W. P., & House, A. D. (1976). Why can't Johnny compute? *Journal of Learning Disabilities, 9,* 210–214.

Dunn, L. M., & Dunn, L. M. (1981). *Peabody Picture Vocabulary Test—Revised.* Circle Pines, MN.: American Guidance Service.

Dunn, L. M., & Markwardt, F. C. (1970). *Peabody Individual Achievement Test.* Circle Pines, MN.: American Guidance Service.

Dunn, R., & Dunn, K. (1978). *Teaching students through their individual learning styles: A practical approach.* Englewood Cliffs, NJ.: Prentice-Hall.

Durkin, D. (1983). *Teaching young children to read* (4th ed.). Boston: Allyn and Bacon.

Durost, W. N. Bixler, H. H., Wrightstone, J. W., Prescott, G. A., & Balow, I. H. (1971). *Metropolitan achievement tests.* New York: Harcourt Brace Jovanovich.

Durrell, D.D. (1955). *Durrell analysis of reading difficulty.* New York: Harcourt Brace Jovanovich.

Dusek, J. (1975). Do teachers bias children's learning? *Review of educational research, 45,* 661–684.

Eaton, M. (1978). Data decisions and evaluation. In N. Haring, T. Lovitt, M. Eaton, & C. Hansen. *The fourth R: research in the classroom.* Columbus, OH.: Charles E. Merrill.

Ekwall, E. E. (1976). *Diagnosis and remediation of the disabled reader.* Boston: Allyn and Bacon.

Ekwall, E. E. (1981). *Locating and correcting reading difficulties* (3rd ed.). Columbus, OH.: Charles E. Merrill.

Ekwall, E. E., & Shanker, J. (1983). *Diagnosis and remediation of the disabled reader* (2nd ed.). Boston: Allyn and Bacon.

Engelhardt, J. (1976). Diagnosis and remediation in school mathematics: Developing continuity among R and D efforts. In J. W. Heddens & F. D. Aquila (Eds.), *Proceedings of the third national conference on remedial mathematics.* Kent, OH.: Kent State University Press.

Engelmann, S., & Bruner, E. C. (1974). *Distar reading.* Chicago, IL.: Science Research Associates.

Engelmann, S., Johnson, G., Hanner, S., Carnine, L., Meyers, L., Osborn, S., Haddox, P., Becker, W., Osborn, W., & Becker, J. (1978). *Corrective reading program.* Chicago: Science Research Associates.

Engelmann, S., & Osborn, J. (1976). *Distar: An instructional system.* Chicago: Science Research Associates.

Enright, B. E. (1983). *Enright diagnostic inventory of basic arithmetic skills.* North Billerica, MA.: Curriculum Associates.

Evans, S. S., & Evans, W. H. (unpublished paper). Rate, proficiency, and instructional decision-making.

Evans, W., & Evans, S. S. (1983). Secondary programs for handicapped students. In R. E. Schmid & L. M. Nagata, *Contemporary issues in special education* (2nd ed.). New York: McGraw-Hill.

Evans, W., & Evans, S. (1983). Using parents in behavior management. *Academic Therapy, 19,* 37–43.

Evans, W. H., & Stritch, T. M. (1983). Video game syndrome. *Academic Therapy, 18,* 533–534.

Farr, R. (Ed.). (1973). *Iowa silent reading tests.* New York: Harcourt Brace Jovanovich.

Fitts, W. (1965). *Tennessee self-concept inventory.* Nashville, TN.: Counselor Recordings and Tests.

Flavell, J. H. (1978, October). *Cognitive model-*

ing. Paper presented at the Conference on Children's Oral Communication Skills, University of Wisconsin, Madison.

Foster, G. G., Reese, J. H., Schmidt, C. R., & Ohrtman, W. F. (1976). Modality preference and the learning of sight words. *Journal of Special Education, 10*, 253–258.

Foster, G., Ysseldyke, J., & Reese, J., (1975). I wouldn't have seen it, if I hadn't believed it. *Exceptional Children, 41*, 469–473.

Foster, R., Gidden, J., & Stark, J. (1973). *Assessment of children's language comprehension*. Palo Alto, CA.: Consulting Psychologists Press, Inc.

Fountain Valley teacher support system in reading. (1971). Huntington Beach, CA.: Richard L. Zweig Associates.

Frank, A. R., Logan, H. L., & Martin, D. J. (1982). LD students' subtraction errors. *Learning Disability Quarterly, 5*, 194–196.

Fries, C. (1963). *Linguistics and reading*. New York: Holt, Rinehart and Winston.

Fry, E. (1977). *Elementary reading instruction*. New York: McGraw-Hill.

Fry, E. (1980). The new instant word list. *The Reading Teacher, 34*, 284–289.

Gallagher, P. A. (1979). *Teaching students with behavior disorders: Techniques for classroom instruction*. Denver: Love Publishing Co.

Ganschow, L. (1984). Analyze error patterns to remediate severe spelling difficulties. *The Reading Teacher, 3*, 288–293.

Gates, A. I., & MacGinitie, W. H. (1972). *Gates-MacGinitie reading tests*. New York: Teachers College Press.

Gates, A. I., & McKillop, A. S. (1962). *Gates-McKillop reading diagnostic tests*. New York: Teachers College Press.

Gillespie-Silver, P. (1979). *Teaching reading to children with special needs*. Columbus, OH.: Charles E. Merrill.

Gillet, J., & Temple, C. (1982). *Understanding reading problems: Assessment and instruction*. Boston: Little, Brown, and Co.

Gilmore, J. V., & Gilmore, E. C. (1968). *Gilmore oral reading test*. New York: Harcourt Brace Jovanovich.

Glaser, R. (1963). Instructional technology and the measurement of learning outcomes: Some questions. *American Psychologist, 18*, 519–521.

Goldman, R., & Fristoe, M. (1972). *Goldman-Fristoe test of articulation*. Circle Pines, MN.: American Guidance Service.

Goldman, R., Fristoe, M., & Woodcock, R. W. (1976). *Goldman-Fristoe-Woodcock Test of Auditory Discrimination*. Circle Pines, MN.: American Guidance Service.

Goodman, L., & Hammill, D. D. (1975). *Basic school skills inventory*. Chicago: Follett.

Goodman, K. S. (1969). Analysis of oral reading miscues: Applied psycholinguistics. *Reading Research Quarterly, 5*, 9–30.

Goodman, Y. M. & Burke, C. L. (1972). *Reading miscue inventory: Manual of procedure for diagnosis and evaluation*. New York: Macmillan.

Gottfredson, G. D. (1984). *Oversight on school discipline*. Hearings before the Subcommittee on Elementary, Secondary, and Vocational Education, House of Representatives. Washington, DC.: U. S. Government Printing Office (C. I. S. No. H 341-77.1).

Gottman, J. M. (1977). Toward a definition of social isolation in children. *Child Development, 48*, 513–517.

Gray, W. S., & Robinson, H. M. (1967). *Gray oral reading test*. Indianapolis: Bobbs-Merrill.

Green, J. A. (1975). *Teacher-made tests* (2nd ed.). New York: Harper & Row.

Greenwood, C. R., Walker, H. M., Todd, N. M., & Hops, H. (1979). Selecting a cost-effective screening device for the assessment of preschool social withdrawal. *Journal of Applied Behavior Analysis, 12*, 639–652.

Gronlund, N. E. (1973). *Preparing criterion-referenced tests for classroom instruction*. New York: Macmillan.

Gross, A. M. (1984). Behavioral interviewing. In T. H. Ollendick & M. Hersen (Eds.), *Child behavioral assessment*. New York: Pergamon Press.

Guerin, G. R., & Maier, A. S. (1983). *Informal assessment in education*. Palo Alto, CA.: Mayfield Publishing Co.

Guthrie, J., Seifert, M., Burnham, N., & Caplon,

R. (1974). The maze technique to assess and monitor reading comprehension. *The Reading Teacher, 28,* 161–168.

Hall, M. (1981). *Teaching reading as a language experience* (3rd ed.). Columbus, OH.: Charles E. Merrill.

Hallahan, D. P., Hall, R. J., Ianna, S. D., Kneedler, R. D., Lloyd, J. W., Loper, A. B., & Reeve, R. E. (1983). Summary of research findings at the University of Virginia Learning Disabilities Research Institute. *Exceptional Education Quarterly, 4*(1), 95–110.

Hammill, D. D. (1982). Improving spelling skills. In D. D. Hammill and N. R. Bartel, *Teaching children with learning and behavior problems.* (3rd ed.). Boston: Allyn and Bacon.

Hammill, D. D. (1985). *Detroit tests of learning aptitude* (Rev. ed.) Austin, TX.: Pro-Ed.

Hammill, D. D., & Bartel, N. R. (1982). *Teaching children with learning and behavior problems* (3rd ed.). Boston: Allyn and Bacon.

Hammill, D. D., Brown, V. L., Larson, S. C., & Wiederholt, J. L. (1980). *Test of adolescent language.* Austin, TX.: Pro-Ed.

Hammill, D.D., & Larsen, S. C. (1974). The effectiveness of psycholinguistic training. *Exceptional Children, 41,* 5–14.

Hammill, D. D., & Larson, S. C. (1983). *Test of written language.* Austin, TX: Pro-Ed.

Hammill, D. D., & Poplin, M. (1982). Problems in written composition. In D. D. Hammill and N. R. Bartel, *Teaching children with learning and behavior problems.* (3rd ed.). Boston: Allyn and Bacon.

Hanna, P. R., Hanna, J. S., Hodges, R. E., & Rudorf, E. H. (1966). *Phoneme-grapheme correspondence as cues to spelling improvement.* U. S. Department of Health, Education, and Welfare. Washington, DC.: U. S. Government Printing Office.

Hannaford, A. E., & Taber, F. M. (1982). Microcomputer software for the handicapped: Development and evaluation. *Exceptional Children, 49,* 137–144.

Hargrove, L. J., & Poteet, J. A. (1984). *Assessment in special education.* Englewood Cliffs, NJ: Prentice-Hall.

Haring, N. (1978). Research in the classroom: Problems and procedures. In N. Haring, T.

Lovitt, M. Eaton, & C. Hansen, *The fourth R: Research in the classroom.* Columbus, OH.: Charles E. Merrill.

Haring, N. G., & Bateman, B. (1977). *Teaching the learning disabled child.* Englewood Cliffs, NJ.: Prentice-Hall.

Haring, N. G., & Eaton, M. (1978). Systematic instructional procedures: An instructional hierarchy. In N. Haring, T. Lovitt, M. Eaton, & C. Hansen, *The fourth R: Research in the classroom.* Columbus, OH.: Charles E. Merrill.

Haring, N. G., & Gentry, N. D. (1976). Direct and individualized instructional procedures. In N. G. Haring & R. L. Schiefelbusch (Eds.), *Teaching special children.* New York: McGraw-Hill.

Harris, A. J., & Sipay, E. R. (1975). *How to increase reading ability* (6th ed.). New York: David McKay.

Harris, A. J., & Sipay. E. R. (1980). *How to increase reading ability* (7th ed.). New York: Longman.

Harter, S. (1979). *Perceived competence scale for children.* Denver: University of Denver.

Hartman, A. (1974). *The effects of pairing olfactory stimuli with words on the acquisition of word recognition skills of kindergarten students.* Unpublished doctoral dissertation, Ohio State University.

Haughton, E. (1971). Great gains from small starts. *Teaching Exceptional Children, 3,* 141–146.

Heilman, A. W. (1976). *Phonics in proper perspective* (3rd ed.). Columbus, OH.: Charles E. Merrill.

Heilman, A., Blair, T., & Rupley, W. (1981). *Principles and practices of teaching reading* (5th ed.). Columbus, OH.: Charles E. Merrill.

Heron, T. E., & Heward, W. L. (1982). Ecological assessment: Implications for teachers of learning disabled students. *Learning Disability Quarterly, 5,* 117–126.

Hewett, F. M., & Taylor, F. D. (1980). *The emotionally disturbed child in the classroom* (2nd ed.). Boston: Allyn and Bacon.

Hieronymus, A. N., & Linquist, E. F. (1974). *Iowa tests of basic skills: Manual for administrators, supervisors, and counselors.* Boston: Houghton Mifflin.

High intensity learning system. (1972). New York: Random House.

Hops, H., & Greenwood, C. R. Social skills deficits. (1981). In E. J. Mash & L. G. Terdal (Eds.), *Behavioral assessment of childhood disorders.* New York: Guilford Press.

Hops, H., & Lewin, L. (1984). Peer sociometric forms. In T. H. Ollendick & M. Hersen (Eds.), *Child behavioral assessment.* New York: Pergamon Press.

Howell, K. W., & Kaplan, J. S. (1980). *Diagnosing basic skills: A handbook for deciding what to teach.* Columbus, OH.: Charles E. Merrill.

Howell, K., Kaplan, J., & O'Connell, C. (1979). *Evaluating exceptional children: A task analysis approach.* Columbus, OH.: Charles E. Merrill.

Howell, K. W., Zucker, S. H., & Morehead, M. K. (1982). *Multilevel academic skill inventory.* Columbus, OH.: Charles E. Merrill.

Huff, P. (1979). Language experience approaches. In J. Alexander (Ed.), *Teaching reading.* Boston: Little, Brown and Co.

Humphrey, J. H. (1966). *Child learning through elementary school physical education.* Dubuque, IA.: Wm. C. Brown.

Hymel, G. M. (April, 1984). A systems-based model provides more scientific approach for designing instruction. *NASSP Bulletin,* 7–16.

Hymel, S., & Asher, S. R. (1977). Assessment and training of isolated children's social skills. Paper presented at the biennial meeting of the Society for Research in Child Development, New Orleans, March 1977.

Idol-Maestas, L. (1983). *Special educator's consultation handbook.* Rockville, MD.: Aspen Systems Corporation.

Irmscher, W. F. (1972). *The Holt guide to English.* New York: Holt, Rinehart, and Winston.

Jackson, P., & Lahaderne, H. (1967). Inequalities of teacher-pupil contacts. *Psychology in the Schools, 4,* 204–211.

Jastak, J. F., & Jastak, S. R. (1978). *Wide range achievement test.* Wilmington, DE.: Jastak Associates.

Johns, J. L. (1978). *Basic reading inventory.* Dubuque, IA.: Kendall/Hunt.

Johnson, M. S., & Kress, R. A. (1965). *Informal reading inventories.* Newark, DE.: International Reading Association.

Johnson, W. (1944). Studies in language behavior. 1. A program of research. *Psychological Monographs, 56,* (2).

Jongsma, K., & Jongsma, E. (1981).Test review: Commercial informal reading inventories. *The Reading Teacher, 34,* 697–704.

Kaluger, G., & Kolson, C. (1978). *Reading and learning disabilities* (2nd ed.). Columbus, OH.: Charles E. Merrill.

Kamm, K., Miles, P. J., VanBlaricom, V. L., Harris, M. L., & Stewart, D. M. (1972). *Wisconsin tests of reading skill development.* Minneapolis: National Computer Systems.

Kanfer, F. H., & Saslow, G. (1969). Behavioral diagnosis. In C. M. Franks (Ed.), *Behavior therapy: Appraisal and status.* New York: McGraw-Hill.

Karlsen, B., Madden, R., & Gardner, E. F. (1976). *Stanford diagnostic reading test.* New York: Harcourt Brace Jovanovich.

Kauffman, J. M. (1981). *Characteristics of children's behavior disorders* (2nd ed.). Columbus, OH.: Charles E. Merrill.

Kaufman, A. S., & Kaufman, N. L. (1985). *Kaufman test of educational achievement.* Circle Pines, MN.: American Guidance Service.

Kerr, M. M., & Nelson, C. M. (1983). *Strategies for managing behavior problems in the classroom.* Columbus, OH.: Charles E. Merrill.

King, R., Wesson, C., & Deno, S. (1982). Direct and frequent mesurement of student performance: Does it take too much time? University of Minnesota Institute for Research on Learning Disabilities. Research Report No. 67.

Kirk, S. A., Kliebhan, J. M., & Lerner, J. W. (1978). *Teaching reading to slow and disabled learners.* Boston: Houghton Mifflin.

Kirk, S. A., McCarthy, J. J., & Kirk, W. D. (1968). *Illinois test of psycholinguistic abilities.* Urbana, IL.: University of Illinois Press.

Koenig, C. H., & Kunzelmann, H. P. (1980). *Classroom learning screening manual.* Columbus, OH.: Charles E. Merrill.

Kolb, D. A. (1978). *Learning style inventory.* Boston, MA.: McBer.

Koorland, M. A., & Westling, D. L. (1981). An applied behavior analysis research primer for behavioral change personnnel. *Behavioral Disorders, 6*, 164–174.

Kopp, O.W. (1967). The evaluation of oral language activities: Teaching and learning. *Elementary English, 44*, 117.

Kottmeyer, W. (1959). *Teacher's guide for remedial reading.* New York: McGraw-Hill.

Kroth, R. L. (1975). *Communicating with parents of exceptional children: Improving parent-teacher relationships.* Denver: Love Publishing Co.

Kroth, R. (1973). The behavioral Q-sort as a diagnostic tool. *Academic Therapy, 8*, 317–329.

Lankford, F. G., Jr. (1972). *Some computational strategies of seventh grade pupils* (Project No. 2-C-013, Grant No. OEG-3-72-0035). Washington, D.C.: HEW Office of Education, National Center for Educational Research and Development (Regional Research Program) and Center for Advanced Study, University of Virginia.

Lankford, F. G., Jr. (1974). What can a teacher learn about a pupil's thinking through oral interviews? *The Arithmetic Teacher, 21*, 26–32.

Larrivee, B. (1981). Modality preference as a model for differentiating beginning reading instruction: A review of the issues. *Learning Disability Quarterly, 4*, 180–188.

Larson, S. C., & Hammill, D. D. (1976). *Test of written spelling.* Austin, TX.: Pro-Ed.

Lee, L. (1971). *Northwestern syntax screening test.* Evanston, IL.: Northwestern University Press.

Lee, L., & Koenigsknecht, R. (1974). *Developmental sentence scoring.* Evanston, IL.: Northwestern University Press.

Lenz, B. K. (1982). *The effect of advance organizers on the learning and retention of learning disabled adolescents within the context of a cooperative planning model.* Unpublished dissertation, University of Kansas, Lawrence.

Lepore, A. V. (1979). A comparison of computational errors between educable mentally handicapped and learning disability children. *Focus on Learning Problems in Mathematics, 1*, 12–33.

Lerner, J. W. (1985). *Learning disabilities: Theories, diagnosis, teaching strategies* (4th ed.). Boston: Houghton Mifflin.

Lewis, E. R., & Lewis, H. P. (1965). An analysis of errors in the formation of manuscript letters by first grade children. *American Educational Research, 2*, 25–35.

Loper, A. B. (April 1982). Metacognitive training to correct academic deficiency. *Topics in Learning and Learning Disabilities*, 61–67.

Lovaas, I. (1968). A program for the establishment of speech in psychotic children. In H. Sloane & B. Macaulay (Eds.), *Operant procedures in remedial speech and language training.* Boston: Houghton Mifflin.

Lovitt, T. (1978). Arithmetic. In N. Haring, T. Lovitt, M. Eaton, & C. Hansen, *The fourth R: Research in the classroom.* Columbus, OH.: Charles E. Merrill.

Lovitt, T. (1977). *In spite of my resistance: I've learned from children.* Columbus, OH.: Charles E. Merrill.

Lyon, R. (1977). Auditory-perceptual training: The state of the art. *Journal of Learning Disabilities, 10*, 564–572.

MacDonald, J. D. (1976). Environmental language intervention. In F. Withrow and C. Nygren (Eds.), *Language, materials, and curriculum management for the handicapped learner.* Columbus, OH.: Charles E. Merrill.

Madden, R., Gardner, E. F., Rudman, H. C., Karlsen, B., & Merwin, J. C. (1973). *Stanford achievement test.* New York: Harcourt Brace Jovanovich.

Mallon, B., & Berglund, R. (1984). The language experience approach to reading: Recurring questions and their answers. *The Reading Teacher, 37*, (9), 867–871.

Maloney, M. P., & Ward, M. P. (1976). *Psychological assessment: A conceptual approach.* New York: Oxford University Press.

Mann, P. H., Suiter, P. A., & McClung, R. M. (1979). *Handbook in diagnostic-prescriptive teaching* (Abridged 2nd ed.). Boston: Allyn and Bacon.

Mash, E. J., & Terdal, L. G. (1976). Assessment for potential reinforcers. In E. J. Mash & L. G. Terdal (Eds), *Behavior therapy assessment: Diagnosis, design, and evaluation.* New York: Springer.

McCandless, B. R., & Marshall, H. R. (1957). A picture sociometric technique for preschool children and its relation to teacher judgments of friendship. *Child Development, 28,* 139–148.

McCullough, C. M. (1963). *McCullough Word-Analysis Tests.* Princeton: Personnel Press.

McLoughlin, J. A., & Lewis, R. B. (1981). *Assessing special students: Strategies and procedures.* Columbus, OH.: Charles E. Merrill.

McMahon, R. J. (1984). Behavioral checklists and rating scales. In T. H. Ollendick & M. Hersen (Eds.). *Child behavioral assessment.* New York, Pergamon Press.

Mecham, M. J., Jex, J. L., & Jones, J. D. (1967). *Utah Test of Language Development.* Salt Lake City: Communication Research Associates.

Mercer, C. D., (1983). *Students with learning disabilities.* (2nd ed.). Columbus, OH.: Charles E. Merrill.

Mercer, C. D., & Mercer, A. R. (1985). *Teaching students with learning problems* (2nd ed.). Columbus, OH.: Charles E. Merrill.

Mercer, C. D., Mercer, A. R., & Evans, S. S. (1982). The use of frequency in establishing instructional aims. *Journal of Precision Teaching, 3,* 57–63.

Mercer, J. R. (1973). *Labeling the mentally retarded.* Berkeley, CA.: University of California Press.

Miller, I. C. (1977). *School behavior checklist.* Los Angeles: Western Psychological Services.

Mills, R. E. (1956). An evaluation of techniques for teaching word recognition. *The Elementary School Journal, 56,* 221–225.

Mills, R. E. *Learning Methods Test,* Fort Lauderdale, FL. 1612 E. Broward Blvd., 1956.

Moffett, J., & Wagner, B. J. (1983). *Student-centered language arts and reading, K-13: A handbook for teachers* (3rd ed.). Boston: Houghton Mifflin.

Mooney, R. L., & Gordon, L. V. (1950). *Mooney problem check lists.* New York: Psychological Corporation.

Morse, W. C., Cutler, R. L., & Fink, A. H. (1964). *Public school classes for the emotionally handicapped: A research analysis.* Washington, D. C.: Council for Exceptional Children.

Morsink, C. V. (1984). *Teaching special needs students in regular classrooms.* Boston: Little, Brown, and Co.

Myklebust, H. R. (1965). *Picture story language test.* New York: Grune and Stratton.

Naslund, R. A., Thorpe, L. P., & Lefever, D. W. (1978). *SRA achievement series.* Chicago: Science Research Associates.

National Council for Teachers of Mathematics. (1980). *An agenda for action: Recommendations for school mathematics of the 1980's.* Reston, VA: Author.

Newcomer, P. L., & Curtis, D. (1984). *Diagnostic achievement battery.* Austin, TX.: Pro-Ed.

Newcomer, P. L., & Hammill, D. D. (1982). *Test of Langauge Development.* Austin, TX.: Pro-Ed.

Newland, T. (1932). An analytical study of the development of illegibilities in handwriting from the lower grades to adulthood. *Journal of Educational Research, 26,* 249–258.

Newman, J. M. (1984). Language learning and computers. *Language Arts, 61,* 494–497.

Nihira, K., Foster, R., Shellhaas, M., & Leland, H. (1974). *A.A.M.D. Adaptive Behavior Scale.* Washington, D. C.: American Association on Mental Deficiency.

Norris, S. P. (1985). Synthesis of research on critical thinking. *Educational Leadership, 42,* 40–46.

O'Leary, K. D., & Johnson, S. B. (1979). Psychological assessment. In H. C. Quay & J. S. Werry (Eds.), *Psychopathological disorders of childhood* (2nd ed.). New York: John Wiley & Sons.

Otto, W., McMenemy, R. A., & Smith, R. J. (1973). *Corrective and remedial teaching.* (2nd ed.). Boston: Houghton Mifflin.

Otto, W., & Smith, R. J. (1980). *Corrective and remedial teaching* (3rd ed.). Boston: Houghton Mifflin.

Petty, W. T., & Jensen, J. M. (1980). *Developing children's language.* Boston: Allyn and Bacon.

Pflaum, S. W. (1979). Diagnosis of oral reading. *The Reading Teacher, 33,* 278–284.

Pickert, S., & Chase, M. (1978). Story retelling: An informal technique for evaluating children's language. *The Reading Teacher, 31*(5), 528–531.

Piers, E., & Harris, D. (1969). *Piers-Harris Children's Self-Concept Scale.* Nashville, TN. Counselor Recordings and Tests.

Pikulski, J., & Pikulski, E. (1977). Cloze, maze, and teacher judgment. *The Reading Teacher, 30*, 766–770.

Polloway, E. A., Payne, J. S., Patton, J. R., & Payne, R. A. (1985). *Strategies for teaching retarded and special needs learners* (3rd ed.). Columbus, OH.: Charles E. Merrill.

Poplin, M. (1983). Assessing developmental writing abilities. *Topics in Learning and Learning Disabilities, 3*, 63–75.

Poteet, J. A. (1980). Informal assessment of written expression. *Learning Disability Quarterly, 3*, 88–98.

Precision teaching project. Skyline Center, 3300 Third Street, N. E., Great Falls, Montana, 59404.

Prescott, G. A., Balow, I. H., Hogan, T. P., & Farr, R. C. (1978). *Metropolitan achievement tests.* New York: Psychological Corporation.

Prescriptive reading inventory. (1977). CTB/McGraw-Hill.

Prieto, A. G., & Rutherford, R. B. (1977). An ecological assessment technique for behaviorally disordered and learning disabled children. *Journal of Behavioral Disorders, 2*, 169–175.

Puccinelli, M. (1965). *Catch a fish.* Indianapolis, IN.: Bobbs-Merrill.

Quay, H. C. (1979). Classification. In H. C. Quay & J. S. Werry (Eds.), *Psychopathological disorders of childhood* (2nd ed.). New York: John Wiley & Sons.

Quay, H. C., Morse, W. C., & Cutler, R. L. (1966). Personality patterns of pupils in special classes for the emotionally disturbed. *Exceptional Children, 32*, 297–301.

Quay, H. C., & Peterson, D. R. (1967). *Behavior problem checklist.* Champaign, IL.: University of Illinois.

Regional resource center diagnostic math inventories. (1971). Project No. 472917, Contract No. OEC-0-9-472917-4591 608. Eugene, OR.: University of Oregon.

Regional resource center diagnostic reading inventory. (1971). Project No. 472917, Contract No. OEC-0-9-472917-4591 608. Eugene, OR.: University of Oregon.

Reid, D.K., & Hresko, W. P. (1981). Language intervention with the learning disabled. *Topics in Learning and Learning Disabilities, 1*(2), viii-ix.

Reid, D. K., & Hresko, W. P. (1983). Written language. *Topics in Learning and Learning Disabilities, 3*(3), vii-viii.

Reinert, H. C. (1980). *Children in Conflict* (2nd ed.). St. Louis: C. V. Mosby.

Reisman, F. K. (1977). *Diagnostic teaching of elementary school mathematics: Methods and content.* Chicago: Rand McNally.

Reisman, F. K. (1981). *Teaching mathematics: methods and content* (2nd ed.). Boston: Houghton Mifflin.

Reisman, F. K. (1982). *A guide to the diagnostic teaching of arithmetic* (3rd ed.). Columbus, OH.: Charles E. Merrill.

Reisman, F. K. (1984). *Sequential assessment of mathematics inventory.* Columbus, OH.: Charles E. Merrill.

Rhodes, W. C., & Paul, J. L. (1978). *Emotionally disturbed and deviant children.* Englewood Cliffs, NJ.: Prentice-Hall.

Roberts, G. H. (1968). The failure strategies of third grade arithmetic pupils. *The Arithmetic Teacher, 15*, 442–446.

Roe, B., Stoodt, B., & Burns, P. (1978). *Reading instruction in the secondary school* (Revised ed.). Chicago: Rand McNally.

Rosenshine, B. (1978). The third cycle of research on teacher effects: Content covered, academic engaged time, and quality of instruction. *78th Yearbook of the National Society for the Study of Education.* Chicago: University of Chicago Press.

Rowe, M. (1974). Wait-time and rewards as instructional variables, their influence on language, logic and fate control: Part 1—Wait-time. *Journal of Research in Science Teaching, 11*, 81–94.

Rupley, W. H., & Blair, T. R. (1979). *Reading diagnosis and remediation: A primer for classroom and clinic.* Chicago: Rand McNally.

Rupley, W. H., & Blair, T. R. (1983). *Reading diagnosis and direct instruction.* Boston: Houghton Mifflin.

Safran, S., & Safran, J. (1984). The self-monitoring mood chart: Measuring affect in the classroom. *Teaching Exceptional Children, 16*, 172–177.

Salvia, J., & Ysseldyke, J. (1985). *Assessment in special and remedial education* (3rd ed.). Boston: Houghton Mifflin.

Samuels, S. (1983). Diagnosing reading problems. *Topics in Learning and Learning Disabilities, 2,* 1–11.

Sattler, J. M. (1982). *Assessment of children's intelligence and special abilities* (2nd ed.). Boston: Allyn and Bacon.

Schell, L., & Hanna, G. (1981). Can informal reading inventories reveal strengths and weaknesses in comprehension subskills? *The Reading Teacher, 34,* 263–267.

Schlosser, L., & Algozzine, B. (1979). The disturbing child: He or she? *The Alberta Journal of Educational Research, 25,* 30–36.

School Utilities, Volume 11. (1982). Minnesota Educational Computing Consortium, 3490 Lexington Ave. N., St. Paul, MN. 55112.

Schumaker, J. B., Deshler, D. D., Alley, G. R., & Warner, M. M. (1983). Toward the development of an intervention model for learning disabled adolescents: The University of Kansas Institute. *Exceptional Education Quarterly, 4,* 45–74.

Semel-Mintz, E. M., & Wiig, E. H. (1980). *Clinical Evaluation of Language Functions.* Columbus, OH.: Charles E. Merrill.

Shuller, D. Y., & McNamara, J. R. (1976). Expectancy factors in behavioral observation. *Behavior Therapy, 7,* 516–527.

Siegel, L. J., Dragovich, S. L., & Marholin, D. (1976). The effects of biasing information on behavioral observations and rating scales. *Journal of Abnormal Child Psychology, 4,* 221–233.

Silbert, J., Carnine, D., & Stein, M. (1981). *Direct instructional mathematics.* Columbus, OH.: Charles E. Merrill.

Silvaroli, N. J. (1982). *Classroom reading inventory* (4th ed.). Dubuque, IA.: William C. Brown.

SIMS Reading and Spelling Program (1978). (3rd ed.). Minneapolis: Minnesota Public Schools.

Slosson, R. L. (1963). *Slosson Oral Reading Test.* East Aurora, NY.: Slosson Educational Publications.

Smith, D. (1981). *Teaching the learning disabled.* Englewood Cliffs, NJ.: Prentice-Hall.

Smith, D. D., & Lovitt, T. C. (1982). *The computational arithmetic program.* Austin, TX.: Pro-ED.

Smith, D., & Lovitt, T. (1973). The educational diagnosis and remediation of written b and d reversal problems: A case study. *Journal of Learning Disabilities, 6,* 356–363.

Smith, R., Neisworth, J., & Greer, J. (1978). *Evaluating educational environments.* Columbus, OH.: Charles E. Merrill.

Spache, G. D. (1972). *Diagnostic reading scales.* Monterey, CA.: California Test Bureau.

Sparrow, S. S., Balla, D. A., & Cicchetti, D. V. (1984). *Vineland Adaptive Behavior Scale.* Circle Pines, MN.: American Guidance Service.

Spivack, G., Haimes, P. E., & Spotts, J. (1967). *Devereux Adolescent Behavior Rating Scale.* Devon, PA.: Devereux Foundation.

Spivack, G., & Spotts, J. (1966). *Devereux Child Behavior Rating Scale.* Devon, PA.: Devereaux Foundation.

Spivack, G., & Swift, M. (1967). *Devereux Elementary School Behavior Rating Scale.* Devon, PA.: Devereux Foundation.

Starlin, C. (1982). *On reading and writing.* Iowa Monograph. Des Moines, IA.: State Department of Public Instruction.

Starlin, C. M., & Starlin, A. (1973). *Guides to decision making in computational math.* Bemidji, MN.: Unique Curriculums Unlimited.

Starlin, C. M., & Starlin, A. (1973). *Guides to decision making in spelling.* Bemidji, MN.: Unique Curriculums Unlimited.

Stauffer, R. (1980). *The language experience approach to the teaching of reading* (2nd ed.). New York: Harper & Row.

Stephens, T. M. (1977). *Teaching skills to children with learning and behavior disorders.* Columbus, OH.: Charles E. Merrill.

Stephens, T., Hartman, A., & Cooper, J. (1973). Directive teaching of reading with low achieving first- and second-year students. *The Journal of Special Education, 7,* 187–196.

Stephens, T. M., Hartman, A. C., & Lucas, V. H. (1978). *Teaching children basic skills: A curriculum handbook.* Columbus, OH.: Charles E. Merrill.

Stephenson, W. (1953). *The study of behavior: Q-Technique and its methodology.* Chicago: University of Chicago Press.

Stoodt, B. (1981). *Reading instruction.* Boston: Houghton Mifflin.

Sucher, P., & Allred, A. (1973). *Sucher-Allred Reading Placement Inventory*. Oklahoma City, OK.: Economy.

Swanson, H. L., & Watson, B. L. (1982). *Educational and psychological assessment of exceptional children*. St. Louis: C. V. Mosby Co.

Swift, M., & Spivack, G. (1972). *Hahnemann High School Behavior Rating Scale*. Philadelphia: Departmental Health Sciences, Hahnemann Medical College and Hospital.

Szymandera, C. (1972). *Sound Foundations Program*. Niles, IL.: Developmental Learning Materials.

Taber, F. M. (1981). The microcomputer—its applicability to special education. *Focus on Exceptional Children, 14*, 1–14.

Tarver, S. G., & Dawson, M. M. (1978). Modality preference and the teaching of reading: A review. *Journal of Learning Disabilities, 11*, 17–29.

Taylor, R. (1984). *Assessment of exceptional students*. Englewood Cliffs, NJ.: Prentice-Hall.

Temple, C., & Gillet, J. W. (1984). *Langauge arts learning processes and teaching practices*. Boston: Little, Brown and Co.

Templin, M. C., & Darley, F. L. (1960). *Templin-Darley Tests of Articulation* (2nd. ed.). Iowa City, IA.: Bureau of Educational Research and Service.

Thomas, O., Thomas, I. D., & Lutkus, A. (1978). *The world of spelling teacher's edition (Level 4)*. Lexington, MA.: D. C. Heath and Co.

Thorpe, L. P., Lefever, D. W., & Naslund, R. A. (1968). *SRA achievement series*. Chicago: Science Research Associates.

Thornton, C. A., Tucker, B. F., Dossey, J. A., & Bazik, D. F. (1983). *Teaching mathematics to children with special needs*. Menlo Park, CA.: Addison-Wesley.

Tiegs, E. W., & Clark, W. W. (1970a). *California achievement tests*. New York: California Test Bureau/McGraw Hill.

Tiegs, E. W., & Clark, W. W. (1970b). *California reading test*. Los Angeles: California Test Bureau.

Tierney, R. J., Readance, J. E., & Dishner, E. K. (1985). *Reading strategies and practices: A compendium* (2nd ed.). Boston: Allyn and Bacon.

Turner, S. (1984). How to look at the testing components of basal reading series. *The Reading Teacher, 37*, 860–866.

Underhill, R. G. (1976). Classroom diagnosis in remedial mathematics: Diagnostic and remedial approaches. In J. L. Higgins & J. W. Heddens (Eds.), *Remedial mathematics: Diagnostic and prescriptive approaches*. Columbus, OH.: ERIC Center for Science, Mathematics, and Environmental Education.

Underhill, R. G., Uprichard, A. E., & Heddens, J. W. (1980). *Diagnosing mathematical difficulties*. Columbus, OH.: Charles E. Merrill.

Urban, W. H. (1963). *Draw-a-Person*. Los Angeles: Western Psychological Services.

Valmont, W. J. (1972). Creating questions for Informal Reading Inventories. *The Reading Teacher, 25*, 509–512.

VanHouten, R., Morrison, E., Jarvis, R., & McDonald, M. (1974). The effects of explicit timing and feedback on compositional response rate in elementary school children. *Journal of Applied Behavior Anaylsis, 7*, 547–555.

Vinter, R. O., Sarri, R. C., Vorwaller, D. J., & Schafer, W. E. (1966). *Pupil Behavior Inventory*. Ann Arbor, MI.: Campus Publishers.

Wahler, R. G., & Cormier, W. H. (1970). The ecological interview: A first step in out-patient child behavior therapy. *Journal of Behavior Therapy and Experimental Psychiatry, 1*, 279–289.

Walker, H. M. (1976). *Walker Problem Behavior Identification Checklist*. Los Angeles: Western Psychological Services.

Wallace, G., & Larsen, S. C. (1978). *Educational assessment of learning problems: Testing for teaching*. Boston: Allyn and Bacon.

Wallace, G., & McLoughlin, J. (1979). *Learning disabilities: Concepts and characteristics* (2nd ed.). Columbus, OH.: Charles E. Merrill.

Warner, M. M., Schumaker, J. B., Alley, G. R., & Deshler, D. D. (1980). Learning disabled adolescents in public schools: Are they different from other low achievers? *Exceptional Education Quarterly, 1*(2), 27–36.

Watson, D. L., & Tharp, R. G. (1985). *Self-directed behavior* (4th ed.). Monterey, CA.: Brooks/Cole Publishing Co.

Wechsler, D. (1974). *Manual for the Wechsler Intelligence Scale for Children—Revised.* New York: Psychological Corporation.

Wepman, J. M. (1973). *Auditory discrimination test.* Palm Springs, CA.: Research Associates.

Westerman, G. S. (1971). *Spelling and writing.* San Rafael, CA.: Dimensions.

White, O., & Haring, N. (1980). *Exceptional teaching* (2nd ed.). Columbus, OH.: Charles E. Merrill.

Wiederholt, J. L., Hammill, D. D., & Brown, V. (1978). *The resource teacher: A guide to effective practices.* Boston: Allyn and Bacon.

Wiens, J. W. (1983). Metacognition and the adolescent passive learner. *Journal of Learning Disabilities, 16*(3), 144–149.

Wiggins, J. S. (1973). *Personality and prediction: Principles of personality assessment.* Reading, MA.: Addison-Wesley.

Wiig, E. H., & Semel, E. M. (1980). *Language assessment and intervention for the learning disabled.* Columbus, OH.: Charles E. Merrill.

Wixson, K., Bosky, A., Yochum, M., Alvermann, D. (1984). An interview for assessing students' perceptions of classroom reading tasks. *The Reading Teacher, 37,* 346–352.

Wood, B. (1976). *Children and communications: Verbal and non-verbal language development.* Englewood Cliffs, NJ.: Prentice-Hall.

Wood, M. (1975). *Developmental therapy: A textbook for teachers as therapists for emotionally disturbed young children.* Baltimore, MD.: University Park Press.

Wood, S., Burke, L., Kunzelmann, H., & Koenig, C. (1978). Functional criteria in basic math skill proficiency. *Journal of Special Educational Technology, 2,* 29–36.

Woodcock, R. W. (1973). *Woodcock reading mastery tests.* Circle Pines, MN.: American Guidance Service.

Woodcock, R. W., & Johnson, M. B. (1977). *Woodcock-Johnson Psycho-Educational Battery.* Boston: Teaching Resources.

Woodruff, E., Bereiter, C., & Scardamalia, M. (1981–1982). On the road to computer assisted compositions. *Journal of Educational Technology Systems, 10,* 133–148.

Woods, M. L., & Moe, A. J. (1977). *Analytic reading inventory.* Columbus, OH.: Charles E. Merrill.

Ysseldyke, J., & Algozzine, B. (1983). Where to begin in diagnosing reading problems. *Topics in Learning and Learning Disabilities, 2,* 60–69.

Ysseldyke, J., Thurlow, M., Graden, J., Wesson, C., Algozzine, B., & Deno, S. (1983). Generalizations from five years of research on assessment and decision making: The University of Minnesota Institute. *Exceptional Education Quarterly, 4,* 75–93.

Zaner-Bloser evaluation scales. (1984). Columbus, OH.: Zaner-Bloser.

Zigmund, N., Vallecorsa, A., & Silverman, R. (1983). *Assessment for instructional planning in special education.* Englewood Cliffs, NJ.: Prentice-Hall.

Index

Note: Page numbers in italic refer the reader to figures and tables in text.